Tioga
Bradford
Susquehanna
Wayne
Wyoming
Sullivan
Lackawanna
Pike
Lycoming
Luzerne
Columbia
Monroe
Union
Montour
Carbon
Northumberland
Snyder
Northampton
Schuylkill
Lehigh
Dauphin
ata
Harrisburg
Perry
Berks
Lebanon
Bucks
Montgomery
Cumberland
Lancaster
Chester
Philadelphia
York
Delaware
Adams

County Chronicles

Volume III

A Vivid Collection of Pennsylvania Histories

by
Ceane O'Hanlon-Lincoln

Published by

Front Cover

"The Courting Buggy" by Pennsylvania artist Helen Crosby (Warmuth) Alt. Prints of the Amish scene from this volume's cover, as well as scenes from the covers of other volumes of the *County Chronicles* Pennsylvania history series, may be purchased by contacting the artist at 724-628-9543. The history of "The Courting Buggy" is discussed in "Amish Country," this volume. Helen Alt was born in Philadelphia in 1918. She began painting during her high school years, and upon graduation received a scholarship to the Pennsylvania Academy of Fine Arts. Her work has earned her numerous awards. Alt has been a resident of Connellsville, Pennsylvania, since 1946.

Author Ceane O'Hanlon-Lincoln with her cover artist Helen Alt, at awards ceremony, Connellsville, PA
Photo by William S. Warmuth II

Published by
MECHLING BOOKBINDERY
PRINTING & BINDING
1124 Oneida Valley Road - Route 38
Chicora, PA 16025-3820
www.mechlingbooks.com
1-800-941-3735

Layout and Design by Kari Anne McConnell

Printed July 2007 in the United States of America

ISBN-13: 978-0-9760563-2-4
ISBN-10: 0-9760563-2-1

Library of Congress Control Number: 2007927210

Book # 674 of 1000

This book is dedicated to my father, who loved stories;
To my mother, who loved books;
To my brother, J. Robert Hanlon, Esq., who loves both;
To time-travelers everywhere,
And to my husband, Phillip R. Lincoln~
Who bought me my ticket.

— Acknowledgements —

As always, my greatest debt is to my husband, Phillip R. Lincoln.

To my cherished readers who continually communicate their delightful feedback for my Chronicles, both to me and to my publisher.

To my treasured muses, especially Jean Minnick, Bill Colvin, Sandra Bolish, Florence Shutsy-Reynolds, and authors Patty Wilson and Bob Cole.

To the historical societies and historic sites all across our great commonwealth.

To an amazing artist and dear friend, Helen Alt, whose paintings for the covers of my *County Chronicles* charmingly beckon the reader to enter and embark on a magic carpet ride into Pennsylvania's exciting past.

To a great lady, "Pennsylvania's Sweetheart," Shirley Jones- a special "Thank you!"

To Charlotte Morrison-Lynn for her kindness and patience.

To a kindred spirit, Marla Mechling, for her guidance in assembling this work.

To fellow authors for the permissions to quote from their works.

To all those who supplied precious photographs and memories for this volume.

To everyone over the long years who advised "Write it your own way."

To all the interesting, colorful people I have met and interviewed along the thrilling road to history- to each of my dear benefactors, I am profoundly grateful.

To the Native Americans, the pioneers, the immigrants, the heroes herein.

To fellow time-travelers everywhere—

And since we are all travelers in this world and the next—*this book is for you.*

— Contents —

— Foreword —

I love history, especially Pennsylvania history. I love researching it. To me, research is like a treasure hunt, because I am forever uncovering gems of yore. Even more, I love writing about our thrilling past; for the past speaks to us- *if we listen.*

My books afford time-travel, something about which I often fantasize. Since nothing is ever lost or destroyed, the great Albert Einstein believed that actual time-travel would one day be possible. Of course, visitors to the past would be observers only. History does not offer revision. It proffers lessons.

Immediately after the premier volume of *County Chronicles* debuted in late October 2004, readers began asking me if I had begun the second volume. The fact that my *Chronicles* would be a *series* had been announced in the Foreword of the first volume, as well as in several newspaper articles round about. Originally, I had intended to stay within the general vicinity of southwestern Pennsylvania; but I decided, after prompting from readers, to loosen those confines.

County Chronicles, the series, discusses historic figures and events that left their dusky imprints across the landscape of our entire commonwealth. I have, on occasion, been referred to as a writer of local history, but I daresay— *all history is local.*

I want to take this opportunity to set the record straight about the premier volume. It is *not* just about my home county of Fayette. It is only natural that the first book of a series on Pennsylvania would have, for its central focus, the author's home region. But in actuality, the premier volume embraces people, places and events from several neighboring counties, including Allegheny, Bedford, Somerset, Washington and Westmoreland, as well as events from a scattering of outlying counties. Hence, Fayette is the central focus, but indeed not the only focus in the premier volume of my *County Chronicles.*

As I did in the first two volumes, I decided to add, at the end of this book, a "Hometown Memories" segment. There are two reasons for this. First and foremost is the fact that Connellsville, one of the most historic towns within the commonwealth, celebrated, in 2006, its bicentennial. The other reason is that our southwestern corner of the state has, for far too long, been the forgotten segment of Pennsylvania. As a writer of Pennsylvania's vibrant past, I naturally want to share with readers a bit about *my* neck of Penn's Woods, which is replete with history and scenic delight.

In keeping with the first two books, this and each subsequent volume of the series will *not* be a chronological history, but rather a bright and colorful tapestry of assorted places, people and events that affected and shaped our state's exciting story. Thus, the reader may skip around, choosing a Chronicle according to interest and mood.

My style is conversational, not the documentary style found in most conventional history books, where this fascinating subject is chronicled with dates and events of politics, war and social issues. History is so much more! *It is the full scope of human experiences.* Politics, war and social issues to be sure; but history is also art, the performing arts, science, industry and innovations, religion, medicine, important achievements in every field of endeavor, love and its opposite, fear; the list is virtually endless. There should be no fences around history; it is a spacious realm with a diversity of fascinating vistas.

Each Chronicle in this and all subsequent volumes will unfold like a story. That is what history is- the *story* of a small town- perhaps one you've never heard of- or a city, a state or nation; and more than anything else, *history is people.* The great historian Richard Ketchum once wrote in a book dedication- "History is us."

I sometimes feel as though I know the historical figures I write about more than I do most people around me today. After all, I don't get to read other people's mail or their diaries, as I often do with many of the luminaries who have long passed over. And make no mistake, I do my homework. "History is not history unless it is the truth," the astute A. Lincoln once declared. History should never hide the truth, and truth can be stranger, more captivating- and ever so much more thrilling than fiction!

I do not presume to apply the lofty title "historian" to my name. To echo an esteemed Pennsylvanian, author David McCullough, I consider myself a writer whose *milieu* is the past. Along with the meticulous research, many of the histories found in this series will be seasoned and warmed with nostalgic memories gained through personal experiences and interviews. In addition, each volume of my *County Chronicles* is a convenient travel guide to Pennsylvania's historic sites.

Concise enough to read in one sitting, each Chronicle is, and will continue to be, complete in itself- ideal for today's busy people who like to read.

I am proud to state that both men and women, teen to senior, enjoy my *County Chronicles.* From the outset of this series, my goal has been to reach a wide range of readers and not just die-hard history buffs. On occasion, I have encountered a wary reader who has expressed doubt: "I didn't really like history in school." "Hold on!" I interpose. "Answer me this: Do you like a good story well-told? Do you like a story replete with mystery, romance, spice, adventure and lots of action? A cliff-hanger at every page-turn?" "Sure!" comes their swift reply. "Well then," I conclude, "you like history. You just don't know you do!"

And so, drawn from a spectrum of counties, each volume will continue to be a vivid- readable- collection of Pennsylvania's true stories.

My main goals with my Chronicles have always been to stimulate pride and appreciation in Pennsylvania's rich, layered history, and to spark further interest in the subjects therein. *It is my hope too that readers will keep these numbered, very collectible books in their families, to pass down from one generation to another.*

Greater minds than mine have distinguished history as the most important subject in school. An *un*awareness of history is akin to planting cut flowers! History not only gives us roots, it teaches us valuable lessons. History teaches us how to behave. History teaches us what America stands for- what we should be willing to stand up for! *And more than anything else, history is love of home- and country.*

Due to my *County Chronicles,* I was nominated and accepted into the *International Who's Who.* It is pleasing and headily gratifying to announce that the premier volume has thus far garnered three major awards, the Athena Award from my hometown of Connellsville, a Citation/Special Recognition Award from the Pennsylvania House of Representatives, and a Congratulatory/Special Recognition Award from the Senate of Pennsylvania for: "... the significant contribution to the citizens of the commonwealth of Pennsylvania.... Whereas a writer of considerable talent, Ms. O'Hanlon-Lincoln penned [*County Chronicles*] in a most professional manner, with meticulously researched stories of... history and landscape.... Ms. O'Hanlon-Lincoln is truly deserving of great respect and gratitude for her book which details this commonwealth's rich history...."

Jay Craig, of the Pennsylvania Senate Library, stated: "*County Chronicles* is a welcome addition to the Senate Library... the history you provide will help anyone researching Pennsylvania."

In addition to the Pennsylvania Senate Library, *County Chronicles* have found several other prestigious homes: in the library and archives at Heinz History Center; the George C. Marshall Library, the Virginia Military Institute, Lexington, Virginia; and the Special Collections Department in the library at Washington and Lee University, Lexington, to name a few.

In March 2005, my hometown mayor, Judy D. Reed, presented a copy of the premier volume of *County Chronicles* to Governor Edward Rendell in gratitude for the generous check he bestowed upon our city in preparation for Connellsville's bicentennial in 2006. The Governor, in turn, sent me a treasured letter in which he stated: "*County Chronicles*... is a beautiful book that demonstrates the love and loyalty you have for your very special home area, indeed 'a unique patch of Penn's Woods.' I am sharing your fine book with members of my staff to enjoy.... I appreciate... your passion for honoring... the history of our great commonwealth."

The feedback from readers, across the state of Pennsylvania and beyond, has been amazing, and I thank each of you who took the time to pen me your impressions. I have been called a "state-of-the-heart" writer. I write from the heart to reach the heart- *I write for you.*

There are many more Chronicles to share; and God willing, I will continue to share with you, in each of the subsequent volumes of *County Chronicles*, the vast wealth of history that is embedded in Pennsylvania's lush, rolling hills and valleys, majestic mountains, and ever mysterious deep woods.

And what wonderful memories I am increasingly reaping with my Chronicles! Like "Dorothy," I have clicked my heels together thrice and repeated that time-honored phrase, "There's no place like home!"

I hope you find the stories of Pennsylvania's past as captivating as I do. It is my ardent desire that by the conclusion of this third volume, those of you who live in Pennsylvania will see home with new eyes, to wit with appreciation and admiration; and those readers from afar will have become cognizant of a magical land- just over the rainbow.

Now, I invite you to open that charming window to the past that beckons on the cover of this book... enter through the tunnel of time and embark with me, across the turning pages along the yellow brick road to history, as we explore this unique corner of our nation once called "Penn's Woods."

Ceane O'Hanlon-Lincoln
Connellsville, Fayette County, Pennsylvania
April 12, 2007

"In days to come, when your children
ask you what these stones mean,
you shall tell them."
- Joshua 4:7

Amish buggies in the snow
Photo by Heather Shedron, Apple Creek, Ohio

"The Holy Experiment"

"My prison shall be my grave before I budge a jot; for I owe my conscience to no mortal man."
- William Penn, Tower of London, circa 1670

Pennsylvania's William Penn was the first great champion of American liberty and peace. During the late 1600s, when Protestants persecuted Catholics, Catholics persecuted Protestants, and both persecuted Quakers and Jews, Penn established an American sanctuary which protected freedom of conscience and worship. Nearly everywhere else colonists stole land from the Native Americans, treating them with varying degrees of distrust and disrespect; but Penn traveled unarmed among the Indians, negotiating peaceful purchases with them. He insisted that women deserve equal rights with men. In addition, he gave Pennsylvania a written constitution which limited the power of government, provided a humane penal code, and guaranteed many fundamental liberties.

This extraordinary man, who gave his family name to a hopeful new colony in America, produced a framework for governing that was far ahead of the political and social standards of his time. Penn welcomed anyone who believed in God, regardless of religious affiliation. *As a result, Pennsylvania became the best hope for the Old World's persecuted people, because it guaranteed religious freedom, ethnic tolerance, and an elected government to all who lived within its perimeters.* This included the Native Americans, the early settlers, such as the Dutch and the Swedes, as well as any new arrivals. Penn wanted those who settled in Pennsylvania to apprehend and appreciate their innate freedoms. To the traditional liberties of Englishmen, he added a further provision: "Government is free to the people under it... where the laws rule and the people are a party to them." He declared, "We put the power in the people."

In keeping with his Quaker beliefs, he required neither the bearing of arms nor the swearing of oaths. The punishment of crime was to be milder than that in English law– and was to be concerned with reform.

The ideals of William Penn that took root in his "Holy Experiment" foreshadowed, in many ways, the democratic government "of, for and by the people" that exists in the United States today. What Penn called his "Holy Experiment," we call Pennsylvania and in consequence– the United States of America.

For the *first* time in modern history, a large society proffered equal rights to people of different races and religions. In fact, Penn's dramatic example caused quite a stir in Europe. The famous French philosopher of this "Age of Enlightenment," Voltaire, himself a champion of religious tolerance, offered lavish praise: "William Penn might, with reason, boast of having brought down upon earth the Golden Age, which, in all probability, never had any real existence but in *his* dominions."

Voltaire was the fellow who fervently avowed, his words inciting the great French Revolution of 1789, "I may not agree with what you say, but I will defend to the death your right to say it!"

However, *William Penn was the only person who made major contributions to liberty in both the Old World and the New.* To learn just how he accomplished this remarkable feat, let us travel back in time to this great man's beginnings.

William Penn was born in London on October 14, 1644, the son of a British admiral, who was at sea more than he was at home. Left mostly to himself, the inquisitive young William, too, embarked on a lifelong journey, into the riveting and fascinating world of books. Reading for long periods at a time, he developed a keen interest in religion– or perhaps a better phrase here might be "a personal set of beliefs and spiritual attitudes." An idealist from early youth, Penn assumed a passionate stance that individuals had the right to worship as they please.

I will endeavor to word-paint an image of this icon of liberty and justice by sharing with you the following from a biographer who described William Penn's "...oval face of almost girlish prettiness but with strong features, the brusqueness of the straight, short nose in counterpoint to the almost sensuous mouth. What gives the face its dominant character are the eyes, burning with a dark, luminous insistence. It is known from verbal descriptions that Penn was fairly tall and athletic. Altogether, the young Penn must have been both handsome and impressive."

Due to his father's social position, William acquired a sturdy education. At age seventeen, as a student at Oxford University, the opinionated lad defied Anglican officials with his visits to John Owen, a professor who had been dismissed for advocating "tolerant humanism." The last straw, the one that got William tossed out of Oxford, occurred when Penn refused to attend services of the established Church of England. Chapel attendance was compulsory.

As a result of his behavior at university, William's parents shipped him off to France, where the rebellious youth was less likely to cause embarrassment, and where, they hoped, their outspoken son would acquire comportment. William was enrolled at *l'Académie Protestante*, the prestigious French Protestant university, located on the Loire River at Saumur in northwest France. It is noteworthy to mention that while in attendance there, he studied with Christian humanist Moïse Amyraut, a kindred spirit who supported religious toleration.

After two years of study and travel on the continent, Penn returned to England in the summer of 1664 to study law at Lincoln's Inn, the most respected law school in London. He learned the common law basis for civil liberties, and here too, he gained courtroom strategy. *He was going to need it!*

Upon completion of his law studies, William's father sent him to Ireland to manage the family estates there. It was during this period of his life when he became inspired by a leader of the Society of Friends, a pacifist group who derisively became known as "Quakers."

This Protestant sect, which was founded in 1647 by the English preacher George Fox, emphasizes a direct relationship with God; that is, its members believe that an individual's *conscience* is the ultimate authority on moral conduct. Not to say that this group dismissed/dismisses the Bible, only that they strongly believe in the power of the conscience/guiding light, the "Light of God"/"Inward Light" (later called "Inner Light") to which every human being has access.

The name "Friends" came from John 15, verse 14: "Ye are my friends, if ye do whatsoever I command you." "... For I call you friends who do my commandments."

In its earliest days, the Society of Friends was subject to persecution due to its dissent from the established Anglican Church of England. During one particular court trial, George Fox, the movement's leader, declared to the presiding judge that he feared no temporal punishments, but did quake and tremble lest he failed to obey God's commands. The judge's tagging of Fox and his followers as "Quakers" has been used ever since, over the long years, interchangeably with "Society of Friends" and "Friends."

In brief, Friends, then and now, believe that everyone who seeks to do so can communicate with God at any time and in any place, needing no clergy or intermediaries, that each and every human being has equal access to the Light of God. This pacifist group holds that everyone has responsibilities toward all other persons. In both relationships- with God and with other humans- Friends rely upon guidance from this illumination which they strongly believe comes from God Himself. Quakers deem that religion is a personal experience, the *most* personal of all human rights. Concisely, love of God and humanity are what, in my opinion, constitute Quaker unity.

From the beginning, Friends had places of worship, though they kept them free of symbols and called them "Meeting Houses," where participants yet meditate silently, speaking when the spirit moves them. One need not be a member to attend. Anyone and everyone is welcome as a friend.

Penn and the other Quakers of his era held that accepting money tainted the purity of testimony; therefore they had no paid clergy. It is my understanding that most Friends, then and now, would say that all are clergy, that there is no laity among Friends.

Despite the fact that the schisms of the nineteenth century have resulted in many branches, this Protestant sect has retained a testimony of simplicity. Today, most Friends have abandoned the plain dress tradition. From their beginnings, Quakers believed in equality of women, and it can be said that they were among the pioneers of English and American suffrage movements.

The Friends' tenets struck a responsive chord in William Penn; and the ardent humanitarian soon became a zealous member, although the English government considered attending Quaker meetings a crime. Within the next several years, Penn emerged England's leading defender of religious tolerance. Once, in the autumn of 1667, police raided a meeting at which William was in attendance. Since Penn looked like a fashionable aristocrat rather than a plain Quaker, he was given leave to go. Immediately, he protested that he was *indeed* a member of the Friends and should be treated as the others. His appeal was swiftly granted.

William Penn was imprisoned at least half a dozen times for expressing his views. So far ahead of his time, they were considered blasphemous. While in prison, he wrote one pamphlet after another about freedom of conscience, vehemently attacking intolerance. His writings significantly contributed to the literature of Quakers, which was distributed throughout the Society's underground. I daresay the Society had been started by passionate preachers with little or no real education. William Penn avowed to aid the Friends by applying his imposing scholarly knowledge and legal training. Meanwhile, his father threw him out of the house.

Drawing on his education in law, Penn proved himself capable of challenging oppressive government policies in court. *One of his banner cases affirmed the right of a jury to come to a decision uninfluenced by a judge.*

This impressive "man-of-the-scales" used his diplomatic skills and family connections to free large numbers of Friends from jail, thus personally saving their lives, because many Quakers during that era died in prison.

In 1668, Penn met the wealthy Isaac Penington and was invited to his home at Buckinghamshire. There, he was introduced to Penington's attractive stepdaughter, Gulielma Springett. It was love at first sight.

Poet John Milton's literary secretary, one Thomas Ellwood, noted in the flowery language of the era, "Miss Springett's innocently open, free and familiar conversation, spring[s] from the abundant affability, courtesy and sweetness of her temper."

William wed Gulielma on April 4, 1672. She was to bear him seven children, four of whom would die in infancy.

All the while, Penn's writings were stirring up more and more controversy. When the Anglican bishop had him imprisoned in the Tower of London, he was ordered to recant. But the bishop did not know our William, who, pulling himself up to his full height, declared, "I owe my conscience to no mortal man."

Like all true writers from the beginning of time, he could not stop writing. During those seven months in the notorious Tower, he wrote pamphlets which defined the principal elements of the Society of Friends/Quakerism. His best known work from this period, *No Cross, No Crown*, is considered a pioneering rationale- a plea- for religious toleration.

While Penn was making a name for himself as a defender of liberty, he traveled throughout Germany and Holland to observe how Quakers were faring in those areas. Holland impressed him because it was substantially free. A commercial center, people there cared primarily about peaceful cooperation. Persecuted Jews and others flocked to Holland. Little by little, Penn began to create a vision of a place where Liberty could flourish.

As others seeking religious freedom, William Penn turned his eyes and heart to the New World, to lands being colonized in America. Before I continue, I feel compelled to state here that despite Penn's remarkable clarity of vision for human rights, he had a mystifying blind spot about slavery. He owned slaves in America, as did several other Quakers. Antislavery eventually did become a widely shared Quaker position, but not until circa 1758, about forty years after Penn's passing. While engaged in the research for this Chronicle, it was surprising to me, in light of their humanitarian views and their fair treatment of the Native Americans, that Quakers owned slaves at all. All I can say is that, shamefully, slavery was an accepted practice of the times, during which slaves, as disgraceful as this sounds, were not thought of as human.

Convinced that religious tolerance could not be achieved in England, Penn's attention turned to a group of Quakers and others who had settled in 1677 in New Jersey. Those

Pennsbury Manor, Morrisville, in beautiful, historic Bucks County, PA
Photos courtesy Pennsbury Manor and the Pennsylvania Historical and Museum Commission

colonists had brought with them a covenant of liberties that reflected his beliefs. In 1681, Penn transferred these ideas- and ideals- to the dense wilderness on the west side of the Delaware River, north of Maryland, where he received a charter from King Charles II for a new colony (approximately the present-day size of Pennsylvania), where roughly a thousand Swedes, Dutch, and Natives lived.

Actually, the charter, which was granted on March 4, 1681, went to William in payment for an outstanding royal debt owed to his now-deceased admiral father. Into the bargain, I am thinking, as have others before me, that the idea of a colony of their own, across the great pond of the Atlantic, likely seemed to the king an easy way to be rid of the "troublesome" Quakers. William would be proprietor, owning all the land, accountable directly to the king. It was agreed that at the beginning of each year, Penn would give the king two beaver skins and a fifth of any gold and silver mined within the colony.

William wanted straightaway to christen his outpost "Sylvania," due to the deep woods that covered it, but the king attached Admiral Penn's name to the colony, thus creating the name "Pennsylvania." William had no problem with that, though he feared Posterity would think he had named it for himself. As it turned out, his feeling was not off the mark.

Penn's Frame of Government for his very special protectorate called for a democratic assembly and council under the proprietor's (that is, *his*) direction and for guarantees of fundamental individual liberties. It provided for the security of individual property, virtually unlimited free enterprise, a free press, trial by jury- and, of course, religious tolerance. *Pennsylvania's was the first constitution to provide for peaceful change via amendments.*

As governor, Penn would retain a veto over proposed legislation; but he declared to those who would settle his colony: "You shall be governed by laws of your own making and live a free and, if you will, a sober and industrious people. I shall not usurp the right of any or oppress his person...."

William Penn set sail for America aboard the good ship *Welcome*, arriving on November 8, 1682. Over the next two years, with assembled Friends, he founded Philadelphia, choosing the name himself, which translates from the Greek, the "City of Brotherly Love." He personally approved the site of the community, between the Delaware and Schuylkill rivers, and it was William Penn who named the major arteries of the town, including Broad, Chestnut, Pine and Spruce.

When Penn had first inspected the wee town, only about ten houses stood near the wharf, although others soon sprang up. More than ever, he believed what he had proclaimed about the colony before he left England: "I am firm in my faith that the Lord will prosper it."

As new settlers poured into Pennsylvania, they cleared the rich farmlands that spread out in every direction, providing commodities for Philadelphia to export, at the same time creating a market for Philadelphia imports.

One of the most important things to stress in this Chronicle is that William Penn achieved peaceful relations with the Natives whose home this was- the Susquehannock, Shawnee, and the *Lenni Lenapé* (Delaware), among others.

Penn appointed his cousin, William Markham, to be his deputy governor. From the onset, Penn *purchased* lands from the Indians. According to the respected historian C. Hale Sipe in *The Indian Chiefs of Pennsylvania*, the first Indian deed of record was a purchase of lands in what is now Bucks County, made by Deputy Governor Markham for William Penn. This deed is dated 15 July 1682. The Native land grantors included fourteen Delaware chiefs or sachems. The payment list of goods traded for the land is a formidable one, and one that the Delaware leaders found highly pleasing.

On 23 June 1683, William Penn himself purchased additional tracts of land from the Indians, and it is on this particular deed that the famous Delaware Chief Tamanend/ King Tammany made his mark- that of a coiled snake.

Tamanend stands tall among the Lenapé chiefs. Not a lot is known about him except that he was greatly respected as a wise man/ sachem, even called by some a "saint." He was head chief of the Unami or Turtle Clan of Delawares prior to 1683 to circa 1697, and is known in the Colonial Records of Pennsylvania as the "King of all the Delawares." He is the Tammany of Tammany Societies that sprouted in the cities of our nation during our early history.

It should also be noted that no strong liquor ever appeared in the lists of trade goods supplied by Penn, as they had on Markham's earlier list. There is no doubt that Penn realized straightaway the harmful effects of alcohol on the Natives. In William Penn's "Great Law," drawn up shortly after his arrival in Pennsylvania, there appeared a provision punishing anyone, by fine of five pounds, who should "... presume to sell or exchange any rum or brandy or any strong liquors at any time to any Indian within this province."

Though no authentic record of the "Great Treaty" with Tamanend exists, it is replete with romantic appeal. Immortalized in Benjamin West's famous painting, the scene depicts Penn, unarmed, clad in somber Quaker garb, addressing the assembled Indians, Tamanend and his associate chiefs, under the great elm at Shakamaxon, within the limits of the "City of Brotherly Love."

According to historian Sipe in the above account, William Penn's words at this significant occasion reflected his passionate beliefs: "We meet on the broad pathway of good faith and goodwill; no advantage shall be taken on either side, but all shall be openness and love...."

Tamanend's words in turn are equally noble: "We will live in love with William Penn and his children as long as the creeks and rivers flow, and while the sun, moon, and stars endure."

French philosopher Voltaire said of this admirable event in Pennsylvania's- *America's*- proud history that it was the "... *only* treaty never sworn to and never broken."

The Historical Society of Pennsylvania in Philadelphia houses a wampum belt-gift to William Penn that his *Lenni Lenapé* friends had presented to him as a token of peace. However, Penn's documents with the Natives were lost within a few decades- likely because future administrators did not want to follow his examples. Thus, there has always been a lack of agreement between historians as to the precise date the Great Treaty took place. Like Sipe, I tend to think it was in November, since it was described well before him by historian George Bancroft that the participating parties met "... under the shelter of the forest now leafless by the frosts of autumn."

I should add, however, that West's rendering shows the trees to be in full foliage, though the painter may have done so for esthetics. Many historians do fix the time of the Great Treaty in June, since that is when Penn's first Indian land purchases took place. Regardless of whether it was summer or fall, the year of the Great Treaty was 1683.

Above all else, Native Americans admire courage, and the fact that William Penn traveled among them unarmed and unafraid impressed them greatly. Natives love games and sport, and legend has it that Penn was a superior sprinter who engaged in races with them, winning the contests along with their lasting respect.

As a former language teacher and world traveler, I know the importance of taking the time to learn a bit of conversational language of the peoples among whom one ventures. Penn learned the Indian dialects, but did at times negotiate with an interpreter.

Each and every one of William Penn's land purchases were via peaceful, voluntary exchanges. And although policies were more strained under his sons, his negotiated peace lasted for some seventy years- which has to be a record in American history.

I can proudly relate that Pennsylvania was a sharp contrast to the harsh treatment of Indians in other colonies. In New England, for example, the Puritans made political dissent a crime. They whipped, tarred and feathered, even hanged Quakers, conducted witch trials and hanged women and men accused of witchcraft; and they treated the Native Americans abominably, hunting them as they did the wild beasts in the forests- even selling captured Indians into slavery.

Pennsylvania, a spiritual haven with a diversity of religions, was, from its beginnings, tolerant of eccentric sects some of which were good herbalists. Thus, it is not surprising that the colony had yet another significant difference between itself and its neighbors to the north. Pennsylvania did not hang witches.

The only witch trial (though not the only occult trial) within the perimeters of Penn's Woods occurred in 1683. The defendant was Margaret Mattson, a Swede, who resided with her husband on a farm west of Philadelphia at what is now Ridley Creek. Mattson, who was also known as the "Witch of Ridley Creek," was brought before the provincial court consisting of both a Grand and a Petit Jury, in addition to William Penn and his attorney general. Mattson's daughter (who seemed to me a greedy as well as a vengeful sort) testified against her mother, stating that the latter was in league with the Devil. The prosecution put forth the usual accusations. During the trial, the haggish-looking Margaret was accused of various forms of witchcraft- bewitching geese, cattle, and people. A verdict was soon reached, but like the old woman herself, it was a toothless indictment. Mattson was found "Guilty of having the comon [sic] frame of a witch, but not guilty in manner and forme [sic] as shee [sic] stands endicted [sic]."

What is most interesting, according to several accounts, is that Margaret had the following exchange with William Penn himself. Straightaway, during the course of the trial, the proprietor asked her these two rather leading questions: "Art thou a witch? Hast thou ridden through the air on a broomstick?"

Mattson nodded, promptly articulating a firm: "Yes." Why she answered Penn thus is debatable. One might well ask History if the crone was simpleminded, intensely sarcastic, or did she believe she could ride through the night on a silver broomstick? We shall never know. Perhaps Margaret was simply not fluent in English, and keep in mind that Penn used the biblical dialect of the Quakers. The most fascinating part of this story again shifts to William. Reportedly, he declared as there was no law against riding a broomstick, Mrs. Mattson had every right to ride one if she so chose. Penn then ordered the lady discharged. I wondered when I read that, if a smile had played at his lips when he delivered the above passage.

Within the comfortable perimeters of Penn's Woods, its far-thinking proprietor insisted on low taxes. A 1683 law established a low tax on cider and liquor, a low tariff on imports and on exported hides and furs. To help promote settlement, Penn suspended all taxes for a year. Then when the time came to reimpose taxes, he encountered fierce resistance and "... had to put it off."

Collecting rents due him was always a headache. These monies came to him only in dribs and drabs, and William never earned enough from the colony to offset the costs of administration which he paid out of his personal capital. Toward the end of his life, he confessed that Pennsylvania was a net loss, costing him some £30,000.

Not long after his first sojourn in his new colony, Penn set about building for himself and his family a mansion, which he promptly christened "Pennsbury Manor." Situated twenty-six miles up the Delaware River, the house was not yet completed when he had to hastily return to England to defend Pennsylvania's boundaries against claims by Lord Baltimore, the proprietor of Maryland. Gulielma, who was pregnant, had stayed behind in England, waiting not only for their child to be born, but for their new home to be readied in Pennsylvania. What William did not know at the time was that he would be forced to remain in England for the next fifteen years.

In 1688, Penn's fortunes took a turn when, in England, the Stuarts were overthrown. Penn had Stuart connections and was subsequently arrested for treason. He was cleared in late 1690, but not long afterward was again labeled a traitor. The harried humanitarian became a fugitive for the next four years, secreting himself away in the squalor of the horrid London slums. Certainly it was a bleak time for William; however, unbeknownst to him, relief was headed his way.

It was his friend, Enlightenment essayist John Locke, who helped Penn restore his good name. You may recall from your history classes that Locke's writings influenced Thomas Paine who, upon his arrival in the colonies in 1776, would write the brilliant political pamphlet *Common Sense* that would urge the American colonists to break with the British monarchy and proclaim their Independence. Paine would make use of the liberal ideals of John Locke (who had exchanged ideas and ideals with *his* friend, William Penn) to press the case for Liberty.

Though Locke had come to Penn's rescue, William's dark days were far from over. No sooner was his name cleared than his beloved wife passed away at the age of forty-eight, after a lingering illness. The disease, thought to be tuberculosis, also took William's firstborn son. The layered trials and tribulations had begun to show in Penn's appearance. His once graceful stance was now bent; and his cherubic boyish face reflected the grief of losing a beloved mate and child. Friends said that he went about with a listless air, in an absent sort of way.

Then, Cupid's arrow found again William's tender heart. In March of 1696, a couple of years after Guli's death, William married twenty-five-year-old Hannah Callowhill, the plain and practical daughter of a Bristol linen draper. There are those who have said that William married Hannah for money. This author does not dismiss that theory in its entirety; for, in all honesty, money was somewhat of a consideration in both of Penn's marriages. Granted, this was not the romantic courtship and passionate union he had had with Guli, but it was a good match. Twenty-seven years his junior, Hannah, in spite of their age difference, would prove herself a capable helpmate.

In 1699, William arrived with his new wife at his "fine, greene countrie towne" of Philadelphia in his fast-growing colony of Pennsylvania.

Pennsbury had been waiting. It was a good homecoming.

Hannah's companionship and his return to Pennsylvania had revived William's spirits, in spite of the fact that nothing or no one could ease his money problems. In his absence, things had changed. The colonists were beginning to buck his authority, and often refused to pay their rents and taxes. In response to protests, Penn negotiated a new frame of government, adopting the Charter of Privileges.

This constitution lasted for three-quarters of a century. It confirmed anew the democratic form of government, guaranteeing individual rights of those living within the boundaries of Pennsylvania. For the first time, it granted the assembly the right to initiate bills. As governor, Penn retained the right to veto an action if he deemed it necessary. When an unfriendly Parliament threatened to annex all proprietary colonies, William made hurried plans yet again to set sail for England.

The truth of the matter was that William had always been sloppy about his business practices. He cared more for people than for money; it was as simple as that. He often could not be bothered with administrative details, preferring to leave them in the hands of a business manager. His was a fellow by name of Philip Ford from whom William, over many years, had borrowed money to cover debts. Each year, Penn spent on the average of twice what he received. Worse, the trusting William signed papers without reading them. The paper he signed with Ford listed Pennsylvania as surety in the event that William could not pay him back. Current scholarship does not paint Philip Ford as quite the snake in the grass he was formerly considered to be. In fact, the manager never acted on the signed agreement.

After Ford died, his wife Bridget found the document and used it in an attempt to call back the loans her husband had made. When William could not pay, she had him tossed into debtor's prison. However, her coldheartedness backfired; and in 1708, the Lord Chancellor ruled that the "... equity of redemption still remained with William Penn and his heirs...."

Shortly before embarking for England in the autumn of 1701, William gathered a large assembly of his Delaware and Shawnee friends at Pennsbury Manor. He wanted to reiterate and reaffirm the covenants of peace and goodwill that had always prevailed, binding them together as brothers. The actual meeting took place in the manse's great hall.

The sachems assured Penn that they had never broken a covenant "... made with their hearts...." When the conference ended, William bestowed upon the Native leaders many fine gifts, before the Indians withdrew to the courtyard. There, under the stately trees, aflame with autumn splendor, Penn's Native guests engaged in ceremonies of their own, including the smoking of their calumets, called by the Whites "peace pipes."

Native Americans did not break a covenant which included this traditional validating of language- their words rising with the smoke, skyward, to Creator- for that would have meant breaking a covenant with God Himself.

There are some historians who have written that Queen Aliquippa of the Susquehannocks/Conestogas was present at Penn's farewell, along with her husband and infant son. When we travel back through the swirling mists of time, people and events are sometimes shrouded in mystery. I can offer no proof of her attendance in this discussion, though Aliquippa may *well* have been there. It should be noted that several spellings exist for the queen's name. I have also read that she was a Seneca. I think I can offer a reason for the tribe confusion. In the late 1600s, the Senecas defeated the Susquehannocks. Since Aliquippa survived, she may have been adopted and/or married into the Seneca tribe. Her history illustrates time and again that she possessed a strong personality, and such a trait was much admired by the Senecas.

We do know for certain that William Penn informed the chiefs at the gathering that this was likely the last time he would meet with them. He related that he had acted, never out of political designs or selfish interests, but always out of respect and true affection. He entreated them to continue in his absence to cultivate feelings of brotherly love with those left in his place, so that the bond between their two peoples "... would grow ever stronger throughout the passing years."

Penn took special care to inform the sachems that the sell or trade of liquor of all kinds would continue to be absolutely forbidden in his colony, and that, according to their desire and his, this law would be staunchly enforced. As mentioned previously, Penn had seen early on the degradation and destruction that strong drink wrought among the Natives, and he had always done all within *his* power to prevent this and other vices of the white man from permeating the Native culture.

Before the conference broke up, William told the sachems that if any person or persons within the boundaries of Pennsylvania broke this law, or any agreements they had made together that day, the chiefs were to immediately inform the leaders of his province, so that the offenders might be prosecuted. He raised his hand then in the ancient sign of *adieu* and eternal friendship, turned and walked inside. He would never see his beloved "Penn's Woods" or his Indian brothers again. It was a sad day for all present- *a sad day for Pennsylvania.*

"Well would it have been for the colony of Pennsylvania," historian Sipe tells us, "had his successors emulated the Swedes and William Penn's noble examples..." in dealing with the Natives!

Penn's time in his colony totaled less than five years, though his negotiated peace, as stated above, lasted for some seventy. William Penn's "Holy Experiment" had been Elysian compared to what was to come between the years 1754 to 1795. That era would leave a bloody smear on the pages of Pennsylvania history books- with its half-century of virtually nonstop Indian warfare, beginning with the French and Indian War and ending, after the Revolution, with the final defeat of the Indians at Fallen Timbers. That crushing blow, in 1794 in neighboring Ohio, would result in the Treaty of Greenville the subsequent year.

During the turbulent period of Indian wars that would befall Penn's Woods, an incident in the future winter of 1763 warrants mentioning here. It would happen in consequence of panic when Pontiac's War erupted, spreading terror and a path of destruction throughout the White settlements from Detroit down to the Carolinas. A group of inflamed Scotch-Irish frontiersmen, known as the "Paxton Boys" after the township where they resided in Dauphin County, would shoot and hack to death, in their fear-rooted fury, a group of peaceful Conestoga (Susquehannock) Indians. Afterward, the "Boys" would torch the gore-splattered log dwelling where they had done the killings. Later, when some local men would be sifting through the ashes, they would discover a charred leather pouch containing the Conestoga's 1701 treaty signed by William Penn's hand. The document pledged that the colonists and their Indian brothers "... shall forever hereafter as one head and one heart... live in true friendship and amity as one people."

To return to William Penn, who was now back in England: In October 1712, Penn suffered a major apoplexy while composing a missive about the future of Pennsylvania. Four months later, he suffered a second major stroke. As a result of the damage to his brain, he had severe difficulty speaking and writing, and this must have caused the great communicator terrible frustration in his attempts to make himself understood.

When Bridget Ford had forced William into court, the court determined a debt figure, less than what the widow Ford wanted, while still a sizeable amount, and certainly more than Penn could pay. To free William from debtor's prison, other Quakers had pitched in, and the Ford debt was satisfied. To repay the Friends who had come to his rescue, William Penn had but one recourse- he had to try and sell Pennsylvania back to the Crown. He almost saw the process through, when, at the last stages, the strokes incapacitated him. And that is how the Penn family kept Pennsylvania until the Revolution.

While the capable Hannah managed his affairs, aided by their colonial secretary, James Logan, William used his final days to bond with his sons whom he had missed during his years of travel. The end, however, was near. He was old now and, to his chagrin, very tired. Like all those, across the bridge of time, whose lives are coming to a close, he *knew* it.

William Penn, Liberator, passed away quietly at the age of seventy-four, on July 30, 1718. He was buried at Jordans, Buckinghamshire, England, next to his beloved Guli. To quote historian C. Hale Sipe from *The Indian Wars of Pennsylvania*: "When his great heart was cold and still in death, the Red Man of the Pennsylvania forests lost his truest friend."

During William Penn's life, there had been no serious Indian troubles in his colony, no actual Indian warfare. In contrast, less than a generation after his passing, the Shawnees with their "grandfathers," the Delawares- who had made their first treaty with William Penn under the great elm at Shakamaxon- would rise in bloody revolt for a series of injustices done them, spreading, rather than the bonds of friendship, terror, devastation and death throughout the Pennsylvania settlements. As high a regard as Indians hold courage, they believed in avenging wrongs; not to have done so would have been against what they held true in their hearts. *This would be an awful truth for Penn's successors to learn.*

However, there were rights and wrongs on both sides, good and evil on each, because both factions, Natives and settlers alike, struggled for *a way of life* along with possession of the precious land. That land was *home* to the Indian, and he revered it like his mother. But when a frontier farmer stood on the land he worked, and he looked out toward the horizon- all he could see was the future. *That* is the simple truth, and History should not hide that truth.

Nonetheless, let us not be too quick to cast full culpability upon Pennsylvania's frontier farmers. During the long and bloody years extending from the French and Indian War to the period following the Revolution, the American colonists were on the receiving end of first the French-instigated then British-incited Native violence. The small, scattered farms on the Pennsylvania frontier were perfect targets for hit-and-run Indian warfare. And know this, readers: Both the French and the English paid the Indians well for settler scalps.

Closer to the moment of our main discussion: After Hannah's death in 1726, the proprietorship passed into the hands of William's surviving sons, John, Thomas and Richard. Thus, as mentioned above, Pennsylvania remained a proprietary colony of the Penn family until it gained its statehood, becoming one of the original thirteen stars on the beautiful flag George Washington commissioned at the time of America's bid for Independence.

Long before William Penn's death, Pennsylvania ceased to be a place dominated by Quakers. Penn's policy of religious tolerance and peaceful coexistence attracted a vivid melting pot of war-weary Europeans- English, Scotch-Irish, Irish, Welsh, German, French, Jews, Catholics, Protestants, and an assortment of Protestant sects, including Dunkers, Huguenots, Mennonites, Amish, Moravians, and more.

The bright and far-reaching light of liberty lit the way for so many immigrants that, by the American Revolution, Pennsylvania had grown to some 300,000 people, becoming one of the largest American colonies. *I can safely relate that Pennsylvania was America's first grand melting pot. We are, and always have been, a true slice of America.* Fortunately, yet today, dozens of ethnic groups have preserved and sustained their unique customs and traditions. Across Pennsylvania, annual ethnic festivals are a highlight of our magnificent cultural milieu. In Westmoreland County, there are the Ligonier Highland Games; in Sullivan County, there's the Delaware/*Lenni Lenapé* Pow-wow; the impressive Irish Festival in Pittsburgh; Scottish, Native American, Irish, German, Italian, Polish, Slovak, and Russian festivals abound. And this is but a wee sampling of Pennsylvania's colorful ethnic celebrations.

Philadelphia, a major commercial center, was Colonial America's largest city. It was our nation's first capital, remaining so until 1800. Prior to and during the American Revolution, the City of Brotherly Love's presses churned out newspapers, pamphlets, almanacs and books, proving it to be an intellectual center, as well as rendering it the "sacred site" for Liberty. Today, people around the world cherish and honor this talisman, and they come to Philadelphia to "touch" it. At Independence Mall, visitors can ponder the symbol of American liberty, the 2,080-pound Liberty Bell.

Indeed the spot where Liberty was born, Philadelphia is the site that inspired the incomparable Thomas Jefferson to pen the Declaration of Independence. It is the location where those courageous men known as the Founding Fathers drafted the Constitution of a new nation- founded on liberty.

If you were to don colonial attire, you would blend right in at Pennsbury, the handsome estate William Penn built for himself and his family on the Delaware River, north of Philadelphia. The manor is typical of that of English gentry (whence the late 1600s-early 1700s) with its Georgian mansion and outbuildings, intricate formal gardens and extensive orchards. William Penn planted hundreds of apple trees, and still today, delicious cider is made at the estate. An interesting fact is that Penn was so skillful at drying fruit that he shared his recipe with his mother-in-law, who raved about it to the rest of the family.

Penn really thought of himself as a country gentleman. "The country life," he wrote, "is to be preferred; for there we see the works of God; but in cities little else than the works of men; and the one makes a better subject for contemplation than the other." William believed the country life best for his children- and children in general.

Penn knew what future generations, who would strike roots in Pennsylvania's kind soil, would all discover. Pennsylvania country living is indefinable in terms of estimated value, its rewards measured in intangibles chiefly. There are no price tags for Penn's ubiquitous Woods with their leafy secret places; for rolling, emerald fields falling away to sparkling rivers; for the sunshade of a willow and the mirrored glass-green of a summer pond; for the splendor of crisp autumn days in the mountains, or the glow of lanterns lit for a winter evening's outing, their gold splashed amid the blue-shadowed trees o'er a snow-blanketed countryside.

According to *Guide to the Homes of Famous Pennsylvanians* by Arthur P. Miller, Jr. and Marjorie L. Miller, in addition to the official Pennsbury Manor web site, after William Penn's death, Pennsbury's buildings collapsed through neglect, and the estate degenerated into ruins. Visitors, however, never stopped coming to the mesmeric locale. Though Penn's descendants had sold the land, the state of Pennsylvania, inspired by the work being done at Colonial Williamsburg in Virginia, purchased forty-three of the original 8,000 acres; and between 1933 and 1942, gave its management over to the Pennsylvania Historical Commission. In the 1940s, the PHC merged with the State Museum and the State Archives to become the Pennsylvania Historical and Museum Commission.

Today, Pennsbury stands as a monument to Pennsylvania's founder, to this creative, committed man who spent his entire life, health and fortune to establish and prove his "Holy Experiment."

At the end of a mile-long lane, the historical site again resembles the original estate, and several pieces of William Penn's furniture and tableware have found their way back home in the reconstructed manse, where stately trees shade, and the Delaware River glides gracefully past the front door. The reconstructed outbuildings include a barn, smokehouse, bake house, brewery, blacksmith shop, icehouse, woodshed, and a "necessary house" (outhouse).

Whilst visitors stroll amongst the delightfully landscaped gardens and orchards, horses crop the lush grass round about. Sheep dot the peaceful, rolling countryside, and gentle oxen plow the richly turned fields. Colonial-attired docents and workers go about their duties in the spirit of three centuries past. The all-round pastoral atmosphere reflects Penn's love of nature; just as inside, the warm glow of flickering sconces and candlelight pleasantly carry visitors on a romantic journey, through the channel of time, to the 1700s. The ambience at Pennsbury is pure *magic!*

An interesting fact I learned from the gracious folks at Pennsbury is that in 1699, William Penn, in order to improve the quality of his horses, imported a regal Arabian stallion named Tamerlane. At this writing, at least one Arabian still adorns the Pennsbury grounds.

Tours, exhibits, workshops, special programs and seasonal events (such as the Manor Fair in September and Holly Nights in December) offer visitors realistic time-travel into seventeenth-century plantation life.

Only twenty-six miles from downtown Philadelphia, Pennsbury Manor, located at 400 Pennsbury Memorial Road, Morrisville, in beautiful, historic Bucks County, is, as stated above, operated by the Pennsylvania Historical and Museum Commission. The site is open year-round, Tuesday through Saturday, 9–5, and Sundays noon to 5; closed Mondays.

Admission is reasonable, free for children under six, with special rates for seniors, families, and other groups. Tours begin at the visitors' center with an interesting and informative video orientation to the site. Here too are an artifact exhibit and the museum shop. Pennsbury is handicapped-accessible; wheelchairs available. There is free on-site parking.

I strongly advise comfortable walking shoes. Visitors should plan to stay two hours, at least, in order to enjoy everything. For more information, call 215-946-0400, or visit online by typing "Pennsbury Manor" into your computer's search engine. I hope you will one day pay a real visit to Pennsbury– it is a true living-history site!

In summary, William Penn was a visionary. Though he had been on a first-name basis with royalty, he made it possible for all classes to settle in his colony. His "Holy Experiment" set a profoundly important example and precedence for Liberty. Penn went beyond the theories of his good friend John Locke to show that a free society can thrive. Pennsylvania demonstrated to the watching world that different races and religions can live and work together peacefully by simply believing in God, themselves– and the Golden Rule.

Due to William Penn's "Holy Experiment of brotherly love," our noble commonwealth is the Keystone of the towering bastion of ideals that have become the great and enduring "United States of America."

"Amish Country"

"Come out from among them and be ye separate."
- II Corinthians 6:17

Charming Lancaster County, the garden spot of America in eastern Pennsylvania, has long been known as the capital of Amish country. Though there are Amish communities in several other counties of Pennsylvania, as well as in other states of our nation and Canada, the largest groups of Old Order Amish live in Lancaster County, Pennsylvania, and Holmes County, Ohio.

The Pennsylvania county and county seat, Lancaster was named for Lancashire, England; and its symbol, as that of its namesake, is the red rose, from the House of Lancashire. The city of Lancaster was our nation's capital for a single day when the Continental Congress met there in September 1777. The Colonial government had fled Philadelphia to escape approaching British troops, stopping at Lancaster city before moving on to York, Pennsylvania. Now, let us embark on our journey to scenic Amish country with the correct pronunciation of the name of these fascinating but "plain" folk: *Ah' - mish.*

Nearly everyone who has ever glimpsed an Amish horse-drawn buggy clopping along a road amidst modern traffic, a bearded Amish man at the reins, and at his side, an Amish woman attired in a long dress and bonnet, is curious about these people. When I was growing up, I often referred to them as "Pennsylvania Dutch." However, they are *not* of Dutch extraction; they are German. The erroneous "Dutch" came about due to the fact that they speak *Deutsch,* which is the German word for German.

The Amish are actually trilingual. They speak a dialect of German at home, which, ironically, is called "Pennsylvania Dutch" or "Pennsylvania German." At worship, they use High German. They learn English in their schools, so that they can converse with the "English," that is, anyone who is not Amish.

The curiosity we have for this group is understandable and expected due to the very simplicity of their lifestyle in such a complex and often convoluted world. Too, their ways are sated with taboos that forbid the use of cosmetics, jewelry, wallpaper, curtains (plain green window blinds being the most common solution for privacy) and frills of all kinds. Those frills include what we think of as *necessities* in our homes, such as electricity, radio, stereos, television and its amenities of VCRs and CD players, telephones and computers. Yet today, the Amish continue to be the most conservative of the "plain sects," which also include the Mennonites and the Brethren.

Harried by persecution in the Old World, it is logical that they found their way to the

Early twentieth-century/vintage postcard depicting Amish at Lancaster, PA
From author's personal collection

New, to "Penn's Woods," "Penn's Paradise," as the Amish came to call it. Indeed, there is a divine little town in Lancaster County named exactly that- *Paradise.*

The Amish have their roots in the Mennonite community. Both originated with the Anabaptist movement in Europe, which came about at the time of the Reformation. The Anabaptists believed that only adults, who had professed their faith, should be baptized. Separated from the larger society, many of the early Anabaptists were put to death as heretics by both Catholics and Protestants, though many escaped by fleeing to the mountains of Switzerland and southern Germany. [See "The Village," *County Chronicles Volume II.*]

Amish horses await their owners who are attending a public auction. Auctions are popular among the Amish for both practical and social purposes.
Photo by Heather Shedron

It should be added that, essentially, Anabaptists advocate, in addition to adult baptism, nonresistance (passive submission/not resisting violence with force), and separation of church and state. In fact, the Anabaptists were some of the earliest folks to espouse separation of church and state.

Church Amish family en route to Sunday service
Photo by Heather Shedron

In the protective mountains of Switzerland and Germany, the Anabaptists began their tradition of farming and holding their worship services in their homes rather than in churches. This practice came about because they believe, as stated in the Bible, "The Lord of heaven and earth dwelleth not in temples made with hands."

In the mid-1500s, a young Catholic priest from Holland named Menno Simons joined the movement; and before long, his writings and leadership unified several of the Anabaptist groups, who were termed, after him, "Mennonites."

Then, in the late 1600s, a Swiss bishop, Jacob Amman, broke with the Mennonites, whom he felt were becoming too worldly. His followers, too, were named for him and became known as "Amish." Though the two groups have split, they still hold the same beliefs concerning adult baptism and nonresistance. They differ in other matters, such as dress, use of modern technology, and interpretation of the Bible to which both groups staunchly adhere.

The important fact that I wish to convey in this Chronicle is that both Mennonites and Amish settled in Pennsylvania as part of *America's first great melting pot- William Penn's "Holy Experiment" of religious tolerance.* The first sizable influx of Amish arrived in Lancaster County circa 1727.

Amish children at spring plowing
Photo by Heather Shedron

Going home.
Photos by Heather Shedron,
P.O. Box 84, Apple Creek, Ohio 44606

Stressing humility, long hours of hard work, family, community, and separation from the modern world, the Amish, to some, may seem trapped in the eighteenth century, the Colonial period. To some, they may appear inflexible, unwilling to change with the times. The fact of the matter is that the Amish *do* change; it is just that their changes come about a lot slower than ours. Amish examine new ideas carefully. If some new gadget or invention threatens the simplicity of their lifestyle or their family unity, they will reject it.

Old Order groups all drive horses and buggies rather than cars, though an Amish will ride in a car if a situation warrants it. If you see what looks like an Amishman driving a car, he's a Mennonite. Amish reject electricity in their homes, and send their children to their own one-room schoolhouses.

The ringing of an old-fashioned school bell, carried across the neat patchwork of rolling fields, signals the time for children to cease farm chores and take up their books. Amish children attend school only through the eighth grade. This is all the education the Old Order feels is necessary– the fundamental "three R's," reading, writing, and arithmetic. This belief is based on the words in the Bible that read: "... the wisdom of the world is foolishness with God."

After eighth grade, the young Amish work on their fathers' farms or in their businesses until they marry. Though they pay school taxes, the Amish have always struggled to keep their children out of the public school systems. In 1972, the Supreme Court handed down a landmark unanimous decision which exempted the Old Order Amish and related groups from state compulsory attendance beyond the eighth grade. However, it should be noted that many Mennonites and Progressive Amish do attend high school and even college.

This might be a good time to reiterate that the Amish do pay taxes. In addition to school taxes, they pay real estate taxes, state taxes where they exist, and Federal income tax. Most Amish vote. The Old Order are exempt from Social Security and Medicare, except when employed by an outside person or concern (non-Amish), since this would automatically be withheld, though they can apply for an exemption. Many Amish use their carpentry and other skills during the winter months to earn extra income. Old Order Amish do not collect Social Security, Medicare, or assistance from any government agency. You'll never see an Amish on relief! *They support and care for their own.* Because they lack insurance, this can be quite difficult, to say the least.

Due to their separateness, they suffer from some uncommon problems. Since theirs is such a closed society, new blood lines are rarely introduced, resulting in various genetic disorders. They are also distinguished by a variety of unique syndromes. And since almost all of the Amish descend primarily from the same few hundred founders in the eighteenth century, genetic disorders among them are from founder effects exacerbated by a degree of inbreeding. Some of these disorders are quite rare (outside the Amish community) and serious enough that they have increased the mortality rate among Amish children.

For decades, the majority of the Amish accepted these problems as "*Gottes wille*," God's will, rejecting any use of genetic tests to prevent the appearance of these disorders. However, there is an escalating consciousness among the Amish of the advantages of exogamy (outbreeding). Increasing genetic diversity reduces the probability of diseases or other undesirable traits that occur due to genetic abnormalities.

In the 1990s, a handful of hospitals created special outreach programs to assist the Amish, the first of which was instituted at the Susquehanna Health System in central Pennsylvania by James H. Huebert. Treating genetic problems is the mission of Dr. Holmes Morton's Clinic for Special Children in Strasburg, Pennsylvania, which has developed effective treatment for such problems as maple syrup urine disease (so called due to the burned-sugar smell to the urine), which previously was fatal.

Smack dab in the middle of a central Pennsylvanian cornfield, the clinic is a marvel of genetic medicine and science. It has been embraced by most Amish and has largely ended a situation in which some parents felt it necessary to quit the community (which normally resulted in shunning) in order to properly care for their children.

The combination clinic for Special Children and Amish Research center, which was raised by hand, rope and horse in the Amish way, is the creation and life's work of Dr. Holmes Morton and his wife Caroline. The Harvard-educated couple surprised colleagues and friends when, in 1987, they announced they were giving up prestigious urban posts in Philadelphia and packing up the family to begin a new life among the Amish and Mennonites. According to several sources, they have never regretted the move. Since their arrival in Amish country, the Mortons' credibility among the sects has been cemented. To the plain folk who travel to the clinic from their homes via horse and buggy, this help in saving their children has been heaven-sent. "This building is really a pillar of the Amish community," Dr. Morton has told the press.

During wartime, the Amish are conscientious objectors. Basically, they believe in keeping God's commands and minding their own business, as well as putting in long hours of hard work- their day begins at 4 a.m.- sticking together and helping one another.

There is no social drinking among the Amish, though a few might make homemade wine for medicinal purposes.

Let's talk a bit about their dress, and be advised that I am speaking in generalities in this Chronicle, for customs differ slightly from district (congregation) to district. Old Order Amish women and girls wear modest, collarless, unadorned dresses made from solid-color fabric depending on the season. Printed material is taboo. Mennonites wear printed fabrics. The print is what I would term "Victorian," such as a delicate floral pattern against a background of maroon, navy or sky blue, green, brown, black, or soft pink.

Dress sleeves are long or mid-arm length, and the rather full skirts fall halfway between the shin of the legs and the shoes. An apron covers the dress, and straight pins or snaps fasten the Amish women's attire.

Their limited articles of clothing are hung on pegs along bedroom walls. There are pegs for hanging coats and hats downstairs as well. The peg method of hanging clothing is found in old Amish homes. In newer Amish homes, there are some closets.

Never does an Amish woman cut her hair, which is traditionally worn parted in the middle. On young girls, a narrow section on each side of the center part is braided, then pulled back from the temples in a plain, tight bun just above the nape of the neck. Women roll that narrow section of hair away from the face, then pull the tresses back into the customary bun.

Over the head is the traditional, heart-shaped prayer cap, gauzy white if the woman is married, black if she is single. Amish females cover their heads with a prayer cap because of the biblical words: "... every woman that prayeth or prophesieth with her head uncovered dishonoureth her head...."

Amish girls and women do not wear makeup or cosmetics of any kind, nor do they adorn themselves with jewelry. Remember, humility and simplicity are key to their tenets. Anything that smacks of vanity is rejected and taboo. "It is not our way," the Amish will tell you.

Men and boys wear dark-hued suits, straight-cut frock coats without lapels, broadfall trousers with buttons not zippers, suspenders and solid-color, plain shirts. Socks and shoes are black, as are the broad-brimmed felt hats they wear in the colder season. Wide-brimmed straw hats are worn in summer. While the men's shirts fasten with buttons, their vests close with hooks and eyes. Suits may have buttons, and Velcro has come into some Amish lives, although most prefer the traditional hooks and eyes.

Amish men do not have mustaches, which are reminiscent of military figures; but they do, as in the Old Testament of the Bible, grow beards after they marry.

To the Amish, their manner of dress and appearance encourage humility and separation from the rest of the world. Their clothing and general appearance is an expression of their faith. Dress and other lifestyle practices comprise the *Ordnung,* the generally unwritten set of rules, which based on the Bible, give the Amish their identity and their separateness. They believe as the Bible states: *"Come out from among them and be ye separate."*

The Amish farm some of the richest land in America. Dotting the countryside, their farmsteads are always neatly painted or white-washed. No electric wires run from house or barn; but near many houses, a windmill stands sentinel against the rolling landscape. Amish believe that the absence of electricity on their homesteads rules out the temptation for using this modern convenience for forbidden entertainment. Brightly colored flowers rim vegetable gardens. Pretty white fences, rather than electric ones, keep peacefully grazing cows and sleek horses in pastures. Most Amish farmers own at least six draft horses, such as Percherons, Belgians, or Clydesdales, and Kentucky or Tennessee mules to pull farm implements, in addition to four driving horses. I have been told that the Amish prefer the Percherons or Belgians to the Clydesdales, due to the long, silky hair on the fetlocks of the big Scottish breed. That long fetlock hair requires grooming time that the Amish cannot spare from their numerous other commitments.

The first tenet that the Amish teach their children is to fear God and love work. Alongside Amish simplicity is found a work ethic that grooms their surroundings to enhance God's creations. The old maxim "Cleanliness is next to Godliness" is one they live by. To gaze upon Amish country is to look at a scene free of the clutter of the modern world- and on a landscape radiantly serene.

The infinite tasks of the Amish farm demand full-time input from the entire family. Parents and older siblings teach younger ones the do's and don'ts of the *Ordnung,* how to go about the various farm chores, and generally how to make a living without exposure to influence that would contradict what they hold to be true and in accord with Divine and moral law.

Since the Amish believe that the land is a gift from God, the farm is not only an enterprise but a means of religious stewardship. The sun, one of God's most vital gifts, is the Amish farmer's guiding light, so to speak. The Amish farmer depends on the sun and daylight hours more than any other energy source. As long as the sun is up, there is the chance to plow, to make hay, to harvest. A lantern, however, dimly lights the area of the barn where milking is done before sunup.

In the gloaming, work slows, and the family gathers round the glow of the table for the evening meal, lit usually by one artificial light, which may be a propane gas lamp.

Modern vehicles and Amish buggies share the roads in Amish country.
Photo by KC Freel

Amish retire early, for even schoolchildren are roused at four in the darkness and chill of predawn to help with the milking and other farm chores.

The Amish home is usually a spacious farmhouse nestled at the end of a postcard-pretty lane in or about the quaint villages of Lancaster or the other rural Pennsylvania counties that harbor Amish communities. Here, women sweep and scrub floors rather than vacuum. Girls learn to master a treadle sewing machine positioned at a sunny window. As with their attire, their homes are devoid of most frills. Homemade rag, hooked or braided rugs grace the bare floors. Heat radiates from the central stove in the kitchen; there is no central heating. Because the Amish are at their work by dawn and retire early, they have little time to sit around shivering in unheated rooms.

The doors separating the rooms on the home's first floor can be opened/folded back to create large spaces to accommodate members for worship services, weddings, and funerals. "Home Amish" hold services every other Sunday in the homes of the various congregation/district members. I use that term because there are "Church Amish" who worship in churches, but the Old Order does not hold with this practice.

In the living room of the "Home Amish," the (members of a district) congregation is seated on simple, backless wooden benches, according to marital status and gender. Opening with hymn singing, in unison and *sans* accompaniment, the service commences around 8:30 a. m. and lasts about three hours. Harmonizing/"part-singing" and musical accompaniment are taboo. There is a short sermon then a long one, followed by testimonials.

As it has been since Colonial times, the kitchen is the heart of the home, and certainly this is even truer of an Amish home. Here, the hearty meals the Amish are known for are prepared to feed the robust appetites of the hardworking farmers. Since the kitchen is the real "living room" for the Amish family, it is the largest room and the warmest, where on cold winter nights, the typical Amishman can be found in the small circle of soft lamplight, reading his Bible or the Almanac, or dozing on the couch that is usually found in that cosy space. In this hearth room, the children do their homework, whilst the women busy themselves making rugs or quilts, or with the darning and sewing that requires so much of their time.

Most Amish homes have an outside kitchen too, known as a "summer kitchen." This is where sauerkraut is made, as well as scrapple (a seasoned mixture of pork and cornmeal set in a mold and served sliced and fried), sausage, and the spicy, brown apple butter so delicious on thickly sliced bread warm and fragrant from the oven. Here too, all the canned goods are "put up." Amish families preserve countless quarts of peaches, cherries and other fruits, a medley of vegetables, jams and jellies; and nearly every household makes its own bottled drinks, such as ginger ale and root beer. Above all, the Amish are known for their fine cooking. If ever you have visited Lancaster County, you *know* how true this statement is!

Shoofly pie is my personal favorite! And speaking of pies, it is not uncommon for an Amish goodwife to bake twenty or thirty pies every week. Easy to understand, when you consider that families are large, men and boys ravenous from working in the fields; and pie, as it was in olden times, is served with every meal. As I wrote in the premier volume of my *County Chronicles*, the pioneers were aptly named, for they consumed pie aplenty, with beef, pork, or chicken and vegetables for a main course, and with a variety of fruits for dessert, breakfast included. Besides the well-known shoofly, Amish-favorite pies include apple, cherry, peach, apricot, rhubarb, and raisin.

The old adage "A woman's work is never done" goes triple for Amish women. They do housecleaning, tend vegetable gardens, bake and cook extensive meals for large numbers of people, make quilts, rugs, and clothing for the entire family, all the while tending the youngest children. Let us not forget that Amish women also launder and repair all the family clothing; and in addition to their extensive canning, they make buttermilk, cheeses and other dairy foods. And the list goes on!

I hope I have not painted the Amish picture to be all work and no play, a somber and dismal life devoid of laughter. There is socializing and sport, of course, though these activities are rather simple, requiring no special equipment. Checkers or pickup baseball are two I could mention; but corner ball, played with a hard rubber ball, is favored by Amish boys over the national pastime. Other juvenile amusements include jumping rope, tag, and tug-of-war. Boys and men enjoy hunting and fishing, even wrestling matches. Girls enjoy the crafts of sewing, embroidering, and rug making. Roller and ice skating are shared with the boys. One would be hard-pressed to find elaborate or any kind of mechanical toys in an Amish home.

Elder Amish enjoy working with their hands. Wood carving, furniture making, quilting, and the creation of colorful crafts to sell in the shops to tourists are all popular pastimes. Be advised that these folks are *expert* wood craftsmen and quilt makers. Storytelling and the verbal wit of riddles are two amusements

Church service on Sunday
Photos by KC Freel

that Amish of all ages seem to enjoy, and at which they also excel.

Auctions, held on a regular basis, barn raisings, husking and quilting bees are Amish occasions for getting together with other "plain" friends and neighbors. These gatherings, though work-filled, are considered "frolics."

When I was about nine years old, my parents took my brother and me to Lancaster County for a two-week summer vacation. We stayed on an actual Amish farm. It was such a pleasant experience, as well as a learning one. Robbie and I watched the farmer milk cows; and we were permitted to help with certain chores, such as egg gathering and feeding some of the farm animals. The food was memorable, and that was my first experience with Amish world-famous shoofly pie.

Both lunch and supper tables overflowed with "roasts" (roasted chicken or meats); chow-chow, a mixture of pickled vegetables; homemade breads, pies, funnel cakes and cookies; pot cheese and other flavorsome cheeses; not to mention a rainbow of shimmering jams and preserves. Oh, the fresh fruits and vegetables straight from the garden! I remember the huge breakfasts as especially enticing, and the salted, outsized pretzels that my brother and I delighted in.

On that trip, Mother purchased, along with other souvenirs, a potholder bright with Amish-style heart, floral and bird designs- *disselfink*- that reads: "Kissin' wears out; cookin' don't!" The colorful item, via a magnet, decorates my refrigerator today; but I am not certain that I wholeheartedly agree with its projected theory. Come to think of it... I don't think Mom did either, but the motif is unusually pretty!

I would recommend an Amish-country vacation to anyone who enjoys good food, tranquil surroundings, and the excitement, grace and charm of time-travel- which brings me to my next point of discussion.

The horse is of great importance to each and every Amish person, since it is their main means of transportation, coupled with the fact that the horse powers their farm implements. From their earliest years, Amish children, boys especially, are taught the care and respect for the horse, one of God's finest creations. The Amish take great pride in their horses, and if you have ever witnessed an Amish horse and buggy on our Pennsylvania roads and byways, then you know how glossy and sleek these animals are.

At age sixteen, or shortly thereafter, an Amish boy receives his first buggy, an open two-seater. This is known, as pictured in the Helen Alt painting on the cover of this volume, as a "bachelor's buggy," or more commonly, the "courting buggy," since it is invaluable in a young Amishman's dating activities. Over the long years, this open buggy has decreased in popularity. The closed carriage has become more the choice of Amish teens; not to say, however, that the traditional, open two-seater has disappeared. Did you know that Amish buggies have windshield wipers? Battery operated. Buggies bear reflectors, too, for driving in murk and darkness.

Dating is permitted at age sixteen. Most Amish youths spend two or more years socializing with others of their age group, in a "supper gang," before becoming engaged. This is referred to, in their terminology, as "running around." Attending singings and other Amish social functions, visiting relatives and friends, taking buggy rides in an open or closed courting rig are all permissible.

During an October 3, 2006, edition of *Good Morning America* largely dedicated to the Amish, I learned that when Amish youths turn sixteen, they are allowed to experience the outside world and decide for themselves in which culture they wish to live. *Ninety percent of them return to the Amish way of life.*

Like so many others, I have always been curious about bundling, a courting custom that has virtually died out. If you saw the 2000 film *The Patriot*, then you can conjure the sequence involving the couple engaged in this old courting practice. In New England where the winters can be long and quite harsh, a Colonial suitor found bundling a practical way to spend more time with his betrothed. Distances between Colonial farms across the frontier were often great, and this old winter custom of courting couples occupying the same bed, without undressing, was a way for them to become "intimate" without sexual contact. I do not believe the custom has survived anywhere else today except with some Amish, though I have been told by a respected Lancaster professor of sociology that the Lancaster Amish do not practice this custom anymore.

Since family is the core of Amish traditions, choosing a mate is *the* most important decision in an Amishman's life. There is no divorce, but a man or woman may remarry, if his or her mate passes away.

November is the traditional wedding month among the Amish in Lancaster County, after the harvest and before deep winter. A whirlwind of activity begins after Fast Day, October 11. Then, after autumn communion the following Sunday, a young couple's wedding date is "published," that is, *announced*, during the Sunday morning service.

A wedding requires much hustle and bustle and is quite a feast day. The home of the bride is the site where the ceremony will take place, and it must be spotless, cleaned from top to bottom. All the food must be prepared, enough for two full meals for the family and the large number of guests. Personal invitations are hand-delivered, via horse and buggy, locally. Plain postal cards are mailed to distant relatives.

Weddings take place on Tuesdays or Thursdays, with preparations and cleanups on Mondays, Wednesdays and Fridays. Weddings do *not* occur on Saturdays, because Sunday cleanups would be considered sacrilegious. No work of any kind ever intrudes on the sacred quietude of Amish Sundays.

A typical Amish wedding day commences at 4:00 a.m. After all, cows still require milking! And there awaits, too, the other farm chores. Besides, there are plenty of last-minute preparations to tend to. The clatter of hooves on the lane leading to the bride's home, circa 6:30 a. m., announces the arrival of the helpers. Within the subsequent half-hour, the wedding party has usually eaten breakfast and dressed for the ceremony.

Blue is the most traditional color for an Amish bridal frock, navy blue or sky blue, though purple is also popular. A bride traditionally sews her own dress, in addition to those of her two attendants. The dresses are always plain, the skirts reaching to mid-calf. No lace, no veil, no train, no flowers- *plain*. An Amish woman's wedding dress- or at least part of her wedding attire- is the dress she will one day be buried in.

The bride and her two attendants wear white capes and aprons over their dresses, black prayer caps (though, once married, the wedded Amish woman will wear daily the familiar, heart-shaped white cap), black stockings and black high-topped shoes. The white cape and white apron are the items she will likely be buried in when her time comes to pass through the portal to salvation.

The groom and his two attendants wear black suits with snowy white shirts and high-topped black shoes with black socks. Amish men usually do not wear ties, though black bow ties are donned for a wedding. The groom sports a black felt hat with a wide, three-and-a-half-inch brim. The attendants, in the Pennsylvania Dutch vernacular, are called *newehockers*, meaning "sidesitters."

At the wedding gathering (likely 200 to 400 people), all the guests' horses will be put to pasture for a restful day of grazing, the buggy's parked in a long, black line between the barn and the bride's house. Inside the bride's family home, the guests- the men in their best black suits, the women in their Sunday dresses- arrange themselves on the backless benches, facing the spot where the preacher will stand. By 8:30 a.m., the three-hour ceremony begins with singing; and again, I remind readers, there is no harmonizing or musical accompaniment. About an hour later, the minister and the bride and groom, with their attendants, come down the stairs from the top level, where the engaged couple have been given marital instruction.

The minister questions the pair about their marriage-to-be. This segment of the service can be equated with the exchanging of vows, after which the minister blesses the couple. [Old Order Amish do not exchange or wear wedding rings, as many Mennonites do.] Following the blessing, other ordained men at the gathering and the fathers of the bride and groom may give testimony about marriage to the assembled congregation. A final prayer draws the service to a close. Then the feast begins, and what a feast- and there is no such thing as an Amish caterer!

Amish wedding fare is known far and wide for its quality and quantity. Whole chickens are roasted and tidbits blended into mounds of flavorful stuffing. Bowls heaped with mashed potatoes, gravy, coleslaw, chowchow, and specially prepared vegetables await. Have you ever sampled Amish celery cooked in a delicate, sweet-sour sauce? Ambrosia! Breads, apple butter, fresh-churned butter, jams and preserves, cheeses- all homemade- grace the long tables. The desserts include apple pie, homemade whipped cream, berry sauce, a tempting array of Amish doughnuts and cookies, put-up peaches and other fruits, and, of course, gallons of freshly ground coffee.

At the wedding feast, the men are seated at one end of the long tables, the women on the other. Amish weddings break up around 10:30 in the evening. Four a.m. comes mighty early; and the next day, on top of their regular chores, there is the cleanup, at which the bride and groom will participate. The wedding night is spent at the bride's home, where they will remain until they set up housekeeping in their own home the following spring.

During the winter, the newlyweds will spend their honeymoon-weekends visiting among family and friends, where they will accumulate most of their gifts, practical items for their own home.

If you have seen the 1985 Paramount film *Witness,* a good portion of which was filmed in Intercourse, Pennsylvania, you would have acquired some knowledge about the Amish, and perhaps it aroused your interest in these God-fearing, hardworking people. One unforgettable sequence of the film depicts a barn raising, and I suppose this is one aspect of the Amish we all think of when their name is uttered.

Courting buggy outside Amish church
Photo by KC Freel

When fire claims an Amishman's barn, all his kin, friends and neighbors gather, from miles around, to build him a new one. As I stated earlier, the Amish take care of their own. Barn raising is a prime example of the "Amish way" of applying Christianity to everyday life- of the brotherhood they share.

It would not be unusual to find hundreds of Amish gathered together on a morning at first light, preparing to labor all day, without any financial reward, in order to build a new barn for a neighbor. Such an occasion is not really looked upon as a drudge, but as a "frolic." Though the barn raising will involve plenty of hard work, it will also include much laughter and what's most important- *fellowship.* Along with the noontime feast, each barn raising is a day worth remembering!

Though it is oft related that at such gatherings a barn is completed in a single day, this is not *entirely* true. There is required much preparation before the gathering meets to start the work. For instance, all the wood is cut and hauled to the site in advance, and much of the finish work remains after the gathering starts home at dusk. Nonetheless, the new barn is up once the sun is down.

It can be rightfully said that Amish give respect, honor and a meaningful place to their aged. Children learn from grandparents, from their acquired wisdom, and youngsters enjoy the companionship of the elders. As with the Irish, among the Amish storytelling is valued.

Funerals are regarded with the biblical words: "The Lord giveth, and the Lord taketh away." Death is viewed as a portal to salvation for those who have remained true to the faith, to God's commands. Like everything else in Amish lives, an Amish interment is the essence of simplicity, devoid of flowers, music, or decorated headstones. The deceased is enveloped in a white shroud- "... and they shall walk with me in white; for they are worthy," Revelation 3:4-5- and placed in a handmade, unlined coffin without handles or any embellishment. The funeral feast is prepared by friends and neighbors of the deceased's family.

As a child, I witnessed a long funeral procession of horse-drawn Amish buggies, and was astounded at its length along the road. The great number of people attending an Amish funeral is due firstly to the fact that they have large families and secondly because it is tradition for all the Amish in the area to come and pay their last respects to one of their own. Family members remain until the last shovel of earth is mounded over the grave, which was dug the day before by friends from their district. Simple granite headstones indicate Amish burial sites.

Before I conclude this Chronicle, I would like to say a few words about hex signs. Over 300 years ago, when the Amish came to Pennsylvania to take advantage of William Penn's "Holy Experiment," they brought with them, along with their language and style of dress, German traditions and art. Mystical bird and floral designs had graced their birth and marriage certificates in the old country. These symbols had also decorated family Bibles, quilts, dishes, pottery, even furniture. Six-pointed stars were quite popular; and perhaps, since the German word for six, *sechs*, sounded to their English-speaking neighbors like "hex," they came to be known as "hex signs." Thus, the belief, passed down through the years by non-Amish, that these symbols were painted on barns as hex symbols for protection against witching is likely a myth. If you were to pose the issue of hex signs to an Amishman, he would probably respond that the colorful symbols are "chust for nice."

I have seen these old-world symbols on a myriad of their crafts but never on *their* barns. I am not stating that the "hex" is never used by them on their barns, merely that *I* have never seen this in my numerous visits to Amish country. I have seen numerous hex signs on non-Amish barns, however. In not-too-distant Berks County, Mennonites decorate their barns with these happy, colorful symbols, as do other farmers of German extraction who came to Pennsylvania at the time of the Reformation. Due to their more liberal ways and their barn-decorating practices, those folks are known as the "Fancy Dutch."

The pretty patterns hold legends. Families chose a "hex sign" based on color, design and meaning. Some of the most popular symbols included hearts for love; birds, called *distelfinks*, for happiness; tulips for faith, and stars for luck. Colors lent added meaning. Blue conveyed protection; white, purity; green, abundance, and red, strong emotion, such as love. For many years, hex symbols were all hand-painted.

In the early 1940s, Jacob Zook, an eleventh-generation Pennsylvania Amishman living in the village of Paradise, successfully pioneered the hand silk screening of hex signs. Four or five colors are used in the process, and each color requires its own carefully designed screen. Zook's invention allowed hex signs to be made in quantity at modest cost. Today, throughout Amish country, there are many businesses that sell hex signs in different sizes for use indoors and out. The brightly colored patterns render hex signs fascinating folk art. I am open-minded about the legends that have come to surround them. I enjoy them for their beauty; and if they, indeed, bring luck, love and laughter, then that too would be nice!

Windmills, old and modern, generate power on Amish homesteads. Photo by KC Freel

If you type in your computer's search engine "Pennsylvania Dutch" or "Amish," a wealth of information will be afforded you. I think PaDutch.com is a good place to begin, which will include a diversity of accommodations. Aside from the hotels and motels, there are lots of charming Bed and Breakfasts, as well as matchless Farm Bed and Breakfasts– shopping, dining, entertainment, and historic sites. Lancaster County boasts a large selection of outlet stores, and as many unique shops as they have horse shoes! Amish quilts, rugs, crafts, pottery, and their handcrafted furniture will both impress and tempt you.

The fresh-from-the-farm goodness of Amish country food and the beautiful scenery are two features that bring visitors back, year after year. Smorgasbords are like nowhere else. "Pass-the-platter" dining is also popular. "Pennsylvania's Sweetheart," Shirley Jones, when I interviewed her for her segment of this volume, told me that one of her most pleasant Pennsylvania memories is the family-style dining found at eateries throughout Amish-country Pennsylvania.

There are many ways in Amish country to explore and learn about the Amish and the other "plain" folk that comprise the "Pennsylvania Dutch." We have Amish in Somerset County, in the southwestern corner of the commonwealth. And near to my home, in Fayette County, is a Bruderhof (German: "Place of Brothers") community at Farmington, in the mountains above Uniontown. As with the Brethren, Mennonites and Amish, the Bruderhof do not serve in the armed forces of any country. Nonresistance and the command

A scenic buggy ride through the beautiful Amish country of Somerset County, PA. Note the windmills along the ridge in the distance.
Photos by KC Freel, Jay, FL (HKTravelinstore@aol.com)

"Love thy neighbor as thy self" are central to their beliefs.

I hope that you will embark on a scenic journey to Pennsylvania Amish country, in Lancaster, York, Mifflin, Berks, Somerset or the other counties of our commonwealth where these fascinating people have their neat and orderly communities.

If you want to get away from it all, the tranquil Amish country will provide the perfect holiday escape. There is something for everyone: farmers' markets, wineries, breweries, auctions, flea markets, outlets, antique and craft shops galore, art galleries, museums, and more. And lest I forget historic sites, including those that will appeal to train enthusiasts, such as the Strasburg Railroad, America's oldest short-line railroad. Here, visitors ride authentically restored passenger cars pulled by a huge, coal-burning steam locomotive. Come to Strasburg and fall in love with trains all over again!

Or come to Lancaster County to fall in love all over again. Amish country has twenty-eight covered bridges, known also as "Kissing Bridges," more than any other Pennsylvania county. Oh, the romantic sound of horses' hooves crossing one of these tunnels of time! Before we became known as the "Keystone State," Pennsylvania was called the "State of Covered Bridges." [See "Tunnels to the Past... Stepping Stones of History," in *County Chronicles'* premier volume.]

Cameras are nearly always a part of any holiday, but please respect that these "plain" folk do *not* want their photographs taken. Images smack of vanity; and this, as we know, is "not the Amish way." *Respect too their horse-drawn carriages on the roads, and well... do as they do and obey the Golden Rule.* Diamond-shaped road signs bearing the silhouette of an Amish horse and buggy is a commonly seen traffic caveat throughout Amish country.

The Amish and other "plain" groups have survived centuries of separateness. They are, indeed, a people apart. Yet, as I have endeavored to point out in this Chronicle– *they are also a people very much together.*

"History's Sweetest"

"Who can take a sunrise/Sprinkle it with dew/Cover it in choc'late and a miracle or two/The Candy Man/Oh, the Candy Man can...."
-The Candy Man, lyrics and music by Anthony Newley and Leslie Bricusse
From the 1971 Paramount film, Willy Wonka and the Chocolate Factory

Milton S. Hershey, the man whose name became synonymous with America's favorite chocolate bar, was born on September 13, 1857, into a Mennonite family descended from immigrants from Switzerland and Germany. The family's Pennsylvania home was nestled in the lush, rolling hills of Derry Township, near present-day Harrisburg. Milton Hershey's only sibling, Sarena, born April 12, 1862, died on March 31, 1867, of an unknown illness. Thus, Milton was the only surviving child of Fannie and Henry Hershey.

Fannie raised her son in the strict confines of the Mennonite faith. Milton's father, whose sole claim to fame was H. H. Cough Drops, failed at a long list of business ventures, including running a fruit farm and nursery. Henry moved the family often, permitting his son a limited education. Though Milton only went as far as the fourth grade, his belief in himself would take him to great heights.

From early on, this extraordinary man *knew* he possessed the talent for making delicious candy, though his work years, after his four years of schooling, began in an entirely different endeavor. His father apprenticed him to the editor of a German newspaper. The problem was that Milton showed no interest in printing, therefore displaying little talent for it. However, as Fate would have it, his hardworking mother took matters in her capable hands and found her son a job with a candy maker in Lancaster. The affable boy spent the next four years learning everything he could about making candy, which he immediately found to be a fascinating trade.

In 1876, America's Centennial celebration in Philadelphia prompted Milton to relocate to that city, where he hoped to sell candy to the thousands of revelers who were expected to come for the hundredth birthday of the Declaration of Independence. The optimistic young man borrowed money from his family; and drawing on his innate Mennonite work ethics, he cooked his candy nights, selling fresh caramels from a pushcart, among the throng in the streets, during the days.

For the next six years, Hershey struggled to keep his small candy business alive. His aunt Mattie came to help out, and even his mother pitched in; but finally, Milton was forced to liquidate in order to pay off nagging creditors.

Denver, Chicago, and then New York were geographical locations added to his mounting list of failures. Be that as it may, Milton Hershey was learning more about the candy business with each futile attempt at gaining a financial foothold. For instance, he discovered that fresh milk added to his caramels greatly improved their texture and taste. Just as milk became a vital ingredient to his candy, an ever-growing *persistence*- the essential ingredient, the quintessence, to greatness- propelled him onward in his pursuits.

Like the path of most champions, Hershey's road to success was rocky with disappointments. In 1886, the Candy Man returned to his Pennsylvania roots in Dauphin County, not far from where he had been reared at Derry Church on his family's farm. He was twenty-nine and penniless- though far from defeated.

His relatives were, by this point in time, tapped out, and no longer wished to aid him in his candy endeavors. It was a friend, William Henry Lebkicher, who loaned him enough money so Hershey could salvage his kettles and other equipment from his last failed venture. The problems that had doomed his finger-licking caramels in New York had been his usual lack of funds coupled with high sugar prices.

Undaunted, Milton leased a tiny room in a dismal, abandoned factory, whipped up his candies long hours into lonely nights; and from a basket, started again selling his caramels with renewed hope and vigor.

Picture, if you can, this handsome man with the dark, wavy hair and thick, handlebar moustache, that basket looped over his arm, peddling his candies in the streets. There was a softness in Hershey's eyes that people remembered. Though he must have harbored hurts and disappointments within their deep-blue depths, his eyes seemed always to smile. It was this warmth, his inner light of honesty, integrity and downright decency that peered out from his soul, as well as the sweetness of his expression, that arrested customers, on their way to and from their destinations, and made them stop and buy his candy.

Each day, in all kinds of weather, over and above the miles he walked selling his goods, Hershey had to make the long tramp to a farm to purchase the five gallons of milk his caramels required. As before, profit threatened to elude him, but he refused to compromise on quality. *Then something extraordinary happened.*

An English importer chanced to taste one of Milton's milk caramels. For Hershey, this would prove to be the sweet taste of success. The Englishman placed the first large order Milton ever received- 500 pounds sterling, enough to give his fledgling little company the boost it needed. It was the turning point in his life. More overseas orders followed, which allowed Hershey to secure a substantial loan. He could now expand his candy business to begin realizing his dreams.

By 1893, Milton Hershey had opened three other plants in addition to his original operation. To his trademark Crystal A Caramels, he added other confections, bestowing on them fanciful names, such as Melbas, Uniques, and Scarlets. More importantly, Hershey introduced mass production.

In leaps and bounds, his business grew, with his candies being shipped all over the world, to China, Japan, Australia, the British Isles, and across the breadth of Europe. It was an amazing turnabout! Milton S. Hershey would soon demonstrate to the world that he was a born entrepreneur. The next sizeable stepping stone on his sweet path of success presented itself in Chicago.

The year was 1893, and the place was the World's Columbian Exposition, the World's Fair. Here, legend has it that Hershey noticed some children discarding the caramel centers of candy they were eating- after polishing off the chocolate exteriors. When I asked the folks at the Hershey Archives about this, they said there was no *proof* of it, and I cannot offer any here, though the story may be rooted in truth. What *is* accepted is that Hershey be-

Vintage photo of Hershey Inn, which served as apartments for Hershey employees

Hershey garage and livery

came infatuated with an innovative German chocolate-making machine. The proverbial light went on in his fertile mind, and I suppose we could even say that visions of chocolate drops danced in his head. He immediately purchased the entire exhibit, along with the copyright.

Once the new machinery was installed in his Derry Township plant, he began in earnest to produce chocolate candies. At the start, he simply chocolate-coated his famous caramels. Soon, he became emboldened and took a chance on chocolate cigars and chocolate cigarettes. The novelties, which provided delicious amusement, became a virtual overnight success.

The flush of business achievement vitalized Milton's personal life as well. In 1897, on a business trip to Jamestown, New York, he met Catherine Sweeney, a pretty girl behind the counter of a soda fountain, where he had stopped to make a sales call. Catherine's hourglass figure and her pert face, framed with a cloud of curly, red hair, captured his full attention. And though it was not Valentine's Day, Cupid was lurking among the shop's confectionaries- and his arrow found its mark. After a whirlwind courtship, the forty-one-year-old German Mennonite bachelor and the Irish Catholic shop girl married, and "Kitty" came to live in Pennsylvania, in the mansion Hershey had purchased with his sweet profits.

Milton Hershey was, by now, full of surprises. In 1900, he sold his longtime caramel business for a cool million. He had other fish to fry... that is, other candies to try. He had been working on a formula for milk chocolate, which, at that time, was a luxury only the rich could afford. Before he sold his caramel business, he had test-marketed a milk chocolate bar, and the feedback- excuse the pun- convinced him that he could mass produce and market affordable milk chocolate candy that had hitherto been a high-ticket item from Switzerland or Germany. Hershey had a gut feeling that chocolate was something everyone would love and even crave. Before long, people everywhere would verify his theory.

In 1903, he began construction of what was to become the largest chocolate manufacturing plant in the world. Two years hence, his new state-of-the-art factory was complete. Hershey had chosen for the site his hometown of Derry Church, Dauphin County, close to the Pennsylvania Dutch country, where he knew the work ethics of the people, and where dairy farms abounded.

Milton Hershey's vision included more than just the world's largest chocolate factory. He envisioned a model town built around it, a place where his employees could send their children to the finest schools- a pleasant, happy town with extensive recreational and cultural opportunities for its residents. He knew in his heart that contented workers are more productive workers.

Unlike so many of the era's wealthy magnates, the oft-called "robber barons," Hershey did not want to build a company-house community, where workers lived a bare existence, owing their souls to the company store, as a popular song related. He was not on the same page with those men. Milton Hershey was on a page of his own!

He wanted a "... real hometown with one-and-two-family brick houses, shady streets, and manicured lawns." With his great success, his sweet inner light shone brighter, with benevolence and a profound sense of moral responsibility.

Hershey's architects laid out tree-lined streets and the water and sewage systems. Though most of his workers rented at modest rates from the company, Hershey sold- on generous terms via a trust he had established- not the sign-of-the-times row houses, but attractive, comfortable homes to his workers.

On April 24, 1907, Hershey dedicated a lovely, landscaped park in his town. Later, fun-filled rides, a swimming pool, and a grand ballroom were added to the leafy, sun-dappled retreat. A bank, a hospital, a free library, a zoo, a laundry, an inn, and a trolley line to transport, from round about, his workers- all- were incorporated into Hershey's town. The idyllic community provided a reliable, inexpensive transportation system, as well as the excellent public school system and the recreational facilities about which he had dreamed. Milton Hershey even built a junior college that was tuition-free to Hershey residents.

Presently, those aforementioned trolleys and special trains were bringing thousands of visitors to the town the Candy Man had built on chocolate.

According to authors Rendall M. Miller and William Pencak in their book *Pennsylvania, a History of the Commonwealth,* "Milton Hershey's paternalism could be overbearing at times. He was known to tour the town in his Cadillac convertible, chauffeur at the wheel, taking note of front yards that were not neatly manicured or homes where occupants had neglected some detail of maintenance." According to the same source, Hershey even went so far as to hire private detectives to find out who was littering the beautifully landscaped park "... or engaging in other kinds of behavior that he disapproved."

If Hershey went too far in his desire for a perfect town, we should bear in mind that he was a perfectionist; and after all, he was paying for everything. In any case, the good *far* outweighed the "downside." Perhaps he was a bit ahead of his time even in those pursuits; because today, littering is fined, and in neighborhoods across America there are local zoning ordinances, rules for property owners in regard to esthetics and maintenance.

Keep in mind too that in the early days, there was no police force in Hershey's town; so naturally, he would have wanted to keep a watchful eye on things. As it were, the town's residents were well aware of what he was providing for them, and trouble with a capital "T" was nonexistent.

Over and above all the previously mentioned benefits, there were no real estate taxes, and utilities were practically free. Hershey provided his workers with insurance against illness, accident or death, plus a good retirement plan. As stated previously- Milton S. Hershey was on a page of history all by himself!

When the Great Depression crippled the American economy, and employers everywhere were laying off workers, Hershey was determined to keep *his* employees working. In fact, it was during the lean 1930s when he kicked off a large-scale building project that included the Hotel Hershey; a community building; a state-of-the-art high school; sports arena; stadium; theater, and a ground-breaking, windowless, air-conditioned office building. The result of what Hershey himself referred to as the "Great Building Campaign" transformed the town into a major tourist attraction that has continued to grow in popularity ever since.

Hotel Hershey, high on a hill overlooking the town, is as elegant as ever. The extensive, adjacent botanical gardens feature seasonal displays that continue to elicit exclamations of delight from each and every new guest.

The Candy Man's humanitarian concerns went further still, as he continued to put his sweet success to work dispensing funds for

Open-air theatre, Hershey Park

more and more philanthropic endeavors. Since he and Kitty were childless, they founded a school, kindergarten through high school, for orphans, recognized today as one of the most generous institutions of its kind in the nation. Three years after Kitty's premature death in 1915, Milton Hershey endowed the orphanage, the Milton S. Hershey School, with the entire fortune of Hershey Chocolate Company stock.

Milton took great pride in his town, in his school for needy children, in each of his business endeavors; *and it must be said that during his entire life, though he became a wealthy man, he placed the quality of his products and the well-being of his employees ahead of profits.*

It should also be noted that every year, the Milton S. Hershey Testamentary Trust makes a substantial contribution to the Derry Township School District, the public school district for the town of Hershey.

His good works did not stop in Pennsylvania. In a bold move, Hershey purchased and built sugar refineries in Cuba. East of the island capital of Havana, he had a town constructed for his workers that he proudly christened "Central Hershey." As he had done in his homeland, he brought in doctors, dentists and teachers, and he built a free school for the children with recreational facilities that included a baseball diamond and a golf course.

In 1935, Hershey established the M. S. Hershey Foundation, a private charity to provide educational and cultural opportunities for Hershey residents. According to the Hershey web site, the foundation supports the Hershey Museum, Hershey Gardens, the Hershey Theatre, and the Hershey Community Archives.

At Hershey Museum, visitors can view exhibits that illustrate Milton Hershey's brilliant career. They can learn how chocolate is made. Other exhibitions highlight Native American artifacts and Pennsylvania Dutch antiques.

Hershey Park, over the years, has become a worldwide tourist attraction, with its rides and its walk-through zoo, which today envelops eleven acres and is populated with over 200 animals from a variety of North American regions.

While reading the interesting *Guide to the Homes of Famous Pennsylvanians* by Arthur P. Miller, Jr. and Marjorie L. Miller, I discovered a colorful footnote to the Candy Man that applies to his later years and his theme park. Employees remembered that, after the last visitor had left the park, they often caught sight of a lone man, a little portly, his rich brown hair and moustache frosted with white, the denim-blue eyes laughing, merrily riding one of the carousel's gilded, antique horses. *It was a wise man who once said it is never too late to have a happy childhood.*

Milton had had no real childhood to speak of. Remember that he had begun to work at a very early age; and perhaps, coupled with his humanitarian nature, that is the reason he acutely felt the need to come to the aid

The Rustic Bridge, Hershey Park, Hershey, PA

of disadvantaged children. When he was growing up, Milton's parents were often at odds. They finally separated when he was older, with his father moving out. Though he always maintained a close relationship with both his mother and his father, this had to have left a mark on the sensitive man's heart.

East of town, at Founders Hall, located on the vast, impressive campus of the Milton S. Hershey School, visitors can view a video that recounts the story of the school, whose mission is to serve children "in social and financial need."

This great man's contributions also extended to our military. He sold chocolate bars to the Army during World War I; and during World War II, Hershey developed what became known as the Field Ration D. The thick, rectangular-shaped energy bar packed a whopping 600 calories and did not melt in the heat when carried into the field. Soon, the Hershey factory was turning out thousands of these bars per day for Uncle Sam.

In 1943, the Procurement Division of the Army inquired about the possibility of obtaining a heat-resistant chocolate bar with an improved flavor. After a short experimentation period, Hershey developed the Hershey Tropical Bar, which remained a standard ration for the United States Armed Forces. The Tropical Bar went to war in Korea and Vietnam.

As a result of Field Ration D and its follow-up Tropical Bar during World War II, the Hershey Company received the Army-Navy "E" Production Award in recognition for its outstanding war effort. As accompaniments to the award, Uncle Sam presented Hershey with congratulatory/appreciation lapel pins for each and every employee, along with a flag that Milton proudly flew above his plant.

The "E" Production Award is *not* an easy honor to win. Milton Hershey received it for exceeding all production expectations in the manufacturing of an Emergency Field Ration. Major General Gregory said of Hershey: "The men and women of Hershey Chocolate Corporation have every reason to be proud of their great work in backing up our soldiers on the fighting fronts."

A former manager once assessed Milton Hershey with these words: "He was never satisfied with the conventional way of doing things. He was always wanting to experiment."

In keeping with Milton's long tradition of testing and trialing, the Hershey Company later developed for the United States Armed Forces the Desert Bar, which can withstand in excess of 60 degrees Celsius or 140 degrees Fahrenheit.

Milton S. Hershey died in 1945 at the venerable age of eighty-eight, thirty years after his beloved wife Catherine. Though she had sought medical attention in a number of cities and traveled extensively to spas across Europe, Catherine had finally succumbed to a mysterious, chronic malady in 1915. "Kitty" and Milton are both interred in Hershey Cemetery.

Today, the Hershey plant uses about 700,000 quarts of milk, from 50,000 cows, for a single day's production of milk chocolate. Hershey's chocolate bars, in their distinctive chocolate-colored wrappers, sold for five cents from 1900 to 1969, at which time the nickel bar was discontinued, and the popular Hershey Bar sold for a dime. I would not be exaggerating to state that to generations, every chocolate bar was a "Hershey Bar"! After a gradual decline in sales, Advertising-Hall-of-Famer Billings Fuess, Jr. boosted Hershey Bars tremendously, in 1977, with the now-classic jingle, "Hershey's, the Great American Chocolate Bar."

I must not neglect to mention that in 1923, Harry B. Reese of neighboring York County became famous for introducing– at Hershey's– the Reese's Peanut Butter Cup. The chocolate/peanut butter combination was a marriage made in heaven! Sales rose again significantly in 1982 with the debut of the film *E.T.* Actually, Hershey Foods established the benchmark for good product placement– Reese's Pieces were used by the character Elliott to tempt E.T. out of hiding.

On February 15, 2007, the Hershey Company announced "... a comprehensive, three-year supply chain transformation program." This forward-looking plan is expected to enhance Hershey's manufacturing, sourcing and customer service capabilities. It will also generate significant resources to invest in the company's growth initiatives, including accelerated marketplace momentum within Hershey's core US business, along with disciplined global expansion. In keeping with the Milton S. Hershey tradition, "The creation of innovative new product platforms to meet consumer and customer needs" is ever in the works.

Nowadays, the town of Hershey is also multi-dimensional. The original chocolate factory is still there, as well as a newer, bigger

Both sides of a vintage Hotel Hershey matchbook, illustrating the hotel's elegance and amenities
The circa 1900 Hershey images from the author's personal collection

one on the western edge of town. I highly recommend taking the tour at Chocolate World, which, open daily, is always free. Here, visitors step into a world bursting with the delectable smell of chocolate; and where automated cars take them on the journey of the cocoa bean, on its magical way into the rich core of a Hershey's chocolate bar. At the end of the tour is a free sample. And who can resist chocolate!

Visitors can also tour the Homestead. This quaint farmhouse, built by Milton's great-grandfather, is the home where the Candy Man was born.

For information on touring Hershey, Pennsylvania, I suggest you go to: www.hersheypa.com. Every question you might have about how to get there, what to see and do, hours, fees, tours, special events, where to stay and more, you will find on the varied menu. You may also call toll-free: 1-800-HERSHEY or email: info@HersheyPa.com.

History teaches us, over and yet again, that there is a reason for everything. As with other great men, Milton S. Hershey had several "failures" before he found his proper niche in life. I always say that triumphs make nice memories, but mistakes provide life's lessons.

More than anyone else, Hershey made chocolate part of the American scene.

Today, his dream of a "real hometown" has survived and thrived in a constantly changing world. Hershey, Pennsylvania, the "town built on chocolate," continues to be, for its residents, a "sweet place to call home." *And it is a very special place to the millions of people who visit it each year.*

The Hershey Company is the largest North American manufacturer of quality chocolate and confectionary products with revenues (2007) of nearly five billion dollars and more than 13,000 employees worldwide. I need not say more; the Candy Man's accomplishments speak for themselves, his innate goodness ever vibrant in the sweetest town in America, where the street names exude chocolate delights- and even the streetlights are candy kisses.

 "Aulos of Athena"

"Twelve Highlanders and a bagpipe make a rebellion."
- Sir Walter Scott

"The bagpipe is my instrument of choice because it stirs my heart, as it has stirred... hearts over the past thousand years. The pipes invoke feelings so basic to the human nature, from festive joyfulness to steadfast determination to mournful sorrow and pathos. The pipes are messengers... they bring memories of times past to the fore. The bagpipes tell us something about who we are."
- George Balderose, founder and director of the Balmoral School of Piping and Drumming

"The Best of Pittsburgh!" (in regard to ace piper George Balderose)
- Honorable Tom Murphy, former Mayor of Pittsburgh

"Time mysteriously returns to us what we have lost- in memories and wisdom," I wrote in "The Pipes, the Pipes Are Callin'!" of my *County Chronicles'* premier volume. When I hear bagpipes, I remember my father and the memories and wisdom he passed on to my brother and me. The sound of the pipes brings back his tale of a young man off to war, descending a troop train somewhere in England near the Scottish border, "... in the blackest night I ever experienced. I could not see my hand in front of my face." He said too that he had felt suddenly lost and more than a bit frightened... until he heard the approaching sound of bagpipes. "They bucked me right up."

There have been times in *my* life when I've switched on pipe music to chase away fears. Thus far, it has never failed me. When my father passed away, I was sharply reminded of the above incident, and I hired an ace piper- George Balderose of Pittsburgh, founder and director of the Balmoral School of Highland Piping- to ease my father's journey through that long, dark tunnel: an Irish medley- "Wearing of the Green," "Danny Boy," "Amazing Grace," and "Going Home." I knew Daddy heard and was pleased.

Perhaps it is in the blood, in our very bones- for if you've Celtic blood, the skirl of the pipes is a wee bit of heaven. And I can personally attest to the fact that the skirl of George Balderose's pipes are the voices of so many angels.

I have often entertained the *pensée* that God's army of archangels, His Celestial Hierarchy, has its own special pipers!

Legend, however, has it that, one fine morn, the goddess Athena awoke to thoughts of what had transpired the eve before. It seems that a sister deity had come round to bemoan her distressing hard life. So sated with sorrow was this tale that Athena decided, over breakfast, to turn it into an art form with the creation of a musical instrument. I might add to this colorful anecdote that Athena, in addition to her imposing title of goddess of war, was also considered the goddess of creativity.

Aries, by the bye, is the male god of war, and though his warrior spirit and bravery are mirrored in his female counterpart, Athena, *her* martial character is tempered with wisdom. Thus, the versatile Athena also wears the crown of goddess of wisdom.

In order to accomplish her task, Athena had first to invent the aulos, a long, hollow reed instrument with finger holes, which emitted a primal sound much like a human cry. The first pieces composed for the aulos were, fittingly, laments. Hence, mythology tells us that Athena was the inventor of the aulos, which, in turn, gave birth to the bagpipes.

Contrary to popular belief, the pipes probably originated in Egypt, Greece or Rome, as alluded to above, and not in Scotland. It is believed that the nomadic Celts/Gaels introduced the bagpipe first to Ireland then to Scotland circa 1 A.D. [The Gaels of Ireland and those of the Highlands of Scotland are of the same Celtic lineage.] And I think most historians would agree that, from the early 1500s to the dawn of the nineteenth century, the MacCrimmon family of the Highlands, their pupils and their pupils' pupils were responsible for elevating Highland pipe music to a whole new level.

The MacCrimmons, it is said, had established a school for piping on the scenic Scottish Isle of Skye, where, washed by a timeless sea, 500 million years of history whisper across the ever-mysterious inlets, mountains and glens. Dusky, ancient footsteps lead to what were once Skye's dense, dark green forests and over the soaring cliffs, where today one can almost hear the echo of ancient pipes; sense, too, the chilling battle cries of fierce Highland warriors.

There is a legend about the MacCrimmons I would like to share with you, dear readers. In his book *Bineas is Boreraig*, published in 1959 in West Lothian, Scotland, Roderick Ross states: "Life is not discovery but re-discovery. As we look back across the bridge of time, we note that in the sixteenth and seventeenth centuries witchcraft persecution in Europe had reached unprecedented proportions. The West Highlands were no exception to this unfortunate behaviour."

It seems that the MacDonald Clan and its septs (subclans), one of the most ancient clans, "bred in less with the Vikings" than most other clans round about. As a result of this association with Norsemen, feelings of culpability and inadequacy permeated among and sank its talons into their neighbors. As a sign of the times, those neighboring clans, such as the MacLeods and the Campbells, felt that witches among the MacDonalds had put curses upon them. As we have all read, the ancient remedy for this shadowy practice in those dark and medieval times was brutal assault on those who harbored "witches"- hence the Massacre of Eigg at the beginning of the sixteenth century and the Massacre of Glencoe at the close of the seventeenth century.

The chief of Clan MacLeod on Skye was, from 1480 to 1540, one Alastair Crottach, called by many "Humpback." He was the leader who orchestrated the horrendous massacre at Eigg. There, nearly 400 MacDonalds, the entire population of Canna, Rum and Eigg, were suffocated in a cave on Eigg Isle. Author Ross tells us that when, at the overture of the nineteenth century, Sir Walter Scott visited the ghostly depths of this crag chamber, he found its floors strewn with bones, his torch casting an eerie light on ancient skulls, their mouths open in silent screams- screams, I might add, that he could never silence in his writer's soul.

As the MacLeods were leaving Eigg after their grisly work, an old MacDonald crone, whose aged joints had prevented her from reaching the "safety" of the sea-cliff cavern with the others of her clan, pointed a claw-like finger at the backs of the MacLeods and flung at them this curse, her straggly grey hair blowing in the strong wind, her face, with its high cheekbones and deep hollows, taking on an intensity beyond words, the faded blue eyes kindling to blue flames: "Humpbacked is the young MacLeod of today, and so long as dry straw will burn, many a hump and crook will there be in your clan hereafter!"

Cruime is the Gaelic for "bend" or "crookedness," and we can draw our own conclusions that the MacCrimmons (in the Gaelic *MacCruimein*) sprang from one of Alastair Crottach's natural children. He bestowed on them the land at Galtrigil, about eight miles from Dunvegan Castle. You see, Alistair felt that by positioning his kith and kin there, and using the name MacCruimein, they could dispel the stark MacDonald curse with their music; that is, by the shrill, piercing sound of their pipes, "rising out of the realm of bottomless darkness."

Both Ireland and Scotland were awash with magical spells, and such a method of dispelling evil spirits was a commonly accepted one in those veiled days replete with superstition. The MacCruimeins/MacCrimmons played their pipes on a high, rock-face precipice, a sheer drop, called Na-Ho that rises 400 feet from the roaring sea beneath. Nightly, the skirl of their pipes drifted out into the ethers to work its magic, echoing from that towering ledge of rock "... with the void canopy of night above..." and the deep ocean depths below.

I have *always* believed, with keen Celtic sentiment, that the pipes drive away evil and keep it at bay. As I stated earlier, many a time in my life have I switched on pipe music to chase away fear– that most negative of human emotions.

In ancient times, during the clan wars of Ireland and Scotland, it was easy to tell who was lining up against whom; because, in addition to their tartans and standards, the clans each had a signature tune, which their brave pipers purposefully skirled as they approached the battle site. The pipes could be heard above the roar and din of battle, and the piper blew signals, via different tunes, on his pipes, at the same time encouraging his troops on to valor.

From the myriad of incidents regarding the pipes and valor, I have chosen a trilogy to present in brief here. The first took place during the French and Indian War, called in Europe the Seven Years War. It was in 1759 at the Battle of the Heights of Abraham for the capture of Quebec. Here, the pipers of the Fraser Highlanders were blowing the most stirring of airs, encouraging the men, who were fighting like wild boars. In the midst of the fray, however, a staff officer, who author C. A. Malcolm tells us in *The Piper in Peace and War,* suddenly ordered the pipers to cease playing. The result was that the Highlanders almost immediately began to weaken in their offensive, then to give way. It soon became clear that the tide of victory was turning, as the Highlanders were being driven back. The unenlightened staff officer became frantic and sharply blamed the officer in command of the Fraser unit. "Well, sir," retorted the Highlander CO, "it's *your* fault in stopping the pipers from playing! Even now they would be of use!"

Without hesitation the staff officer shot back: "Let them play then!" Play the pipers did, and to such purpose that the regiment responded in perfect harmony. Shaking off their inertia, they poured over the enemy like a raging mountain torrent after a deluge of spring rains. The Highlanders' renewed spirit and dash staggered the enemy, who fled before them, beaten and broken. "Thus," says Malcolm, "the pipers saved the day, and helped to gain the Dominion of Canada for the British Crown."

The second incident occurred at the Battle of Waterloo on 17 June 1815. This bloody engagement involved the 79th Cameron Highlanders, who first saw action in that battle in the early afternoon. Ramming through a hedge, they had engaged the French with a heavy volley of fire, then followed up with a ferocious bayonet assault. The French turned tail and retreated down a slope with British cavalry hot on their *derrières.*

French cavalry subsequently launched a determined counterattack; and the 79th, as per their pipers' clarion call, immediately formed into the classic "defensive squares," ready with fixed bayonets to receive the heavy horse charge. The instant Napoleon's formidable horsemen thundered forward, Piper Kenneth MacKay coolly stepped out of his protective square and, exhibiting no fear, began playing the traditional rallying tune, "*Cogadh no Sith*" ("War or Peace, the True Gathering of the Clans"), marching round and round the bristling bayonets of his soon-to-be-victorious comrades. The incident thrilled all who saw it and all who heard it, and long was it toasted and talked of thereafter.

As a result of his valor, Piper MacKay was presented with a set of silver-mounted pipes from King George III, and it should be noted that the 79th was one of only four regiments specifically mentioned by the Duke of Wellington in his Waterloo dispatch. Moreover, Piper Kenneth MacKay's action was the subject of a magnificent, emotive painting that was put on display at the Royal Academy in 1893. The painting was afterwards purchased by the officers of the regiment for their mess.

The third incident took place in India and involves the Gordon Highlanders. Of all the campaigns in which the Gordons have borne a distinguished role, none outshine the Dargai War of 1897. In fact, author Malcolm tells us that "The eyes of the world were drawn to it." At Dargai (in the northwestern frontier of India, now a part of Pakistan), when the moment came to advance, the Gordon Highlanders dashed straight up the hill they were ordered to take, headed by their pipers, the Highlanders shouting their fierce Celtic battle cries. At the crest, they met a murderous gunfire, and as the Gordons burst into action, Piper George Findlater earned his worldwide fame. Bullets smashed both his ankles. Findlater fell, clutching his pipes. Unable to stand, he leaned against a rock, and amidst all the heavy firing, he continued to play the regimental march, as the blood ran from his wounds, soaking his kilt and staining it crimson. Findlater played until he lost consciousness, resulting in his winning the distinguished Victoria Cross. When he returned home, the valiant Gordon piper "... found himself famous." His handsome, mustached likeness was sold by the thousands, "... and Scotsmen in London would have let him swim in champagne...."

Bagpipes have traditionally gone to war, stirring the blood of the armies they accompanied and chasing away their fears, as well as their enemies. They also served to mourn those who were killed in battle. The clans traditionally used the pipes to lament their dead, "Sayin' 'goodbye' in their own special way." The more things change, the more they remain the same, for the bagpipe tradition of bidding farewell is embraced yet today by Celtic- and deep-feeling- hearts everywhere.

If you are a movie fan, you saw evidence of this in *Braveheart*, a story about the Scottish hero William Wallace. The pipes heard in that inspiring film are, in reality, the Irish pipes called *Uilleann*, not the Highland Pipes shown. Mel Gibson, when asked about this, replied, "*Braveheart* was filmed in Ireland, and the Irish pipes sounded better over the Irish landscape!"

Unlike the Highland Pipes, *píp uilleann* are played sitting down; and the piper uses the elbow (which is what *uilleann* means in the Irish language) to pump in the air with a bellows under one arm, then force it out of the bag with the other arm. The Irish call the great pipes, translated verbatim, *piob mor*. 'Twas an ancient type of *piob mor* that sounded in the magical mists round and about the sacred hill and Hall of Tara, where resided Ireland's (*ard ri*) high kings. And I daresay it was at the legendary Battle of Falkirk in Scotland, where the incomparable William Wallace, "Braveheart," noted the rousing effect of the great pipes on the brave Irish troops who had crossed the water to throw in with his Scottish force.

The pipes are traditionally made of hardwood. Mr. Balderose related to me that the earliest pipes he has seen, in Scottish museums, were all of native hardwoods. However, for centuries, quality pipes have been made from African blackwood or ebony, known widely for their resonant qualities, and used also for fine oboes, clarinets and flutes. Bags, once fashioned from the whole skins of sheep, goats, or other small animals, are, in our modern age, cut from leather or Gortex, a synthetic material that allows moisture to escape while retaining air.

The bagpipe is not an easy instrument to play. In my years of attending the various Highland Games in Pennsylvania, Maryland and Virginia, I have spoken to a number of pipers who say virtually the same thing: that the key is a keen desire to learn coupled with perseverance. Practice on the chanter (the melody pipe with finger holes and reed) should be a *daily* ritual, and practice on the pipes with drones, weekly, in order to become top-notch.

Personally, I am moved more by the pipes than by any other musical instrument. I never attend a concert or Highland games of massed bands without a pocketful of tissues. And sure 'twas the luck o' the Irish to have met the virtuoso piper Balderose.

It is the belief of many that the Great Pipes do not sound exciting and moving when played by just anybody. With that I am in *complete* accord. Precise fingering goes without saying, but really great piping is only produced by those pipers who can hear- *feel*- Athena's aulos *in their very souls*.

If ever you have heard Pittsburgh's George Balderose play "Amazing Grace" or "Going Home," there would be no words that I would need to supply- that I *could* supply. The skirl of his pipes at my father's funeral service tugged at my heart strings and loosened my held-in tears, the notes enveloping me in their warmth, as only good music can do. To be sure, the pipes, as Mr. Balderose has avowed, are messengers; for I *knew*, at the conclusion of his medley at Dad's gravesite, that at the other side of that long tunnel my father was traveling, another piper, an ancestor from our clan who had gone before, welcomed my father home.

Bagpipe music falls into three basic types- *Ceol Mor* (pronounced kyoll-more), which is the classical or, by exact translation, the "great music"; *Ceol Meadhonach* (pronounced kyoll med-a-noch) meaning "middle music" that includes hymns and airs; and *Ceol Beag* (kyoll-bek) the popular "little music" of dances and marches. Whichever, this ancient art is as electrifying today as ever it was.

Now, let us cross the bridge of time to a concise history of Pittsburgh's Balmoral School of Piping and Drumming, founded by

"Virtuosic piper" George Balderose in an array of performances round about the SW Pennsylvania area. For Balmoral school-related queries, private or group lessons, weddings, funerals, Celtic gatherings and concerts, Mr. Balderose can be reached at 1414 Pennsylvania Ave., Pittsburgh, PA 15233, or by telephoning 412-323-2707.
Photos by Peter Wolff, G. McBride and Matt Freed.

George Balderose in 1978. Firstly, I would be remiss if I did not recount for my readers the school's lofty mission. Their goals have always been "... to raise the standard and preserve and promote the appreciation of bagpipe music and its related musical activities throughout the United States of America." Balmoral accomplishes this "... by providing world class instruction, cultivating excellence in youth, presenting innovative musical events, and fostering *tradition*," ingrain to both piping and drumming.

Perhaps, as the school's web site suggests, the best place to begin the institution's history is with the "Bobs of Balmoral," pipers Robert U. Brown and Robert B. Nicol, who served as pipers at the noble Balmoral Estate in the Highlands of Scotland from 1927 until their deaths in the 1970s. The "Bobs of Balmoral," just as the Scottish Highlands themselves, were the stuff of bards and storytellers, their layered histories a vital part of the rich heritage of Celtic music and legend.

In 1978, when Balderose founded the Balmoral School in Pittsburgh, he wanted to honor those eminent pipers whom he so greatly admired. In their lifetimes, the "Bobs of Balmoral" achieved legendary greatness in Scotland and abroad for their piping, particularly via the *classical* bagpipe music. It was only natural to name his school after them, since those men had inspired *generations* of dedicated pipers.

One of the Balmoral Bobs' most notable students, James McIntosh, is a cofounder of the Pittsburgh Balmoral School. Other Brown/Nicol students who have taught at the Pittsburgh location are Donald Lindsay, formerly of the United States Air Force Pipe Band that played at President John F. Kennedy's funeral; John McDougall, champion piper with the Queen's Own Cameron

Highlanders, and P/M (master piper) Jimmy MacGregor of the Gordon Highlanders, also a piping Gold Medalist, who led the Gordon pipers at the Battle of El Alamain. *Impressive,* to say the least.

Since 1978, the Balmoral School has been operating under the auspices of Calliope House, Inc., the nonprofit, tax-exempt Pittsburgh Folk Music Society that the energetic Balderose also founded.

During the school's second decade (1988-98), the staff was significantly increased; and it should be noted that from 1979 through 1988, there were at least two separate entities, staging summer piping sessions, that used the "Balmoral School" in their titles. In 1988, those two entities amalgamated. The northern session's summer school location, for many years, had been located at Edinboro University of Pennsylvania. Today, sessions are held at East Stroudsberg University of Pennsylvania, as well as at the Saint Joseph's Retreat Center located off US Route 30, near Greensburg. I can personally attest to the charm of the latter locale, since my brother Rob attended prep school there in the 1970s when it was operating as such an institution.

Since the early 1990s, Balmoral has extended to several other regions. Currently, the Balmoral Schools hold five sessions each year, coast to coast. As of this writing, there are Balmoral Schools at Thomas More College, Crestview Hills, Kentucky; Sonoma State University in Rohnert Park, California, and at Lewis University at Romeoville, Illinois.

In 1990, under the laws of the Commonwealth of Pennsylvania, the Pittsburgh Balmoral School was incorporated as a not-for-profit corporation. Two years hence, the school's application for tax-exempt school status was approved by the IRS. The Pittsburgh Balmoral School of Piping and Drumming is one of the first in United States history, if not *the* first, to be incorporated as a nonprofit, tax-exempt educational and charitable corporation.

In addition to being Balmoral's founder, George Balderose is the school's executive director, and he works closely with a board of directors to plan each year's activities.

In 1993, instruction in smallpipe playing was added to the curriculum of all the Balmoral sessions. For many years now, ace piper Balderose has been teaching the various Celtic smallpipes, Scottish and Irish.

It is understandable that Mr. Balderose, in addition to his other duties, is also a teacher at the Balmoral school. He has had the privilege of studying with some of the world's top Highland piping instructors for more than two decades. A man dedicated to his craft, George has spent considerable time developing methods of teaching this ancient art, and it is significant to relate that several of his students have gone on to win firsts at renowned piping competitions, such as the Highland Games in Ligonier (Westmoreland County), Pennsylvania, held annually, for the past half-century, the first Saturday after Labor Day. Actually, these exciting, fun-filled games are held at rustically beautiful Idlewild Park, located just three miles west of Ligonier.

Balderose has performed with the Pittsburgh Symphony, as a soloist for the Metropolitan Museum of Art in New York City, and with championship Scottish and Irish dancers at concerts and Celtic festivals throughout the eastern United States. Four-times winner of the prestigious MacCrimmon Quaich for Grade One *Piobaireach/Ceol Mor,* George Balderose is, indeed, a winner, in every sense of the word.

In 1980, the Clan Donald Educational and Charitable Trust awarded Mr. Balderose a fellowship to travel to Scotland and study with master piper James McIntosh for a year in 1980-81. In 1985, Jim McIntosh emigrated to Pittsburgh, and was hired by Carnegie-Mellon University to revive the defunct Kiltie Pipe Band. Not long afterward, Jim teamed up with Eldon Gatwood, who played oboe for twenty-five years with the Pittsburgh Symphony, and to whom Balderose had taught the pipes.

McIntosh and Gatwood proposed that a student seeking a Bachelor of Performing Arts at CMU could choose the bagpipe as an instrumental major. This was the first B.A. degree for bagpipe music offered at any university in the entire world. Jim McIntosh received the M.B.E. in 1994 for this accomplishment. M.B.E. stands for Member of the British Empire medal, a Queen's Honor, bestowed each year for cultural contributions to Great Britain.

As the person who invited Jim McIntosh to the United States for the first time in 1978, George is justly proud of his mentor's accomplishments. Since, George has produced three cassettes and CDs, along with an instructional video of his mentor's music magic.

To return to our main focus: In 1981, the year subsequent to his traveling fellowship, a deserving Balderose was awarded the Senior Certificate in Piping from the College of Piping at Glasgow, Scotland. Currently, George serves as a Trustee of the Clan Donald Educational and Charitable Trust, a nonprofit foundation that awards scholarships for Americans to study at Scottish universities. The Clan Donald Educational and Charitable Trust is also the sponsor of the Ligonier Highland Games.

As if all the above were not enough, in 1984, the tireless Balderose founded, directed, and served as piping instructor for Scottish Week at the Augusta Heritage Center in Elkins, West Virginia.

Since 1989, Mr. Balderose has been a member of the Pennsylvania Governor's Heritage Affairs Commission's Traditional and Ethnic Arts Touring Program.

The teaching staff at Balmoral of Pittsburgh is beyond the description "impressive" and includes a bright spectrum of instructors, each with a long list of awards and accolades.

The Pittsburgh Balmoral School of Piping and Drumming proffers scholarship assistance to teenage students of the bagpipe on a competitive basis. Applications for scholarships are obtainable upon request. For information about scholarships, tuition and fees, discounts, schedules, room and board, please go to the Balmoral School of Piping and Drumming web site: www.bagpiping.org, or you can visit George Balderose on his web site at: www.Pittsburghpiper.com, or at the web site of the musical group this multitalented man has also founded at: www.roadtotheisles.org. Or you can contact George at 1414 Pennsylvania Avenue, Pittsburgh, PA 15233; telephone: 412-323-2707.

Perhaps the most significant implication of the ideals and goals of the Balmoral school is this: Each Balmoral School of Piping brings to the United States, from Scotland, the winner of the Scottish Solo Piping Junior Championship so that he or she may study with the champion instructors who teach at the Balmoral summer schools.

What's more, the Balmoral Board of Directors has decided to produce a National Junior Solo Scottish Piping and Drumming competition in Pittsburgh during November of 2007. It is their objective to attract the top young American competitors from all across the country to compete in Pittsburgh for this prestigious national title. Presently, Balmoral is engaged in a fund-raising campaign to make this event financially possible, stimulated by a $100,000 Challenge Grant by Ed and Julia Littlefield and the Sage Foundation of Arlington, Washington.

The grant will match on a one-to-one basis every dollar contributed to the Balmoral School. Since the school is tax-exempt, all contributions are tax deductible. Donations to the Balmoral School are always needed and most welcome.

If *you* want to learn to play the bagpipes, George Balderose is available for private lessons at his home at Calliope House, 1414 Pennsylvania Avenue, on Pittsburgh's historic, charming North Side (once known as "Allegheny City"). There are also small group classes that Balderose teaches, through Calliope, at Chatham College in Pittsburgh. Private lessons are usually conducted on Sundays, and the group sessions Tuesdays. George utilizes traditional teaching methods, together with more modern approaches, many of which are his alone. An additional option for aspiring pipers is to attend an intensive weeklong (or longer, depending on the individual student and his/her needs) summer session of the Balmoral Schools, which are held, as touched on above, at colleges and/or conference centers in Pennsylvania, Kentucky, Illinois and California.

As stated earlier, the pipes are not a particularly easy instrument to master; but Mr. Balderose and Balmoral believe that anyone can learn to play who has: self-motivation, the ability to count steadily, a minimum of thirty minutes a day to devote to practice, and- very important- a good teacher.

Now, don't panic in those households where a would-be piper may reside! One begins his or her training with a quiet instrument called the practice chanter. This instrument is what all hopeful pipers start with and learn on. Even advanced players learning new tunes or refining existing tunes use the chanter. The pipes, understand, have the same number of finger holes as the melody pipe or chanter. Blowing into the practice chanter, however, rather than into a bag(pipe), produces a lot less volume. So, take heart, mothers and fathers and families of novice pipers. The beginning piper can quietly learn the basics, the correct fingering of pipe music, without blowing hard into a bagpipe and producing a tempest of terrible noises.

After the student has memorized about half a dozen tunes on the practice chanter, playing them correctly and smoothly, then it is time to make the transition to the pipes. This is normally done after three to six months, or more, of weekly or biweekly lessons on the chanter, accompanied by daily practice sessions at home.

There are simply too many skills to learn at once on a set of new bagpipes. Blowing with force, squeezing the bag, and coordinating these two activities so the pressure of one equals the pressure of the other, in addition to learning the music and fingering- all simultaneously- would be impossible. Thus, it is strongly suggested to learn the music and fingering *first* on the practice chanter, then graduate to a set of pipes, wherein the blowing pressure is greater, and learning to blow into and alternately squeeze the bag at the same pressure is requisite to keep the instrument in tune.

It is highly advisable to begin your training with a good teacher- right from the outset- otherwise bad habits may be acquired, making it impossible to play good music. As we all know, bad habits are hard to break! Wisdom dictates in all aspects of life that mastering one thing at a time brings the best results- this is especially true for the pipes.

Another thing I want to make would-be pipers aware of is cost. A major feature of the practice chanter is that it is much less of an investment than the Great Highland Pipes, around $100 as opposed to $1,000 or more for a full set of new pipes. Be advised that occasionally used sets can be found for less, though many antique sets are prized and thus *quite* costly.

I remember when I was finishing and decorating our basement. I looked everywhere for a used set of Great Highlands, never finding them- or any I could afford. I learned back then that bagpipes don't come cheap. And here, I must extend an important caveat: Beware of cheap sets made of inferior materials. A proper set is always going to cost the buyer at the very least $1000. The cheap sets are light in weight with inferior materials and craftsmanship. Bagpipes are always purchased *with a teacher* at Balmoral, who knows how to identify shoddy craftsmanship by, for example, examining the inside of the drone and chanter bores for unpolished roughness.

Bagpipes, Balmoral and Balderose are, to many Pittsburgh folk, synonymous and nearly interchangeable, and I think George Balderose loves Pittsburgh and its environs as much as Pittsburgh loves him- and he loves the bagpipes! For over thirty years, he affirms, he has "... enjoyed playing the pipes for many audiences, friends, and families in this wonderful region." A few years ago, I was enthralled with his magnificent performance in *Brigadoon* with the Pittsburgh Civic Light Opera at the Benedum Center. George has also appeared at Carnegie Music Hall in Pittsburgh and in concert with the River City Brass Band.

A reviewer for the *New York Times* once described Balderose as having "a virtuoso's gift." And in the words of another critic he is a "virtuosic piper." His great gift for the pipes, as I stated in the premier volume of my *County Chronicles*, is truly divine for the way his music stirs the soul. It awakens in my genetic memory hundreds of Celtic ancestors. Their tears, their laughter, and their battle cries pulsate in my blood as they echo across the great portal of time.

The pipes are visceral- in my opinion, the *most* visceral of musical instruments. Like their mother, the aulos of Athena, they have the power to kindle human emotion like nothing else on this earth. This is why the pipes are so ofttimes an integral part of military, police, and fire-men-and-women's funerals. They conjure, among other human emotions and virtues- *valor,* the strength of mind and spirit that enables a human being to encounter danger with firmness and resolve.

To quote George Balderose: "The bagpipe is my instrument of choice because it stirs my heart, as it has stirred... hearts over the past thousand years. The pipes invoke feelings so basic to the human nature, from festive joyfulness to steadfast determination to mournful sorrow and pathos. The pipes are messengers... they bring memories of times past to the fore. *The bagpipes tell us something about who we are.*"

"THE MAGIC WATER"

"The maple syrup of Pennsylvania's Somerset County is the sweetest I have ever tasted."
- Kate Smith, April 17, 1947 (via her noontime radio show)

Small-town America has long conjured, due largely to artist Norman Rockwell, the nostalgic image of a country store complete with a potbellied stove and a handful of old-timers spinning, round its warmth, a bright circle of yarns and palaver. In his own words, the famous American illustrator was showing the America he "... knew and observed to others who may not have noticed."

The picturesque town of Meyersdale in Somerset County, Pennsylvania, is no exception to the above rural-America reflection. A recounting of the normally quiet town's Pennsylvania Maple Festival has its roots in just such a Rockwell-like tableau; for it was around the potbellied stove of the Shipley Hardware Store, in the gloaming of a snowy January night in 1948, where the notion of an annual Meyersdale celebration to promote the sweetest of all Pennsylvania's natural resources- Somerset County maple syrup- was conceived. On that memorable, blustery winter's eve- locally known since as the "potbellied stove summit"- those farseeing men envisioned and warmed to the festival idea around Shipley's old-fashioned heater. It would not be long until their dream became a reality, one that has transformed Meyersdale into "Maple City, USA."

Though the stove summit kindled the dream, the festival had its *actual* beginnings elsewhere. Meyersdale's colorful story of development and growth was, fascinatingly, sparked by Kate Smith's popular daytime radio show, *Kate Smith Speaks.* Ms. Smith's news and commentary program, to which thousands of fans across America tuned in, aired at noon daily.

I know my older readers will fondly remember Kate, but I think I should pause here to introduce my younger audience to this American icon.

The star-spangled Kathryn Elizabeth Smith was born May 1, 1907, in the nation's capital. From an early age, she loved to sing and entertain. In 1926, after performing in a string of theaters and nightclubs, a New York City producer "discovered" her. Soon after, Columbia Records' vice president, Ted Collins, became cognizant of the plucky singer with the big heart and a set of lungs to match. Collins became her partner and manager, and he was the one who wisely put her on the radio.

"Kate," as she was known, became an *instant* success on the air. However, her star had only begun to shine, for she was destined to break the longevity record for capturing the hearts of American audiences everywhere. Movies were next on her bright horizon; and in 1943, she belted out a memorable rendition of "God Bless America" in Irving Berlin's *This is the Army.* It would become a signature tune.

From the beginning (1926) of her long and brilliant career to the late 1960s, Kate made several recordings, many of them top-of-the-chart hits. She helped to write the lyrics of "When the Moon Comes Over the Mountain," which emerged as her theme song. Irving Berlin regarded the song she had made famous, "God Bless America," as *his* most important composition. And Kate herself predicted that the stirring anthem would "... still be sung long after all of us are gone."

Smith's was the most popular variety program, *The Kate Smith Hour,* which aired weekly from 1937 to 1945. At the same time, she had the number-one daytime radio show, the midday *Kate Smith Speaks.*

When television became a fixture in American homes, Kate went with it by way of her sparkling variety shows that ran to 1960. After that, she made hundreds of guest appearances on such television programs as the *Ed*

Sullivan Show, the *Tennessee Ernie Ford Show*, the *Jack Paar Show*- the list is extensive.

During the final decade of her life, Kate gave dozens of live concerts. She ended her career on a high note as the good-luck charm for the Philadelphia Flyers (the hockey team whom she called "my boys") with her rousing rendition of "God Bless America," inspiring them to two successive Stanley Cups, in 1974 and again in 1975.

In 1976, the year of our nation's Bicentennial, America's grand dame was named Grand Marshal of the Tournament of Roses Parade. Fittingly, the last song she delivered was Irving Berlin's classic for a Bicentennial special prior to July 4, 1976. Kate Smith passed away in 1986. In 1987, the Flyers erected an eight-foot bronze statue of the internationally known singer outside the Spectrum, their arena, in Philadelphia.

To return to the main focus of our Chronicle: One day, early in 1947, during her daily noontime radio broadcast of *Kate Smith Speaks,* Kate happened to mention that she would sure appreciate a taste of some "...good Vermont maple syrup." A few of Meyersdale's local citizenry took her offhanded comment as a challenge; and picking up the gauntlet, they sent the radio star a sample of Somerset County's maple syrup.

On April 17, 1947, during her radio show's national broadcast, Kate sang more than the era's popular tunes. She sang the praises of Somerset County's gift to her, pronouncing their syrup "... the sweetest she had ever tasted."

The stellar publicity with its star-dusted fallout spurred the incentive for a promotional campaign which began that May, under the auspices of the Meyersdale Chamber of Commerce. However, the initial fervor began to wane as the long winter days loomed ahead. Then came the "potbellied stove summit," on January 20, 1948, mentioned at the overture of our tale; and with enthusiasm rekindled, the campaign received a needed shot of adrenaline to set it on its "yellow brick road" to success. Chamber of Commerce President W. Hubert Lenhart took charge. A planning committee was formed, and energetic preparations for the very first Pennsylvania Maple Festival finally got under way.

On March 18, 1948, the premier festival opened with glowing words of praise from Pennsylvania's Governor Daniel B. Strickler. A crowd of approximately 1,500 had gathered on Main Street to hear him speak and to witness the coronation of Pennsylvania's first Maple Queen, Miss Agnes Jean Hornbrook.

As we are prone to say in our neck of Penn's Woods, the Maple Festival put Meyersdale "on the map." Certainly, it played an important role in the postwar development of the town and surrounding communities. From a crowd of 1,500 to tens of thousands of visitors annually, the Pennsylvania Maple Festival is not only a tale of growth but of strong community spirit as well. Every year, Meyersdale basks in the fact that more and more of its townspeople pitch in and work together for the same cause. And each year the festival has made the town more and more famous- and an even *sweeter* place to live.

Now, let us travel even further back in time, to the pre-colonial period and the earliest beginnings of the celebration of maple syrup. As I have stated in previous volumes of my *County Chronicles* history series, Native American words and expressions were/are illustrative. The Indians celebrated the "Maple Moon" with the return of spring. Legend has it that the Native Americans accidentally discovered the sweet stuff when an Indian struck a sugar maple tree with a tomahawk, in spring, while the sap was running. Out came this clear liquid that looked like water. The surprised Indian ran to get a crude bowl to catch Earth Mother's offering. It is suspected that the Natives set the sap-filled bowl near the campfire, perhaps on heated stones. Or perhaps heated stones from the campfire dropped into the wooden trough containing the sap liquid, condensing it. And before they knew it, the Indians had maple syrup.

Like the discovery of the sap itself, the heating process was accidental, as History continuously tells us many findings and inventions are. When the Natives tasted the condensed sap, they were delighted with its sweet rewards and instantly christened it the "Magic Water."

In 1970, Meyersdale began staging an historical, musical pageant about the Indians' discovery of the sweet water, calling it, appropriately, *Legend of the Magic Water.* Over a hundred local volunteers make up the cast and crew. Today, the play, which tells the history of maple syrup through story, dance and song, is an integral and colorful facet of the Pennsylvania Maple Festival. The pageant continues with the exciting tales of the pioneers and travelers of the early railroad. The entire program is vibrant with dancing girls, entertainers of all kinds, and the remarkable settlers of Meyersdale, complete with their impact on the Somerset area. No one in the region wants to miss the pageant, which is provided by a gamut of talented local people. The *Legend of the Magic Water* is easily the largest, all-volunteer community musical in the district, and the audience leaves annually with positive comments- and lasting memories.

Sap-hauling wagon at Maple Festival Park

Though Europeans knew how to tap trees, it was the Native Americans who discovered how to make maple syrup. The making of maple syrup is truly an *American* art! Indians from New England to Canada were producing maple syrup from the early to mid-1600s. They made a sloping gash, about two inches deep and between two and three inches in length, in the trunk of a sugar maple tree. Then a knife was inserted into the bottom of the cut, so that the sap flowed down the cut, onto the knife and into a positioned wooden receptacle on the ground. These "buckets" were fashioned either of tree bark caulked with pitch or hollowed out logs. The Indians placed these receptacles on the snowy ground at the base of each tree.

According to the Pennsylvania Maple Festival web site, by 1765 the settlers changed the Indians' tapping to what they called "tree boxing." They trimmed off the bark and carved out a half-inch-deep square or rectangular cavity into the tree trunk. A sloping trough was put into the tree trunk to gather the sap from this "box"/cavity to a spout that carried the liquid from the trough to a receptacle. Boring holes (into a tree for the sap) began sometime around 1774.

By 1950, the present-day tapping was accepted. Spouts, called "spiles," were inserted into the trunks of the sugar maple trees to draw off the sap. Originally, they were made of wood. Over the years, they have been replaced by first galvanized cast iron, and then- you guessed it- plastic.

As previously stated, the Indians used tubs from hollowed-out tree bark or logs as collecting receptacles. The colonists used crude wooden troughs until sometime in the late 1840s, when wooden buckets replaced them. Actually, wooden buckets were used as early as 1748, but were not in common use until much later. The "good ole" wooden buckets persisted until 1935, when they were replaced by tin-plated buckets. Bear in mind that the wooden receptacles dried out and leaked if they were not painted every year. Bucket covers were utilized from early on, to keep leaves and debris from polluting the sap. Since 1965, modern plastic tubing carries the sap directly to a gathering vat or storage tank.

The old way of collecting sap

I think this is a good time to pause and tell you about "spotza." Ever tasted it? If you had, you would remember it. It is a sort of taffy, and one of the unique foods derived from maple syrup. Spotza is made by boiling maple syrup down to the soft-ball stage (about 238 degrees F) and then pouring it over crushed ice. This forms soft, clear taffy, which should be eaten *immediately* to savor its full flavor and texture rewards. The early settlers learned about spotza from the Indians, who poured boiled maple syrup onto clean snow. The word *spotza* comes to us from the Pennsylvania Dutch, which translates, as you may have surmised, "spot on the snow." Annual visitors can watch spotza being made and taste its delicate flavor at the Pennsylvania Maple Festival Park at Meyersdale.

The year 2007 pridefully marks Somerset County's 60th Pennsylvania Maple Festival. The yearly celebration embraces many events and activities, including a horse-pulling contest, a popular Pennsylvania sport with muscular equine athletes. Like all good athletes in training, these horses in competition are worked every day to strengthen and condition their muscles and tendons. Keep in mind that these are draft horses bred for power and agility to pull heavy loads, and the short distances they pull in this contest does not harm them. Local farmers have remarked to me how proud these horses are after a competition. "Just watch them strut their stuff when they are unhitched!"

In addition to their daily workouts, like human athletes, the quality and quantity of the horses' food is important. Along with their oats, which is an energy food, comes supplementary vitamins and minerals for stamina. A good supply of hay, of course, is a given, with alfalfa for protein; and this combination is fed twice a day.

For draft horses, the proper fit of collar, harness and bridle is of the utmost importance as well. Each horse is different, and the gear must fit each properly, so that sore muscles do not result. Horse-pulling is a sport; but I daresay, it is also a science with much more than meets the untrained eye of the observer.

Another feature of the Pennsylvania Maple Festival is the annual pancake and sausage event. This is the brainchild of the Meyersdale Lions' Club, and it has been, from its introduction, a welcome addition to the festival. Each and every year, the entire proceeds of this event go toward a current community project, with all the supplies for its success purchased from local businesses. And let me tell you, readers, this is no ordinary pancake meal. The select ingredients and the manner in which the food is prepared will make this meal memorable- golden, lacy-edged, mouth-watering pancakes, topped with real melted butter; seasoned-and-roasted-to-perfection, homemade sausages, and Pennsylvania's best maple syrup all washed down with good, hot coffee in an all-you-can-eat supply. The Lions' pancake-and-sausage project is one more example of the strong community spirit that exists and persists in Meyersdale.

The Quilt Show is another festival attraction. Quilters from all over the area put their beautifully crafted quilts on display for the public throughout the days of the celebration. The fire hall, which houses these vivid coverlets, is open during the entire festival from 10 a.m. to 5 p.m. Registration for entry must be done ahead of the time the festival opens. Cash and ribbon awards are bestowed on the quilt winners.

Artists and crafters come from all over the country to proffer their wares at the Pennsylvania Maple Festival. Along with the aforementioned quilts, some of the crafts that visitors can expect to see are wood carvings, knitted and crocheted items, ceramics and pottery, caned chairs, leather crafts, hand-fashioned brooms and baskets, dried flowers, homemade candies, handmade dolls, water and oil paintings, prints... and the list is ever-increasing.

Several years ago, a cobbler/shoemaker shop was acquired by the Maple Festival; and it has since become a permanent part of Festival Park, presently occupying its own building.

Once the property of Charles A. Dively, the cobbler shop is unique and was reputed to be the "... most complete cobbler shop east of the Mississippi." This exhibit consists of a cobbler's bench, sewing machine, and more than 100 wooden patterns and lasts for shoes and boots. A "last" is a metal form shaped like a human foot, over which a shoe is shaped or repaired.

The outsized wooden boot that once attracted clients to Mr. Dively's shop today attracts modern festival visitors to the cobbler shop building. On cold days, the old potbellied stove that warmed Dively's shop over a century ago, as he diligently labored at his craft, now warms visitors and the cobbler-shop guide.

An interesting item I uncovered was that a hundred years ago, a pair of good, leather, handmade shoes or boots cost a man from $4 to $7; a woman circa $3, while children's footwear ranged from fifty cents to about $2.75. Repairs cost anywhere from ten cents to $1.25.

I want to add here that finding a shoe repair shop today is nearly impossible! It is a craft lost to history. I suppose we could say that the reason shoe repair shops are practically nonexistent is due to the fact that nowadays, for the most part, shoes and boots are not handmade; thus, we can purchase a new pair for less than the cost of repairs. I don't know anyone who gets their shoes and boots resoled anymore. Remember when we did that?

In my hometown of Connellsville, Fayette County, there were several shoe repair shops. Lanzi's, Vona's, Spicola's, Petrilla's, Verdone-then-Pistilli's were a few of the Italian "heel bars" that existed while I was growing up. Take into account that Italy and Spain have always been known for exquisite leather goods, including footwear; and in the "old country," one had to learn a trade from an apprentice. Therefore, it is understandable that southwestern Pennsylvania, with its many Italian immigrants, would have had, at one time, several shoe repair shops.

An antique doctor's office shares the building with the cobbler's shop. It would be impossible to list all the vintage items within this permanent exhibit, though a more-than-a-century-old set of surgical instruments complete with celluloid handles certainly attracted my interest. There are also old office ledgers, leather medical bags [Remember when the doctor carried such when he made house calls?], medicine bottles, a complete Edison Dictaphone, and early X-ray equipment, to mention a few of the numerous things this exhibit houses. There are no reproductions in the doctor's office.

My personal favorites were the saber, gold arm insignias, uniform buttons, and jewelry that President Abraham Lincoln presented to Dr. Clay McKinley. Dr. McKinley was one of the local doctors whose instruments were donated to this permanent exhibit. McKinley served during the Civil War in the Medical Corps, and he and his wife became close friends of Abraham and Mary Todd Lincoln.

Speaking of the Civil War, visitors can tour, while at the festival grounds, the historic Meyers Manor. Though, over the long years, the old house hosted many celebrities, its most famous guest was none other than Ulysses S. Grant. While traveling through the region, he once stopped overnight at the homestead. Constructed at the turn of the nineteenth century, the house is chiefly associated with the Meyers family, who added to the original log structure, and who, due to several business ventures, became leading citizens of the Meyersdale area.

Maple Festival visitors will discover many things. At Festival Park, you can learn– hands on– how to tap a sugar maple, boil sap into syrup and sugar off, even how to make delectable sugar cakes, twirl spotza, and so much more! The park complex is the heart of the festival, which is located on scenic Meyers Avenue, charming with its Victorian homes and its canopy of majestic trees.

The nice folks of Meyersdale will tell you that maple production is a labor of love. The process of making maple syrup has undergone many changes over the long years since the Native Americans discovered the "magic water." And though new innovations and technology have made maple production more efficient, it continues to be a laborious, painstaking and ultra-careful endeavor.

Visitors learn, hands-on, how to tap a sugar maple tree.
Photos by author's husband, Phillip R. Lincoln

I am proud to relate that Somerset County produces more maple products than any other county in the commonwealth of Pennsylvania. This is due to the abundance of sugar maples in the area, as well as the region's seasonal temperatures. I cannot refrain from mentioning that scenic Somerset County is nicknamed the "Roof Garden of Pennsylvania," because of its fertile, high-elevation farmland.

Like farming, the maple industry is also subject to Mother Nature's capricious temperament. Frigid, late-winter snows; fluctuating temperatures; too much rain; too little rain, and a too-short tapping season can wreak havoc on the industry from year to year. But once the sap is collected and evaporated into desired form, Somerset producers can proudly sell their sweet delights, locally and nationally. It is important to note that a high volume of each year's yield is purchased by large, commercial syrup manufacturers who transform the syrup's consistency to match that of their own name brand.

I think it significant to mention also that the sugar maple is one of America's most stately trees. Did you know that a sugar maple is at least thirty years old before it is tapped? The tapping process does not harm these trees. If a tree is ten inches in diameter, it can support one tap; fifteen-inch trees can support two taps, and twenty-inch trees, three taps. I was amazed to learn that an average maple tree will produce fifteen gallons of sap from each tap per season.

When is the time right to tap? Cold nights and warm days. When the weather is such that there is a freeze at night and a thaw during the day, then it is time for sap collecting. The maple season may last for eight to ten weeks; but during this period, the heavy sap may run only from ten to twenty days. The harvest of sap concludes with the advent of spring's warm nights, and the first stages of bud development of the sugar maple trees.

Throughout rolling, scenic Somerset County, there can still be glimpsed pail-carrying men, who collect from each tree and empty the buckets into covered tanks hauled on trucks or tractors. A great deal of sap is pumped from roadside tanks into a tank truck, to be hauled to central storage tanks at the "sugar house." Here, germicidal lamps over the tanks prevent bacterial growth until the sap can be evaporated.

Unlike the Native Americans who used heated stones to evaporate sugar-water and the settlers who used iron kettles fired with wood, maple workers today use fuel oil to boil the water. As the sap flows at a steady boil, the water escapes in the form of steam, and the sugar-water becomes ever sweeter, changing to the familiar amber hue with the increasing sugar content.

Direct from the tree, the sugar content in the liquid is about two to two-and-a-half percent. After the boiling process, the sugar content is about sixty-five percent. One gallon of maple syrup weighing eleven pounds was condensed from forty to fifty gallons of tree-given sugar water.

Transferred next to flat pans for final processing, the syrup is forced through special filters to remove any sediment. It is then stored in 550-gallon, sterile metal tanks that have germicidal lamps beneath the lids. Later, it is pumped back to finishing pans and reheated to 185 degrees F, refiltered and packed into cans, bottles, ceramic or plastic containers ready for purchase.

This final packaging continues throughout the entire year, providing jobs for many in the Meyersdale area. Once the Somerset maple syrup is packaged, it may travel around the world, or it may appear on your table, via your hometown grocery store.

Pure maple syrup varies in color. It can be light, medium, or dark amber, each jewel-like in hue.

Unopened containers of maple syrup can be stored (up to two years) in any cool, dry place. Opened containers *must* be refrigerated. Refrigerated maple syrup can last about a year, but be sure to watch for mold growth. *If mold occurs, discard immediately.*

Every visitor to the Maple Festival is welcome to see the sugar camp demonstration in the building across from historic Meyers Manor at Maple Festival Park. This building is easily recognizable by the smoke issuing from its chimney and the sweet smell permeating the air. Here, visitors can learn virtually everything about maple syrup.

With over 31,000 sugar maple trees to be tapped each year in Pennsylvania, and less than a month and a half for harvesting the sap, the process *must* be done quickly. Since most Pennsylvania syrup producers no longer use the old galvanized buckets to catch the sap, the plastic tubing that leads, like a sap network from tree to tree, to the holding tank in the processing plant is a modern time-saver.

Here are some uses I have discovered for pure maple syrup. Over pancakes, waffles and French toast is the most common use, of course, but there are several others. Maple syrup sweetens applesauce in the most delightful way. Try adding a bit to milkshakes or eggnog! Add it to your morning grapefruit- much better than sugar! Mix a little with butter to glaze baked squash, yams or sweet potatoes. Maple syrup makes a nice topping for ice creams too, especially the maple nut flavor.

Have you ever added pure maple syrup to baked beans? Give it a try; I am certain you will like it. The Pennsylvania Maple Festival web site lists several maple recipes free, including those for baked beans, maple cream puffs, maple rolls, and even maple spring chicken.

At their web site, you can acquire the dates, each year, that the festival will run, including the date and times of the Grand Parade. I suggest you begin your inquiries *before* March, so you will have time to make arrangements, and if you are planning to attend the festival one day only, I recommend you go on parade day. At the Pennsylvania Maple Festival web site, you can discover even more about maple syrup, plus the answers to your questions about the annual Pennsylvania Maple Festival. If you are not a computer person, then telephone the festival office at 814-634-0213, and they will be happy to answer any of your queries, including quilt registration.

I will leave you with a maple recipe I picked up at the Pennsylvania Maple Festival.

Maple Date and Nut Bread

1 cup dates
3/4 teaspoon soda
1 cup boiling water
1 well-beaten egg
1/2 cup pure Pennsylvania maple syrup
1 teaspoon salt
1 cup pastry flour
1 cup whole wheat flour
1 teaspoon baking powder
1/2 cup chopped nuts
1 tablespoon melted shortening

Beat all ingredients together, then bake at 350 degrees for 60-75 minutes. Remove from the oven and brush top with a light glaze of maple syrup. Makes one loaf. Enjoy!

On the way up to the festival, from our home in neighboring Fayette County, my husband and I took in the rustically beautiful Pennsylvania countryside complete with the occasional Amish horse and buggy. We spent an entire day at the festival, learned all about sugar maple trees and the making of maple syrup, enjoyed seeing all the crafts and sampling a variety of delicious foods. At day's end, we started home; and like Kate Smith, we were warmed by the friendliness of the Somerset County folk and the indubitable conclusion that our Pennsylvania maple syrup is the sweetest we ever tasted!

"A Sentimental Journey or Praise the Lord and Pass the Ammunition!"

"Yesterday, December 7, 1941- a date that will live in infamy- the United States of America was suddenly and deliberately attacked by naval and air forces of the Empire of Japan...."
- President Franklin Delano Roosevelt

"Nothing will ever be the same."
- Columnist Marquis Childs, at the time of Pearl Harbor

Before the Japanese attack on Pearl Harbor, the United States was a nation of approximately 132 million people. We had an armed force of about 1.4 million men, primarily the result of the Selective Service Act, which had been signed on September 16, 1940. Hitler's *blitzkrieg* had been steamrolling across Europe since September of 1939, and America was divided as to whether or not we should enter into another of Europe's wars.

Then, before 0800 hours (Hawaiian time) on a quiet Sunday morning, December 7, 1941, while Japanese diplomats were in Washington, guaranteeing us peace, Japan delivered a surprise attack on the American military base in Honolulu, known as Pearl Harbor.

In Washington, President Roosevelt had just finished his lunch when a call came through for him from the Secretary of the Navy, Frank Knox, who insisted on speaking to the President immediately. Roosevelt took the call.

When more information of the attack filtered through, the President called for a joint session of Congress to be held the following day- for the express purpose of asking for a declaration of war. He then called in his secretary, Grace Tully. "Sit down, Grace. I am going before Congress tomorrow, and I want to dictate my message. It will be short." It was that. It was also destined to become one of the most famous speeches of the twentieth century, giving birth to one of the most legendary phrases of the era.

By early evening of December 7th, hundreds of anxious men and women had gathered in the chill outside the White House. So great was the crush of people, they were standing five or six deep on the sidewalk beyond the tall iron fence surrounding the presidential grounds. The cold deepened with the agonizingly slow passage of time. In watchful silence, however, the crowd remained, peering at the executive mansion's lighted windows in hopes of spotting movement inside, scrutinizing the arrival of each automobile to see if they could identify passengers. Devoid of stars, the ink-black sky, with its misty and indistinct moon, seemed to symbolize the uncertainty of the moment.

In 1942, during the dark days following Pearl Harbor, when the fear of a Japanese invasion harried Hawaii and the West coast; when Evil wore a human face, and Hitler was nearly in Moscow; when German submarines were right off our East coast, from Maine to Florida, sinking our oil tankers, along with anything else they could target; and no one knew if the Nazi war machine would ever be stopped- could be stopped- Americans everywhere took refuge in our history, well stocked with our heroes of the past.

History has always been a great source of strength in times more trying, and it is a constant reminder to a troubled present of the courage of those who have gone before. Winston Churchill once said, "We have not journeyed all this way because we are made of sugar candy!"

Back in 1936, Franklin Roosevelt, speaking at the Democratic National Convention in Philadelphia, told the nation: "This generation of Americans has a rendezvous with Destiny." Nineteen-thirty-six had been a year of ominous signs and headlines. Hitler had marched unopposed into the Rhineland. Spain had exploded into civil war. The Italian dictator Mussolini, using planes, mustard gas and 250,000 troops, crushed Ethiopia, whilst his son crowed over the victory, declaring to the press that bombing the Ethiopian cavalry was "exceptionally good fun"!

In September 1939, Hitler displayed the same sick sentiments after Germany's victory over Poland. Contrary to the propaganda in Italian and German newspapers, the Polish cavalry did not *charge* panzers with sabers and lances. In fact, the Polish cavalry had made a successful, whirlwind attack against a German infantry unit, albeit there were armored vehicles involved. When the order flew down the lines, "Draw sabers... " reins were gripped tighter, men leaned forward in their saddles, and one of the last great cavalry charges in history rushed forward at the gallop. The loss to the men was rather minimal. The horses got the worst of it from the frantic German machine-gun fire. About forty brave, beautiful horses lay dead or badly wounded, bleeding and gasping for air. After the battle when reporters were shown dead Polish cavalrymen and horses on the battlefield onto which German tanks had since appeared, the Italian newspapers broke the Hitler-enhanced story that the dictator fanned, as I said, to spread propaganda coupled with fear.

But who can ever forget another of FDR's haunting quotes: "The only thing we have to fear is Fear itself"? History is replete with the rich voices that reach out to us to stand up for what is right and just and to lift our spirits- sometimes from the distance of centuries.

A month before Hitler invaded Poland, on August 2, 1939, Albert Einstein addressed a letter to President Roosevelt at the White House. The historic missive warned that Germany was attempting to develop a terrible new bomb, that the German government had already stopped the sale of uranium from the mines in Czechoslovakia. Einstein urged FDR to speed up scientific research under government supervision. Shortly thereafter, the President initiated what would become the top-secret Manhattan Project. The world would change forever. To quote author David McCullough from his *Brave Companions, Portraits in History*: "Politics and physics had been joined irrevocably."

Indeed, history is many things. It is about leaders and leadership, yes. And it is about change- the only thing we know for certain will happen. But history is also a teacher, our greatest teacher. It teaches us lessons in appreciation and admiration.

History teaches us what we stand for- *and, more importantly, what we should be willing to stand up for.*

History is vital to sustaining our freedom. History is another word for "Patriotism." *History is love of home and country.*

With this Chronicle I hope to recreate a vivid picture of the World War II era. Interspersed with my comments and historical data, this segment will mostly contain oral histories that I have garnered through a host of interviews, from family, friends and neighbors from my home area of southwestern Pennsylvania. However, these memories could have been collected from just about any small town or rural section of America. As I unlocked memories from the war years via these discussions, I felt, more and more, like an archaeologist unearthing a precious past; or like someone who had just discovered a secret drawer in an old desk. With each reading of letters yellowed with age or carefully preserved newspapers brittle to the touch, with the pondering of each vintage photograph faded by Time, I was discovering cached-away gold.

In conjunction with the heroism of our fighting men, I want to say, "Hail to the women of America during World War II!" You took up your heritage from the brave and stalwart women of the past, women such as the "Molly Pitchers" and Captain Molly Cochran Corbin about whom I wrote in the first two volumes, respectively, of my *County Chronicles* Pennsylvania history series. But unlike "Captain Molly," who manned a cannon for George Washington in his desperate battle to hold on to New York during the

Revolutionary War, the women of the Second World War were warriors without guns.

Necessity propelled more than six million women into the American workforce. In 1943, a fictional character emerged who embodied the ideal of the 1940s American woman worker. Her name was "Rosie the Riveter," and she was everything Uncle Sam wanted in a wartime woman. She was highly patriotic and loyal, close-lipped, hard-working and efficient, even pretty.

Apart from those in the workforce, thousands of women became Army and Navy nurses, and many others were accepted into the WAC, WAVE, SPAR, WASP, and other female military-affiliated units. And though women in that era did not go into combat, many were thrust on or near the frontlines, such as the heroic Army and Navy nurses on Bataan.

From the farms and factories to those frontlines, from film actresses to Gold-Star mothers, the women of America took the proverbial bull by the horns and did what had to be done for the war effort, providing an unparalleled panorama of patriotism, courage, obligation and stamina.

Rosie's bright poster with her muscle-flexed arm and the bold words "We can do it!" said it all- *and they did do it all.* Each in her own way, the women of this nation were invaluable to the war effort; and though not all of them faced bullets, like Wonder Woman (the first comic book superhero, created in 1941, to fight Nazi evil) they helped to win the greatest war in our history. Collectively, these valiant women were the "other American warriors of World War II." God bless them, our veterans, and everyone who contributed to the war effort!

"We had to choose between what was right and what was easy... more often than not, it was as simple as that." So many of those I interviewed stressed to me how every American man, woman, and child "pitched in" during the war years, doing whatever he or she could, no matter how small. Even a small star shines out of darkness.

America was never more united than it was during World War II. It was a time when the choices were clear; a time when death was closer and life was more precious. It was a time of courage and honor- of passion and sacrifice.

I hope this Chronicle will trigger the memories of my older readers; and I hope they, in turn, will pass their World War II memories down to their children and to their grandchildren.

It is my ardent desire too that these stories will help to instill strength and courage, inspiring my readers in our terrorism-troubled present.

~ ~ ~

"I was just a kid, a preteen, but I recall jitterbugging with the soldiers at dances sponsored by the ladies' circle in my hometown of Smithton. This club, in which my mother played a major role, sold tickets to fundraiser dances, the proceeds of which were used to purchase gifts for our young men departing for war. I remember helping to stuff big duffle bags full of those 'little pieces of home' that the boys being deployed took with them. It didn't matter who you were; everyone in our little town pulled together for the war effort. In addition to the above, my mother was also an air-raid warden. Our whole family has always been extremely patriotic. I began developing my deep love-of-country during those patriotic war years."

– "Pennsylvania's Sweetheart," Shirley Jones, singer/actress, formerly of Smithton, PA

~ ~ ~

"I can vividly recall where I was when I first heard the news of the attack on Pearl Harbor. I was with friends in an automobile en route back to Connellsville from Duquesne University in Pittsburgh. I remember we were all singing the "Hutsut Ralson" song along with the car radio, when, all of a sudden, the commentator broke in with the news about Pearl Harbor. I remember he said that it was located at Honolulu, Hawaii, or we would not have known where Pearl Harbor was.

"I was only eighteen at that time, and though my friends and I realized that the state of affairs was serious, we did not realize the full significance of the situation until much later. For instance, we never thought that the war would last as long as it did, and we had no idea- *no idea at all-* of the horrors it would bring to so many."

– Gloria Rock, Connellsville, PA

~ ~ ~

"It was the Sunday of the Pearl Harbor attack when I heard the news. My brother had graduated not long before from California State Teachers' College, and my sister and I had driven my parents to Washington [Pennsylvania] to see the school where my brother had obtained a teaching position, his classroom, and the house he had rented in the town.

"Upon our arrival at the high school, my brother greeted us; and we had just started to enter the door of the industrial arts department, where my brother's classroom was located, when one of his students came running across the lawn toward the IA building like there was some sort of trouble, an accident somewhere or something. I can still see him running across the winter-grass, shouting and waving his arms. At the door, he blurted the news about Pearl Harbor. After a shocked silence, we all began asking questions very nearly at once: 'Where did you hear this?' 'When did it happen?' 'How bad is it?'

"I felt immediately that the attack would mean *war.* I also recall that the boy did not know anything more, only that there had been an early-morning surprise attack on our base at Honolulu by the Japanese. I can still image him, very antsy and anxious to deliver the dire message to others. The news took the wind out of our sails, and we cut short our tour of the school in order to get to the nearest radio set, which was at my brother's residence nearby.

"There, huddled around the radio, we gleaned what information we could. The news was scant, and we did not get a detailed report until much later. Remember, there were no televisions in those days, no CNN, or any round-the-clock news channels, and even newspapers did not have the *full* story until a day or so later."

- Florence Shutsy-Reynolds, Connellsville, PA

Author: I want to interject here that Florence Shutsy was the first woman from my hometown of Connellsville to earn a pilot's license. She would go on to earn a place in history herself as one of the WASP (Women Airforce Service Pilots), a select group of young women who, during World War II, became pilots, pioneers, heroes, and role models for women across America. WASP were the first women in history to fly American military aircraft. I wrote about the brave-hearted Florence Shutsy-Reynolds and her sister WASP in "Wings of Athena," *County Chronicles Volume II*, and I am proud to state that since, we have formed a wonderful friendship. Shutsy-Reynolds is one of Pennsylvania's finest!

"Wings of Athena," Florence Shutsy-Reynolds, the picture of WASP pride, courage and confidence!
Photo courtesy Florence Shutsy-Reynolds, Connellsville, PA

When Pearl Harbor was attacked, Florence was already a licensed pilot. She had scored in the top five percent for flight school, which earned her a flight scholarship; but she was not old enough to enter the WASP program. Following the Japanese attack, the age requirement was lowered; and the determined young woman began her WASP career December 7, 1943, on the anniversary of Pearl Harbor.

"I had signed a document stating that I would join the service and use my flight skills in case of war. And I have to state here for the record that there were those, at that point in time, who thought women-in-the-service was a big joke. Despite the derision, we proved that women were physically and psychologically capable of flying any aircraft Uncle Sam had to offer, and we opened the door for women in combat.

"Once they lowered the age requirement, I had the entire requisite- pilot's license, my education, and flight training. I met the height and weight requirements, and I had passed the physical. There was also an intense interview, which some of the girls did not pass, and an additional army physical to get through. I passed the lot and was on my way!

"I had a strong will and a desire to serve, but keep in mind that the WASP was strictly an *experiment*, mostly to free men up for combat. However, my sister WASP and I *knew* in our heart-of-hearts that the WASP carried more than personnel and matériel- *we carried the future.*

"To focus for a moment on a personal war memory: I fondly remember FDR's fireside chats. These regular radio broadcasts kept America's morale up and running, and they helped keep the country together. When it was time for one of the President's chats, the nation, collectively, stopped what we were doing and gathered attentively around the radio to hear what the President had to say.

"Before Pearl Harbor, the country was divided on whether we should get involved in another of Europe's mêlées. World War I, the 'war to end all wars,' was not really so distant in the past. I remember that Roosevelt had a heck of a time getting his Lend-Lease Act passed, though he had been a bit of an isolationist himself before Hitler's Blitzkrieg rolled over Poland. When the Japanese attacked Pearl, anger and vengeance overrode the objections of the isolationists.

"Getting back to your original query, my personal reaction to Pearl Harbor was *outrage.* I knew I was going to get into some military outfit. I had originally wanted to join the Marines, but I was destined to become a WASP, and I have always been proud to carry this distinction."

- Florence Shutsy-Reynolds, Connellsville, PA

~ ~ ~

"The night of the Japanese attack on Pearl Harbor, I was downtown Connellsville at the Eagles, playing in Amedeo Molinaro's band. I had already heard the news over the radio at home; so that evening at the dance, I announced the news at the microphone for the benefit of those who had no idea that we had been attacked. After the pronouncement, we played patriotic tunes for the remainder of the evening. I want to add that right after I made the announcement, you could almost have heard a pin drop. I think everyone, or nearly everyone, was in shock. 'Nobody would attack the United States of America!'

"Of course, most of us knew it would mean war, but I don't think anyone realized, at that point in time, the total concept of war, especially a long, bloody war, such as it was. No, that had not penetrated our minds.

"In those days, the men had to register for the Draft at the Selective Service Office. In my hometown, it was located on the second floor of the post office. My number was in the 900s; and I figured that Uncle Sam wouldn't be calling me for another eight or nine months, at least. I was called up within three months. All in all, I spent thirty-eight months overseas. I was sent first to Scotland, to the area where Rudolf Hess had landed several months before. Of course, *that* was the talk of the region. The event was outlandish and... *unexplained.* It still is, in fact."

-William DeMiere, Connellsville, PA

Author: In May, 1941, Deputy Fuehrer Rudolf Hess, closest to Hitler in the Third Reich inner circle, boarded an unarmed *Messerschmitt Bf 110* and took off solo from Augsburg, Germany. His destination was Scotland. After avoiding the flack of anti-aircraft fire and a British Spitfire, Hess parachuted out of his plane over Scotland, at Floors Farm just south of Glasgow, where he was immediately collared by a Scottish farmer armed with a pitchfork. The incident remains one of the most mysterious of World War II.

Hess told British authorities that he was seeking a meeting with the Duke of Hamilton and Brandon to negotiate a peace between Germany and England. There was, most certainly, more to his story than that.

For decades, there has been talk that the Duke of Kent, the fourth son of King George V, was also entangled in the strange happening. Some believe, however, that Kent had been working with British Intelligence in a plot to fool the Nazis into believing that the Duke was plotting with others to overthrow Winston Churchill.

If Hess had been attempting to rendezvous with one or more of the British royals with whom he was involved in a conspiracy, the world will likely never know; for authorities in Britain have kept it a well-cached-away secret over the long years.

The British locked Hess straightaway in the Tower of London, as a POW, the *last* person to be held prisoner there. After the war, Hess stood trial at Nuremberg, where he received a life sentence. Rudolf Hess died in 1987, the *last* remaining prisoner at Spandau Prison in West Berlin. He was ninety-two.

There have been those who thought that sentence rather harsh. Was it? My personal opinion is that it was *not*.

Yet today, Hess' mysterious flight sparks theories ranging from his *alleged* mental illness to British royal conspiracies.

William DeMiere continues: "I was in what I call a 'bastard outfit.' What I mean is that, essentially, we were the 'navy for the army,' an idea that had originated with FDR's cousin, Brigadier General Theodore Roosevelt. Actually, there were two of these special army outfits, the 591st and the 592nd. The 591st Boat Regiment, of which I was a part, was sent to the European theater of war, and the 592nd was sent to the Pacific theater.

"As I said earlier, I was first sent to Scotland. Our uniforms were somehow lost in transit, and as odd as it may seem, we were issued English army uniforms until supplies came through. I must say the Scots were the most hospitable people I ever encountered in the war. And I'll say this for the English- come four o'clock in the afternoon, they had to have their tea, war or no war, the military included. Rainbows are another... well, *vivid* memory I have of Scotland. It would drizzle, and the sun would come out, and there would be a rainbow. It was nothing to see ten or twelve rainbows a day. At the time, I kept hoping they were a good omen. I saw more rainbows the eight months I was in Scotland than I did the sixty years since I came home.

"It wasn't all rainbows, however. I had heavy guard duty in Scotland. The Germans knew that we had a floating drydock. In fact, there were only *three* in the entire world of the huge size we had there. This floating dock was large enough to accommodate battleships, cruisers, and aircraft carriers, actually any size craft the Navy had. The Germans knew it was there all right, and they tried their best to destroy it, mostly with night raids. I have to say that nights in Scotland during the war were the blackest I ever experienced in my life. We were so close to the ocean, so there was a lot of cloud cover; and, in addition, blackouts were a must, so the darkness was *absolute*. Nights there were pretty darn scary, what with the total darkness, the constant air raids with their screaming sirens, the roar of the German bombers, and the loud explosions of their dropped loads.

"From Scotland, I was sent to Liverpool, England, and from there to North Africa. Uncle Sam was preparing for an invasion of Sicily and Italy, and there were quite a few American ships headed for Africa, which was the staging point for that invasion.

"We were at sea over a month, because we had to zigzag our way there to avoid German submarines. For some reason, I never got seasick, but a helluva lot of the fellas did. I remember that we played cards a good bit of the time, and I learned how to play an English card game called 'cribbage.'

"As it turned out, we didn't have to exchange shells with any German subs; though we did encounter some pretty severe sea storms, one of which nearly capsized our ship. I truly believed we were goners that night, and I remember uttering what I thought was my final prayer before meeting my Maker.

"When we finally docked in Africa, my main duty was to help unload the ship. While I was on the 'Dark Continent,' I kept a diary... so I wouldn't forget. Along with the others in my outfit, I unloaded some two hundred ships.

"It wasn't too long before we were moved from Oran to nearby Mers-el-Kébir, a former French port that is now Algeria. I should mention that back in early July of 1941, the British navy had sunk or put out of action a number of units of the Vichy French fleet at Oran and Mers-el-Kébir, in order to prevent their falling into German hands."

- William DeMiere

Author: FDR's dynamic cousin, Brigadier General Theodore Roosevelt II, was the most successful son of President Teddy Roosevelt. In France, on 6 June 1944 (D-day), he earned a Congressional Medal of Honor for gallantry and intrepidity at the risk of his life, above and beyond the call of duty. The general rallied the troops storming the Normandy beaches during the invasion- shades of his famous father leading the "Rough Riders" up San Juan Hill!

Vichy was the puppet French government that collaborated with the Nazis after France capitulated in the spring of 1940. The Vichy government (named for its location in central France), to the chagrin of most of the French people, was headed by WWI hero Henri Pétain, who was, after France was liberated in 1944, tried for treason and sentenced to death, though his sentence was later commuted to life in prison. Shamefully, one of the provisions of Pétain's agreement with the Nazis was the surrender of all Jews living in France.

As for Scotland, both DeMiere and my father told me that nights there during the war were the blackest they ever experienced in their lives. Both men related to me that they drank the richest milk they ever tasted there, "... thick with cream, it was," Dad remarked to me years ago.

And here, I cannot help but share with you a little WWII story my father often told. Dad liked to play darts, a game found in nearly every pub throughout the British Isles. One evening, he happened to beat a Scot at darts, several games in a row. "Bloody hell!" exclaimed the brawny Scotsman, disappearing in a rush through the door. In a short while, he reappeared, his naturally ruddy face even redder, and my father eased his back against the wall, preparing for a fisticuffs. Instead, what he got was a solid gold medal with the words "Marston's Dart League 1935-36 Champion, W. Stapleton" engraved on the back. "You take it, Yank," the towering Scot insisted to my father, giving him a friendly "slosh" on the shoulder, which nearly knocked Dad off his feet. "Y' prr-oved yerself a better player than meself, laddie."

"It was at Mers-el-Kébir where my battalion did most of our unloading of troops and supplies, ordnance mostly," Bill DeMiere informed, again taking up his story. "As I said earlier, this was the staging area for the invasion of Sicily and Italy. My unit was supposed to be sent to Anzio, but Fate intervened in the guise of all things- *seasickness.* The sea was so rough that nearly our entire crew got seasick- and I do mean *sick.* By the time we put in at Naples, everyone was so badly afflicted that we ended up replacing the outfit in charge of Naples Harbor; and those poor fellas were shipped to Anzio, which, as you know, was no picnic on the beach!

"I always say that God did not have a hand on my shoulder. He had His hands on *both* my shoulders! Though we were spared the hell of Anzio, my outfit ended up with seven Battle Stars and a Presidential Commendation for the job we did for Uncle Sam. We were, in essence, the main suppliers of ammunition for the Army at the crucial hour of many important raids and invasions, when our guys really needed that ordnance."

- William DeMiere, Connellsville, PA

~ ~ ~

"My brother was one of the first to be called up from Connellsville. His draft number came up, and he was immediately on his way to war. I remember how sad and how worried we all were.... I recall vividly, too, the rationing. It seemed like *everything* was rationed- sugar, meat, gasoline, even shoes. Sometimes that was not easy to deal with; however, I want to state for the record that we *never* complained. I remember well that we all did without, and we rationed what we had to willingly. Our country was at war, and each and every one of us complied. It was all part of the war effort; and the country pulled together and did what had to be done, as I said- *willingly.*"

- Carmel Caller, Connellsville, PA

~ ~ ~

"Men had to register for the Draft at eighteen years of age, at which time they were each assigned a number and called up accordingly. It was sort of like a lottery. I was the clerk at the Selective Service Office in my hometown. I remember getting up before daybreak many times to dress and hurry down to the B&O [Baltimore and Ohio Railroad] Station to get the boys on the train to Pittsburgh. The train left around 5:00 a.m., and it always seemed like the middle of the night, especially in winter.

"I want to stress that the patriotic spirit of my hometown was exceptionally strong during World War II. After Pearl Harbor, so many of our men came into the draft office and volunteered to go ahead of the time of their normal sequence... *so many.* It was precisely as that Japanese admiral had remarked after their attack on Pearl- that 'Imperial Japan had only succeeded in awakening a sleeping giant'!

"Since I was the clerk, my duty was concerned mostly with the tons of paperwork that government jobs seem to require. At the railroad station with the draftees, after making certain that each had reported for duty,

I then appointed a group leader to carry the paperwork with them to Pittsburgh, where they would get their physicals. In the fog-shrouded chill of those predawn musterings, I always held my breath that each draftee would show up. I am proud to relate that was *not* a problem.

"I didn't linger at the railroad station after my paperwork duties were complete with each group of men being deployed. Once my job was done, I went home. In that way, I did not interfere with the goodbyes between the departing young men and their loved ones. That was heart-wrenching to witness, let me tell you. I didn't like to gape at those saying what might be their final farewells.

"Without regard to the hour or the weather, Connellsville's Italian band, the Molinaro Band, unfailingly showed up at the station to honor our troops. That always brought tears to my eyes.

"The dedicated ladies of the Connellsville Canteen were there too, any hour of the day or night. They never missed a train during the period of the Canteen's operation.

"Mine was a difficult job– frustrating sometimes, heart-wrenching nearly all the time. But *someone* had to do it. In fact, before it was over I drafted myself and joined the WACs! Uncle Sam needed all the help he could get to fight the Axis forces lined up against us."

– Adeline George, Connellsville, PA

Author: The folks in my hometown of Connellsville will never forget patriotic heroine Rose Bailey Brady, a former schoolteacher, who initiated and orchestrated the Connellsville Canteen during World War II. Rose's daughter Ann Riley told me when I interviewed her for the premier volume of *County Chronicles* that her mother, who was already active in hospital volunteer work, came up with the canteen idea while engaged in conversation with her brother, a priest. Rose and her brother, Reverend Francis Bailey, thought how helpful it would be to servicemen and women coming through the busy railroad town of Connellsville, if they had a place where they might find, as one reporter stated, "warm smiles and hot coffee."

Rose galvanized into action, obtaining the cooperation of the proper authorities, then recruiting volunteers and organizing them into shifts. The tireless woman contacted all the local merchants. Rose found them to be most cooperative; each of them *enthusiastically* supported the Canteen.

Connellsville became swept up in a new wave of patriotism! Within a few weeks, the old Boyts-Porter Building, opposite the B&O Station, was converted into the spic-and-span Connellsville Canteen.

Cognizant of train timetables, the Canteen was *always* prepared, even in the wee hours. It operated twenty-four hours a day, seven days a week; for the troop trains rolled into Connellsville's B&O Station day and night. Serving coffee, tea, sodas, donuts, home-baked cookies, cakes, pies, thick sandwiches, soups, and fresh fruit, Rose's ladies, their aprons ever clean and crisp, labored admirably. Their reward was the countless letters and poems of thanks, appreciation and praise from "our men and women overseas" who had stopped, for a fleeting moment in time, at this "home away from home."

For many, the Connellsville Canteen was the last taste of home before being hurled into the jaws of death. I am proud to say that my

A group of the Connellsville Canteen volunteers Image of the Connellsville Canteen courtesy the Connellsville Area Historical Society. This reprinted image, as well as other vintage photo-postcards, are available for purchase from the society.

grandmother, Mary Bello; my mother, Jennie B. Hanlon, and several aunts and cousins worked at the Canteen. And they all had the highest regard for Rose Brady.

From 1944 to 1946, approximately 800 women, of all ages, met some 600,000 troops, furnishing them with, in addition to food and drink, much-needed conversation and chauffeured rides to their doorsteps for open-arm homecomings.

Among the members of the Drivers Corps was Rita Smyth Ross, who told the Connellsville *Daily Courier* in a 1994 interview, "Driving the soldiers home was enormously satisfying." Ross delivered them on angels' wings. "Most of them were on furlough, so they only had a limited amount of time to spend with their families."

Today, a familiar, blue Pennsylvania historical marker, dedicated April 23, 1994, designates the spot on Water Street, where the Connellsville Canteen provided a welcoming oasis to those en route to and from war.

The guest speaker that dedication day- fifty years after the Canteen had begun- was Florence Shutsy-Reynolds, the former WASP whom I have cited in all three volumes of my *County Chronicles.* Florence compared the Connellsville Canteen with its famed Hollywood counterpart. She recalled how female soldiers were shuttled aside at the celebrated "Stage Door."

"I never liked being discriminated against," Shutsy-Reynolds told me.

When a duty assignment brought her East, she took advantage of the opportunity to visit her family in her hometown of Connellsville. "After the conductor announced the stop, he added, 'The ladies of Connellsville invite all military personnel to be their guests at the Connellsville Canteen for free refreshments.' Word carried through the train quickly; reactions were loud and joyful. I felt a warm glow of pride in my hometown! As I gathered my gear to disembark, I glanced out a window and was *amazed.* I had expected a couple of volunteers with a pot of coffee. What I saw, however, was a large number of volunteers- ladies who presented a snappy, disciplined appearance and more than enough food to feed the entire train. I didn't know what to expect (after the Hollywood experience). I needn't have concerned myself, the Connellsville ladies could not have been more gracious. I was young, tired and hungry. They not only gave me food and coffee; *but for the first time since putting on my uniform, I was being treated on an equal basis with all other military personnel.* No discrimination here! The Connellsville Canteen was ahead of its time!

"Travel was difficult during wartime," Shutsy-Reynolds continued, "and food was scarce and very expensive, so a canteen that offered genuine hospitality and good, home-made- free- food was a bright spot on many a long journey for GI's. Everyone in Connellsville supported the Canteen. Merchants gave foodstuffs and equipment; farmers dropped off fresh produce daily; women prepared and brought fare from their own kitchens- all this in a time of shortages and strict rationing. It is amazing how the Canteen operated in the face of such obstacles!"

Author: My Pennsylvania home, as the rest of America, had to cope with the tragedies that only war can bring; and yet, my hometown found it in their hearts, as Shutsy-Reynolds so stirringly expressed, "... to offer comfort to other mothers' sons and daughters, as they paused in our town on a trip to uncertainty. During that brief passage of time, Connellsville strengthened their resolve and renewed their faith in the American way of life."

The Connellsville Canteen, which became known far and wide, was, in my opinion, the finest chapter in my hometown's rich history.

An "Air Force brat," I grew up on wartime stories; and to this day, when I hear from my Connellsville home, those nocturnal- somehow nostalgic- train whistles from the not-too-distant railroad station, I image those laudable ladies hustling to make ready for yet another troop train.

Rose Brady passed away in 1992 at the venerable age of ninety-five. Ah, Rose, how right you were: "Even a war cloud can have a silver lining!"

~ ~ ~

"I worked at the Connellsville Canteen. Our canteen became known nationwide for its generosity and hospitality. I did not put in the long hours that many of the ladies did, but I did pitch in when I was off work. My sister, Jennie Hanlon, and my mother, Mary Bello, also worked there. I remember that a strong sentiment, a determination to each do our part in the war effort, prevailed all during the war years... even when the war dragged on.

"I was quite young, only seventeen, when Pearl Harbor was attacked; but if you want to know my reaction, it was one of shock. 'How could anyone *dare* to do this to the United States of America and get away with it!'

"Like a lot of people, my initial thoughts were that we would get into the war and end it in no time flat. Never did we think the war would last as long as it did. Since I was so young, a teenager, with no brothers, father, husband or sweetheart away at the front, I and many of my friends, at first, were caught up in the excitement of the era. The whole country pulling together spurred by the high patriotic sentiment of the times was electrifying; but it did not take us long before we began to realize that war translated 'death and destruction,' along with so many other terrible things.

"I loved the songs of the war era. There were so many really good ones, classic songs now: 'Sentimental Journey,' 'I'll Never Smile Again,' 'Ac-cent-tchu-ate the Positive,' 'The Three Little Fishies,' 'Mairsy Doats,' 'Boogie Woogie Bugle Boy,' 'Don't Sit Under the Apple Tree with Anyone Else But Me,' 'In the Mood,' 'Moonlight Serenade,' 'Pennsylvania 6-5000,' 'The White Cliffs of Dover,' and 'I'll Be Seeing You,' to name a few. *That was music...* not like the noise pollution that exists today! And there were several patriotic tunes too: 'Over There' was revived from World War I, and there was a song to commemorate all the women working in factories to free the men for combat– 'Rosie the Riveter.' And, of course, 'Praise the Lord and Pass the Ammunition!' "

– Frances Bello Ondrus, Parma, Ohio,
formerly of Connellsville, PA

Author: "Praise the Lord and Pass the Ammunition," according to the Smithsonian web site, was inspired by the Japanese attack on Pearl Harbor. During the cacophony of battle, the low-flying Japanese planes attacking a Navy ship prompted the Navy chaplain aboard the vessel (who had been attempting to say a prayer of protection and who later wished to remain anonymous) to shout those words from his needed position in the ammunition line. The Navy chaplain's bellowed phrase became the emotive title of Frank Loesser's popular song written the following year.

Three other popular tunes of the era were "Take the A-Train," "I Left My Heart at the Stage Door Canteen," and Glenn Miller's "String of Pearls," which he wrote, consistent with popular belief, after he presented his wife with a string of pearls for a special-occasion gift.

Glenn Miller disappeared over the English Channel on a cold day in December 1944. The beloved bandleader was en route from England to Paris where he was scheduled to do a Christmas concert for the allied troops. His body was never found.

An American patriot *extraordinaire*, Major Miller had already entertained more than a million troops in England. At the beginning of the war, Miller, too old to be drafted, had convinced the army to take him so he "... could put a little more spring into the feet of our marching men and a little more joy in their hearts." Pennsylvania-born Jimmy Stewart portrayed Miller to perfection in the 1953 award-winning film, "The Glenn Miller Story."

It was only recently that the Glenn Miller mystery was "solved" when a navigator's logbook from a Lancaster bomber was discovered among several WWII items at auction. I might add that this "Lancaster" theory about Miller's vanishing had surfaced back in the 1980s, and though this is the most popular and certainly most logical explanation as to what happened, there can be no real proof, since no evidence was ever recovered of the plane or Miller's body.

On the day of Miller's disappearance, 15 December 1944, a squadron of Lancaster bombers had aborted their raid over Germany, due to heavy fog and the fact that their fighter escorts never got off the ground to accompany them. Returning home to England, the big four-engined RAF bombers could not safely land with their bombs still aboard; thus, they flew over the Channel's bomb-jettison zone in order to drop their staggering loads.

In that same time and space, Miller was being piloted across the Channel in a Noorduyn "Norseman" C-64, a small, single-engine bush plane, rare for that area of the world. The heavy fog could well have put Miller, the pilot/Flight Officer John Morgan, and Lt. Col. Norman F. Baessell, the third American officer on board, off-course into the very dangerous no-fly zone that was avoided by all planes and ships. I have read that the pilot was not an expert on instruments, and compasses were rather unreliable, in addition to which the Noorduyn had no de-icing capability.

The British airman's log stated: "I saw the small plane flick over to port in an incipient spin and... disappear into the Channel." The log revealed the lost aircraft to be a "Norseman" clearly recognized by this flier who had trained in Canada where those planes were prevalent. The bombardier and the rear gunner also saw the Norseman below them, as the bombs were dropping from their Lancaster. Seeing the Noorduyn in trouble, the gunner had called over the plane's intercom: "There's a 'kite' just gone in, down under!" A "kite" is British airman vernacular for "small plane."

The "Norseman" may have gone into a spin and into the drink due to the powerful jets of water from the dropped bombs. Or its spin and subsequent crash into the Channel may have had nothing whatsoever to do with the falling bombs. The Noorduyn could well have been in trouble on its own. We will never know.

Since there was no debriefing after the aborted mission, the incident was virtually lost in the maelstrom of bombing activity that the Lancaster squadron was involved in as WWII was winding down. Miller's band showed up two days later at Orly Field in Paris, expecting Major Miller to meet them; but, of course, he did not. No one had reported his plane missing! After speaking at length with an historian at the United States Air force Historical Research Agency, I feel one explanation for that might be because there had been no flight plan. Basically, Major Miller had hitched a ride to Paris (to take care of preliminary matters for the scheduled concert) with two American officers whom he had met the evening before.

Miller had had an eerie premonition before boarding the aircraft that foggy December day, and voiced his doubts about the little plane to the pilot, asking, "Where th' hell are the parachutes!" Laughing it off, the American officer quipped with an old military utterance oft delivered before an engagement, "Do you want to live forever? Lindbergh flew in a single-engine plane across the Atlantic. We're only going across the Channel!" This exchange was overheard by Miller's friend and band manager, Lt. Haynes, who stood watching the Norseman speed down the runway then lift off into the fog- *and disappear.*

~ ~ ~

"I was only thirteen when the war broke out, but I can sure verify that Molinaro Band played anytime of day or night when Connellsville's troops departed for war. Some winter mornings it was so cold that the horns froze up. My brother Carmen came up with the solution of putting a bit of antifreeze in the valves of the horns so that our musicians could play. We have a family 'Tale of the Antifreeze,' which in brief goes like this: The Connellsville High School Band volunteered to throw in with us; but the first frigid morning they showed up at the railroad station, they played two notes, and their horns froze up, while we played on. We happily shared with them our antifreeze trick; and after that, when the high school band joined us, their horns blew with no problem, even during the coldest sendoffs.

"As the war wore on, our ranks were constantly thinning, so it was good that the school band helped swell our numbers. One by one, our members were either drafted or enlisted to serve voluntarily, and that left few in our family to play. Then, the band consisted of those family members either too old or too young to go to war, along with, as I said, a mixture of volunteer musicians, such as the fore-mentioned high school band members. I recall a time or two when we had a single trumpet and a drum, but we still showed up to play. Those times, we were very much akin to the 'Spirit of Seventy-six'- a single fifer and a drummer playing, in spite of it all, with fervor.

"We had a devoted group in the band, I will say that. *Devoted.* Keep in mind that these musicians had regular jobs. Nevertheless, they pulled themselves out of their warm beds, in the wee hours, to hurry down to the railroad station- in their haste sometimes in pajamas under overcoats- to play for an hour or so in the rain or snow. Then they'd return home and get ready to go to work at either West Penn or Anchor Hocking for the early shift. It was sacrifice, but it wasn't, if you know what I mean. It was for 'our boys,' as we used to say.

"My brother Amedeo was thirty-two and exempt. Nonetheless, he enlisted and served with distinction. Many who went didn't have to go, but that is an example of the kind of patriotism Connellsville, Fayette County... *Pennsylvania* has consistently displayed. It is part of *who we are*, as you say in your *County Chronicles* history series.

"I know you have been asking many of the people you have interviewed for this segment about Pearl Harbor. My memory of the *end* of the war is ever so much more vivid. It was an August day in 1945, when my brother Carmen, who had taken over the band when Amedeo enlisted, burst into the house, yelling for us to get our instruments and follow him down to Brimstone Corner. 'Brimstone?' I questioned. 'Why not the station?' 'It's over!' he shouted. 'What's over?' I asked, looking up from my comic book, puzzled. 'The war's over! The Japanese have surrendered!'

"Germany had already surrendered, and this was the most wonderful news I had ever heard. Everyone would be coming home! We grabbed our instruments and all sprinted down to Brimstone Corner where we set up and played- and played and played. I am not exaggerating when I tell you that we played so hard and so long that my ears rang for a week. It's really true.

"Ole Connellsville was brimming with people, shouting, cheering, singing, laughing, hugging, kissing, and even kneeling down, right there in the street, for a brief prayer of thanksgiving. Many folks were rushing to their churches; and if they didn't have a church, to *any* church to kneel and say prayers of thanks.

"All the church bells were ringing; the whistles on the trains down at the B&O were screaming with the news; car horns were blowing, and people were throwing confetti out of the upper windows of the town buildings. I can recall it all, and it was wonderful, a treasured memory, bright and vivid as the day it happened. *It was over.* Our brave men and women would be coming home- and Molinaro Band was there to welcome them."

- Henry Molinaro, Director of the Molinaro Band, Connellsville, PA

Author: Always a military-type band, Molinaro's soul-stirring music gave those departing young men and women an extra measure of courage to take with them from their hometown. Reaching out with heart-swelling notes to cloak with appreciation- almost like a protective shield- in a *rousing* sendoff, Molinaro Band was *there* each time troops boarded trains and streetcars bound for war.

This was also true when troops returned home from the front. The Molinaro Band was there to greet them, sending out on melodic swells, along with the waving flags, shouts of joy and embraces from loved ones, the thing that only good music can convey, a soaring white-light of emotion that reaches down and deep into those intimate chambers of the human heart.

I can honestly state that there was not an equal in the nation to the Connellsville Canteen during the WWII era. Service men and women across America heard about the Canteen. Via word of mouth, it became synonymous with *patriotism* and *home*. And, there at the B&O Railroad Station, the Molinaro Band literally set the tone for that soaring patriotism that existed then- and yet exists- in my Pennsylvania hometown.

~ ~ ~

"I was drafted into the US Navy in March of 1943. I fulfilled boot camp at Great Lakes, Illinois, followed by further training at St. Louis. There, for a brief but memorable moment in time, I was a guard for movie star Judy Garland. As it happened, I was among approximately fifty sailors who were appointed to act as crowd-control when the popular actress was appearing at a Saint Louis hotel. My memory tells me she was conducting a major bond-rally there for Uncle Sam. This was something many of the big-name stars did for the war effort. From Saint Louis, I was stationed at St. Pedro and Long Beach, California, respectively, where I acquired mine-sweeping training, and that led to my tour on the *USS Compel,* a mine sweeper.

Harry L. Porter, Electrician's Mate, 2nd Class Petty Officer

"Later I did a tour of duty on an oil and fuel tanker. Tanker duty was never pleasant. High-octane aviation fuel meant that you didn't need to concern yourself with your swimming abilities, because if a tanker took a hit, *it was all over.* There were usually no survivors. We would go out to sea for the purpose of pumping gas into aircraft carriers. We also put diesel fuel into countless submarines.

"At one point, we put in at Pearl Harbor for repairs. After three weeks in dry dock, we departed with a fourteen-ship convoy. It took us twenty-three days, zigzagging to avoid enemy subs, to reach our destination of the Marshall Islands, over two thousand nautical miles southwest of Honolulu, in the

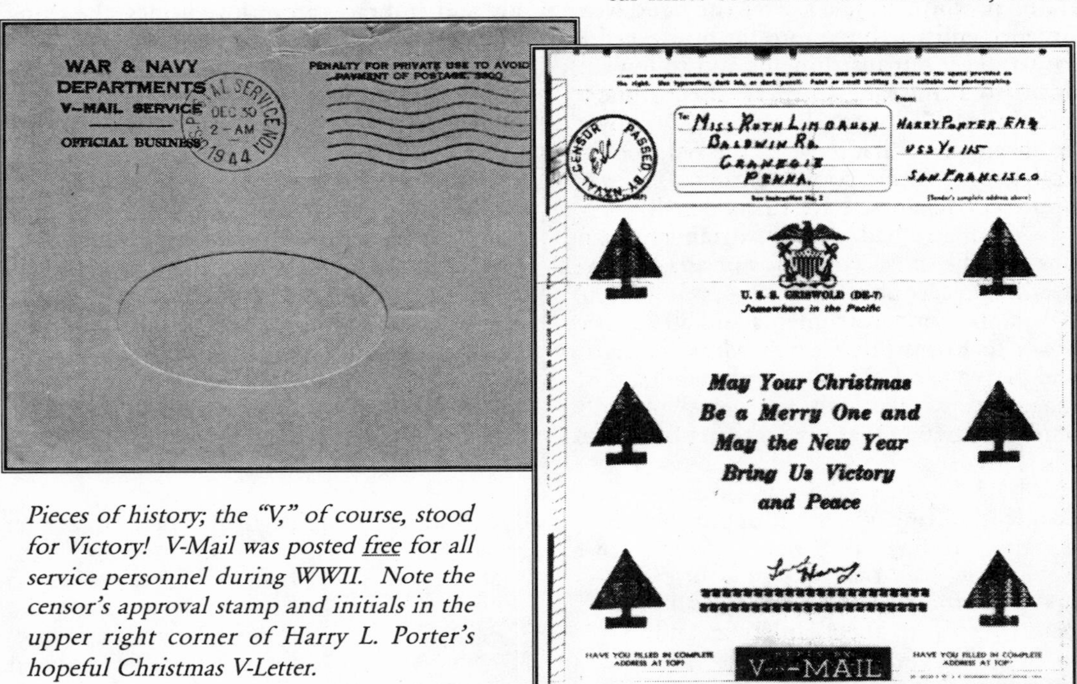

Pieces of history; the "V," of course, stood for Victory! V-Mail was posted <u>*free*</u> *for all service personnel during WWII. Note the censor's approval stamp and initials in the upper right corner of Harry L. Porter's hopeful Christmas V-Letter.*

V-Mail, photo, and vintage postcard courtesy Harry L. Porter, Connellsville, PA

West Pacific. I remained at Kwajalein, the world's largest atoll, located in the Marshalls, for over two years, where I continued fueling ships day and night. For weeks at a time we fueled amphibious landing crafts- virtually nonstop. The Marshall Islands, by the way, were the first ones liberated after Pearl Harbor had been bombed back in '41. The United States captured Kwajalein in February of 1944 and used it as a naval supply base for the remainder of the war. Later, it was on Bikini in the Marshall Islands where the United States tested the first hydrogen bomb.

"A colorful mention of my time in St. Pedro [California] is the fact that our base, a small-craft training center, was commanded by the famed actor Robert Montgomery. I have to state for the record that Montgomery was a tough, no-nonsense CO. Some might think that an actor, such as he was, would be lenient and easygoing, but that was not the case. He was a strict disciplinarian, a remarkable CO- *military to the core.* Another interesting fact is that, due to strict gas rationing, service men and women were provided, by the municipality of Hollywood, the free use of bicycles to get around and see the various sights. I took advantage of this, which afforded me the opportunity to see several movie stars, including Edgar G. Robinson, who was known for his gangster roles; Betty Grable, who was the most famous pinup girl of the era; George Raft; Dick Powell, and Humphrey Bogart.

"V-Mail is another thing I would like to mention. The 'V,' of course, stood for Victory! Letters were handwritten, then photographed on V-Letters. The paper was similar to Kodak paper, and the text was impossible to alter. While serving in the Navy during the war, I often wrote to my cousin in Carnegie, Pennsylvania, which is just outside of Pittsburgh. Recently, when she passed away, I discovered that she had saved all my letters, and as it turned out, I am glad she did, because V-Mail is an important piece of World War II history. All mail from overseas was censored, and you will note on each piece of V-mail the approval stamp and initials of the government censurer who read it. V-Mail was free to all service personnel. However, any non-military person who attempted to use the familiar brown V-Mail envelopes to avoid paying postage was penalized."

- Harry Porter, Connellsville, PA

~ ~ ~

"*Do* I remember where I was when Pearl Harbor was attacked? Who could ever forget! I was a high-school senior in December of 1941, and I vividly recall that I was on my way to the movies when first I heard the news about Pearl Harbor. My friends and I had stopped at Woody Wrote's newsstand for some gum or candy. The radio was on in the store, and over the waves came the news that the Japanese had attacked Pearl Harbor, our naval base in Honolulu, Hawaii. I remember it was about 12:30 in the afternoon that infamous Sunday. I recall too that it was only about twenty minutes later when the *Courier* had an Extra out on the streets, with the newsboy shouting the news for all to hear.

John "Wally" Schroyer, a Pennsylvania- American- hero
Photo courtesy John "Wally" Schroyer, Connellsville, PA

"My first reaction was shock, as was most people's. My friends and I went to the movies, wondering where it would all lead.

"In January 1942, during my senior year at Connellsville High School, Johnny Lujack and I were invited to attend the Rose Bowl. That was the one-and-only time the Rose Bowl was played on the East coast. The Japanese had been dropping bombs from balloons along the West coast, and that was the reason in 1942 the parade and the game were hosted at Durham, North Carolina. Many of your readers might not know that.

"I was home from the service and back at Penn State when the Japanese surrendered at the end of the summer in 1945. My initial thought was *relief.* I was extremely thankful the United States did not have to invade Japan. That would have meant a loss of many more American lives. The Japanese were so well fortified."

- John "Wally" Schroyer, Connellsville, PA

Author: I included Mr. Schroyer in "The Right Stuff" of the premier volume of my *County Chronicles* Pennsylvania history series. After playing football brilliantly during his high school years, John "Wally" Schroyer played *outstanding* varsity football as a freshman at Penn State before he entered the service. It was wartime, and that "terrific camaraderie," that team spirit... that *heart* he told me had spiraled his high school team to their 1941 and 1942 championships would serve him well again– this time in something ever so much bigger.

Schroyer served in the African-Italian Campaign in the Army's 45th Infantry Division. He lost a leg to machine-gun fire in the hell that was Anzio Beachhead and was captured and held as a prisoner for thirteen months, during which time he was moved from Italy to Austria, Czechoslovakia, Poland, then finally to Germany.

"The unknown was the worst," Schroyer told me. "In spite of the nagging fear, the desire to live and get back home, along with my faith in God, kept me going. I was freed in a wounded-prisoner exchange. I weighed about 118 pounds at the time, but I had made it. I came out via Switzerland, sailed from Marseilles, and landed stateside in March 1945. I was detained in a hospital in New York for a short while, then transferred to Atlantic City, New Jersey, where several hotels had been converted into VA hospitals. I got back to my Pennsylvania hometown of Connellsville in August 1945."

Author: Anzio was hard-fought and harder-won. The operation helped tilt the balance in our favor at the end of World War II, and contributed to the drive that led to the fall of Rome. "Anzio Beachhead," wrote Naval historian Samuel Eliot Morison, "should endure in our memories as a symbol of heroic tenacity." The soldiers and sailors there prevailed against heavy odds, adding the name "Anzio" to the proud list of American battles won, to American courage and honors.

Wally Schroyer earned a Purple Heart, a POW Medal, and two Bronze Stars for Valor with Oak Leaf Clusters for his service to his country at Anzio Beachhead.

~ ~ ~

"I was a seventeen-year-old farm boy, living with my parents on their farm at Alverton, near Scottdale, when I heard the news about Pearl Harbor. I recall that we had gone to church that morning, and were just finishing up with our dinner, when my dad turned on the radio. The news came over the waves, on KDKA. We would not have known where Pearl Harbor was if the announcer had not told us it was in the Hawaiian Islands.

"I remember that everything during the war was rationed; and you had to have stamps, tokens and tickets for just about everything you needed, even to purchase a pair of shoes.

"I remember too that we collected tin foil, saved from cigarette packs; scrap iron; grease, and we took these saved items to collection centers to go for the war effort. People are spoiled today; but back then, we did this without complaining. It was all for the war, you see.

"We walked everywhere, or we bicycled. Two and three cars in a family were unheard of then. And we took the streetcars. They were cheap, clean, well-maintained, and they ran on time. You could set your watch by them.

"There was no television back then. We counted on newspapers and the radio for our news; and the radio was nearly always on in the evenings, right after supper till bedtime. I want to say, though, that newspapers in those days were more respectful of troops and troop movements than they are today."

- Tom Adams, Uniontown, PA

Author: I agree with Mr. Adams that, for the most part, the press, in the past, was more respectful of our military during wartime. However, there were incidents of newspapers reporting information that hurt our troops, much like we hear about today, as far back in time as the Revolutionary War. One incident that comes to mind happened during the Civil War. General Grant complained loudly to President Lincoln that when reporters descended on his camp, they ferreted out battle plans and troop movements, and then reported in the newspapers "... as if the rebels can't read English! They're worse than a pack of spies... spies I can shoot!" Lincoln's retort was to treat anyone who was acting like a spy as a spy.

~ ~ ~

"I was a junior in high school when World War II broke out. I attended Scottdale High School- that's what the school was called in that era. [Today, Scottdale is part of the Southmoreland School District.] On the Sunday the Japanese attacked Pearl Harbor, I recall clearly that I heard the news in the afternoon. We had come from church and had just finished our meal, when we heard it on the radio.

"That Sunday evening, when I attended youth group at our church, I discovered, as several of us were talking about the news, that the pastor's wife was not cognizant of the attack. As she absorbed the information- what little we knew- she became filled with dread and visibly upset.

"I was young, so the impact of it was not as devastating to me. I felt safe with my parents in our home, here in America, with the broad Atlantic on one side of us, the endless Pacific on the other. I had a strong faith in God, in our country and its leadership, in our troops; and I felt, at first anyway, that we'd get into the war and end it right quick. I don't think any of us thought it would last as long as it did.

"Another thing I recollect is that the following school year of 1942-43, my senior year, many of our male classmates wanted to enlist in the service of our country, and our school district wanted to make certain that these young men finished high school and got their diplomas. Therefore, my senior class doubled up on our studies, and our class graduated on April 30, 1943. We may well have been the only high school class in the nation who did that to accommodate our would-be warriors during that war."

- Elsie Kern Ghost, Connellsville,
formerly of Scottdale, PA

Author: After a bit of research, I discovered that other high schools across America held graduation ceremonies early during the war years, so that their senior young men could enter the service of their country and still get their diplomas.

Elsie Kern Ghost continues: "I remember we had to adhere to blackout regulations. Blinds, shades, curtains and drapes had to be closed tightly. There were regular drills in case of a real air raid. Thank God our mainland never came under attack!

"Meat, sugar, gasoline, just about everything was rationed. This was accomplished via stamps, tokens and tickets for the various items. We all saved grease from bacon, sausage, and other fatty meats to be processed into ammunition for the soldiers in the field. Rubber, tin foil, and metal items, all were to be turned in for the war effort; Uncle Sam had a use for each and every one of them.

"By the way, ladies' stockings in those long-past days were made of silk; and that is why they were so scarce, because silk was needed for parachutes. Just the same, we ladies had ways around that! There existed a liquid leg makeup- 'stockings in a bottle' it was called, I believe. This or regular pancake makeup was applied to the legs, and then 'seams' were penciled up the backs of the legs. We learned to improvise in those days, in more ways than one. Situations like that always prompt creativity. After all, necessity is the mother of invention!

"For us, gas rationing was not such a terrible hardship. I can count on the fingers of one hand the young folks I knew who had access to an automobile. Families who did own a car had *one* car. We walked, and we bicycled, or we rode the trolley to and from destinations. Trolleys ran about every half-hour to points all around, so we weren't really strapped.

"As for 'Victory Gardens,' I was born on a farm, so we always grew our own vegetables, tomatoes, corn, green beans, lettuce and such. But I do remember that even folks in town, as long as they had a yard, turned part of their property into a Victory Garden.

"I can recall with pride that our high school band, the Scottdale High School Band, played at the trolley and train stops in Scottdale, where our local boys embarked for war.

"I attended Franklin Commercial College for fifteen months after high school, then took the Civil Service Exam and immediately departed for Washington, DC. Thousands of young women were going there to work at the Pentagon, State Department, the White House, and other government areas. I was always glad I went; it was a great experience for me, a growing experience.

"As it turned out, I worked as a stenographer at the Pentagon. I had undergone intense clearance, and my work involved both 'Secret' and 'Top Secret' information. The kind-hearted colonel in charge of the 10th Mountain Division, to which my husband-to-be, Eugene Lloyd Ghost, was attached, often informed me of Eugene's whereabouts, though I was not permitted to discuss that or any other military information with anyone; and I can honestly state that I never did. I was thoroughly conditioned, because the information that came across my desk was all *vital* to the war.

"While in the nation's capital, I caught sight of the imperious General Patton strutting down a Washington street; another day, I saw 'Ike' when he returned from the European theater of war; and I was *there* when our President, Franklin Roosevelt, passed away. That was such a sad, ineffaceable occasion to have lived through. Roosevelt had taken us through the Great Depression, and he had been an outstanding wartime leader. He never exploited fear for political advantage. Rather, he soothed the nation's nerves by assuring us that the only thing we had to fear was Fear itself. His fireside chats had been so good for the nation at war. I shall never forget his funeral procession, the Washington streets lined with people openly weeping; it was *heartrending*.

"I lived in a nice, respectable boarding house and roomed with two other girls, both 'neighbors' from Pennsylvania, so to speak, one from Mill Run and the other from Dunbar. The only drawback was that we had no cooking privileges; thus, we had to take all our meals out. I came home to visit for a few days, and was in the process of returning to DC– in fact, I was just entering Union Station, May 8, 1945– when I heard that Germany had surrendered. Union Station was overflowing with people celebrating VE Day. Everyone was ecstatic, and perfect strangers embraced with the intense camaraderie of the hour. *It was a great day... a great day!*

"We joined in the celebration, only to discover that all the restaurants and stores had closed. There was no place to get a bite to eat. We walked into a bar that was open, hoping to order something; but we were unable to get a meal, not even a sandwich. Finally, on the morning of the tenth, two days later, we headed out for an early breakfast, our stomachs empty. However, our prayers were being answered, so our hearts were full. The war was winding down. By mid-August, the Japanese too would surrender.

"During the war years I spent in Washington, the government workers, we girls, could go to one of the nearby army bases in Virginia to dances. That was fun. We would catch a bus from DC. This bus wasn't part of the Washington transportation system; rather it was a Virginia passenger line. I remember the first time I rode that particular bus. My girl friends and I boarded and took seats in the back, as was our habit. But after we were settled in, we noticed a sign on the back of one of the rear seats. It read: 'These seats are reserved for our colored patrons.' We exchanged looks, thinking, 'We're in the wrong seats?' *We weren't in Pennsylvania; that was for certain!* I had just been initiated into the heartbeat of bigotry. Those 'colored,' as African-Americans were then called, were being drafted to fight for a nation that made them sit, in certain areas of that country, in the backs of buses. It just wasn't right. For a long time afterward, I had mixed feelings about the South. Here we were in a war, all of us together, and we were *all* pulling together. I saw, though, that we were going to have to make some vital changes to our country when the war was over– and I believe we have.

"Nevertheless, I want to stress that in those days during World War II, people did not complain. I never heard anyone complain about rationing or anything else. We did not look upon what we were doing as 'sacrifice.' Everyone *wanted* to pitch in for the war effort, to do his or her share. That was America's finest hour. And I believe the unity we experienced then was due to one of the most outstanding traits we Americans possess– *we pull together in times of crisis.* I saw it again after September Eleventh, and it made me proud, as it always has and always will, to be an American."

- Elsie Kern Ghost, Connellsville,
formerly of Scottdale, PA

Author: During the Revolutionary War, George Washington's army was an *integrated* army, the likes of which America would not see again for nearly two centuries.

During World War II, the armed forces had become the nation's largest minority employer, yet existing policy supported *segregated* units, in training and at facilities. In the autumn of 1945, racial problems were examined within the Army. In its final report, the established board adopted integration as a long-term goal and recommended that qualified Black soldiers be included in special and overhead units, and that Black officers be assigned the same tasks as White officers. Nevertheless, the Secretary of the Army took that recommendation as a "separate but equal" approach to military units, following the lead of the nation at the time. Further action was required to bring about substantive change.

By the summer of 1948, several factors came together to force a new racial policy within the armed forces, chief among them a significant number of Blacks in the military, as well as the growing strength of the Civil Rights movement. President Truman responded with Executive Order 9981. There came, as a result, an end to much of the discrimination in the armed forces. *However, segregation in the military officially ended in 1954 with the disbandment of the last all-Black unit.*

~ ~ ~

"I certainly do remember where I was and what I was doing when I heard the news about Pearl Harbor! I was at the home of a friend, *that* Sunday afternoon, helping to clear away the dinner dishes. We had no sooner turned on the radio and gone into the kitchen to do the dishes, when my friend's father called to us in an excited voice from the living room: 'Are you listening! Did you hear! They're attacking us!' We rushed into the front room, and he continued in an agitated manner, 'The Japanese are attacking our naval base in Hawaii!'

"At that, we gathered around the radio to get the details, and the announcer repeated the news of the attack. Our thoughts went immediately to our sweethearts who were in the service, stationed in Virginia. We kept listening in shocked silence, trying to absorb the bad news and make sense of it. I remember that we all voiced our thoughts about how it would affect the country- and each of our lives.

"At the end of the war, my husband was wounded in a mopping-up expedition in Germany. He was first scout, first platoon who had entered a German village to clean up any German military stragglers who might have remained in the town and surrounding area. A sniper, from his lookout position in an upper window, shot John in the leg. My husband was really lucky he wasn't killed, though he subsequently lost his leg.

"John notified me when and where he would be coming home, not long after he was wounded; it was to an army hospital on Staten Island, New York. I was living and working in Philadelphia in those days. Philly is my hometown- where John and I had met before he left for overseas- and Staten Island was not that far away. I took the train to New York; and from Manhattan, the Staten Island ferry; then I was there- at the vast army hospital.

"When I arrived, I kept asking various people where to go to get to the section where my husband said he would be. After finally locating the right area of the hospital, I will never forget the scene that stretched before me. All those amputees- *so many*! I was overwhelmed by the sheer number of young men missing an arm or a leg, some with both limbs missing. It was heart-wrenching! I've never been able to erase that sight from memory. *It is burned there forever.*

John Warmuth and Helen Warmuth (Alt) at an army hospital, Atlantic City, New Jersey, August 1945

Artist Helen Alt during the World War II era
Photos courtesy Helen Alt, Connellsville, PA

"I made up my mind then and there, however, as I looked over that sea of maimed and battered warriors, that I would not cry. I would not cry in front of John. I swallowed hard, collected myself and prepared to meet my husband, whom I had not seen for several months.

"Turning around, I saw a young man on crutches, making his slow but purposeful way toward me, his left pajama leg pinned up. 'It's John!' I exclaimed inwardly. I almost had not recognized him; he had lost so much weight. I rushed forward and embraced him. I did not cry, not then, not ever. John was alive, and we were together again. That was all that mattered.

"When the Japanese surrendered, toward the end of the summer of 1945, I was in Atlantic City, visiting my husband in the hospital, where he had been transferred. After John had been sent there to recover, I took a small apartment near the hospital and traveled back and forth to Philly every day to work, so I could keep my needed job. It was about an hour on the train, each way.

"The news of the surrender spread like wildfire across Atlantic City. The joyous pealing of church bells could be heard all over town. Sirens and horns sounded for hours on end, and baskets of confetti were thrown from the upper floors of many of the buildings, including the hotels that had been converted into military hospitals. The streets looked as though they were blanketed with big- incongruous- snowflakes under the brilliant rays of August! Everyone, even perfect strangers, hugged and kissed and patted one another on the back. *We had done it!* We had won the greatest war in history! I remember that a lot of people ran to church to say prayers of thanks that the boys would be coming home. I believe that was the scenario in every town across America."

- Helen Crosby Warmuth Alt,
Connellsville, PA, formerly of Philadelphia

Medals presented in 1945 to the extraordinary woman who became my cover artist, Helen Crosby Warmuth (Alt), for her dedicated service as a volunteer with the Anti-Aircraft Coast Artillery and the Army Air Forces-Air Raid Warning Systems. At Philadelphia, while working days at her insurance job, Helen served every night, from 6 to 10 p.m.

Author: My talented cover artist, Helen Alt, of whom I lauded in "The Right Stuff" segment of my *County Chronicles Volume II*, married serviceman John Warmuth in 1943, when she was serving as an air-raid volunteer in Philadelphia, for which she was subsequently decorated. As night-shift supervisor, her job was to oversee the tracking of all aircraft from New York to Washington, DC, and 400 miles out to sea.

"We all had to pass a test to qualify as an Army Air Force-Air Raid Warning System Volunteer," Helen informed. "Once you were cleared, then you could serve. Those of us accepted were each given an identification badge. That badge was my pass into the Planning Map Room where I worked nights."

It is easy for me to imagine Helen during the war years, for she is still, at this writing nearing ninety, very much a goal-setter.

"The most exciting incident that occurred during my four years as a volunteer," Helen shared with me, "was the night when a German submarine was detected offshore. That was early in the war. Sometimes, a German sub's purpose in coming in close was to discharge spies called 'Fifth Columnists,' who came onto the beach in a rowboat. That night, as they were putting in to shore, they were all immediately apprehended by the United States Coast Guard, who had been summoned by our volunteers."

Fifth Columnists were spies who infiltrated many aspects of American life, their job to blend in- many disguised themselves as priests and nuns- to gain as much intelligence as they could before their designated rendezvous (pickup) with another U-boat. They rendezvoused by signaling with a light, from a deserted beach, to the German submarine offshore.

"That's one of the main reasons our job was so very, very important," Helen stressed to me during our interviews. "It was an exhilarating feeling of a job-well-done the night we rounded up those German spies!"

~ ~ ~

"During the war years of 1941 to 1945, I was eight to twelve years old. I remember my mother baking cookies and pies to be donated to the Connellsville Canteen. I was never permitted even one of those goodies, for sugar and other food stuffs were all strictly rationed. *Those treats were for our soldiers!*

"In May 1942, sugar was the *first* food item to be rationed. We used molasses, and eventually honey, in place of sugar much of the time for baking cookies for the Canteen; and I recall that gingerbread cookies were popular fare then, due to the molasses they called for.

"We had a 'Victory Garden,' and we canned and preserved as much as we could. Anyone with a bit of a yard had a Victory Garden; and that was a true sign of the times.

"My dad was a Civil Defense Warden, and I remember we had dark green window shades on the windows all over our house. When we heard the loud siren issuing from down at the fire department, we knew to turn out all the lights, pull all the shades down tight, and wait till the 'all-clear' signal. Understand that these were regular air-raid drills, so that we would be prepared as to what to do, and not do, in case of a real attack, which never came; thank God. We always knew, when the fire whistle blew, the location of a fire by the number of blasts of the siren, but a drill was a totally different sound. It was a long, uninterrupted, screaming, whirling sound that meant business. My father had instructed us well, and of course, we complied completely.

"No lights were permitted to escape from any window or door. Total blackouts were especially important at seacoast towns. Lights there would silhouette any passing ship, allowing marauding enemy subs to get a bead on those shadow-ships and pick them off like shooting ducks in a barrel. Total blackness was the order of the day.

"Outside, the Civil Defense Wardens in our town, my father among them, went around and made certain that everyone was abiding by the rules. The C.D. Wardens wore metal helmets and armbands for identification.

"I seem to recall that women would sell their hair for the crosshairs in the bomb sights on bombers, though I believe spider silk was used as well... it was much thinner and stronger than hair.

"I rode my bicycle most everywhere, and I recall that I had to have my bike tires patched all during that period. Rubber and tires were hard to come by.

"We peeled tin foil from gum wrappers and from cigarette packs. We collected copper, any kind of scrap metal really, grease, and rubber for the war effort. I recall that grocery stores were collection centers, as were schools. We took rubber bands, old rubber shoes and boots and old tires to school to be sent to the war effort.

"Encouraged by our teachers, we gave a dime at school, whenever we could, to be used to purchase individual stamps that we put in a book toward war bonds. I can still mind-conjure those war-bond stamps with their image of a soldier holding a rifle. The school-purchased bonds were the special ten-dollar bonds. I recall that twenty-five dollar bonds could be purchased in that era for a tad over eighteen dollars. Everyone was encouraged to buy war bonds; and several popular film stars toured the country, promoting them.

"Tin cans were washed and cleaned out well. Then we pushed the two lids inside, put the can on the floor, stood on it and flattened it. We finished by smashing it down as flat as we could make it, and that is how tin cans were delivered to the collection centers. In Connellsville, you could take items down to Abe Daniels' junk yard. He was the Daniels who became a future mayor of that city.

"We never thought of those things as sacrifice, not even the rationing. We never felt we were denying ourselves. Everyone, from children to adults, wanted to support our troops and be a part of the war effort.

"Collection centers had assigned days of the week for the various items. For instance, Monday was for copper, Tuesday for rubber. Mind, I can't recall what day was for what item, but I do remember that there were assigned days for certain items.

"I nearly forgot about the milkweed pods! We collected them too. They were used as fill in life jackets.

"And let's not forget the stars in home-front windows. During the war years, a blue star meant that household had someone in the armed forces. A gold star was symbolic of a fallen hero.

"Women knitted like mad during the war for the soldiers overseas. I remember the yarn was the military khaki color, olive drab, for those woolen knitted caps worn under helmets and for mittens and gloves. Ace bandages too were fashioned from white wool or white colored thread.

"It is important to state here that during the Great Depression and the war years that followed, *no one ever wasted anything.* Everything was saved and used. I remember that we never even threw away string from the butcher's. It was rolled on a ball and stored on a pantry shelf for its many uses. Remember, we did not have the different kinds of tapes and adhesives we have today. We saved the grocer's brown paper bags for our lunches- and even the waxed paper. If that paper got a bit of mayonnaise or mustard on it, we prudently wiped it off, let it dry, and folded it up for the next day's sandwich.

"I recall that we made candles from honeycomb wax. Many of us made our own laundry bar soap from lye, water, and fat. Soap powder was scarce. Grocers saved it for their regular customers, when they did get in a shipment. I recollect that I had to fetch it for a few of the elderly women in my neighborhood.

"We cooked our own wallpaper paste from flour and water. We made most of our clothing and even our rugs from rags we saved. I've noticed that rag rugs have become trendy- and quite expensive nowadays!

"We canned a lot too in those more frugal times. There was a brightly colored poster, widespread during the war years, that depicted a cheerful housewife holding an armful of sealed mason jars of what she had *put up*- that's how we worded *canning* or *preserving* back then- with the encouraging words at the bottom of the picture: 'Of course I CAN! I'm patriotic as can be- And ration points won't worry me!'

"I remember when the war dragged on that the President, in one of his radio fireside chats, asked the country to refrain from decorating a tree for the Christmas holidays in honor of the troops. That year, we took an evergreen branch, *just a branch*, and decorated it with little white balls we fashioned from old quilting batting. It was a sort of compromise; and with the family gathered together, we sang carols and said prayers for the safety of our boys in the field and the war's victorious end.

"My sister, who was an Army nurse, was stationed at the Halloran Army Hospital on Staten Island, New York. She often wrote us about the wounded and amputees coming home from the front. It was all so sad. But how proud we were of her! She was doing her part for the war, as were so many other Army and Navy nurses, stateside and overseas. Those women were a godsend. They had to endure so much, both physically and emotionally.

"Newsreels, before and after movies, were one way we kept abreast of the war news, though by the time we saw those reels, the war news they contained was weeks old. I remember that there were often collections made at the movie theaters after a newsreel for the war effort.

"The most popular way to get war news was, of course, via the radio, and we always gathered around ours after supper every night. We never missed the President's fireside chats either. His leadership kept the country together at that stressful time. Newspapers were another means of news. That, of course, is a given; but in those long ago days, there were Extras out on the streets, with newsboys shouting, 'Extra! Extra! Read all about it!' Now mind, the front page of the Extra carried the *breaking* news; the remainder of the paper was repeat news. Just so you know.

"Everybody walked, bicycled, or took the trolley, which meant some walking in addition; and we were likely healthier for it, just as we were likely healthier eating less meat. Anyway, we walked a lot more. It was safe in those days to walk the streets after dark, though we had a curfew due to the war. Even a child was safe on the dark streets in those days, if an errand needed to be run.

"We had had a lot of training doing without during the Great Depression; so, during the war years, we never gave rationing a thought. No- definitely not denial or sacrifice. We never applied *those* words to what we did. We were dedicated to our boys in uniform and to *their* sacrifice and *their* valor. There was a war on, and by the grace of God, we were determined to pull together- as one nation- to win it."

-Nancy Stafford, Dayton, Ohio,
formerly of Connellsville, PA

~ ~ ~

"I was close to nine years old when I heard the news about Pearl Harbor. We always went to church Sunday nights, and the preacher announced it at that indelible, December 7, 1941, service. I can recall exactly where I was sitting that night. The church is no longer there. Yet, I can clearly see, with my mind's eye, every detail of my surroundings that fatal Sunday. I remember the devastation mirrored on the faces of the congregation, while everyone exchanged worried looks.

"Keep in mind that in those days news filtered through to us a lot slower than today. Then, there were no televisions with round-the-clock news channels. It was a day or so before we got any real details of what happened at Pearl Harbor; and when we finally did, it was even more shocking than the early report.

"In our classrooms, we made scrapbooks of everything that was going on in the war. In order to do our part, we kids gathered milkweed pods to turn in, at school, for the war effort. Uncle Sam needed it for fill in life jackets, and we knew our milkweed efforts would save American lives... it was a *good* feeling.

"Each week at school we gave a dime to be used for the purchase of savings bonds. This too contributed toward the war effort.

"I can still image the colorful 'Rosie the Riveter' poster, symbolic of all the women working in factories to free men up for combat. The widespread poster depicted a pretty lady, her hair tied up in a scarf, making a muscle with her arm, and the bold words 'We Can Do It!'

" 'Loose Lips Sink Ships,' and 'Uncle Sam Wants YOU!' were other vibrant posters we saw everywhere. I remember that we all had the proud, hopeful feeling that the country was pulling together- including, as I said, America's schoolchildren- to win the war.

"One particularly vivid memory, during the war years, is the youth group to which I belonged at our church, the Indian Head Church of God. These gatherings were always on Wednesday nights. When some of our young

The highly decorated "Flying Tiger" Merle Peck (front row, far left) with his famed squadron. Note the calendar with the question mark on Peck's B-24 Liberator that he named "Time Will Tell." Photo courtesy Dorothy Johnson Peck, Hopwood, PA

men in uniform were home on furlough and in attendance, it made those evenings all the more special. Then, we would have these rousing sing-alongs; and I can still picture how happy the fellas were to be home–alive and well. The songs were always of a stirring nature, and the boys especially joined in with gusto.

"So many homes in our little village displayed, in their windows, those patriotic banners with blue or gold stars. Each blue star proudly stated that a member of that household was in active service. A gold star or stars represented a fallen hero or heroes.

"School teachers, clergymen, political leaders– everyone in a leadership position– ceaselessly sparked enthusiasm for doing our part, each of us, for the war effort– President Roosevelt most of all. No one balked; everyone wanted to do something; it was a *shared* effort. *I do not remember a time in our history when we were more united than we were during World War II.*

"People constantly gave blood. All the women I knew knitted items for the soldiers in the field. We saved, collected, and turned in anything and everything we could to help Uncle Sam to win the war. We all complied with the rationing regulations. A lot of people planted Victory Gardens. Most of all, we prayed every day for our victory against the evil that was the Axis forces... and for our men and women in uniform to come home.

"Air-raid drills and blackouts were often experienced, and we all knew this was necessary. The loud sirens meant lights out in no-uncertain terms. Everyone obeyed that summons. I recall that some people had even built air-raid shelters to take refuge in. They stocked them with supplies too. My family, like most, bought those dark green window shades; and at the shriek of the siren, we pulled them down snugly and made sure no lights were on.

"I just remembered that when I was a child and a preteen during the war years, I had a close friend, almost like a family member. She was a school teacher, and I fondly recall that she was the one who had taught me to read even before I started school. When the war broke out, she joined the WACs; and lo and behold, she found her true calling in life, serving her country– along with a husband in the bargain!

"After the war, I eventually married a man who had been a pilot with the famed 'Flying Tigers.' The man who was destined to be my husband, Merle Peck, served in the China-Burma-and-India theater of war. As had been the case in World War I, numerous Americans took advantage of the opportunity to fly and fight without waiting for their country to enter the war. That's how it was with Merle.

"Merle piloted B-24 Liberators, transporting fuel and flying on bombing missions. He and the other 'Flying Tigers' are discussed in a book entitled *Chennault's Forgotten Warriors: The Saga of the 308th Bomb Group in China* by Carroll V. Glines. I always keep this book on my coffee table. Included in the book is one of Merle's many dangerous fuel-ferrying missions.

"At war's end, my husband received the Distinguished Flying Cross among several other decorations. The Distinguished Flying Cross is awarded for heroism or extraordinary achievement, both of which evoke Merle Peck.

"My husband's B-24 Liberator was named 'Time Will Tell'; and the name was boldly painted on the plane, along with the image of a calendar with a page flipped back that bore a big question mark.

"Hollywood even made a movie [in 1942] about *The Flying Tigers*, which starred John Wayne. I think the film captured the public's attention and brought some well-deserved recognition to this very impressive group of American flyers.

"After the war, Merle became a school teacher. He taught social studies at the local high school. My husband was nine years my senior. We met after the war in our little mountain village of Indian Head, Pennsylvania, where we both attended the same church. Merle never talked about the bombing aspect of his time with the 'Tigers.' Essentially, he thought of his wartime service as a job that needed to be done to preserve America's freedom and our American way of life. In war, Merle Peck's strong patriotism, along with his strong faith in God, kept him going in the job he felt he had to do."

-Dorothy Johnson Peck, Hopwood, PA,
formerly of Indian Head, PA

Author: During the summer of 1941, about 300 men posing as tourists and teachers boarded a ship bound for Asia. Training began at Rangoon in September of 1941, about three months before Pearl Harbor.

Two of the three squadrons moved to Kunming, China, to protect the Burma Road, the only ground route into China; and on December 20, 1941, the Flying Tigers received their "baptism under fire" when they inflicted heavy losses on Japanese bombers attempting to attack Kunming.

A retired Air Corps major who had served as a special advisor to the Chinese Air Force, Claire L. Chennault, who became a major general, is the man who formed this American Volunteer Group (A.V.G.). Nicknamed the "Flying Tigers," the unit consisted of approximately 100 pilots and about 200 ground crew personnel, most of whom had been released from the US Army, Navy and Marines to volunteer for the A.V.G. At first, these men were equipped with near-obsolescent P-40s. These were the pursuits/fighter planes that engaged the Japanese aircrafts that attacked Pearl Harbor. P-40s had been the foremost fighters that were in service at the outset of World War II.

I want to state for the record that the Flying Tigers were greatly outnumbered in the air; and most of the time, they operated under adverse conditions. There were no replacement pilots and practically no spare parts for repairing their aircrafts, yet they scored a *very* impressive record against the enemy. The Tigers shot down nearly 300 Japanese planes at a cost of twelve A.V.G. pilots killed or missing in action.

It is interesting to note that their winged tiger logo was designed by Walt Disney Studios. The men, at first, poked fun at it; but it didn't take long before they wore it with pride.

As for military aircraft nose art: American fighters and bombers were adorned with nose art during WWII. Often these paintings were "inspirational"- "cheese cake"- renderings of voluptuous fantasy women with the plane's name a fitting match.

~ ~ ~

Author: Letters from overseas were always censored; so it was not unusual for a wife, mother, sister, or sweetheart to open a soldier's letter that bore razor cutouts- censored words or phrases that had been cut from the missive, such as military positions or troop movements. The censors were military personnel who had been assigned to the task of cutting out all text from overseas letters that contained anything of a military nature. "Somewhere in Europe" became a popular home-front phrase, as had "Somewhere in France" during World War I.

There was an old saying in the military during the war years that soldiers who did not like to write letters, but wanted to let their loved ones know they were well, would pen the letter's salutation and the farewell with their signature at the bottom of the page, and then finish by clipping out a big "censored" segment in the middle.

My mother was one of a multitude of war brides the war created. After Pearl Harbor, young, unmarried women were cautioned about wartime romances and hasty marriages, from parents, from clergy, from magazines and other sources, "not to tie their fates to an uncertain future." But if a woman loved a man, she was bound to his destiny whether she was married to him or not. As one Army Air Force wife stated in a letter to a marriage-contemplating friend: "Everyone, in peace and war, runs a risk when he or she falls in love. If it's meant to be, a mate can be killed crossing a street. If you want emotional insurance, then don't fall in love at all."

For many years after both my parents passed away, I refrained from reading the letters my father had penned my mother from overseas during the war. I stashed them away in a drawer, still tied with the faded pink ribbon, as they were when I had discovered them in an old trunk in the attic. It was only while working on this Chronicle that I decided to read them. Somehow, I do not think either of my parents disapproved.

Here is a fragment of a letter my father sent my mother late in 1944 from Blackpool, located in Northwest England on the Irish Sea, where he was stationed during the war with the Eighth Army Air Force.

My Darling Wife,

How much longer can it last? Another Christmas separated from you by an ocean and a war. Did you get the gift I sent? I saw it in a bombed-out shop window with a "Business as Usual" sign on the door, and knew it was meant for you.

I pray we will be together next Christmas. I wonder how many soldiers whispered that same prayer this Christmas Eve- American, English, Canadian, Australian, Scots and Irish, Russian, even German and Japanese? "Peace on earth, goodwill toward men." Will it ever be so?

Author: My father, John Robert Hanlon, Sr., of Connellsville, Pennsylvania, was a deep-feeling, rather poetic person. When he was a very old man, and I was taking care of him after my mother had passed away, his Irish-green eyes followed the graceful flight of a white butterfly one summer day as we were sitting on his porch: "There," he pointed, "is your mother. She comes every day to see me. She never misses."

During WWII, my father was exempt from the service due to his age and his job at a Pittsburgh steel mill, where he was then employed. However, soon after Pearl Harbor, this intensely patriotic man enlisted and was thereafter stationed in England as part of the Eighth Army Air Force, the "Mighty Eighth," as it became known. As chief of the engine-parts section of the AAF Command Depot's vast internal supply division, Master Sergeant Hanlon supervised the receiving, storing, and issuing of the thousands of engine parts needed to keep our fighters and bombers in the air. Soon after his arrival in July 1943, he was given that important charge and saw the Depot's engine-parts section grow from a corner of one hangar to the largest engine-parts section in the United Kingdom, occupying two giant hangars.

I am proud to state that my father, at the war's end, received a Commendation, the top rating possible for a noncommissioned officer, for his "... outstanding devotion to duty, technical knowledge, and initiative..." at the Air Service Command Depot in a ceremony attended by hundreds of soldiers.

~ ~ ~

Master Sergeant

SGT. JOHN HANLON

Master Sergeant John Hanlon, who is with the Air Service Command Depot in England, has attained the top rating possible for a non-commissioned officer, according to word received from him by his wife, the former Miss Jennie Bell of Brookvale. He has charge of engine parts at the depot. Sergeant Hanlon, son of Mrs. Mary Hanlon of Brookvale, has been in England for the past year. Prior to entering the service in March, 1942, he was employed at the Duquesne steel mills.

Two articles in Connellsville's Daily Courier, Aug. 25, 1944, and a longer piece, Feb. 24, 1945, told of Master Sergeant John Robert Hanlon's "outstanding devotion to duty" at the AAF Command Depot, Eighth Army Air Force, England, which earned him a Commendation. From the author's personal collection

"I was in my car en route to work on the Sunday when the Japanese attacked Pearl Harbor. It was in the afternoon... around two-thirty. I remember because I was working the three-to-eleven shift at the Cleveland Twist and Drill Factory. I knew immediately it would mean war. We had the Draft then, and I was called up into the service not long after.

"I went into the Army Air Force. Due to a bad right knee, I was sent to Denver, Colorado, for a month of training as a medic. From there, I went by train to Mississippi, where I was stationed at the airbase at Clarksdale, which is directly south of Memphis. Mostly, I was a pencil-pusher, a receptionist-clerk, there to deal with the paperwork in the infirmary at the base, which was a primary training site. Our nine-bed infirmary served as an emergency hospital for the cadets in training there. If someone came into the infirmary with a serious condition, he would immediately be sent to the airbase at Greenville, Mississippi, the nearest army hospital facility. By the way, 'primary training,' just as the name implies, was the *initial* military aircraft training for would-be pilots.

"While I was there, there were two crashes. I made the ambulance run to both crash sites. One of those crashes was fatal; the pilot was killed. I can still see the plane, which had hit the ground like a dart, nose first. The engine was buried in the ground. The pilot had been pulled out of the wreckage, and it was my job to take his body to the local morgue in Clarksdale. The pilot in the other crash was luckier. He had parachuted out, into a field. When I picked him up, he seemed fine; nonetheless, it was my duty to take him to our infirmary.

"It really is a small world. When I was at Fletcher Field there in Clarksdale, I encountered a fella from my hometown of Connellsville. He was one of the student pilots in primary training there. I can vaguely picture him in my mind... but now, for the life of me, I cannot recall his name. Time robs you of so many things when you get to be my age. What's that they say? 'Time's a peddler, deals in dust.'

"One of my strongest memories is of a particular doctor at the base, a second lieutenant. I won't mention his name, but he was always chewing someone out, and he could be quite nasty about it. The cadets hated him above all other officers on base. One day, when it was just he and I in the infirmary, I had a heart-to-heart talk with him. It must have done some good, because after that he went about his duties with a whole different attitude- like a doctor should.

"I was one of the last ones to leave Clarksdale, to close down the base at the war's end. When that lieutenant doctor was taking his leave- his wife was with him- he passed by my desk at the infirmary, paused and nodded his head, saying in a quiet sort of way 'Thank you.' I knew what he was referring to; and I stood, shook his hand and wished him luck in his civilian life.

"When the war ended, our whole base was shut down. The CO was afraid the men would go into town and raise hell to celebrate, so no one was allowed to leave the base.

"The thing that I carried with me from the military for the rest of my life was my interest in watch repair. I know that sounds odd coming from a medic, but I had befriended a Jewish fella in the service, who was a watch repairman at the PX. When I expressed an interest in watch repair, he took me under his wing, and I learned from him. I even sat in for him a couple of times. After the war, he telephoned me- I had returned to my old job at the drill factory- and, as he had promised he would, he invited me to go to work with him. I immediately took him up on it, relocating then to Fort Hood, Texas, where I started out doing repairs, such as minor watch repairs and cleaning, as well as ring sizing. All the while, I was learning more and more. I decided to go to school for watch repair, after which I stayed in that business for the rest of my life, eventually acquiring my own jewelry store. A lot of GIs took with them career skills that originated in the service; and many took advantage of the GI Bill, which afforded them the opportunity to go to school."

-Daniel J. Ondrus, Parma, Ohio,
formerly of Connellsville, PA

Author: The GI Bill, officially known as the Servicemen's Readjustment Act of 1944, was designed to provide greater opportunities to returning war veterans of World War II. The bill, signed by President Roosevelt on June 22, 1944, provided federal aid to veterans so that they could better adjust to civilian life. The act included aid for hospitalization, the purchase of homes and businesses, and especially education, providing tuition, subsistence, books and supplies, equipment, and counseling services for all veterans who wished to continue their education.

~ ~ ~

"I entered the service in 1943, in the AAF [Army Air Force], with the hope of becoming a flight nurse; but due to imperfect eyesight, I was then transferred to the ground forces. The year I joined the service, I was already a registered nurse. I had graduated in 1943 from Georgetown University Hospital, where I had completed my nurse's training.

"At the outset of my service career, I was attached to the 130th Evacuation Hospital, as it was called; then I was sent to Fort Dix, New Jersey.

This is the stalwart group of nurses with whom Mimi Finnerty (left, hatless, looking down) served overseas during WW II.

"Upon completion of my basic Army training, I received my overseas assignment, which of course, was my main motivation for joining. On an unforgettable, grey, frigid day in December 1944, our convoy of ships, carrying medical personnel, supplies and equipment, departed from New York Harbor, headed for England. I was soon sent to Tenby, South Wales. There I underwent further training, more specialized, for what I was about to undertake. We were all nurses in my outfit. There were doctors, of course, as well as a few technicians.

"After we nurses completed our advanced training, we boarded a military ship for France, where we disembarked at Le Havre, a port in Northern France on the Channel. From there, we rode in military vehicles overland to Sedan, a town on the Meuse, near the German border. By this point in time, the war was winding down, with the Allies pushing hard into Germany. Nevertheless, we nurses were needed more than ever. There awaited for us a *very* important job.

Army Nurse Lieutenant Finnerty

Mimi Finnerty at Moosberg, 1945

"If you're curious about what we wore, our uniforms were olive drab and consisted of a skirt and jacket that bore our nurse's insignia on the lapel. Officers had badges on the left arm of their jackets. We also wore olive drab, beaked military caps with the Army insignia on the front. Overseas, when we were working, we wore olive drab slacks with matching flannel shirts.

"At the border town of Sedan, we underwent a bit more training for what we were about to face; then we were assigned to the 15th US Army, and shortly afterward, to the 3rd Army. I should mention that before we ever set up as a hospital, we were constantly checking supplies and equipment. We would need them!

"Along with the 3rd US Army, we pushed forward to bivouac at Moosberg, in the Nuremberg area of Germany. There we became operational for the first time. It was the first of May 1945. The Germans would surrender in a week.

"Now our main duty was to care for American and Allied prisoners of war, who had just been liberated from Moosberg's Stalag VII B by the 14th Armored Division. How happy those poor men were to see us! Most of them had been captured when they were shot down over enemy territory. I think the very fact that they were *free* again, with American nurses and other American military personnel around them, significantly bolstered their morale and did a lot to put them on the road to recovery. The *unknown* was no longer their greatest fear, but most were in urgent need of medical care.

"We were two weeks at the POW camp at Nuremberg, after which we were moved to Mauthausen, the horrific concentration camp in Austria.

"I have heard and read that there are those who want the world to believe that the Holocaust never took place. I want to state, for Posterity's sake, right here and now: THERE WAS A HOLOCAUST! I was *there!*

"Mauthausen, an extermination camp, was one of the worst. Classified as a 'Category Three' camp, Mauthausen translated *Death.* Survivors showed us crematories, gas chambers, and mass graves. As in other camps, the inmates at Mauthausen were not only starved and worked to death with forced labor, but were tortured, experimented on, and mass-murdered.

"There was a stone quarry there. Prisoners had been forced to haul heavy slabs of granite or cement up the hundred-eighty-six steps to the summit, only to have their captors hurl them backwards into the pits!

"Those who survived all bore the same hollow-eyed expression, their skins stretched over skeletal frames- *indescribable specimens of humanity.*

"The death camps are a hideous moral blemish on the face of Europe- *and no one should ever forget that they existed.*

"While we were there, from the fourteenth of May to late June, the horrors we learned of were so cruel, so unbelievably subhuman, that I have never been able to erase them from memory. I won't go into details... suffice it to say, they were *pure evil.*

"The inmates were *overjoyed* to see the US Army come to liberate them; and we nurses did everything we could to help those pitiful, suffering people. Due to the horrendous conditions they had endured, many were in such bad shape that they did die. Each morning when we came on duty, we'd begin our day by taking count of those who had perished overnight. We did manage, however, to save lives.

"We had rounded up several German military nurses, and they were detained to help us treat the liberated concentration camp prisoners-turned-patients. This seemed especially satisfying to some of the Jewish inmates, though others felt wary about it. I remember that the inmates we were treating in our tent hospitals could not at first grasp that they would be able to eat every day, so many of them hoarded their food, hiding it under their pillows and such. For sanitary reasons, we used to have to 'shake down' those food items daily. It was a while before we convinced the former prisoners that it was okay to eat all the food we gave them, that we would give them more. To say it was sad... well, there are no words to adequately describe what we encountered at Mauthausen.

"I have to say, however, that we had no trouble with those German nurses. They did their jobs, as they were instructed to do, as healers to the sick, the suffering and the dying. They presented us with much-needed hands and no problems.

"I recall especially a teenage Jewish boy who had sort of latched on to one of our American nurses. He took to calling her *schwester.* Perhaps she reminded him of his own sister, who may have been lost to him somehow. Perhaps his own sister had been separated from him never to be seen again, or she may have died in the horrors of the camp. I will never know.

"Those who were strong enough to walk out of that nightmare place did so. From the time we had entered Mauthausen, we never stopped anyone from leaving in order to find family or whatever they could of home... or go wherever they wished to go. They had been through enough.

"Toward the end of June 1945, my unit was sent to the Atlantic coast of France, to what was termed 'Camp Twenty Grand,' where we were readied to return home ourselves.

"I came home a second lieutenant but made first lieutenant shortly afterward. I was discharged from the Army in the fall of 1945. I am very proud to have served our nation during the time of her greatest need, and to have helped as many war victims as I could. Yes, looking back on that era, I am so glad that I did what I did."

- Mimi Finnerty, Scottdale, PA

Author: Between forty and sixty million people were killed during World War II. With that war, something was added to the annals of organized slaughter– the dead included millions of civilians. Honor in war was a thing of the past.

Tent Hospital at the liberated death camp Mauthausen, Austria, 1945
Photos courtesy Mimi Finnerty, Scottdale, PA

Though Hitler's plan for the "complete elimination of Jews from Europe" had been reported years earlier, only when the camps were liberated shortly before the German surrender was the truth exposed. Documentation would come with the Nuremberg Trials (1945-49). Approximately eleven million human beings had been exterminated in the hell-on-earth places such as Auschwitz, Belsen, Buchenwald, Dachau, and Mauthausen. Over six million were Jews. A new word entered the dictionary, a word as ugly as the camps themselves- *genocide.* It had been invented to label the process. Prisoners, including children, had been shot, beaten to death, hanged, starved to death, buried alive and systematically herded into gas chambers. Photographs taken of the camps and the survivors by their US Army liberators were published in magazines and newspapers- *never to be forgotten.*

Mimi Finnerty reenlisted and headed to Alaska for a second tour of duty a year after her discharge from the Army. "I couldn't stand it," she told me during our sequence of interviews. "I loved every second of my service career. I wanted to do more. I wanted to see the world... and I did."

Abraham Lincoln once said, "It is not the years in your life that count, it's the life in your years."

Dorothy Seese Landman's WWII ID/pass to enter top-security Connellsville Airport grounds, a war bond ad, and a "Blue Streak" label for shipping gunnery materials
Courtesy Dorothy Seese Landman, Connellsville, PA

The nurses in the field, in each of America's struggles, were angels of mercy; and, in my opinion, were just as heroic as any decorated soldier with a gun. To steel themselves to do what Mimi Finnerty and her sister nurses did took heartfelt dedication to God and country, requiring an extra measure of courage and stamina enveloped in a true warrior spirit.

It is people like Mimi who make this nation great. Mimi Finnerty envelops all that is good and decent about America, and I am honored to have interviewed such a great lady.

As for those German military nurses: I always remind readers that there is good and evil in every race of man. My father often told the true story of a fellow employee at West Penn Power Company, who had been a WWII POW en route, via a prisoner train, to a German *stalag.* When the train made a rest stop; and the thirsty, hungry captives were given water, some German women, who had come to the stop on bicycles, insisted to the guards that they be permitted to give the American and Allied prisoners something to eat. Though the German soldiers in charge forbade them to do so, those brave, kind-hearted German women did accomplish their errand of mercy.

~ ~ ~

Author: Connellsville Airport, designated Specialized Supply Depot # 805, played an important role during World War II. In an interview for the premier volume of my *County Chronicles* with longtime Connellsville resident Dorothy Seese Landman, who worked at the airport during the war years, I learned that *vital* gunnery materials for war planes were packed and shipped from several Pennsylvania airfields, such as the historic Connellsville Airport.

"We painted significant blue stripes on the outside of certain crates," Landman informed. "For example, one blue stripe meant that the box would be shipped to England; two blue stripes translated 'Russia.' Codes were memorized and used in lieu of addresses for overseas shipments; and if a shipment was urgent, a 'Blue Streak' label was attached to it, which read 'Immediate Attention Requested.'

"Needless to say, security was *tight* at the airport in those days; no one could enter without a pass. In order to work there, we all had to take Civil Service exams. Half of the civilians were from Connellsville, the other half from surrounding areas.

"There were twenty soldiers stationed at the airport with a major in charge of operations, along with a few other officers. A barracks was provided for military personnel; and a small brick house was constructed on the airport grounds, near the administration building, for the major and his wife. The house was torn down after the war," Landman recalled. "The administration building housed a switch board, the CO's office, and a commissary. Everything else was in the big hangar... more offices; a teletype where the orders came in, after which they were sent to shipping; a first-aid station, and a small PX, where the soldiers could purchase cigarettes and such. In addition to the gunnery materials, we packed and shipped honor medals. I especially remember handling purple hearts and oak leaf clusters.

"I remember that bond drives were quite popular in those days, and we had a few Hollywood luminaries stop at our airport for the purpose of selling bonds for Uncle Sam. One of those bright stars was Robert Preston. That was exciting! I should mention that most employees had bond-purchases taken out of each pay... I did.

"Connellsville Airport was the most expensive depot to operate during the war because the crated materials had to be trucked in and out, to and from the various railroad stations. Every so often a government inspector showed up to look for some excuse to shut us down. Ours, however, was a 'tight ship'; we always passed the literal 'white-glove' inspections with the proverbial 'flying colors.' Moreover, we had J. Buell Snyder, a congressman from Perryopolis, on our side. He had the clout to keep us going to the end of the war. Our hero Snyder even visited us at Connellsville Airport during operations, and he made it a point to shake everyone's hand and congratulate each of us on our important contribution to the war effort."

- Dorothy Seese Landman, Connellsville, PA

Author: Under President Franklin Delano Roosevelt, Fayette County's Congressman J. Buell Snyder was in charge of War Department appropriations.

~ ~ ~

"I went to Japan after the war in 1946. The country was still devastated at that time.

"I had a job at General MacArthur's headquarters in Tokyo, in the Civil Intelligence Section, known as the 'CIS.' The CIS was the final repository of all reports and intelligence data accumulated by the various CIS units. These files were extensively used by all organizational segments of Army Intelligence and other staff representatives.

"I had about sixteen GIs working for me there in my office. Actually, I was the Assistant to the Chief of CIS Files there in Tokyo; and I was sometimes referred to as a

The cinders of war, Tokyo, 1946

Dai-Ichi Building, Tokyo, Occupied Japan, General MacArthur's Headquarters with Imperial moat in foreground

'DAC,' which stood for 'Department of the Army Civilian.'

"Our office was in the Dai-Ichi Building, which faced the Imperial Palace. I worked on the seventh floor, and General MacArthur worked on the floor just below me. I used to like to watch, from the windows or outside, when MacArthur exited or entered our building. The Japanese in the district would line up for over a block just to catch a glimpse of him.

"The general was not what you would call 'sociable.' He was every inch a soldier, very authoritative in his bearing. His wife, however, was a warm, personable individual- extremely likable.

"It is of historical interest to mention that, when first I arrived in Japan, I visited the International Military Tribunal- Far East. The judges were from the United States, Great Britain, Australia, Canada, France, the Netherlands, the Philippines, New Zealand, China, India, and the USSR. The Tribunal's function, of course, was to try war crimes, and among the twenty-six defendants were Tojo and Hashimoto. I remember they, along with most of the others, were subsequently hanged. Yamashita was hanged in 1946, I believe in Manila, for allowing the massive atrocities during the Bataan Death March.

"Some of the things that came across my desk in Intelligence, I have to state, were absolutely horrific; but I had taken an oath, and to this day, I can make the truthful statement that I have never discussed classified information with anyone, not even with the man who became my husband.

"I had been in Occupied Japan for over a year when one of my friends called me to go on a blind date with her and her friend. Though I informed her that I did not like to go on blind dates, she literally begged me to go and proceeded to tell me about the gentleman in question, whose name was Dick Pitzer.

"At that time, I was in residence at the Osaka Hotel, a womens' billet, and no men were permitted above the main floor. I thought I had understood that *Dick* was to meet me in the hotel lobby, but when I approached the man I thought was he, by my friend's description of a 'big man,' I discovered I had the wrong person... sort of. What I mean is that this other gentleman, it turned out, was my escort for the evening, so I looped my arm through his, and we headed for the Officers' Club.

"When we entered the club, I saw a good-looking man, of the stature that fit Dick's description, seated on a couch, with a mug of beer and a redhead. Nevertheless, he and I were eventually introduced; and he asked me to dance. That same evening, when he invited me out, I had to decline, due to my heavy schedule. Never a quitter, Dick persevered, and we finally began dating. He later informed me that the first time he saw me, when I had walked through the door of the Officers' Club, he had declared to himself, 'That's the girl I am going to marry!'

"Dick Pitzer was with the 7th Calvary (Custer's old unit). He was a lieutenant, about a year out of West Point. He had been sent to Occupied Japan after the war, where

Tokyo's Imperial Palace Bridge that Dick Pitzer guarded in Occupied Japan

Dick Pitzer at Imperial Palace Bridge with Dai-Ichi Building/Gen. MacArthur's HQ in background, 1947

he executed a number of important duties... he was a company commander. Among other things, his duties involved food surveillance to prevent black marketing; and he guarded the Bank of Japan, as well as the Imperial Bridge to the Imperial Palace. For a time, he was also the Recreational Officer. In addition to his main duties, he played service football for the Army during his stint in postwar Japan.

"My office, as I said before, was on the seventh floor of the Dai-Ichi Building, facing the Imperial Palace and providing me with a bird's-eye-view of the royal residence. One day, as I was penning a letter to my mother in Texas– I am from Texas; Dick was from Pennsylvania– I witnessed a Japanese girl hurl herself into the moat that surrounds the palace. Though I was in Intelligence, I never discovered the true cause of her attempted suicide. She was hauled out of the water and survived.

"Another day, a second Japanese girl jumped into the moat. But this one stripped completely naked first before flinging herself into the cold, deep water. As I mentioned earlier, I had sixteen GIs working for me in my area; and during that occasion, there were sixteen pairs of eyes strained at our windows. As it turned out, both girls were rescued.

"My duties in Japan extended from October of 1946 to October 1949. Dick was there from October of 1947 to October of 1949.

"Yes, we did marry. We were married in Occupied Japan– twice. We exchanged vows the first time on July 23, 1948, presided over by the American Consulate at Yokohama. Our second wedding, two days later, was a beautiful church wedding at Saint Luke's Chapel in the 49th General Hospital, Tokyo. That is the chapel where most of the Americans were married. Our wedding was followed by a lovely garden reception at Mudge Hall, which had been one of the royal residences before the war.

"We honeymooned north of Tokyo, at the resort town of Karuizawa. We were a week at the Mampei Hotel there, after which Dick's general, General Chase, graciously gave us the use of his home, a mountain lodge that was also located at picturesque Karuizawa, for an extended honeymoon sojourn of a second week.

"Mount Asama, the second largest active volcano in Japan, over eight thousand feet above sea level, is at Karuizawa. The scenery was... *is* gorgeous, and our time there was absolutely delightful, a dream honeymoon.

"I witnessed history in Occupied Japan. I witnessed vital changes that took place in that devastated country after the war, as Japan set out from the Chrysanthemum Empire on its path to a thriving democracy. In fact, the Japanese were in the process of writing their constitution while I was there. It was very much history in the making. The people were permitted to retain their emperor, though

Dick and Tena Pitzer at their garden reception in Tokyo, July 1948

he did not have the power he once had. He became more of a figurehead.

"I remember, when I had first arrived in Japan, how struck I was by the devastation. I can still picture little children roaming the streets, nights. I remarked at the time to a friend that they should be home in their beds. 'What homes?' 'What beds?' she answered me. 'They have no homes, Tena.' It was heartbreaking.

"The women still wore kimonos during that postwar period, and their ways were so different from those of the war-liberated American women.

"I want to conclude that Dick and I returned to Japan for our thirty-fifth wedding anniversary and stayed at the same hotel where we had honeymooned. What changes had occurred in those thirty-five years! It was truly *amazing*, and it did my heart good.

Mount Fiji/ Fujiyama

"Dick and I subsequently resided in other foreign countries due to my husband's career. For instance, we lived for five years in South Korea and a year in Hong Kong, among a variety of other places we became acquainted with on the globe; and I want to state for the record that we always put our best foot forward to be the very best ambassadors we could be for America abroad. *At all times, in all of our homes-away-from-home, that was of the utmost importance to us both.*

"As for Occupied Japan, it wasn't all work and no play. There were some wonderful times there. From my office windows, I could see Mount Fuji, also called *Fujiyama*, and it was a breathtaking sight! Before we departed Japan, Dick and I actually climbed to the top of Fuji– no easy task, to be sure! As I wrote to my mother stateside, 'Fuji was UP, with capital letters!' What a challenge to climb it! I am proud to declare we actually did it, made it to the top where so many had failed to go. I remember the little bowl of steamed rice, at the end of our Fuji quest, that tasted better to me than anything I have put into my mouth, before or since.

"Just as the Marshall Plan helped to rebuild war-torn Europe, America extended a strong helping hand to lift Japan up and out of the cinders of war. My duties in Occupied Japan were a small part of America's momentous role in helping to rebuild that war-torn nation, but I have enormous pride in what we Americans accomplished there."

– Tena Pitzer, Sun City Center, Florida

Author: In a speech, June 5, 1947, at Harvard, George C. Marshall outlined a blueprint for what History christened the "Marshall Plan": "Our policy is directed not against any country or doctrine, but against hunger, poverty, desperation and chaos. Its purpose should be the revival of a working economy in the world so as to permit the emergence of political and social conditions in which free institutions can exist."

As a result of the Marshall Plan, the Fayette County native, whom Truman called the "Great One of the Age," became the *only* professional soldier ever to receive the Nobel Prize for Peace. Marshall, about whom I wrote in "Soldier of Peace" in the premier volume of *County Chronicles*, was appointed Chief of Staff in 1939 by President Roosevelt, followed in 1944 by General of the Army, rendering him America's first five-star general. I know "they say" no one is indispensable, but during World War II and the postwar period, Uniontown, Pennsylvania's favorite son George C. Marshall was indispensable.

As for Tena Pitzer: I can readily believe that she was an *excellent* ambassador for America. I do not think I have ever met anyone with a fairer or a more positive outlook. Speaking with her never failed to boost my spirits. Her humanity, her infectious good humor, along with her wonderful Southern charm envelope a truly great lady.

And Tena's husband: Pennsylvania-born Richard "Dick" Pitzer went from playing championship football at Connellsville High School to West Point, where he made the varsity team as a freshman, and played first-string left end when West Point was, in 1944-45, National Collegiate Champions. In 1999, the Gannett News Media named that 1945 West Point squad the "Second Greatest College Football Team of the Century."

Tena and Dick Pitzer in 1998, Pittsburgh, PA

After graduating from West Point in 1946, Pitzer was committed to the Army for four years. He chose to remain eight. His first assignment was with the Army of Occupation in Japan, after which, he came back to the States to teach Officer Candidate School at Fort Riley, Kansas. From there, Pitzer became an assistant football coach at West Point. Los Alamos, New Mexico, was next, where he was part of the very important test division for the Atomic Bomb. Actually, he was in three different- crucial- operations for weapons testing, including Bikini Atoll.

When Pitzer retired from the military, he continued his significant work, taking a position with Westinghouse in the atomic energy field, which essentially meant building reactors for nuclear Navy and for commercial nuclear power plants. From 1980-86, with Westinghouse, he and Tena resided overseas. Pitzer retired from Westinghouse in 1987. During their years together, Tena and Dick adopted two children, Mary Ann Pitzer-Leslie and Greg Pitzer. At this writing, there are four Pitzer grandchildren and four great-grandchildren.

For several years, Dick Pitzer, then a near-octogenarian, volunteered his time to teach mathematics to battered women at the Mary Martha House, a women's shelter near his Florida home. He helped countless abused individuals to attain self-worth, along with their GED's (General Equivalency Diploma), so that they could become self-sufficient.

I had interviewed Mr. Pitzer for "The Right Stuff" Chronicle in *County Chronicles'*

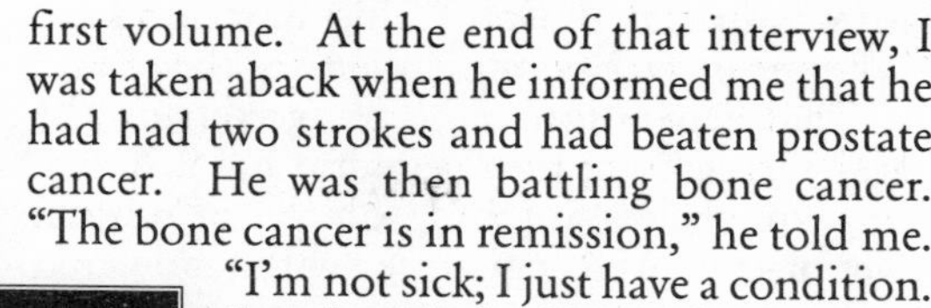

first volume. At the end of that interview, I was taken aback when he informed me that he had had two strokes and had beaten prostate cancer. He was then battling bone cancer. "The bone cancer is in remission," he told me. "I'm not sick; I just have a condition. I'm the kind of guy who laughs a lot. Laughter is God's medicine. It has been known to put cancer into remission. Laughter in large doses," he concluded. "Besides," he added as an afterthought, "unless a man has something to lift, he can never find out how strong he is."

Sadly, before the debut of the premier volume of my *County Chronicles*, I learned, during the 2003 holiday season, that Mr. Pitzer had quietly passed away on December 17 in Florida. That extraordinary man, like all the "Right Stuff" individuals, saw life's hurdles as challenges, not obstacles; the kind of person who never failingly saw the donut, not the hole; the kind who made life as sweet as he could for those around him- for everyone he touched- with compassion, assistance, and cheer. *Dick Pitzer's splendid spirit will persevere whenever and wherever laughter rings true.*

~ ~ ~

Author: History is about the course of human events; therefore, in truth, it includes struggle, suffering, and sacrifice- and History should never hide the truth. I continually endeavor to show, through my word-paintings in each volume of *County Chronicles*, that Freedom never, ever, came cheap- that it is entrusted to each new generation like a precious jewel, a precious legacy to nourish and protect.

Tom Brokaw, in his best-selling book, *The Greatest Generation*, does not laud that generation who fought America's greatest war as "perfect." He reminds us that it is marred with McCarthyism and racism; but says he, "They gave so much and asked so little in return." They won World War II, turned the lights back on in the world, and went on to build modern America "... the America, because of *their* duty, honor and courage, we live in today."

There is no question in this author's mind that the World War II generation of Americans was special. Ralph Waldo Emerson said: *"When it is dark enough, men see the stars."*

That generation came of age during the Great Depression; they were not handed anything, much less anything on the proverbial silver platter. Well acquainted with hard work, they were not afraid of it, because it was certainl, not an unknown. "Families were poor. Everyone had to learn to share and to pull together," one of those whom I interviewed for "The Right Stuff" of the premier volume of this series told me. "It was an era when families were closer-knit."

Let us not forget either that we had heroic leaders during that era. When faced with the enormous challenges of the Great Depression and then World War II, President Roosevelt unfailingly united the nation and brought out the best in his countrymen. Truman, in my opinion one of our finest Presidents, picked up the presidential torch to lead the nation out of the darkness of war with the light of a truly great leader.

Perhaps it was the fact that our nation was attacked at the outset of World War II that rendered Americans so patriotic and willing to sacrifice. A strike against us has always underlined and revitalized our moral strengths and capacities. Historically, America has unceasingly reacted with courage in times of crisis; and it has been heartening to see that, though we are not the America we were before September 11, 2001, we are the same breed of Americans who have continuously stood tall and defiant against the perniciousness of the Kaiser, Hitler, Mussolini, and Saddam Hussein.

When America entered World War II, Hitler made the snide remark to one of his minions that they did not have to worry about the Americans. "The Americans," he said, "are a nation of mongrels." As others of his sort, that dictator found out that there is something to be said for mongrels!

I prefer to call us a bright tapestry of ethnic peoples. And that is what makes us strong. It is largely why we are the survivors we can rightfully call ourselves.

Pennsylvania, as I have often written, is a true slice of America. Indeed, we were the first grand melting pot, William Penn's "Holy Experiment," which, in turn, became the Keystone for the towering bastions of ideals that have become- *the great and enduring United States of America.*

What good men died for at Ticonderoga and Valley Forge and later at Bull Run and Gettysburg, what the WWII generation of Americans sacrificed and died for at Anzio, Bataan and in the Battle of the Bulge- *Freedom*- has come at a high cost with each of our nation's struggles. Remember, however, that we are living under the world's oldest established democracy. It is an ongoing government set down by our remarkable Founding Fathers. We have faced many tests, many challenges, but we have *endured.* "We hold these truths to be self-evident."

Dick Pitzer (right) and classmate Johnny Lujack (1947 Heisman Trophy winner) at 1941-42 high school football reunion, 1994, Connellsville, PA Photos courtesy Tena Pitzer, Sun City Center, Florida

There is a dream called "America," bright with abiding hope, in which I wholeheartedly believe- and I know will not die.

On we go....

"The Hand of God"

"[John] Adams died on [the fiftieth anniversary of the adoption of the Declaration of Independence], July 4, 1826. And so did Thomas Jefferson. People at the time took this as a clear sign that the Hand of God was involved with the fortunes of the United States of America."
-American author/historian extraordinaire, David McCullough, July 2006

Today, as I sit here writing this Chronicle, it is the 4th of July 2006. A couple of days ago, my husband, who habitually reads the newspaper from front to back, noted for me to read an article that appeared in the Sunday, July 2, 2006, *Tribune Review's USA Weekend* magazine, entitled "Declaring Our Freedoms." The piece, in essence, was a discussion between direct descendants of a few of America's Founding Fathers and twice-Pulitzer Prize-winning author, David McCullough.

Steve Moyer, the great-great-great-great-great-grandson of Thomas Jefferson, asked McCullough if he thought the Founding Fathers- if they could do so today- would change anything about the original Declaration of Independence and the Constitution.

"No," America's preeminent historian answered, "both have stood the test of time. In the end, I think they would be very astonished and very grateful that the government they put in place still stands."

The whole article was interesting, but what struck me most was this: *John Adams, America's second President, and Thomas Jefferson, our third President, both died on the same day, July 4, 1826, the fiftieth anniversary of the adoption of the Declaration of Independence.* In fact, James Monroe, America's fifth President, also passed away on the 4th of July, in 1831, the third President (of our nation's first five Presidents) to die on the anniversary of America's Independence.

"People at the time," says McCullough, "took this as a clear sign that the Hand of God was involved with the fortunes of the United States of America."

There were other signs as well. As I penned in the premier volume of my *County Chronicles*, George Washington, America's first President, signed his one and only surrender document on the 4th of July 1754, at Fort Necessity, (now) Fayette County, Pennsylvania, at the outset of the French and Indian War. Humiliated after the embarrassing events at Fort Necessity, the proud, aristocratic and aspiring Washington vowed and declared that *never* again would he surrender. This very persistent leader would keep that promise- to himself and to his country.

In my opinion, as well as that of many other students and writers of history, Fort Necessity played a *vital* role, not only in the overture of the French and Indian War, the War for Empire and essentially the first global conflict, but in the subsequent- *consequential*- struggle for America's Independence. The lessons of war that Washington learned during the French and Indian War in Pennsylvania, molded him into the man he became- the "Father of Our Country."

Experience was his great teacher, and Washington was one man who *learned* from mistakes. Twenty-two years after that character-molding July 4, 1754, incident at Fort Necessity, Washington was chosen, at the onset of the Revolutionary War, as commander-in-chief of the American/Continental Army. It was not because he had such a great military record to his credit. Actually, he did not. It was because the Continental Congress knew the *man*. George Washington was, above all, a natural leader.

As I discussed at length in "A Divine Destiny" of *County Chronicles'* premier volume, Washington escaped harm and disaster so many times, it has not escaped historians that he was destined to lead America in her struggle for Independence and become her first President. As the impossibility of his task increased, so did Washington's sense of responsibility to the "sacred cause." The majority of George Washington's army was very young, farmers mostly, whose youth, during that bloody period of history, passed quickly away. Those boy-soldiers became old with the aging that only the intimate knowledge of war and death can bring. But Washington's army was a marvel! To defeat the greatest-equipped and best-trained military in the world at that time; and when we consider just one facet of what Washington had to deal with–Valley Forge where so many of his soldiers died of starvation and exposure whilst the British fed themselves on the bounty of Pennsylvania's farms in the comfort of Philadelphia– it was as though the concept of America was under the guiding Hand of the Almighty– as many believed it was. *What Washington and his ragtag army would accomplish was nothing short of a miracle.*

In the grey dawn of April 19, 1775, about seventy-seven Minute Men formed a thin line on the Lexington Green, the site of the first battle of the Revolutionary War, there to face a task force of 700 well-equipped British regulars who had marched from Boston to confiscate weapons and powder the Americans had stockpiled. Alerted by Paul Revere (and other riders) the night before, the Minute Men had gathered to *stop* the British; and when the sun rose that historic morning, revealing an enemy that outnumbered them nearly ten to one, the Americans heard their commander shout: "Stand your ground, lads. Don't fire unless fired upon. But if they mean to have a war, let it begin here."

Then and there, the war began. The monument on Lexington Green memorializes that moment with these unforgettable words: "Sacred to Liberty and the Rights of Mankind!!! The Freedom and Independence of America. Sealed and Defended with the Blood of Her Sons." So sacred a war was this!

Our Founding Fathers signed the Declaration of Independence on July 4, 1776. Let us discuss, in brief, two of those valiant men who later became our second and third Presidents, and who both died, fifty years hence, on the same day.

There was a huge celebration in Quincy, Massachusetts, on the fiftieth anniversary of the signing of the great document that had declared America's Independence from the mother country of England. Many of the local dignitaries round about came to John Adams, then in the twilight of his life, to ask him what they should say at the ceremony on his behalf.

Pursing his mouth, Adams was pensive for a long moment before answering, "Independence forever."

His visitors exchanged looks, and then asked him if he would like to add a bit more to his response.

"Not a word." he told them. "Not a word!"

Adams was thinking, I am certain, about freedom of thought– the freedom to think for oneself– and resultantly of the freedoms of religion, speech, and the other basic rights our Founding Fathers set down, rights they so ardently believed were the *basic* rights of mankind.

Undeniably, John Adams was a thoughtful and learned man. The truth is he was more remarkable as a political philosopher than as a politician. "People and nations are forged in the fires of adversity," he declared, doubtless thinking of his own life experience, in addition to the American experience of the Revolution.

According to the White House history web site, Adams was born at Braintree, now Quincy, in the Massachusetts Bay Colony, on October 30, 1735. A Harvard-educated lawyer, he became identified with the patriot cause early on. As a delegate to the First and the Second Continental Congresses, he *led* in the movement for America's Independence.

During the Revolutionary War, he served his infant country well as a diplomat in France and Holland, and he helped to negotiate the treaty of peace at the end of the long and grueling eight-year fight for our Independence.

After the Revolutionary War, from 1785 to 1788, Adams was Minister to the Court of St. James, returning home to be elected Vice President under George Washington.

But serving the new nation for two terms in that office was frustrating for this man of such vigor, intellect and yes– vanity. He complained to his wife Abigail, "My country has in its wisdom contrived for me the most insignificant office that ever the invention of man contrived or his imagination conceived."

When John Adams became America's second President, France and England were warring, which was causing great difficulties for the United States on the high seas, as well as intense partisanship among contending factions within our new nation.

In France, the Directory government (the heads of state in charge after the overthrow of the monarchy via the French Revolution) had refused to receive the American envoy (the representative of our government); and the haughty French rulers had suspended all commercial relations with America.

Adams sent three commissioners to France to reestablish friendly relations with that country; but in the spring of 1798, word arrived that the French Foreign Minister Talleyrand, with the Directory behind him, had refused to negotiate with them- unless the American representatives first paid a substantial bribe!

Adams, in turn, reported the outrageous insult to Congress, and the Senate subsequently printed the correspondence, in which the offending Frenchmen were referred to only as "X, Y and Z."

As a result of all this, the nation broke out in what Thomas Jefferson called the "X, Y, Z Fever," which increased in intensity, due to Adams' exhortations. His language so incited his listeners that the crowds cheered themselves hoarse whenever and wherever the President appeared. Never had the Federalists been so popular.

During his time in office, Adams took matters in hand. Congress appropriated money to complete three new frigates and to build additional ships. It authorized the raising of a provisional army. What's more, it passed the Alien and Sedition Acts, which were intended to frighten foreign agents out of the country.

Though President Adams did not call for a declaration of war, hostilities flashed over the ocean waves. At first, American shipping was nearly defenseless against French privateers; but by 1800, armed American merchantmen and warships were clearing the sea lanes. Despite several naval victories, war fever subsided.

Word had reached Adams that France had no stomach for hostilities with America. French leaders received the American envoy with the proper respect, and negotiations ended the quasi war.

However, sending that peace mission to France to avoid an actual war brought the full fury of the Democratic-Republicans down on John Adams; and in the presidential campaign that followed, the Republicans were united and effective, the Federalists badly divided. Nevertheless, Adams managed to rake in only a few less Electoral Votes than Thomas Jefferson, who emerged victorious, as America's third President.

During those early years of our nation, Jefferson was very concerned about our democracy, our republic (thus the name of his political party, the "Democratic-Republicans"), enduring. His greatest fear was that a monarchy would eventually evolve. There were others who felt likewise. When Jefferson and John Adams were in their most heated state as political rivals in their race for the Presidency, Jefferson accused Adams of being a monarchist, which Adams was certainly not.

Keep in mind, readers, that "monarchist" was the worst thing an American politician could call another in that era. It was akin to someone calling another a "communist" during the McCarthy "witch-hunts" and the Cold War of the 1950s.

In the later part of their lives, however, Adams and Jefferson reconciled and became close friends. After Adams retired to his farm in Quincy, the two Founding Fathers penned elaborate missives to one another. *These are some of History's greatest letters.*

On November 1, 1800 (just prior to the presidential election that year), Adams arrived in the new capital/Capital City, which had been relocated from Philadelphia to Washington, DC, to take up residence in the not-yet-completed White House. On his second evening in the manse's damp, unfinished rooms, he wrote to his wife: "Before I end my letter, I pray Heaven to bestow the best of Blessings on this House and all that shall hereafter inhabit it. May none but honest and wise men ever rule under this roof."

From his farm in Quincy, Massachusetts, where he had retired, John Adams' whispered final words, on July 4, 1826, were about his old rival-turned-confidant: "Thomas Jefferson survives." But Jefferson too had died at his home in Monticello just a few hours earlier.

In the thick of party conflict, back in the presidential race in 1800, Thomas Jefferson had written in a private letter: "I have sworn upon the altar of God eternal hostility against every form of tyranny over the mind of man."

This powerful advocate of liberty was born April 13, 1743, in Albemarle County, Virginia, inheriting from his father, a planter and surveyor, some 5,000 acres of land; and from his mother, a Randolph, a high standing in society.

Jefferson studied at the College of William and Mary, and then read law. In 1772, he married Martha Wayles Skelton, a widow, and took her to live in the majestic mountaintop mansion he had lovingly christened "Monticello."

Freckled and red-haired, tall and lanky, Jefferson was a tad shy about speaking in public. His eloquence flowed through his pen, and that is how he so greatly contributed to the patriot cause. At the age of thirty-three, Thomas Jefferson drafted the Declaration of Independence. This most significant American document was a mélange of both Jefferson's and Benjamin Franklin's making.

In 1785, Jefferson succeeded Benjamin Franklin as minister to France, and it was his sympathy for the French Revolution that prompted the conflict with elitist Alexander Hamilton, when Jefferson was Secretary of State in President George Washington's cabinet. The clash of minds and hearts between Jefferson and Hamilton resulted in Jefferson resigning his position in 1793.

The winds of political conflict brought about the emergence of that era's two political parties, the Federalists and the Democratic-Republicans, with Jefferson gradually assuming leadership of the Republicans who sympathized with the revolutionary cause in France. Championing states' rights, Jefferson opposed a strong centralized government.

Though his arguments were ofttimes quite heated, Jefferson was a reluctant candidate for President in 1796. As touched on above, he won the election by a mere three Electoral Votes.

Once the crisis in France was over, President Jefferson slashed Army and Navy expenditures. He also cut the budget and eliminated the tax on whiskey- a levy violently unpopular in the western portion of the new nation.

I must interject here that Thomas Jefferson's Secretary of the Treasury was Albert Gallatin of my home county of Fayette. I wrote two separate Chronicles about the phenomenal Gallatin in the first volume of *County Chronicles,* in which I stated that it was his financial wizardry that finally pulled the infant nation out of debt following the long and costly Revolutionary War. [America would not be involved in so long a struggle until Vietnam.] And it was Gallatin who lobbied Jefferson to repeal the hated Whiskey Tax, which was ruining frontier farmers. Fayette County, Pennsylvania, had been especially troublesome over the tax.

"Good will prevail."
-President George W. Bush, September 11, 2001

While in office as President, Jefferson sent a naval squadron to fight the Barbary pirates, who were playing havoc with American commerce in the Mediterranean. He purchased the Louisiana Territory from Napoleon in 1803, greatly enlarging our nation. Also through the financial know-how of Albert Gallatin, he financed the Lewis and Clark Expedition, which, as I penned in the premier volume of my *Chronicles,* became an unparalleled success, becoming the first overland exploration of the American West. The unknown was no longer unknown; and as a result, western expansion began.

After his second term, Jefferson retired to Monticello, where he never actually stopped working; writing, of course, and inventing (such things as America's first macaroni machine).

During his second term, Jefferson had been preoccupied in keeping America from any involvement in the raging Napoleonic wars, even though *both* England and France interfered with the neutral rights of American merchantmen. Jefferson's attempted solution, an embargo upon American shipping, worked poorly and was unpopular, to say the least.

Our Founding Fathers demonstrated a miscellany of weaknesses and strengths. Though brave and stalwart- since by declaring Independence, they were openly declaring themselves traitors to the mother country of England and would be hanged if caught- they were men, not gods. Washington himself was an imperfect god. They did not really know how their efforts would turn out- if America would endure.

In the above *Tribune* article, author/historian David McCullough mentioned that if John Adams visited modern America, he would be *outraged* over the role of money in politics today. "I think that he would find it appalling, or more so, than we do. Many say that is how it has always been. But it hasn't. When you have people who get elected... because they spend millions of their own dollars, as well as other people's... that is *not* the democracy the Founding Fathers intended." *Amen!*

McCullough, a Point Breeze/Pittsburgh native was awarded, in December 2006, the highest honor for an American citizen- the Presidential Medal of Freedom. "I've spent a good part of my working life writing and thinking about Presidents," the prolific, very readable author commented to the press, upon learning that he would receive the prestigious award. "So often things in life come full circle," he concluded.

In conclusion here, it is important to remember that the first words of the Declaration of Independence are "When in the course of *human* events..." To paraphrase the eloquent McCullough, the Founding Fathers were, when all was said and done, *human.* Though regarded as paragons, they were not perfect. But they left us a guiding star- an architectural plan- of what we could ideally create.

It is up to each generation to work toward that lofty goal.

As for *patriotism*: This Fourth-of-July word translates *love of country*, and *that* ideal is as pure and unspoiled as ever it was.

Happy birthday, America- and may God continue to hold you in the palm of His hand!

"SACO... A DIFFERENT KIND OF WAR"

"This was a different kind of war."
- Commander Milton E. Miles, USN, head of the SACO Agreement

"It has taken a long time for me to write about my years in the service," Guy Tressler began in his World War II memoirs. Mr. Tressler, born and reared in South Connellsville, Fayette County, Pennsylvania, was one of a select group of men who were scouts and raiders with the Sino-American Cooperative Organization known as SACO (pronounced "socko"), a covert unit organized by President Franklin Delano Roosevelt and Chinese Generalissimo Chiang Kai-shek, for intelligence and guerilla operations against the Japanese in the China-Burma-India theater of WWII. [*Sino*, akin to Sanskrit, translates "Chinese."] To relate to my readers that these missions were "dangerous" would be a gross understatement.

While harvesting World War II memories for "A Sentimental Journey or Praise the Lord and Pass the Ammunition," this volume, my research led me to Guy Tressler. Research is like that; each discovery unearthed is a stepping stone to yet another treasure.

Most people do not realize that not only was China an important ally in the fight against the Japanese during World War II, but the Chinese theater was one of the most critical- yet least known- of the entire war.

The United States Navy had a long tradition in China of keeping Chinese rivers and ports open to free commerce by using US gunboats. Soon after the Second World War began (and prior to the development of the atomic bomb), our naval leaders felt that an amphibious invasion of Japan would be necessary to end the war; and they believed that China would be the best springboard for such an invasion. Too, the Navy wanted to provide accurate weather information to our submarines and surface fleets operating in the western Pacific. Therefore, throughout China, they set up weather stations operated by US Naval personnel who worked closely with the local Chinese.

America wanted to keep a close eye on Japanese ship movements. Dozens of SACO scouts acted as "coastwatchers," secretly reporting the movements of Japanese ships. Though Japan controlled few areas of inland China, they controlled all of the Chinese seaports, a fact that led to the construction of the Burma Road, a vital supply line from India to China during the war era. And SACO trained hundreds of Chinese guerilla troops to fight the Japanese.

The organization's main proponent, US Naval Commander Milton Miles, had served in China for many years following World War I. Miles had a deep respect for the country and its people. SACO was born when Miles suggested the idea to his superiors, including President Roosevelt, who, upon hearing it, fully supported the plan.

Guy Tressler was one of a mere 2,500 valiant special-forces sent to China, the Gobi Desert and India to gather intelligence, ferry supplies, and report to the famed Flying Tigers, as well as to the Army and the Navy at sea. Tressler's guerilla demolition unit, together with other naval special units, evolved into today's elite Navy Seals. As with so many aspects of life, in war or peace, for Guy Tressler it all began with a twist of Fate.

It was December 1942, and Guy had just turned nineteen. "I didn't want to wait to be drafted," he told me. "I wanted to join the Marines. I had graduated from Connellsville High School the previous year and was working at the local glass plant, Anchor Hocking, from the time I was a senior. Due to the war, the plant had six-hour shifts. I worked from 7 p.m. to 1 a.m. So many boys had already been drafted, and so many others had joined. My oldest brother, Arn, was at Pearl Harbor when it was bombed. I simply could not stand by and wait to be drafted. I told my employer that I was going to volunteer for the service."

When Guy and two of his friends arrived in Pittsburgh at the Marine recruiting office, the enlistment quota was already filled, so they went across the way and joined the Navy. "It was destined to be," Tressler told me. "That wasn't the first time I had attempted to join the Marines to find their quota filled. The recruiting office was actually closed when we got there. I banged on the door, only to come face-to-face with a big gunnery sergeant, who bellowed, 'It's five o'clock; the office is closed! Come back tomorrow. Our quota's filled for t'day anyhow.' Well, I wasn't about to spend train fare to Pittsburgh again to make another try for the Marines, so the Navy got me."

Theirs was a delayed program, which afforded the three pals the opportunity to enjoy the holiday season with their families in Pennsylvania before departing for boot camp at Sampson Naval Base on Lake Geneva, New York.

"There, we lined up and received all of our clothes, dress blues, whites and dungarees, along with a seabag. Uncle Sam shipped our civilian clothes home, and from that point in time, we were strictly Navy," Guy laughed.

Boot camp stretched over ten weeks, beginning with shots. "Boot was tough," Guy told me. "But not nearly as tough as what I would endure later. The one thing that sticks out in my mind from that initial period of my service years is the fact that three recruits tried to go AWOL by crossing the frigid, rough waters of the lake in a makeshift raft. The trio drowned. The whole episode was quite a shock to all of us 'boots'."

A ten-day leave was the reward at the end of boot camp. However, Tressler had no sooner arrived home in Pennsylvania, when he received a telegram calling him back to camp without delay. Straightaway, he was sent to Brooklyn Armed Guard Center and from there to Norfolk, Virginia, where he entered gunnery school. Once that training was complete, it was back to Brooklyn at the Naval Ship Yards. Armed Naval Guards are those military personnel stationed aboard merchant ships during wartime to protect those ships from the enemy, mostly from submarines, but from air attacks as well.

"We had a lieutenant, j. g. (junior grade), in charge of us. We were twenty-five enlisted men, including signal and radiomen. Our ship was the *USS Brunswick*, a high-test gasoline and oil tanker– one of the very worst tubs to get on. Understand that when an oil tanker takes a hit, there is such a horrendous explosion that usually there are *no* survivors.

"Our first trip was to Cartagena," Guy informed, "a port in northwest Columbia, South America. Going down, in our fifteen-ship convoy, was without incident; we were empty. But coming back off Cape Hatteras was quite another matter. This route was known as 'Torpedo Alley,' and that is where we encountered our first enemy subs. In such a convoy, oil tankers and ammo ships are always in the middle for protection. As it turned out, we lost but one tanker on that return trip from Columbia, to a wolf-pack German U-boat.

"We proceeded on, clean up to Nova Scotia, to drop off our oil, zigzagging to avoid any more German submarines. I never got seasick in my life; but I saw a lot of fellas so sick ..." Guy shook his head, remembering, "well, I really felt sorry for them. It would not be right if I didn't tell you we were all pretty scared. I remember that, for days, coming up the coast, I could not sleep for the fear of being torpedoed. All of us were greenhorns except for our signalman, petty officer first class. He had been torpedoed twice, once on a tanker; thus, he kept us pretty well up on what to expect and do; though his tales did not make good bedtime stories, if you get my drift.

"Another thing I want to say," Tressler continued, "is that no ship wanted to fall behind a convoy. If one did, she was on her own; and the enemy always watched for this situation, so they could pick off that ship. There were times when we could not see our escorts or the other ships in the convoy; and there was no radio contact, only radar for detecting position. I recall a particular sea storm that caused the convoy to regroup, after which one ship was missing. We never did learn what happened to it."

Guy Tressler completed a total of six months of the dangerous duty on oil tankers, making one trip to Columbia; one to Venezuela; one to Gulfport, Mississippi, and another to Galveston, Texas. He was a gunner on each of those oil missions, on a big 20 mm that required three men to operate it. There were usually ten big guns on each vessel- at the stern (rear) of the ship; at the forward (bow) of the ship; four portside (left side, looking forward); and four starboard (right side, looking forward). Again, a well-earned leave was granted him. This time, Tressler got to take the whole leave, which was a fifteen-day reunion with his family in Pennsylvania.

"After I returned to Brooklyn, I was transferred to Solomons Island, off the coast of Maryland and Washington, DC. There, I was to await my next ship/tour of duty. The Navy, understand, doesn't allow for idle time; and before I knew it, I had become a gunnery instructor on the twenty and the forty millimeters. You see, I had twenty-twenty vision, and I was a crack shot. In fact, I had made third-class gunner's mate my first time out. From the onset, I had developed the nickname 'Trigger'."

The indefinable thing that propelled Guy Tressler into the China-Burma-India theater of war was, as touched on earlier, Destiny. "I had fallen out with my girl; and I was bored after several long months with being an instructor, stateside- bored with the day-in, day-out routine of teaching new recruits on the guns. My problem was that I was a damn-good shot. When I asked for an overseas assignment, I was told, in no-uncertain terms, by my commanding officer that I was needed right where I was; that I was slated to be kept on as a gunnery instructor; and the only way off that island for me was to volunteer for something... something big.

"Fate," Tressler declared to me during one of our interviews, "in the guise of a visiting, high-brass Navy officer, appeared before us on the drill field at 0800 the very next morning. He was asking for volunteers, and here is how he worded it: 'How would you like to be parachuted out of a plane into China behind the Japanese lines and live off the fat of the land?' I had my doubts about that last segment of his offer, but I immediately stepped forward. I might add that this officer was accompanied by a contingent from the War Department in Washington, DC."

Such was Guy Tressler's ticket into a shadow world of sinister jungles, secrecy, suspense, and constant danger. Before he shipped out, he had leave coming to him again, and he headed home for Pennsylvania. "Where Destiny had something else in store for me,"

Guy Tressler, Rogers One, somewhere in India, 1945

the ex-ranger smiled. "That weekend, I met Rose, who later became my wife."

"He wouldn't have volunteered for that special unit, if he had met me first," Rose added. "We fell in love at first sight."

When his all-too-short leave was over, Tressler was deployed to Fort Pierce, Florida, for underwater demolition and scout and raider training. He still did not *really* know what he had volunteered for, what his mission would actually entail, only that it required ten weeks of very special- very strenuous- training to meet the hazardous type of warfare he was about to participate in. That period of his time in the service proffered no leaves nor weekend passes. The specialized training was all hand-to-hand combat training, in addition to building physical endurance.

"And that is where they separated the men from the boys," Guy stated, remembering. "When swimsuits were the uniform of the day, we always cringed inwardly, because we knew it was going to be a tough day, to say the least. We would run out on a rock jetty, plunge into the water and swim the mile or more back to shore."

The unit was trained to hit the beaches in rubber boats. And their intense scout preparation was patterned after the Native American/guerilla-type warfare the legendary ranger Robert Rogers had skilled his men in during the French and Indian War.

For those readers who are movie buffs, the film *Northwest Passage* (in which sports hero Jim Thorpe played a minor role) illustrated the rigorous training Rogers required of his incomparable rangers in the dark American forests of the 1700s.

Since they were a scouting outfit, as well as demolition raiders, that aspect of their duty was also emphasized. Jungle missions would necessitate scouts on point.

Each new day began with one hour of physical exercise. For instance, the would-be raiders arranged themselves in two lines, facing one another, then lifted a twenty-foot coconut log and began tossing it back and forth, back and forth, from one group to the other. "... until the drill instructor felt we had had enough. We also did calisthenics using that log," Guy added.

"Physical fitness comes via daily conditioning," Tressler stated adamantly. "Learning the ropes on the obstacle course was hard work. There was a wicked series of obstacles, including cargo-net climbing. Too, we ran every morning, about a mile along the shore. Now, I don't mean to give the impression we jogged close to the water's edge. Oh, no! We ran on *dry* sand, which was hot, sweaty, and tough on the legs. Yes, it was rough-going; but I knew, once I got into action, it would all pay off.

"Swimming back to shore that mile or more proved an impossible task for some of the men, and a few flunked out of the program because of that. I felt pretty lucky about the swimming segment of the training," Guy related. "I went in a strong swimmer, because of the 'training' I had undergone before I even joined the service. Summers, in the Connellsville area, I swam back and forth across our Youghiogheny, and up and down that infamous river, often against the current. For those readers unfamiliar with the Yough, it is a *wild* river, raging at times, contrary all the time, with many deadly undertows. Growing up during the Great Depression, swimming was our favorite warm-weather pastime, when jobs were scarce and money tight. Those summers thus spent rendered me a darn good swimmer, and enabled me to pass the underwater-demolition requirements."

The raiders' training, which followed the conditioning program, commenced with hand-to-hand combat instruction. "We were taught how to protect ourselves when attacked at close range. One of the basic moves, when an enemy soldier attacked face-to-face, was to cross the arms at the wrists," Tressler demonstrated, "warding off a blow to throat or chest with a knife; and at the same time, hooking the right leg behind his, downing him with a combined shove at his chest; thus flipping the enemy backwards, giving us time to wield our knives."

Much of this segment of Guy Tressler's preparation consisted of Judo/self-defense training. The men were hardened to be alert and vigilant at all times. "The vigilance aspect of our schooling seemed almost unnecessary to some, yet helpful to others," he said, "as we were to discover later. It was constantly drilled into us to be in the best physical condition that we could each attain; to be ready, each of us, for the real thing, and to have a serious mind-set about our duty- whatever it might entail."

There were some who could not endure the rigorous training that the scouts and rangers demanded. Not all who volunteered made it through, and those men were transferred to duty elsewhere.

Arms training followed, and the would-be rangers who had not had any training in small arms would now have to qualify in the use of the .45 caliber pistol, the .45 Thompson submachine gun, the 30.06 rifle, and the M-1 carbine.

"Again, I was lucky. This phase of the training was, for me, no problem," Guy pointed out, "because I had entered the program as a gunnery instructor and had already qualified in those weapons at gunnery school and afterwards during sea duty in the armed guard. I remember that several men in my rubber boat crew expressed that they planned to stay close to me in combat. When they asked me how I had gotten to be such a crack shot, I told them that at home in Pennsylvania, I hunted a lot. Game came in handy back in the Depression to supplement our table; and I had always liked to target practice in the mountain area where I had been raised. Sweet home Pennsylvania had come through for me again."

Next came demolition training. This would be a good time to insert that Mr. Tressler stressed to me that the men never knew what to expect next, that everything was always "mum" and a "surprise." He reiterated too that "After lights-out each night, just when you thought you were settled in for a good, well-deserved sleep, the lights were flicked on- 0400 hours came mighty early! And let me tell you that when we hit the showers to clean up for chow at 0800, we had already put in what felt like a full day of intense training."

Florida's rustic Indian River in the Everglades was the scene of many a mock raid for those special forces during their training. Guy recalled waking one morning, while camping for a day and night on the river, to find a large rattlesnake at his feet. "From that day on, I was even more alert, and never once let down my guard," he told me. "In this Indian River area, our worst enemies were the sand flies, mosquitoes, and the snakes. There was no respite from them, *none.* But we were trained to keep still, in the event we were ever pinned down by our human enemy. And trust me, it is difficult to remain still and quiet when insects and other varmints are eating you alive! Even so, we had to learn to withstand this abuse so as not to be detected by the enemy."

One particular morning, after 0800 muster, the men set out with full gear- rifle, canteen, bedroll, pup tent, and helmet- on a forced twelve-mile march, alternating walking and running with a ten-minute break once in awhile. "I remember," Guy began, picking up his story, "our officer, a young ensign, whom many of us did not especially like, saying to me that he didn't know if he was going to be able to make it due to the blisters on his feet. I locked eyes with him and said, 'If I can make it, you can surely make it.' Among the many things I learned in my specialized training is that a person can always go further than he thinks he can... and that is a basic fact of life for everyone to become acquainted with. It has been the motivating thought that has accompanied me in my life's journey... but *every* life is a journey. Everyone can reach down and deep into his or herself and pull up a reserve of energy and warrior spirit that he or she never knew was there. And *that* is a darn good thing for anyone to be cognizant of."

When the intense conditioning and training came to an end, the scouts and rangers headed back to Fort Pierce for a good rest and a three-day liberty. Guy had received a letter from his serviceman brother that he too was in Florida, on the western coast. Tressler, not knowing if he would ever see Arn again, headed to Sarasota, only to discover that his brother had already shipped out. "When I returned to camp, his telegram was waiting for me: 'Shipping out. Don't come.' I still have that telegram."

Now it was official. Tressler's unit of scouts and rangers were christened "Rogers One." Attached to the Sino-American Cooperative Organization/SACO, Guy Tressler's outfit would now be deployed to fight. There were 125 in his Rogers One unit, and only about 2,500 total of combined Navy and Marines, along with several Coast Guard personnel in SACO during the war.

I must inform my readers that each of those men had a hefty price on his head of what was equivalent to a thousand American dollars, without a doubt, a tempting sum. Commander (later Vice-Admiral) Milton E. Miles of Naval Group China, the man who gave SACO their orders, persevered as his personal bounty escalated from $5,000 to a *million* (American) dollars before the war's end.

Those courageous SACO warriors made up the core of the guerilla-amphibious organization of Americans and Chinese operating in the China-Burma-India theater of war during World War II. They were only a few specially trained men, but the influence they had on the final outcome of that war was no small feat.

After taking a sooty, five-day train ride to San Pedro, California, Tressler and his unit awaited a transport, which materialized within two weeks in the *General George C. Norton*, a ship which had been given the soubriquet "Galloping Norton," due to the fact that it made so many trips back and forth to the China-Burma-India theater of operations.

"After a few days out at sea, I could clearly see the difference between the Atlantic and the Pacific, the Atlantic being so green, the Pacific so blue and so much warmer," Guy reflected. "In fact, I did a lot of *reflecting* on the *Norton,*" Tressler quipped when I read him that passage. "*A lot.* It was my first time in the Pacific, and this tour of duty would be much different than previous ones. We still didn't know our exact destination; and, as it had been with German subs in the Atlantic, we were constantly on the alert for Japanese submarines in the Pacific.

"Our first stop was Pearl Harbor, where we stayed one day with no liberty, taking on supplies. And it was at Pearl," Guy recalled, "where we saw our first Japanese sub. It had been captured and brought in and was tied up alongside us. We were no sooner out to sea when we had to turn around and come back. An Army colonel, who had been down on C-Deck, gambling with the Black soldiers, had gotten himself killed in a crap game. Since we were only three days out, we returned to Pearl with his body and the alleged murderer."

The *USS Norton* had three decks. In 1944, the United States armed forces were segregated, and C-Deck carried the Black soldiers on that ship.

"The trip to China, after that, was without incident," Tressler remarked, "the days filled with refreshing our training. After some time, the destroyer escorts left the *Norton* on her own, as we zigzagged our slow way toward Australia. Japanese subs were spotted several times, and we were constantly on alert. When the general alarm sounded, we all rushed to our gun stations, ready for action. One of the enemy subs surfaced for air and to recharge. Suffice it to say that Japanese sub was what we called a 'dead duck'."

The days were long and hot, the nights a bit cooler. "For the sailors on board ship who were crossing the equator for the first time, there was a special ritual," Guy laughed with the remembering. "You become an 'old salt' in our Navy once you've crossed the equator. For sailors who had crossed *both* the equator and the International Date Line, they entered the elite membership of the Pollywogs, Neptunes, and Shellbacks... it was all great fun."

As the *Norton* rounded the southern tip of the vast continent of Australia, Aussie pilots were picked up to guide it safely into the port of Melbourne. As at Pearl, no one was permitted off the vessel, and again supplies were taken on, including fresh water, which had been rationed. Thirty-six hours later, the *Norton* was back in the open arms of the sea, her bow pointed due west then north into the South Indian Ocean.

"Many days later, the blue Indian Ocean faded away, off our stern. We had been at sea so long now, I quit keeping track of the days; like the blue of that ocean, they seemed to fade, one into the next, and it was easy to lose track," Guy penned in his memoirs.

After a timeless time, the ship slowed and took on another pilot whose job was tricky, to say the least, for the *Norton* had entered the Ganges-Brahmaputra Delta, a massive Indian swamp fed by three large rivers and a variety of small streams. "In the center of high ground stood the sparkling city of Calcutta, a *massive* port, within the province of Bengal. The haze that hung over the area was from the cow dung used for cooking fires. The sights, smells, sounds, customs, clothing, the animals... and oh yes, the oppressive heat- hottest place I have ever experienced in my life- were nearly unfathomable. Calcutta was an experience I could *never* have imagined," Guy affirmed with zeal. "The people looked as though they were from another world... a constant source of amazement and awe."

I could read that awe on Mr. Tressler's face and on the timbre carried on his voice. In fact, his face and voice were replete with memories, recollections of the experiences that had molded him into the man he became.

"Being Navy on A-Deck, we were the first on the muster list," Guy related. But it was not until the following morning that his unit of 125 rangers disembarked and boarded their transportation, Army 6x6s, for a place just a few miles outside Calcutta called "Camp Kanjupara."

"Our quarters were temporary," Tressler recounted. "Sleeping cots were set up in six-man tents. Darkness fell almost immediately, and everything became extraordinarily still. Except for the sounds of the animals- elephants, tigers, jackals and other wild beasts- the silence of an Indian jungle on a dark night needs to be experienced to be realized. It is most impressive. After awhile, I fell into a fitful, dreamy slumber that harmonized with my surroundings. All of a sudden, I was startled out of my reverie by a noise and a rushing gust of air. My first night there I could not sleep for the jackals running in and out of the tent.

"We were warned to check our shoes before putting them on each morning. The deadly poisonous cobras, it seemed, liked the warmth and the smell of leather, and would slither into footwear and curl up inside," Guy remembered vividly. "It was at Camp Kanjupara where we packed away our uniforms. Now, we were issued army khakis minus any insignias, though we kept our dog tags. Now, too, we were initiated into the world of secretness."

Dressed for the hot, stifling weather and jungle warfare, Tressler's unit, Rogers One, fought a hit-and-run, stealth war far behind the fluid Japanese lines. Often they donned

Chinese coolie garb, complete with wide straw hats; and, thus disguised, went into the field with the Chinese in order to succeed at a mission. "The Chinese hid us on their sampans [flat-bottomed skiffs used in eastern Asia, usually propelled by two short oars], and that's how we navigated the rivers, right through the Japanese lines," Guy gestured with a flutter of his hand. Japanese spies and people in their pay were everywhere. In addition, the men also had to worry about the Chinese Communists, "... who were even worse."

As revealed earlier, Tressler's unit received their orders directly from Commander Milton Miles, who received his directly from Admiral Ernest J. King, Chief of Naval Operations. China's General Tai-Li (pronounced "die lee"), who was, at that time, in charge of China's version of the C.I.A., was *very* influential in SACO operations.

Tai-Li wanted Americans to come to China to train Chinese guerilla troops to fight the Japanese; and shrewd commander that he was, he was thinking about the long-term benefit of having a well-trained army of Chinese Nationalist troops to fight the Chinese Communists after the war. Miles and Tai-Li forged a friendship that transcended the suspicions held by colleagues and superiors on both sides. Brutal and feared but fair and honest, Tai-Li was one of the most enigmatic characters in the Chinese theater of World War II.

Tragically, General Tai-Li was killed in a plane crash in March 1946, and three years later, China fell to the Communists. Several leading historians believe that if Tai-Li had not died in that crash, the fate of China might well have taken a different turn- and after completing the research for the MASH/Korean War Chronicle, this volume, I think they might be right.

Though it was not as strict as training camp had been in Florida, and no military insignias sported Rogers One attire, Camp Kanjupara was still very much the Navy. The men were mustered early every morning, received briefings, and kept in top physical condition for what was yet to come.

"What spare time there was could be spent in Calcutta, learning the customs and soaking up that Far-Eastern civilization," Tressler informed me. "I will never forget the natives in their white attire, *dhoti panjabi* and turbans... *sparkling white*; the Brahma cattle free to roam the streets due to the religious beliefs; the dead lying in the open, covered with sheets, until the people tossed sufficient *annas* [a former monetary unit of Burma, India and Pakistan equal to 1/16 rupee] on them [the fee for someone] to take them to the burning ghats on the Houghly River, where their remains would be cremated; the cremation fires ever-burning, and the magnificent temples, *dazzling* amidst the dusky- unimaginable- poverty. As unpredictable as the Indians could be at times, we really could not help liking them.

"There were five of us in my unit who stayed together much of the time during our tour of duty with SACO, and over the long years since, we five have remained close, catching up with one another at our annual SACO reunions. India was still under British rule during the war, quite different than it is now. Though the Indian populous were not especially fond of the British, they depended on them back then," Tressler remarked.

Finally the day came when Guy's unit was moved to a camp from whence they would be involved even more deeply in the stealth war they had volunteered to fight. The new camp was not quite completed when Rogers One arrived. Located about ten miles from Calcutta, its name was "Camp Knox."

"I remember that it was guarded by the Gurkhas [soldiers from Nepal], who were fierce little men with wicked-looking curved knives. It was rumored around camp that the Gurkhas were not initiated into their corps until they could sever the head of a water buffalo in a single stroke. I don't know for certain about that; but I know one thing for fact- they sure hated the Japanese.

"Again, our mission, basically, was to gather intelligence, above and beyond the raider and scout work we did involving guerilla warfare," Guy revealed. "Intelligence included Japanese troop movements. We'd spy on them to see what they were up to, note their supplies- anything and everything we could observe, really; and we'd report weather conditions to the famed 'Flying Tigers' and to Admiral Nimitz, who was in charge of the US fleet of operations in the Pacific. Our 'coast-watchers' constantly reported on Japanese ship movements, and this led the US to destroy a tremendous number of Japanese vessels."

SACO was a *highly* secret organization. Even their flag was mysterious with its trio of question marks, exclamation points and asterisks. The banner fittingly translated "What the Hell?" And suffice it to say that "hell" is what SACO gave to the Japanese.

Commander Milton Miles himself created the pennant in 1934 when, in the Pacific, he was a junior officer aboard the destroyer *USS Wickes.* The story goes, according to the SACO web site, that occasionally during tight maneuvers, one of the ships in the fleet would do something unexpected. During such incidents, Miles wanted to send a pennant up the mast, asking the pithy question "What the Hell?" Milton asked his wife to create such a pennant without using obscenities. She suggested using the symbols that make up the unique flag, telling her husband that when journalists wanted to symbolize an obscenity that is what they did.

Miles used the pennant in a lighthearted way for years- until 1939. Then, he was skipper of the destroyer *John D. Edwards,* off the coast of southeast China in the South China Sea, where the Japanese Navy was harassing the coastal town of Hainan, which included a number of American missionaries. When the *Edwards* arrived at the scene, Miles saw several large Japanese naval vessels bombarding the village. The Japanese flagship hoisted a pennant warning the American destroyer to leave, which put Commander Miles in a bit of a quandary. He had been given orders to protect the American missionaries in that village. After considering the situation for a few minutes, Miles decided to ignore the Japanese threat and hoisted a pennant of his own- "What the Hell?"

Taken aback, the Japanese halted their bombardment, giving Miles time to maneuver his destroyer between the Japanese naval ships and the village. The Japanese commander was confused over the strange banner, since it was not in any code book he had. Wisely, he decided to err on the side of caution and backed the Japanese fleet away from the defenseless village. Milton Miles went ashore and gathered up the missionaries, then departed the subsequent morning, with the Japanese, out on the lapping waters, still trying to decipher that confounding visual message. Throughout World War II, Miles' unusual pennant became the unofficial emblem of SACO.

When the orders came from Milton Miles for Rogers One to go over the Hump into China, they were more than ready. The Hump is that portion of the Himalayan Mountain Range that separates India from China. SACO had a base in northern Assam (in NE India) in the foothills of the Himalayan Mountains. "There, the Navy made oxygen needed for flights over the Hump. This same base served as a supply camp for our groups inside China," Tressler told me.

Close to the border of Burma, the town of Jorhat was nestled deep in the shadows of a jungle, with the Japanese only about twenty miles distant. Here, Japanese patrols were often attacked and killed by the bearded Sikhs, Indians who fought with ferocity and distinction in the British army. "My mission," Tressler said, taking up his story once again, "was to ride shotgun on the ammunition train to Jorhat. The train consisted of the engine with attached tender, two cars loaded with ammo, and my car in the center. There were two .50 caliber machine guns, loaded and ready to fire, one at the door on each side of the car I was in, along with my bunk, and a supply of rations. The trip took four days, during which we made several stops, one to transport the train, one car at a time onto a barge, to the other side of the river, where the train was put back on tracks again. I could never understand why there was no bridge across that river.

"I remember too" Guy pointed to a faded photograph in one of his scrapbooks, "that we stopped at this particularly remote village to take on charcoal, water and supplies. It was during that brief pause in our rail journey when I learned that this village was one of the camps that the renowned white hunter, Frank Buck, used when he captured his tigers."

Texan Frank Buck (1883-1950) was a notorious adventurer, white hunter and animal collector, as well as a movie director and producer, most famous for his 1930s and 40s jungle adventure films. When I asked Mr. Tressler if he had ever encountered a tiger in the wilds, he answered, "I wasn't concerned with tigers, though on one occasion, I did spot a crouching tiger in the tall grass- an unforgettable sight, to be sure. Stealthy humans were my main concern... and considerably more dangerous. I will say that big cats are like communists, you wouldn't want to turn your back on either.

"While on this particular ammo run," Guy continued, "I developed a large carbuncle under my left arm, which started to hurt badly. In fact, it had gotten so I could hardly keep my arm at my side. I told the engineer about it, for I was afraid if we did get hit by a Japanese patrol that I would not be able to operate the machine gun properly. Thank God there was a base at the next stop, where I had it lanced, giving me full use of my arm again. I remember that the British doctor at the base, while treating my arm, asked me to what branch of the service I was attached. When I told him, 'I'm Navy,' he exclaimed, 'What th' hell is Navy doing here in the bloody jungle!' I declined to answer that question.

"We finally reached the railroad yards at Jorhat with our load of ammo. Not long after, I was back at Camp Knox, where I asked, since I had come close to not being able to use my gun arm, why I was sent as the *only* gunner on that train of important cargo. 'Better to lose one man than two,' came the rapid-fire response to my query.

"Two weeks later I came down with malaria and dysentery, and I can truthfully tell you," Tressler avowed, "that was the sickest I have ever been in my life. I figured I would be left behind, because the men in my unit were being called up as replacements in camps throughout China. While still back at Camp Knox, it came over the loudspeaker that President Roosevelt had died."

The date was April 12, 1945. Vice President Harry S. Truman was sworn into office at 7:09 p.m., a firm hand on his family Bible, the weight of the world on his shoulders. Truman looked straight ahead through his thick, round glasses, repeating with intensity the concluding words after the Chief Justice, "So help me God." The sudden, fervent way the passionate little man from Missouri kissed the Bible at the end of the ceremony impressed everyone present. It had all taken less than a minute. After the swearing in, Truman asked Mrs. Roosevelt if there was anything he could do for her. Her sincere reply, after laying her hand on one of those weighted but capable shoulders, was "Is there anything I can do for *you*, Mr. President?" Death had warranted that the buck be passed- while he was in office, it always stopped with Harry.

"When Rogers One crossed the Hump into China, I was with them after all," Guy stated with satisfaction. "It seemed like a century, ever a long time, since our scout and ranger training in Florida. Thank God we repeatedly refreshed that training. We would need it as 'coastwatchers,' weather observers, radiomen, and teachers/trainers for the Chinese guerillas. We also picked up many downed flyers, and we reported to our fleet at sea and the 14th Army Air Force any information vital to the invasion of China. When all was said and done, Rogers One lost but one man, Al Parsons, though he lived to tell his tale.

"Al and a Chinese captain had been cautiously making their way through some tall grass, when a Japanese patrol sprang up, overpowered them and took them captive. Al was eventually taken to Japan," Tressler revealed. "Though he suffered many tortures, he survived it all, was liberated after the war, came back home and lived to be ninety-one... a perfect example of the inextinguishable human spirit. China's General Tai-Li and his guerillas tried more than once to free Parsons, right after he had been captured, but to no avail."

Guy Tressler today, holding SACO's famous "What the Hell?" pennant

Unique and unprecedented, SACO's joint military effort between the United States and the Chinese Nationalist forces is one of the most interesting stories about the Chinese theater in World War II. SACO's mission in China was *so* highly secretive that ten years after they were discharged from the service, its members were still under a gag order. Their missions often took them deep into the jungles, far behind enemy lines, and hundreds of miles from supplies. In addition to their extraordinarily nerve, those stalwart rangers were incredibly resourceful. This was the first and only time in American history that an American military unit had been completely integrated into a foreign military force. In so many ways was SACO remarkable- and it was also one of the most *effective* combat forces in World War II.

At this writing, 2007, there are less than 2,000 SACO still alive. They are all in their eighties, and yearn to keep in touch with one another via their SACO newsletters and magazines. In addition, many attend the annual SACO reunions.

Pennsylvanian Guy Tressler performed numerous dangerous missions along the coast of China, after going over the Hump with Rogers One, volunteering several times to go deep into the tangled web of secrecy and danger behind enemy lines, in the heat of war to 1946.

I am proud to call him "friend." Proud, too, to state that there were several other Pennsylvania men in Rogers One and SACO.

"What I missed most was my mother's good home cooking. And what got me through some of the most precarious times, when my life dangled from a thread, were my good mother's prayers, my own faith in God, and my intense combat training. As difficult as that conditioning and training had been, as I told you, it saved my life on many occasions.

"In retrospect, I am proud to have answered my country's clarion call at her time of need and peril; and I am even prouder to have served in such a *vital* covert intelligence unit.

"I want to say for the record," Guy said with eyes that had become suddenly moist, "I never hated the enemy. My motto has always been that a person cannot have both God and hatred in his heart. I simply and quite honestly felt that no nation should try to rule the world. I felt compelled to duty, to my country and to Freedom, which is a God-given right to all humankind." Again, Mr. Tressler's face was readable, mirroring the emotion he was feeling. "And I especially wanted to do *my* part to bring about an earlier end to the war... and *that*, in essence, is what I felt we did."

Guy Tressler was impressively decorated and honorably discharged from the Navy on March 9, 1946, coming home to marry his cameo-pretty sweetheart, Rosemary Capo. The Tresslers have been married, at this writing, for sixty years. They have three grown children, Sandra Tressler-Russell, Guy D. Tressler III, and Mark D. Tressler, and at this point in time, two grandchildren, Brennen and Devon Tressler.

"There's something else," Guy told me before our interview concluded. "Something of which I am most proud. My grandson, Brennen Tressler, just graduated from the Navy Great Lakes boot camp in Illinois. He has keenly expressed his intention of becoming a Navy Seal. 'I want to be like *you*, Pap.' That's what he has always told me."

When I asked to see Guy's medals, he brought them out; and I indicated the largest and most conspicuous of the honors, remarking that I had never seen such a decoration. "Likely you haven't," the enigmatic Tressler responded with a slight smile. "General Chiang Kai-shek gave me that medal for my service to his country during World War II."

 "Haunted Pennsylvania"

"Issue the orders, sir, and I will storm Hell!"- Gen. "Mad" Anthony Wayne in response to Gen. George Washington over the taking of the British garrison at Stony Point, NY, 1779

"I am the very man you want."
- Gen. Wayne to President Washington, regarding Wayne's command of the expedition into Indian /Ohio country, 1794

"It pleases me greatly to build this fort in the very midst of this grand emporium of the hostile Indians of the west. When it is finished, I defy the English, the Indians, and all the devils in Hell to take it!"
-Gen. "Mad" Anthony Wayne, August 1794, in regard to Fort Defiance (now Defiance, Ohio)

He is one of Pennsylvania's favorite sons, the stuff of legends, and a dynamic hero of the American Revolution and subsequent Indian wars. Anthony Wayne was born near Philadelphia, at what was Waynesborough, in Chester County, Pennsylvania, on January 1, 1745. He was named for his grandfather, who, before immigrating to America, had fought with the British Army in the Irish-lamented Battle of the Boyne.

Not much of Anthony Wayne's early life indicated that he would become a legend. Any outstanding boyhood accolades he owed to his family's social position. Due to that position, he received a good education, though he was not an especially good student. He liked mathematics, and this is likely why he trained as a surveyor, which accounted for the physical endurance he acquired even before he joined the army.

In 1765, when his studies were complete in Philadelphia, Wayne journeyed, at the request of Benjamin Franklin (who owned land there) to Nova Scotia, to survey the land and catalogue its natural resources. However, Wayne relinquished the project after a year and returned to Pennsylvania to help out with the family farm and tannery, in partnership with his father.

My research revealed that the only thing that really stood out about Wayne in his youth was his fervor for all matters military. Like all great military figures, Anthony Wayne was born to lead a wartime army; "failures" at other endeavors thrust him toward that destiny. Wayne would get his chance at a military career- for the winds of war had begun to howl.

He had already started to make a name for himself as a leader while on the Pennsylvania Legislature for his fervent, ofttimes fiery, belief in Liberty and Independence. He served from 1774 to 1775; then, with the outbreak of the Revolutionary War, he raised a military unit of his own, of which he was promptly made colonel. The date was January 3, 1776. The unit was the Fourth Pennsylvania Battalion.

During the American Revolution, George Washington needed every man he could get, as well as every good leader he could muster. All a man needed for rank and privilege in the Continental Army was influence and an ardent desire to serve. Wayne had both, and though clichéd as the phrase has become, I cannot help stating here that he most assuredly had what it takes to lead men into battle and to inspire them to victory.

During his first command, he saw action with General Benedict Arnold in the Battle of Three Rivers, covering, in a rear-guard action, the American retreat from Quebec. Wayne was wounded in that fight, and was subsequently promoted to brigadier general.

At Brandywine Creek, he fought like a lion, while Washington and his defeated force retreated again to safety. Remaining in the thick of the action till the end of the bloody eight-year struggle that was America's fight for Independence, Wayne was well on his way to becoming a legend in his own time.

He shared the terrible hardships, the inconceivable suffering, of Valley Forge with George Washington and the Continental Army during the long, frigid winter of 1777-78. And Wayne was the undisputed hero of Stony Point, New York, when he and his troops captured the garrison there, a fortress one writer called the "... strongest British post on the Hudson River."

It was during that period when Wayne earned the lasting soubriquet "Mad Anthony." The general's troops christened him thus owing to his fearlessness and his quick, fiery temper.

Anthony Wayne, like George Washington, was one of an elite few military figures who never exhibited the least bit of nerves in the heat of battle. Though he appeared fearless and was often audacious in his strategy, Wayne was neither foolhardy nor reckless. His movements were always well-thought-out, and this *must* be emphasized, due to his mad moniker.

Allow me to share with you a bit about the Battle of Stony Point, which elevated "Mad" Anthony Wayne to the status of hero, and wove around him a shimmering legend, one that was told round many a Continental campfire and Yankee pub hence.

At King's Ferry loomed the formidable British-held Stony Point. The fort occupied a site about one hundred and fifty feet high, atop a rocky bluff on the western side of the Hudson River. Three sides were bordered by water, the fourth by a murky swamp. The fortress possessed a series of redoubts and a large number of cannons- placed strategically to drive off attack. The garrison was made up of about 500 well-equipped British, who had been making it quite hazardous for American troops to use the Hudson. Are you starting to get the bleak picture?

Washington felt that it was *imperative* to destroy the British post at the Point; but at the same time, he was more cognizant than anyone of what a *dangerous* undertaking it would be. Knowing the importance of this battle, Washington saw "Mad Anthony" as the *only* choice for the near-impossible feat. When he put the subject to Wayne, that general drew himself up to his full height and replied with his characteristic, unbridled zeal, "Issue the orders, sir, and I will storm Hell!"

Actually, Wayne had been contemplating the capture of Stony Point for some time, and he did not have to *convince* Washington that he could do it. The plan was kept unusually secret. Special troops were selected- from Connecticut, Massachusetts, Virginia, North Carolina and, of course, from Wayne's Pennsylvania.

On the night of 15 July 1779, General Wayne and his men began their march from Fort Montgomery. For eight hours, they struggled over narrow mountain trails, securing any civilians they encountered en route to the Point. Washington had always said that New York and New Jersey were full of spies and Tories, the willing ears and eyes of the British; so the securing of anyone they happened upon was absolutely necessary to avoid detection and consequently losing the vital element of surprise.

When the Americans arrived at Sprintsteel's Farm, two miles from Stony Point, they were told, for the first time, just what their mission was.

Under cover of darkness, the plan was a three-pronged assault. The smallest force attacked first, firing their muskets at the center front, this to draw the attention of the British and create an all-important diversion. From the south, a silent approach was made toward the garrison, stealthily, from Haverstraw Bay. Led by Wayne himself, this was the largest of the 340-man force. A second silent approach, from the north, occurred concurrently, across the bridge at King's Ferry.

The two silent groups had no loaded muskets, only fixed bayonets and pikes, so that no over-anxious shot or shots and no accidental discharges would alert the enemy.

Musket fire from the center column was the signal to the silent units to each begin their approach. To avoid confusion in the blackness of the night, the silent factions, north and south alike, sported pieces of white paper in their hats.

At midnight, the storming of Stony Point commenced with the sharp reports of American musket fire. Inside, the British shook off sleep and scrambled in the darkness, with the roused garrison soon showering death upon the stalwart Americans via cannon and musket fire of their own. Despite the heavy opposition, the carefully planned attack persisted, for each American present knew what his duty was.

Wayne's force was briefly fired upon as they waded across the sandbar, and "Mad Anthony" was grazed when a bullet shrieked across his forehead. Nevertheless, he remained in control of the assault, though his men carried him over the parapet. The heroic efforts of Wayne and his troops resulted in the British flag being hauled down from its staff over Stony Point. When the boys ran the American Stars and Stripes up the pole, Wayne gazed at it a long, thoughtful moment. It was a *beautiful* flag. No painting, no sculpture, no poem or piece of music could equal it. It took his breath, as it had already captured his heart.

British prisoners numbered 543. Sixty-three British were killed in the action; the number of British wounded is unknown. The Americans lost only fifteen men, while eighty-three were wounded. General Wayne sent a joyous message to General George Washington when Stony Point was captured: "The fort and garrison with Col. Johnston are ours. Our officers and troops behaved like men who are determined to be free."

Stony Point was not only a resounding victory, it was a major morale boost for the American Revolution. Succinctly put, it was just the shot of adrenaline Washington's army needed at that express moment- that precarious moment- in time.

After seeing more heated action in South Carolina and thence in Georgia, Wayne distinguished himself even further, ending the war as a major general, a promotion long overdue.

When he returned home to Pennsylvania in 1783, his health was poor. His time in the field had taken its toll. However, the redoubtable Wayne recovered sufficiently to take an active part, then, in the Pennsylvania Assembly, as well as in the Constitutional Convention.

Civilian life, as it had been before the war, was not his cup of tea. I can imagine that he considered himself lucky that sufficient unrest on the frontier- especially to western Pennsylvania- warranted an army to subdue the Indians in neighboring Ohio country.

The British, still an irritating presence in the west and to the north of the newly formed United States, were smarting from the loss of their American colonies and were urging the Indians to evermore atrocities against the American settlers. In fact, due to British incitation, the Pennsylvania frontier was aflame with Indian aggression.

When George Washington chose Wayne for commander-in-chief of the country's first standing army, "Mad Anthony," ever-lastingly duty-bound, replied: "I am the very man you want." The feisty general also affirmed to Washington that another Native American victory over federal troops "... would be irredeemably ruinous to the reputation of the Government." He was referring to the back-to-back fatal expeditions of Harmar and St. Clair, which had been ignominiously tromped by Native forces. Thus Wayne began at once to reorganize the army.

As always, he was a strict disciplinarian; and by August 20, 1794, his grueling preparations had come to fruition.

This was the day, too, when the long-waiting Indian confederation would meet "Mad Anthony" in battle. The Native force was led by an influential Shawnee chief named Wehyahpiherhrsehnwah, Blue Jacket, in association with Little Turtle, a Miami chief, and Buckongahelas, a Delaware.

It should be noted that Cornplanter, the great Pennsylvania chief, kept his Senecas from lining up against the fledgling new nation of the United States. If the Senecas would have thrown in with the above Native confederation, it is not likely that Wayne would have been as successful.

Let it also be said that General Wayne sent peace invitations to the Native chiefs *before* the big fight at the Timbers, but his olive-branch petition was rejected for two reasons. Firstly, the Indians had become keyed up for a good fight; and secondly, the Natives believed they would be aided by their British allies.

When the skies opened, and a deluge of rain fell upon the large Indian camp at Fallen Timbers, the Natives received their first bad omen of what was to come. Across the turning pages of history, weather has been the "Great Determinator" at more than one significant juncture.

The Americans under "Mad Anthony" were about 4,000 strong. At dawn the day of the battle, the general's troops rose to the visceral beat of the reveille drum. Within an hour, they had formed their battle lines; but again the skies poured rain, so heavily, in fact, that their march was delayed an hour.

At seven that fateful morning, the rain had diminished to a descending mist. Wayne's force started forward, following the Maumee portage trail downriver- like a great and powerful mowing machine- toward Fallen Timbers. There, Blue Jacket and about 2,000 Indians awaited him amidst a tangle of forest and a jumble of downed trees, their war paint smeared and streaked by the Great Spirit Manitou's tears, rendering those painted faces even more frightening.

Indians were never known for their patience, and before Wayne's army arrived, the Native force, waiting in the damp chill, had dwindled down to somewhere around 1,000 warriors. There are those historians who would quote an even smaller number. It should be noted that the Sauk (also Sac) and Fox had departed earlier, since there was not enough food to sustain the original numbers of Indians who had gathered.

The great clash of the two worlds, Red and White, took place in Ohio country (just south of Toledo), in a spot where a tornado had hacked out a swath of forest, thus the name "Fallen Timbers."

The odds were with Wayne; and his resounding victory over the Native Americans led to his Treaty of Greenville the following year, opening the western territory to settlement.

At the end of the Battle of Fallen Timbers, the defeated Indians were driven, under Wayne's guns, to the British Fort Miami, about three miles distant, where they called to the British regulars to assist them. The gates remained closed.

When the Americans, in full strength, came into view a short time later, drums beating, General Wayne took note of the situation and issued crisp orders. His troops spent three days burning the Natives' crops, including their vegetables- i.e., the "Three Sisters," beans, corn and squash- the grain and the orchards, as well as the Indians' trading posts and stores round about.

The watching British were taken aback by the *effrontery* of the Americans. In fact, Wayne and his aide, William Henry Harrison, boldly rode in plain sight of the garrison, while a few of the Pennsylvania and Kentucky sharpshooters hurled a loud volley of curses against the British. This so angered those inside that a captain therein grabbed a torch and was about to put it to a cannon pointed directly at the "rabble in arms," when his commanding officer stopped him, threatening to run him through.

In spite of his intervening action, the CO, one Major Campbell, sent a biting message to "Mad Anthony," complaining of the profanities and insults and demanding by what authority Wayne's troops trespassed upon the precincts of the British garrison. [Ohio was not yet part of the United States.]

Let's just say that "Mad Anthony" replied in terms even less cordial than the oaths of his sharpshooters, informing Campbell that his only chance of safety was silence and civility, asserting that Fort Miami had been constructed in contravention to the Treaty of Paris (which was supposed to have ended hostilities at the close of the Revolutionary War).

Beyond breaking the might of the western tribes, another of the results of the Battle of Fallen Timbers was the surrender to the United States of Miami, Niagara, Detroit, Mackinac, and other posts hitherto held by the British, from which they had assisted and encouraged Native hostilities against the Americans.

Settlers began pouring rapidly into the Ohio country, known yet as "Indian country," felling the trees and turning the soil, while the Shawnee and other Native tribes were pushed ever westward before this great White tide of immigration, further and further away from the Ohio River Valley they had so loved.

It was the end of the half-century of virtually non-stop Indian wars on the Pennsylvania frontier. As with all wars, hostilities did not terminate with the swiftness of a pen touched to parchment or a candle quenched by a sudden gust of wind. Historian Allan W. Eckert aptly points out in his spine-tingling *That Dark and Bloody River* that there were scattered hit-and-run attacks after Fallen Timbers, up and down the Ohio.

The beaten, despondent Indians apprehended for some time that they were well on the path of yesterday. After Fallen Timbers, there was no doubt that it was over. The old ways were now lost forever.

With their defeat at the Timbers went their lands and their way of life. Only Tecumseh, the eminent Shawnee chief, had held out, still, and to his own death would hold out, refusing to enter any and all agreements with the Americans. He stated, at the time, to Blue Jacket, a whistling cold wind the symbolic accompaniment to his words: "You are my friend, Blue Jacket, and you will always be so, but this is a matter that goes beyond friendship. If you make peace with the Americans... you will live to regret it."

As for Wayne, some historians believe that his popularity was so great after his victory at Fallen Timbers that even the Presidency was within his reach.

Unfortunately for him, however, the rigors of the field had taken again a serious toll on his body. In 1796, he was fifty-one, past middle age in an era when most did not live beyond sixty. Gout and other health issues plagued him. In the autumn of that year, on his way to Pittsburgh, from fighting Indians in the west (Michigan), he became seriously ill with stomach gout at Erie. Several excruciating weeks later, he passed away there, at the quarters of the post commander, in the newly constructed blockhouse on Presque Isle, now Erie, Pennsylvania. The date was December 15, 1796.

In accord with his petition, he was buried beneath the flagpole. Actually, the general had formally requested that he be buried, wearing his uniform, in a plain wooden coffin, at the foot of the flagstaff of the post's blockhouse. His initials were carved into the top of the coffin, his age and the year of his death marked on the lid with brass tacks. And thus his body remained for the subsequent twelve years.

But his tale does not end here. A dozen years after Wayne's passing, his daughter Margaretta, thirty-eight, became ill, and from her sickbed, beseeched her brother, Colonel Isaac Wayne, who was a year her junior, to bring their father's remains back home, to be placed in the family burial plot in their home area of Radnor, Pennsylvania.

In the spring of that year, Colonel Wayne set out, in a light two-wheeled buggy, on the long journey from the southeastern corner to the northwestern corner of the state.

He enlisted the services of Dr. J.C. Wallace to handle the disinterment. Wallace was the physician whom his father had requested from his death bed. However, at the time of General Wayne's final illness, Dr. Wallace had been stationed at Pittsburgh, about 100 miles distant, and he had not made it in time to aid the dying hero. Anthony Wayne's son, preferring to remember his father as he had been in life, opted not to attend the disinterment.

What follows is a series of events that can only be described as bizarre and macabre. Firstly, when the general's coffin was opened, to the astonishment of all present, it was discovered that his body had not decomposed. With the exception of a bit of decay on one leg and that foot, the body was preserved. Clearly, Colonel Wayne could not transport his father's body the long, rough way back home in a sulky!

Wayne's son had believed he would be carting his father's *bones* across the state, not a body that would surely rot or fall out onto the rutted road during a journey that would take weeks to navigate.

At first unbeknownst to Colonel Wayne, Dr. Wallace's solution to the problem was (after removing "Mad Anthony's" boots and uniform) to boil the body in a cauldron, thus enabling him to separate the flesh from the bones, after which he easily packed the bones into a trunk for the long journey to southeastern Pennsylvania.

Dr. Wallace was assisted in this bizarre procedure by four other people; and, as hinted at above, there were several spectators.

A captain of the garrison's wife, according to the American Revolution web site, requested and was granted a lock of General Wayne's hair. Years later, as she neared the century-mark of her years on this planet, when so often the mind takes a turn down that one-way lane called "senility," Mrs. Dobbins possessed still a clear recollection of the Erie/eerie event. "The hair pulled out of the head had the appearance of plaster of paris. The body was not hard, but rather more the consistency of soft chalk."

Mr. Henry Whitney, in a letter he wrote on the grisly subject, dated October 24, 1809, stated, "The flesh on [General Wayne's] backbone was four-inches thick and firm like new pork."

One of the general's boots had partially rotted away. The other boot was in good condition. James Duncan, another of the spectators at the blockhouse operation, noted that the undamaged boot would fit his own foot, thus he took possession of it, and later had a boot maker fashion him a match for it. His prized possession, Duncan wore those boots until he could wear them no more.

Having removed the general's uniform, Dr. Wallace and his assistants sawed "Mad Anthony's" body into expedient pieces; and after the large cauldron of water was good and hot, they continued dropping those body parts into the boiling pot. As the flesh separated from the bones in the steaming, foul-smelling water, Dr. Wallace and his helpers scraped the bones clean. Then they dried them and packed the bones into a trunk, ready for Colonel Wayne to transport them home to the Wayne family plot at Radnor.

The flesh; the water in which the body had been boiled; the saw and knives; in fact, all the instruments used in the operation were put into General Wayne's original coffin and then back into the original grave.

I have read in several accounts, including *The Indian Wars of Pennsylvania* by esteemed historian C. Hale Sipe, that Isaac Wayne deeply regretted his decision to disinter his father's body. Had he known of the state of preservation of the body, he confessed to more than a few people he would have allowed it to rest in peace at Erie, under a monument he would have had erected to his father's memory.

At any rate, the colonel set out, with his father's bones in the light sulky, home to Chester County, where they were to be interred in the churchyard at Saint David's Episcopal Church. Soon afterward, the Society of the Cincinnati appropriated a sum of $500 to erect a monument there to the grand memory of General Anthony Wayne.

The Cincinnati, by the way, is a prestigious, Philadelphia-based society of Revolutionary War officers and their descendants. On 5 June 1811, the association dedicated the monument over Wayne's grave, which still stands today, though badly weathered.

A huge crowd turned out for the ceremony at the Chester County gravesite, which included a funeral procession over a mile in length.

And still, the tale of "Mad" Anthony Wayne, with his flesh in one grave, his bones in another, does not end here. On November 10, 1853, the then-abandoned Erie blockhouse mysteriously caught fire. It may have been set aflame by arsonists, but there was no proof of that at the time it burned to the ground. Then, in later years, the old parade ground was leveled off, and the site of Wayne's original grave lost.

Round about 1878, a local Erie physician, one Dr. Germer, investigated the location of the famed Indian fighter's burial spot. He found it, and consequently caused the grave and coffin to be opened a second time. The coffin lid bore Anthony Wayne's carved initials and the brass tacks illustrating the general's age and the date of his death. Most of his flesh, at that point in time, had rotted away.

Vintage postcard of the old blockhouse, Erie, PA, and General "Mad" Anthony Wayne's original gravesite, where his boiled flesh was buried
From the author's personal collection

In 1880, the State of Pennsylvania rebuilt the Erie blockhouse as a memorial to General Wayne. Actually, the blockhouse has been rebuilt several times, the last time in 1984. On display in the museum are the original coffin lid, some remnants of General Wayne's uniform, and Dr. Wallace's instruments used in the grisly operation of separating "Mad Anthony's" flesh from his bones.

I think it interesting to note that the word *Erie* translates from the Native tongue *Erieehronon/Eriechronon* to "Cat with a Long Tail." The Erie Indians were often referred to as the *Nation du Chat*, the "Cat Nation," the long-tail cat referring to the panther/mountain lion. I have also read that Erie means "Raccoon," but the Indians thought of that animal as a wild cat and depicted it as such on the Erie totem pole. Early French maps of North America refer to Lake Erie as *Lac du Chat*– the "Lake of the Cat."

The Erie vanished into history. Though their language was an Iroquoian dialect, they were traditional enemies of the mighty Iroquois, whose fierce reputation was known to the four winds. The Iroquois, however, recognized the Erie– who were said to have used poison arrows– as formidable warriors. During the mid-1600s, in a series of battles, the Iroquois defeated the Erie, and any survivors scattered. It took many years for the Iroquois to ferret out the last of the cat people, who surrendered in southern Pennsylvania around 1680. Where those Erie had been hiding for twenty-four years is still a mystery. There are some who say there is a Shawnee link with the Erie. There could well have been some intermarriage. What does all this have to do with "Mad Anthony's" ghost? Read on for *that* connection.

Firstly, what of the large cauldron used to boil Wayne's body? My research produced no firm answer to that question. All I can say is that over the long years, it was lost to Time. In the 1950s, a large kettle was displayed by the Erie Historical Society as that used to process the body of Anthony Wayne. But it has since come to light that particular kettle was not authentic. Today, the Historical Society has no record of having the sinister Wayne cauldron among its collection.

It is a common-enough practice to disinter the remains of a deceased member of a family, by request of a relative, in order to have it moved to another burial site. In fact, history has related to us that sometimes whole cemeteries are moved, when the area upon which they occupy is slated for a building or highway project. In most cases, however, the remains are carefully and respectfully removed for reburial. In other cases, decomposition has done its ashes-to-ashes job, and there is nothing to move. In those instances, a symbolic sampling of the earth is withdrawn from the grave for reburial. Conversely, no instance of removal of a body for reburial can rival the bizarre event that got its claws around that of Major General Anthony Wayne.

As I penned in the premier volume of my *County Chronicles,* the library in my hometown of Connellsville was constructed over a site that was once a cemetery. Did that render the place haunted? My unequivocal answer is "Yes." And that response is based on several interviews I conducted about that library– tales I recounted in the first volume of this series.

And now, dear readers, allow me to unfold for you the most awesome segment of this mad, layered tale of our hero. As his son, Colonel Wayne, traveled southeast with his father's skeletal remains rattling behind him in the trunk (which had been placed on the rear of his light sulky), some of "Mad Anthony's" bones were jolted from the buggy, falling out along the deeply rutted road (now US Route 322).

Countless sightings and a persistent legend dictate that in the wee hours every New Year's since his burial in Chester County, General "Mad" Anthony Wayne's ghost rises suddenly– like a blast from a Revolutionary War cannon– out of his grave in the old Saint David's Churchyard. In a whirlwind, his magnificent warhorse thunders forth, pawing the frozen ground in its eagerness to set out on their annual quest. With all the vim and vigor of his youth, General Wayne leaps into the saddle, his phantom steed rearing, and then they are off at the gallop, along Route 322, to the blockhouse at Erie and back again to Saint David's.

Indeed, certain historians of those parts, who have been careful in collecting and collating the ethereal facts concerning this specter, allege that the ghost rides, in the gloom of predawn, in quest of his lost bones, and in a great hurry to return to the churchyard before cock-crow.

According to the persuasive *Ghost Stories of Pennsylvania* by Dan Asfar, the general's specter "tears down the highway at incredible speeds, passing through anything in its path without breaking stride." Though the general races his steed along as if on the wings of the wind– stones flying and sparks flashing– he is ever and anon seen by the country folk the length of his course. Some witnesses have even been able to catch a clear glimpse of his uniform, the epaulets on the shoulders, the tricorne hat atop the powdered wig, the saber jangling and slapping at his side.

Author Asfar and others have related that those same eyewitnesses to this fleeting phenomenon have stated that, along his flight, the general's eyes constantly scan the road, from side to side, as if he is searching for something that is lost, something so important to him that he is *compelled* to ride that road during the witching hours, back and forth, for all eternity.

As pointed out above, the popular theory has always been that the general is seeking his lost bones that were not buried with the others at Saint David's Churchyard. It would stand to reason that "Mad Anthony" would be discontent at how his remains were handled at Erie, followed by his bones being strewn across Pennsylvania, and then his original gravesite disturbed for a second time. Certainly, he was not permitted to rest in peace.

If you are a reader of ghostly tales, then you know that one of the most common denominators, where ghosts are concerned, is that those spirits had their graves disturbed... or that there is some unfinished business the restless soul feels compelled to accomplish here on earth.

Both of those motives fit the bill for Wayne's ghost. Surely, after so glorious a victory at Stony Point, then at Fallen Timbers, this lion of the field must have felt frustration to have met such an untimely and humble end. His body, once so conditioned to endurance and combat, had finally failed him, and as he agonized in pain on his death bed, his thoughts must have lighted on the then-out-of-reach political rewards he might have reaped for his efforts, even that of the Presidency. It had to have been difficult for him to know that he would never harvest the fruits of his heroics.

And what of a Native American curse? For years, a legend has persisted that there was uttered after Fallen Timbers and later after Tippecanoe- after the battles lost; after Indian lands were acutely diminished; Indian villages, orchards and crops burned; Indian trading posts and stores surrendered and burned- a Native curse against the American Presidents.

It all began with the death of President William Henry Harrison from pneumonia. The curse is commonly attributed to Shawnee leader Tecumseh, "Panther Leaping Across the Sky After Its Prey," but it could well have been uttered by his brother Tenskwatawa, a reformed alcoholic who, after falling into a trance, in which he declared he had been visited by the Master of Life, became known as the "Prophet." The curse is said to have proclaimed the death of all Presidents elected every twentieth year, since the election of Harrison in 1840. One colorful fact is that the coincidental twenty-year pattern was noted in *Ripley's Believe It or Not*, published in 1934.

Do your own research, and see what you think. Begin from 1840, with William Henry Harrison, the first of the Presidents to succumb to the legendary curse, who had been "Mad" Anthony Wayne's aide-de-camp at the Battle of Fallen Timbers. Harrison was the man who took Wayne's place as commander-in-chief of the US Army, resigning from the service to fulfill political ambitions. He died only a month after his inauguration, after succumbing to pneumonia contracted from delivering his lengthy (nearly two-hour) inaugural speech in a freezing March rainstorm (shades of the deluge at Fallen Timbers). Thus, Harrison had the shortest-ever Presidency in American history. I might add that Indian-fighter Harrison (who had burned Native homes, crops, orchards and other food stores, resulting in winter starvation and agony from the cold), suffered from what may have been ulcers. He could only eat dairy products. In fact, he had so much trouble eating that he was actually enduring malnutrition; and this attributed to the cold he caught developing so quickly into pneumonia. Indeed, it had been hard work, the dying- for both Harrison and Wayne.

Twenty years later, President Abraham Lincoln was elected and, in 1865, after being elected to a second term, was shot and killed by John Wilkes Booth in Ford's Theatre, Washington, DC. Twenty years after Lincoln, President James Garfield, elected in 1880, was shot in July of 1881, which led to his death soon after, in September of that year. Reelected in 1900, President McKinley was shot on September 6, 1901, and died a few days later. In 1920, President Harding was elected, his time in office riddled with scandals; in 1923, while still in office, he died of mysterious causes. FDR was reelected in 1940 and died of a cerebral hemorrhage in 1945 before his fourth term was up. JFK, elected in 1960, was murdered in Dallas in 1963.

President Reagan, elected in 1980, came awfully close to being killed when he was shot by a would-be assassin in 1981, the only President to foil the mysterious malediction. There are those who say that, if there was indeed a curse, it is now broken.

This presidential blight is known by several names- the Twenty-Year Curse, the Zero-Year Curse, as well as Tecumseh's Curse and the Curse of Tippecanoe, named for the defeat of Tecumseh's brother Tenskwatawa, aka the "Prophet," by William Henry Harrison at the Battle of Tippecanoe in 1812- at the time, a crushing blow to Tecumseh's growing Indian confederation and his dream of a united Native nation with a return to the old ways.

Legend has it that the "Prophet" pronounced, or repeated, the above deadly curse before witnesses, while sitting for a painting by celebrated artist George Catlin. He also remarked to Catlin that his brother Tecumseh was a great general, and that nothing but his premature death had defeated his heroic plan to come to the rescue of Native Americans, uniting them and taking back what they had lost.

When all was said and done, the brothers Tecumseh and Tenskwatawa did not- could not- halt the misfortunes overwhelming their people. They did succeed, as had their adversaries, "Mad" Anthony Wayne and William Henry Harrison, in leaving their marks upon the times and to history. *Passion* was the common denominator for these four historic figures. They each passionately believed in the goals they had set for themselves. However, there are no *true* paragons. Each of these very human men had their faults. Such were the main protagonists in this Chronicle- "Mad" Anthony Wayne, William Henry Harrison, Tecumseh and Tenskwatawa/the "Prophet."

I have advocated that there is good and evil in every race of man, rights and wrongs on both sides of any conflict. The erstwhile Pennsylvania frontier was the setting for the bloodiest Indian invasion in American history. First the French, then the British encouraged the Natives to horrendous bloodlust against the settlers, with only brief respites, from 1754 to 1795; and to this day, the accounts of those atrocities can cause the flesh to creep.

But lest we forget the attack on the Delaware and Shawnee village of Kit-Han-Ne/Kittanning (1756); the butchery of the peaceful Conestogas (Susquehannocks) by the "Paxton Boys" (Scotch-Irish frontiersmen, 1763); General Sullivan's Expedition (1779) into Seneca lands against the Six Nations of the Iroquois, or the massacre of disarmed Delawares at Gnadenhuetten (1782), to name four of the hostilities against the Indians. And we must not neglect to mention, with the exception of William Penn's dealings with the Natives, the countless broken treaties and the incidents of defrauding and cheating that were perpetrated against the "Red" race by the White.

The protracted Indian wars in Pennsylvania were not only a bloody tug-of-war for land, they were a bitter struggle for a way of life. And both sides- *each exhibiting what Americans have come to be known for*- were willing to die for what they so ardently sought.

A Native American curse? Consider this: Wayne had been called by the Indians the "Chief Who Never Sleeps." Said Little Turtle of him, "The night and the day are alike to him, and during all the time he has been marching upon our villages, notwithstanding the watchfulness of our young men, we have never been able to surprise him."

Indeed, so stealthily had "Mad Anthony" advanced, the Natives bestowed a second nickname on him- the "Blacksnake."

Did the Indians fear that their intrepid nemesis would ride his warhorse across the hanging road to meet them over and yet again in eternal battle?

With his lofty dream of a great, multi-tribe Indian confederation foiled, did Tecumseh, "Panther Leaping Across the Sky After Its Prey," and/or his brother, the "Prophet," send a curse to the land of the Cat Nation (Erie) to stop "Mad Anthony" in death? And then, via this bane, render Wayne's body dissected, so that the ardent general's spirit could not relentlessly pursue the Natives in the Shadow Lands on the other side? There are those who believe that the Shawnee siblings did swear vengeance against the Americans and their leaders after Fallen Timbers.

Tecumseh's brother, Tenskwatawa/the "Prophet," who advocated complete separateness of the Red and White worlds, pronounced that all those who consorted with and/or followed the ways of the Americans, along with all those who did not accept his teachings, were witches. His Prophetstown (located in Indiana Territory, the Shawnees' new homeland at that time) became the center of a new religious fanaticism, where some say hideous dances and sinister ceremonies of Indian magic took place under the wide wings of darkness. To be sure, the "Prophet" himself- who had the look of one possessed- was frightful in appearance, since he had but one eye, blinded as he was from a wayward arrow in his youth. His sightless eye was a bluish-white orb that seemed to see into the inner reaches of whomever he fixed with his mystical gaze. Tenskwatawa had often declared that he could shape-change into a large cat.

Conjure, if you can, readers, this image of Tenskwatawa: a panther pelage draped over his forehead, the big cat's great teeth open in a silent snarl; as, shaking an animal rattle to his guttural utterances, the "Prophet" chants a spell, snarling and growling the strange words over his fire. Suddenly, he tosses something into the flames, rendering an explosive sibilant sound that prompts the "Prophet's" own mouth to open in a prolonged hiss; whilst his fearsome painted visage, the ebony mask evocative of an incited long-tail cat, glows fiendish in the flickering firelight of the shadowy lodge.

After declaring his dissenters witches, Tenskwatawa went a huge step further by capturing those Natives who disagreed with him, torturing them and burning them alive. One old woman was slow roasted for days! To be fair, the "Prophet," though deservedly and significantly associated with this horrific witch-hunt, was not the only one involved in it. Tecumseh, on the other hand, loathed torture.

Needless to say, the "Prophet's" witch-hunts did nothing to endear him to the Americans, whom he declared were a race of witches. Fully deserved or not, Tenskwatawa has passed through time into folklore and history as a devious charlatan exploiting the superstitious and lurking in the shadow of a nobler brother.

After accusing so many, from a variety of tribes, of witchcraft, the "Prophet" was accused of witchcraft himself, though he was not burned for it... not literally anyway. The finger pointing would begin as a result of a blistering petition to Native leaders from William Henry Harrison. It would finally come to pass that the majority of the Natives would feel that Tenskwatawa's was a case of perceiving others as self. In the interim....

When Harrison had first gotten wind of this witchcraft delusion, its sharp claws reaching further and further, he feared a major Indian uprising. The same kind of religious fervor and rage had enflamed the frontier during Pontiac's war back in 1763. Then, the Natives had united to cut a path of death and destruction from Detroit clean down to the Carolinas. There was one difference that Harrison could see between then and now: Tenskwatawa, unlike the prophet Neolin, did not have to wait for a Chief Pontiac to come along. He had his brother, the respected and skilled military leader Tecumseh. The situation was, to say the least, precarious.

Thus, Harrison penned his bold missive, urging the tribes to banish Tenskwatawa as a false prophet: "Ask him to cause the sun to stand still, the moon to alter its course, the rivers to cease to flow, or the dead to rise from their graves."

Regrettably for Harrison, the letter fleetingly backfired. As strange as this will seem, it happened; but then again, we know that truth can often be stranger than fiction; and this is one of the reasons I find history so fascinating.

The "Prophet" gleefully picked up William H. Harrison's gauntlet and announced that on a certain day, he would cause darkness to cloak the sun. Word spread to a myriad of Indian villages; and a vast Native assemblage, from far and near, gathered to witness the "Prophet's" great miracle. Long about eleven in the morning of the selected day, Tenskwatawa, attired in dazzling splendor, strode to the center of the great circle of Indian witnesses. A murmur of anticipation carried round the assembly like the loud drone of an enormous beehive. Soon a hush descended upon the gathering, as hundreds of eyes focused on Tecumseh's more obscure and wholly enigmatic brother. Extending his arms skyward, his up-tilted face solemn, the "Prophet" muttered an unintelligible incantation. A few seconds later, a disc of darkness began slowly to cover the sun. To the shrieks and exclamations of all present, it grew darker and ever darker. The witchcraft that swirled round that blackened circle was a very ancient sort, and the large Indian gathering gave themselves over to it with a fervor that goes beyond any words I can offer. At the moment of total darkness, Tenskwatawa cried out, "Behold! Did I not prophesy truly!"

How he could have learned that there would occur a total eclipse of the sun *I* cannot say for certain. According to the Ohio History Central web site, Tecumseh learned about the predicted eclipse from a couple of Ohio scientists; and then informed his brother of it, suggesting that he perform his "miracle" to firmly unite the tribes behind them in their goal of a confederation of all tribes west of the Alleghenies. This, of course, was to prevent further White encroachment into Indian lands.

Lacking the military skills of his brother, and after giving surety to the Natives that the Master of Life had told him that the Whites' bullets would not touch them in the ensuing fight, the "Prophet" attacked Harrison's force, losing the battle, after which Harrison and his men drove the Indians off and burned Prophetstown to the ground. Tecumseh, who had been away (recruiting more tribes into his confederation) at the time of the Battle of Tippecanoe, attempted, in a lonely quest thereafter, to resurrect the confederation– but his efforts were in vain.

As a result of Tippecanoe, most of the Indians no longer believed in Tenskwatawa. And, as I said, there were those, after his defeat by William Henry Harrison, who accused the "Prophet" of black magic.

Of course, I cannot say with any degree of certainty whether or not the "Prophet" was involved in the black arts, though from what I uncovered about him, he most assuredly had a dark side. I will state for a fact that Harrison took from the victory the slogan for his presidential campaign: "Tippecanoe and Tyler too!" [John Tyler was Harrison's running-mate.]

If a curse did, or does, exist, I would opt for the "Prophet," an unlikable fellow, rather than Tecumseh (whom I have come, through my research, to admire) as its originator; but who can say for certain about any of the mystical segments of this Chronicle?

What is certain, to recap, is that the events involving General Wayne's disinterment could not have been much more bizarre. Even in death, "Mad Anthony" and the two Native brothers' other key adversary, William Henry Harrison, are unique. Lasting only thirty-one days, Harrison's Presidency was the shortest in American history; and Wayne, robbed by Death of his chance at the highest office in the land, possesses the distinction of being the only legendary person in our history to be buried in two separate graves.

So if Wayne is racing his fire-breathing warhorse across Pennsylvania, in the fog and mist of predawn New Years', his burning eyes frantically searching the roadside in nightly quests of his lost bones, I can well understand why.

Let me conclude this Chronicle with this caveat: Travelers on Route 322, *beware.* You could just find yourself momentarily traveling alongside that ghostly horseman, "Mad" Anthony Wayne. If you do, to echo author Asfar, I strongly suggest you yield to that zealous general the right of way– for what chance is there of escaping such a phantom who can ride upon the wings of the wind?

"The Right Stuff"

"If I had to be philosophical, I would say I've been given a great deal of responsibility, and the question begging is 'Will I be able to handle it?' I intend to give it my best shot." - Gen. Lewis A. Mologne, 1982, prior to assuming his role as Commander of Walter Reed Army Medical Center in 1983

"Lew was a humanitarian. He always put others before himself. Yes... he was a great humanitarian."
-Longtime Mologne friend, Dolores Demarco-Jones, to author O'Hanlon-Lincoln, 2006

"My husband was known as the 'Soldier's General,' among an array of other acclaims and awards, but I seldom brag about him, because that was something Lew never did. The great Lew Mologne was the humblest of men."
- Wife Rose Marie Galiardi-Mologne to author O'Hanlon-Lincoln, 2006

In the first two volumes of my *County Chronicles*, I lauded several Pennsylvania natives whom I greatly admire. The title of those Chronicles is "The Right Stuff," and I intend to include a "Right Stuff" segment in every volume of my *County Chronicles* Pennsylvania history series.

What exactly do we mean by the "Right Stuff"? I defined the phrase as the essential or requisite qualities, such as self-confidence, courage, stability, dependability, organizational skills, and specific knowledge appropriate for application in a given field or situation. I have researched the lives of many Pennsylvania as well as national heroes, such as George Washington, Abraham Lincoln, and George C. Marshall, to name a few. I discovered that these exceptional people had common denominators. They all had a strong belief and faith in God; and by extension, faith and belief in themselves and their own capabilities; however, each was a humble person.

Abraham Lincoln once said, "I have been driven many times upon my knees by the overwhelming conviction that I had nowhere else to go."

And certainly "Right Stuff" people possess courage. Lincoln retorted, in the face of relentless adversity, "I say 'try'; if we never try, we may never succeed."

My grandmother used to say that is all anyone can do. At the end of my life, I do not want to lament via Rebecca McCann's rhyme: "It's not the things I failed to do/That make me wipe this eye/It's the things I should and could have done/And simply failed to try."

This reminds me of a story Harry Truman liked to tell of a tombstone he happened across in an old graveyard in Arizona: "Here lies Jack Williams. He done his damnedest." Not a bad epitaph to work toward. It was the long-standing conviction of America's thirty-third President that if you did your best in life, did your "damnedest" always, then whatever happened you would at least know it was not for lack of trying. Truman was also a great believer in the role played by luck, by the forces quite beyond effort or determination. His greatest biographer, Pennsylvania-born author/historian David McCullough wrote of this great President: "[Truman] stood for common sense, common decency. He spoke the common tongue. As much as any President since Lincoln, he brought to the highest office the language and values of the common American people." And there was nothing passive about Harry Truman. He was the Commander in Chief in law- and in fact.

"Right Stuff" candidates do the best they can, one day at a time, to be the best they can be. These valiant companions have polished skills and accumulated knowledge, yes. Stability and dependability, most certainly. Yet, something else led to the greatness of each of these matchless individuals— something *extra*. And that, I soon perceived, was *persistence*. When actress Hattie McDaniel won the Oscar for Best Supporting Actress for her brilliant portrayal of "Mammy" in *Gone with the Wind* (1939), she said: "I did my best, and God did the rest." Ms. McDaniel was the first African-American to win an Oscar.

Lewis Aspey Mologne, football captain, president and "king" of Connellsville High School class of 1950

Another discovery I made was that Time does not alter these essential, requisite qualities. The same basic qualities were necessary for greatness in George Washington's era as they were in George Marshall's. Shakespeare said of great men: "Some are born great; some achieve greatness, and some have greatness thrust upon them." Philosopher Eric Hoffer once said, "A great man's greatest good luck is to die at the right time."

Personally, I believe being in the right place at the right time has something to do with it. And by "it," I mean luck, or destiny, the *magic* that helps to spiral individuals to eminence. I believe in God. I believe in Destiny. I believe in that magic we call "luck." However, I think "luck" can be spelled out in two other ways, both of them four-letter words: w-o-r-k and g-u-t-s. In a word— *persistence*.

Successful people make their own luck.

In each "Right Stuff" Chronicle of my Pennsylvania history series, the peerless individuals therein will be drawn from a variety of life's callings. How proud we should all be of these shining stars! Usually, I include several

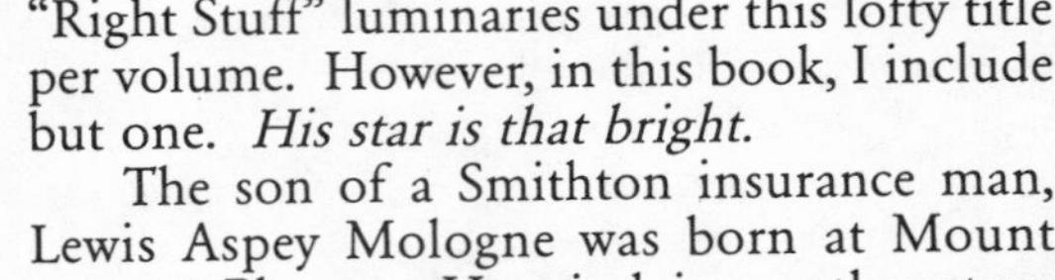

"Right Stuff" luminaries under this lofty title per volume. However, in this book, I include but one. *His star is that bright.*

The son of a Smithton insurance man, Lewis Aspey Mologne was born at Mount Pleasant Hospital in southwestern Pennsylvania. His unusual middle name was the surname of a physician family-friend. Though Lew resided and was reared in Smithton, Westmoreland County, he attended Connellsville High School just over the border in the county Fayette. "In those days, you could choose where you wanted to go to high school, and Lew rode the train from Smithton to Connellsville and vice versa every day," several of his friends told me.

According to Lew's former classmate Dick Smith, who also rode the rails into Connellsville to attend high school, "The locals called that train the 'Jerkwater' or 'Milkrun,' due to the fact that it stopped at every little burg from Pittsburgh to Connellsville. We commuters always had a study hall the final period of each day, so we could leave early to catch our train back home. As for Lew," Dick interjected, "he was one heck of a guy. He turned the whole system around when he was at the helm at Walter Reed... on behalf of our veterans. Lew was like that; he never did anything halfway. Yet, with all his education and his laurels, he was forever 'Lew,' always down-to-earth and affable to his friends... to everyone."

"We can be proud of the fact that some pretty extraordinary people came out of this Fayette-Westmoreland region of Pennsylvania" is a phrase I have heard countless times since I began my *County Chronicles* series. And I heartily agree.

Blond, handsome and popular Lew Mologne was the captain of the football team, elected president, and the crowned "king" of his senior class at Connellsville High School. He and two other varsity football stars, the aforementioned Dick Smith and Bruce Hayes, seeking to play higher caliber opposition, and because Connellsville was an accredited school, traveled to attend classes. The trips were made the first three years by train, and their senior year via an old, rather dilapidated auto designated "for school travel only."

When the clunker was down for the duration, then hitchhiking and walking filled the gaps. "I never had to tramp the entire eighteen miles to [or from] school," Lew told a Uniontown *Herald-Standard* reporter during a September 30, 1982, interview, "although a couple of times, I was covered with snow when my father picked me up," he had laughed with the memory.

Lew had fond reminiscences of his grammar-to-high-school sweetheart Shirley Jones, who is the focus of the subsequent Chronicle in this volume.

"We came from the same small Pennsylvania town, where everybody knew everybody," Mologne related to the *Herald-Standard* in that same September 1982 interview. "Shirley is a very lovely lady who has charm to match her beauty."

Major General Mologne and wife Rose Marie, 1986

"I remember he brought Shirley Jones to our school one day," Nick Manzella, a Connellsville resident who was in Lew's class, told me. "I can't recollect for what function, but I do recall that we were all excited to meet her. Of course, she wasn't famous yet. In fact, she was a sophomore at South Huntington, when Lew and I were seniors at Connellsville, but he had told us how pretty his girl was. We all agreed wholeheartedly upon meeting her. She was not only pretty, she was very personable. I recall that Lew escorted her to his senior prom at Connellsville and to a special Christmas party. I think that holiday dance was held at the old Connellsville/Pleasant Valley Country Club.

"Lew always came home to Pennsylvania for his high school reunions, and he never changed. He had risen to the top of his career, yet he wasn't arrogant or haughty. I never met anyone who had more genuine concern for others, or who possessed more class and dignity than Lew Mologne. He carried those traits with him his whole life," former Mologne classmate Nick Manzella concluded.

Lewis A. Mologne graduated with honors, at the top of his class, from Connellsville High School in 1950. As a result of his hard work and sterling character traits, Mologne won an appointment to the United States Military Academy at West Point.

Though Shirley visited him at the Point, there to attend a "Ring Dance" and other functions, the pair went in different directions from that juncture of their lives, Shirley to her stellar stage, film, and television career, and Lew to a luminous career in the military as a doctor. However, the two remained friends until his passing in 1988. So often, when there is a breakup between sweethearts, the friendship that existed between the pair dissipates. I think it speaks volumes about the characters of these two extraordinary people that, along the ofttimes complex and highly successful paths of both their lives, their friendship never faltered.

Once when Mologne and his sons were traveling back East from Colorado, he happened to notice a marquee in Columbus, Ohio, advertising a play in which Jones was appearing. Lewis' widow, Rose Marie, told me he pulled off the road, telling the boys, "We have to stop and see someone." However, as it turned out, they were too late to catch the actress, who had gone for the day. Mologne decided to leave a message with the stage manager. "He asked him to tell Shirley that Lew had stopped on his way back to western Pennsylvania," Rose Mologne related to me in one of our interviews. "The stage manager wanted to know 'Lew who?' Rose laughed, continuing, " 'If Shirley asks *that* question, then there's no message,' Lew quipped. That was Lew. He had a wonderful sense of humor, a quick wit."

Mologne graduated in 1954 from West Point, fourteenth in a class of 633. After fulfilling his service duties the subsequent three years in the Army Corps of Engineers, Lew then went on to the University of Pittsburgh's medical school, *graduating first in his class,*

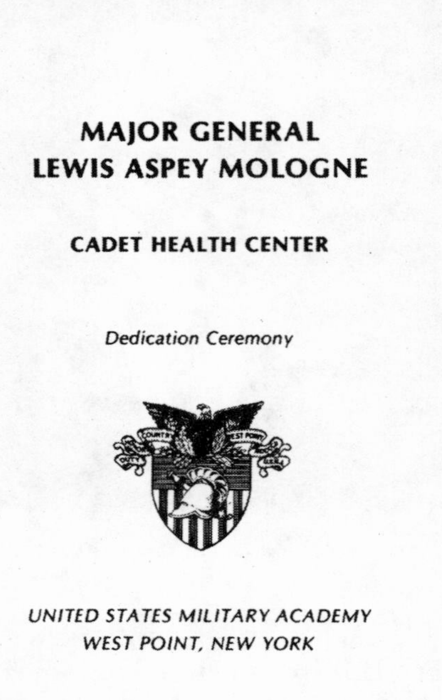
MAJOR GENERAL
LEWIS ASPEY MOLOGNE

CADET HEALTH CENTER

Dedication Ceremony

UNITED STATES MILITARY ACADEMY
WEST POINT, NEW YORK

1400, 24 APRIL 1992

Dedication program for the Major General Lewis Aspey Mologne Cadet Health Center at the United States Military Academy at West Point

CADET SERGEANT

USMA CLASS OF 1954

LEWIS ASPEY MOLOGNE

Cadet Sergeant, USMA Class of 1954, Lewis Aspey Mologne

in 1961, to resume his military career as a doctor. Years later, in 1987, the University of Pittsburgh would proudly confer on Lewis A. Mologne, one of their most outstanding alumni, the "Bicentennial Medallion of Distinction" for so greatly honoring that institution of higher learning.

Mologne was the first West Point graduate to become a general in the Army Medical Department.

Ironically, Lew did not originally intend to make the military his career. "I wanted to go to Walter Reed Army Medical Center only for my residency," he once said in regard to the required apprenticeship for doctors. "But one thing led to another, and here I am," he told that Uniontown reporter in 1982, "still in the Army twenty years later."

Not that Major General Mologne ever regretted his choices. He *loved* both the military and his work in medicine and surgery. "[What I do is] particularly gratifying, with experiences and challenges that could not be duplicated elsewhere," he declared to several sources over the course of his star-studded career.

It is important in this segment to mention that, in 1992, West Point renamed their campus clinic– the Mologne Cadet Health Center– to pay homage to Lew Mologne for his outstanding service to the army medical corps. The center was dedicated on April 24, 1992, with West Point Superintendent Lieutenant General Howard D. Graves presiding over the ceremony and Lew's widow Rose Marie Mologne assisting in the unveiling of the plaque.

The highlights of Major General Mologne's impressive medical career include: Chief of Surgery at the 130th General Hospital in Nuremberg, West Germany, from 1970 to 1973; Surgical Consultant for the United States Army Medical Command in Europe from 1972 to 1973; Commander of a MASH test unit in Texas in 1979; the US Army Medical Command-Korea from 1980 to 1981; two terms of duty at Fitzsimmons Army Medical

Mrs. Rose Mologne and presiding General Graves flank Mologne Cadet Health Center dedication plaque at West Point, 1992

Center in Denver, where he served as Chief of Surgery, Deputy Commander and deputy for medical activities and medical education, and ultimately as Commander at Walter Reed Army Medical Center in our nation's capital.

While only a lieutenant, Lew attended, at Walter Reed, General Douglas MacArthur and former general and the thirty-fourth President of the United States, Dwight D. Eisenhower. Just prior to his becoming Commander of Walter Reed, Mologne told the press, "If I had to be philosophical, I would say I've been dealt a great deal of responsibility, and the question that is begging is 'Will I be able to handle it?' One thing I intend to do is give it my best shot."

According to his West Point biography, Lew Mologne's prominence had escalated during the decade of the seventies, whilst he taught at the Fitzsimmons Army Medical Center. And following his outstanding tour in Korea, he had gained a *widespread* reputation as one of the best and most demanding teachers in military medicine.

Commander of Walter Reed was Lewis Mologne's last assignment, where he was effectively in charge of approximately 5,000 Army doctors, their education and the overall quality of Army medical care. The hospital had fallen on desperate times due to staff and budget cuts, in addition to years of inefficient record keeping.

Bernard S. Little of Walter Reed told reporter Judy Kroeger of the Connellsville *Daily Courier* in a February 21, 1998, interview: "He [Mologne] set about to reinfuse a sense of purpose and values coupled with an increased feel of teamwork and goal sharing. He also increased security, which led to a widespread crackdown of illicit drugs, pilferage and misuse of government supplies." To use a popular phrase: "Lewis Mologne turned Walter Reed around."

Lew's final command, at WRAMC, extended from June 1983 to August of 1988. Sadly, Major General Mologne died that same month, at the age of fifty-six, after a long bout with chronic hepatitis resulting in the cancer that destroyed his liver. Mologne had received a transplant a few months earlier at his alma mater, the University of Pittsburgh, which had been a successful operation. Tragically, however, his health did not improve; and he resigned his post at Walter Reed on August 1 of that year.

Hepatitis is known as the "surgeons' disease," due to the fact that infected needles and

The Mologne House at Walter Reed Army Medical Center, Washington, DC, dedicated May 2, 1997
Photos courtesy Rose Marie Mologne, Bethesda, MD

sharp surgical instruments sometimes puncture protective gloves. That is what happened to Mologne. Possessed of a warrior spirit, he persevered, determined to overcome what had befallen him. "He fought back hard" was a phrase related to me by all those who knew this exceptional man.

I have spoken to a multiplicity of family, friends and coworkers who believe that, had Lew Mologne lived, he would have been the next Surgeon General of the United States. In March 1988 when his liver finally failed, he was close to being appointed to the office that he had assisted countless times on a variety of issues, while serving as Commander at Walter Reed; and I would not be exaggerating in the least when I state that Lewis Mologne was the Surgeon General's right-hand man.

At each assignment of his career, Mologne was presented with a medal of honor for outstanding performance of his duties. He earned, to name a few, a Meritorious Service Medal, three oak leaf clusters, the Legion of Merit for his 1980 Korean duty, and the Distinguished Service Medal. The award he treasured most, as befitted a humble man, was the least impressive honor, an Army Commendation Medal he earned in 1955 during his first tour of Korea, when he was a lieutenant. The decoration was for service "... above and beyond," an axiom that most certainly set a precedence in his military medical career- and in his life.

The incredibly modest Lew Mologne stated more than once, with eyes that always reflected his empathy for his fellow man, that the medal he wore with the most pride was his caduceus, the winged staff which proclaimed him a physician. *It is only from the heart that one can touch the sky.*

Drawn from my interviews with those who knew Lew Mologne well, including his widow Rose Marie, I can state unequivocally that he was a highly skilled and sympathetic healer, as well as a dedicated researcher and scholar who incessantly asked the "why" of something, as he ferreted out the answers to vital issues. Even more notably, Mologne habitually asked "Why not?" in regard to his deep concern for soldiers, veterans, and their families; and like all optimists, he took "Now" for an answer.

After working tirelessly for decades, Lew Mologne became known- *throughout the entire United States military*- as the "Soldier's General." He battled for years to improve the quality of living and medical care for service members and their families. An outstanding soldier, clinician and educator, Mologne gave over thirty years of military service to his country, after which a special award was created to pay tribute to him. The Lewis Aspey Mologne Award is given annually at the Graduate Medical Education Conference to those officers who most emulate the great man for whom the honor was named.

At Walter Reed Army Medical Center, there is- also created in Mologne's memory- the 200-room, state-of-the-art, Georgian Revival-style hotel, which was built with non-appropriated funds rather than taxpayer dollars, I might add. Dedicated on May 2, 1997, Mologne House, with its reasonable rates, is a haven for outpatients and families visiting patients who come to Walter Reed. It is open to active duty military families, retirees, and Department of Defense civilians. With war raging in Iraq, Mologne House is filled with amputees and other wounded service members and their families.

"Living [at Mologne House]... has only made me appreciate more Major General Mologne's efforts to make a difficult time for soldiers at Walter Reed a little more pleasant and comfortable," stated a young military wife in a commentary which appeared in the Uniontown *Herald-Standard* on February 20, 2006. Her husband had been wounded in Iraq the previous April.

One of Connellsville's most eminent alumni, *Major General Lew Mologne, Army surgeon and scientist extraordinaire, left a lasting mark on the care that America's warriors receive every day.* Unfortunately, as mentioned earlier, Mologne's later years of treating soldiers infected with hepatitis eventually destroyed his liver. While Lew Mologne's record of performance and accolades are truly impressive, they are exceeded by his passion for his work and his love and compassion for humankind.

In a letter to the West Point superintendent, James C. Burris, an Army retiree and former classmate of Mologne at the Point, wrote: "Lew Mologne was one of the finest human beings to ever enter West Point; and [he was] one of the greatest leaders the Academy has ever graduated. The number of physicians he trained and taught to become soldiers as well as surgeons is legend. Lew had that special gift of being able to explain what he knew into visual concepts so that others could more easily grasp them and understand," Burris continued. "Call it the ability to communicate, the ability to teach, or whatever skill label best fits. Lew had this gift in spades."

Lieutenant Colonel James S. McHone, M.D., who had been a surgical student of Mologne's, echoed what so many others had declared about this heroic and self-sacrificing man. "*He really cared about us*- students and patients alike, both personally and professionally. And he wasn't afraid to show his feelings."

Lew Mologne is survived by his wife, the lovely Rose Marie Galiardi-Mologne formerly of Connellsville, Pennsylvania, and their five children. An extremely kind and affable lady, Rose frequently visits injured soldiers at Walter Reed; and at this writing, she still does a lot of work for the Red Cross. Thus, she is continuing her husband's long tradition of serving our men and women in uniform, who have so valiantly served our nation.

"Major General Mologne has given thirty-four years of selfless service to his country," Army Chief of Staff Carl E. Vuono, a native of Monongahela, Pennsylvania, declared at Mologne's interment at Arlington. "He was a soldier first, then a leader, a scholar and a surgeon."

To each of those endeavors, Lew Mologne gave 110 percent. He was *a role model in every sense of that phrase.*

"You know how respected Lew was when both the President and the Vice President visited him at his sick bed," longtime Mologne friend Dolores Demarco-Jones related to me. "Lew Mologne was a humanitarian; he always put others before himself. Yes... he was a *great* humanitarian."

When Lew was in the hospital for the last time, both President Reagan and Vice President Bush visited him to thank him for his long and distinguished leadership and service to his country. And when, on August 22, 1988, Lew Mologne passed from this world to a better place- *and into history*- the nation's soldiers lost their best friend.

The "Soldier's General," Major General Lewis Aspey Mologne, rests amidst his fellow warriors at Arlington National Cemetery.

"Pennsylvania's Sweetheart– the Inimitable, Indomitable Shirley Jones"

"I was eighteen when I entered the Miss Pittsburgh Contest... one of the youngest, if not the youngest, of twelve contestants. I won five hundred dollars... a charm bracelet, and a scholarship to the drama school at the Pittsburgh Playhouse. For me, that was the big one...."

"I made a few appearances across the country, and then I went on to the Miss Pennsylvania competition, where I was the runner-up. Finishing second really changed the direction of my life. I wanted to study drama... I already knew what I wanted to do with my life."
- Shirley Jones, 1952

"My partner is at home, and I would like to have him hear you. Can you wait a while longer? It will take about twenty-five minutes for him to get here."- Richard Rodgers (of Rodgers and Hammerstein)

"Well... that's fine. And what is your name?"
- Shirley Jones, 1953

It was a hot Sunday afternoon in July 2006, when the telephone rang just as my husband and I were about to sit down to dinner. In fact, I nearly didn't answer the phone. As it turned out, I was so glad I did. "Hello," I said into the receiver.

"This is Mr. Ingels," came the raspy voice over the line. "I am calling in regard to your request for a personal interview with Shirley Jones." Needless to say my heart did a somersault, and for a moment, I was speechless– a condition from which I rarely suffer. Marty Ingels is Shirley Jones' second husband, a Brooklyn-born comedian turned superagent who possesses an inspirational story of his own.

Mr. Ingels laid the groundwork for the interview, which would take place on November 25, 2006, when Ms. Jones would be visiting her home county of Westmoreland, Pennsylvania, in order to do a live show at Greensburg's Palace Theater.

A singer from the time she learned to talk, Shirley Mae Jones was born on March 31, 1934, in industrial Pennsylvania. Though most folks would name her birthplace as Smithton, she was actually born in Charleroi, in the smoky coal region of the "Mon"/Monongahela River Valley. Shirley was the only child of Marjorie and Paul Jones, who named their beautiful, blonde daughter after the child luminary Shirley Temple.

When Shirley was three years old, the Jones family moved to Smithton, a small town located on the banks of the Youghiogheny River. Smithton was– is– a charming place in

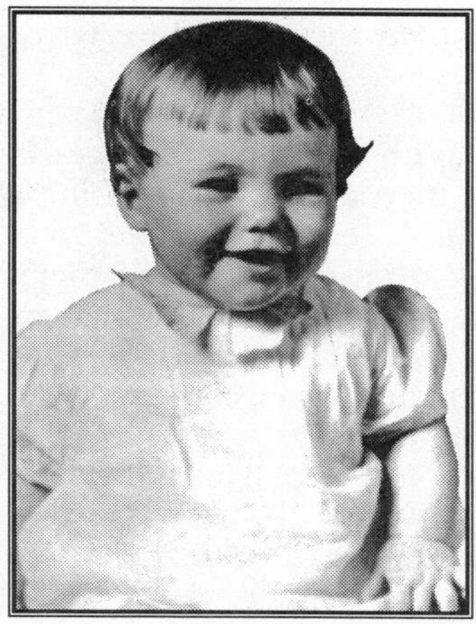

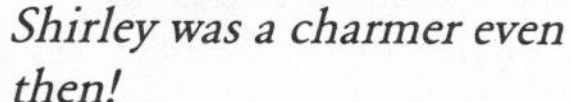

Shirley was a charmer even then!

Teenage Shirley Mae Jones

which to come of age. The tidy little village has five streets, town center, and five churches. Smithton people, then as now, are friendly and caring, and I can say this from firsthand experience.

When I began gathering material for this Chronicle, my husband and I made the less-than-twenty-mile journey, as a Sunday outing, to Smithton from our Connellsville home. Once there, we pulled over to one of the immaculate yards so that I could ask a woman, who was working in her flower bed, where Shirley's house used to be.

"Go to the end of the street. You're on Second, and this is her street. The red brick dentist's office on the corner is the site where Shirley's house once stood." With a smile, the same lady directed me to the old Shepp Theater, around the next corner, where Shirley attended movies, and to the former Jones Hotel– in fact, to all the "Shirley" sites round about the small town.

I wish her house were still there. I wish too that Smithton would erect some sort of permanent tribute to Shirley Jones. Southwestern Pennsylvania is no longer the forgotten corner of the state; and more and more, tourism is bringing visitors to this very special corner of Penn's Woods. When one considers the success of the Jimmy Stewart Museum in Indiana, Pennsylvania, Smithton might well consider a Shirley Jones museum.

Shirley's was a carefree, happy childhood in that pleasant hamlet abounding with friends and family. There, Shirley's grandfather, William B. "Stoney" Jones, a Welsh immigrant, had founded the Jones Brewery in 1907. Shirley's father and an uncle ran the establishment, which produced the brewery's flagstaff Stoney's Beer. The original name had been Eureka Gold Crown Beer, but the locals always asked for "one of Stoney's beers," so Stoney changed the name.

I remember that my father drank Stoney's because he said it contained less sugar than other beers. Via a bit of research, I discovered that Stoney's had no sugar, nor any preservatives or additives.

After Shirley's grandfather died, Jones' Brewery passed to her father Paul and his brothers. A landmark in the town of Smithton, the brewery remained in the Jones family until 1988, at which time it was purchased from the Jones estate by Gabriel Podlucky. Mr. Podlucky has since passed away; and from 2002 to this writing, Jones' is no longer functioning as a brewery. Though their license has been maintained, their orders are contracted out. Presently, Stoney's is being brewed at the Pittsburgh Brewing Company (home of that city's Iron City Beer) and across the state at Lion Brewery at Wilkes-Barre.

In addition to the brewery, Shirley's grandfather owned and operated, in Smithton, the Jones Hotel, formerly known as the Smith House. Today it is a private residence.

Shirley attended the local public schools. At the age of six, she became the youngest member of Smithton's Winnett Methodist Church Choir. Today, as it was in the 1950s, the church is picture-post-card pretty, gleaming white, its tall steeple reaching skyward, its windows diamond-paned.

It is interesting to note that Shirley's heritage, the Welsh, unlike the Irish and the Scots, are not known for the bagpipes. This group of Celts is celebrated for their voices, and yet today, Wales is known for its choral art form.

"I was raised to be a 'good little girl,' " Shirley stated in *Shirley and Marty, an Unlikely Love Story*, a refreshingly candid dual autobiography written with author Mickey Herskowitz. "[I was] raised to act the way a well-bred young lady is supposed to act. So, I figure there is a little demon ... a basic rebel inside me that likes to strike out; it surfaced when I was a child. And I was *never* a follower," she declared with gusto.

In regard to her childhood antics: "Oh, it was all very 1950s, tame by today's standards. I never did anything I knew would cause my parents grief." Well, almost never....

An outspoken child who grew up to be a forthright adult, Shirley was five when she experienced an adult pretense for the first time. The perpetrator was her beloved Aunt Ina. The story goes, according to the above autobiography, that Shirley was suffering from a toothache but refused to be taken to the dentist, whose office was located on the second floor of the five-and-dime store. Ina babysat Shirley often, and the child trusted her. The "great tooth deception" was for her own good, so Aunt Ina told Shirley a fib- that she knew a secret entrance into the dime store. Through the shadowy hall and up the dimly lit stairs they went, Aunt Ina, Shirley's mother, and "innocent" little Shirley, to the dentist's office, where the doctor was waiting. As soon as they entered, the dentist grabbed the blonde mop top, and over her face went the gas bag. Shirley was asleep in jig time, and out came the offending tooth.

When the angelic-looking little girl opened her eyes, her expressive brows rushed together as she focused on her aunt, fixing the adult with a most disgruntled look and the unexpected- incongruous- words: "Damn you, Aunt Ina." Even at age five, Shirley was a straight shooter.

Aunt Ina told author Herskowitz that after little Shirley awoke from a nap she would dress the child up and take her for a stroll around Smithton. "People would just stop and look at her. She was such a beautiful child."

The raid on the Smithton Fire Department is another example of the rebel that dwelled within the reaches of Shirley's heart. She was nine the night she orchestrated this action, and that "... was about as wild as the action got in Smithton..." with its estimated 500 population now and during the time of Shirley Jones' childhood. At around seven in the calm of a summer's evening, Shirley and two of her pals sauntered over to the fire station. Shirley had the naughty idea to pull the fire alarm "... just to see what would happen." Before her friends could object, Shirley reached out a small, dimpled hand, the manicured nails lacquered scarlet, and set off the alarm. Then the trio high-tailed it the block or so down to the Jones Hotel, where they dashed for cover under a bed.

One of her cohorts was a Jones cousin who resided with her family in an apartment at the hotel; and before they knew it, the Smithton fire engine, its siren screaming, came to a screeching halt in front of her grandfather's quiet inn. Racing into the lobby, the firemen asked a startled desk clerk where the fire was. The frantic room search began, and one of the girls squealed.

The "terrible three" were hauled down to the local constable's office. When all the parents arrived, everyone began talking nearly at once; a few were crying, and all were in accord that a "dreadful thing" had just happened.

Bucking up under the strain, Shirley asked the grim-faced constable, "Are you going to put us in jail?"

"Well, I could, you know." He didn't, but his lecture was a doozie.

When we see Ms. Jones on the silver screen in such classic films as *Carousel* and *The Music Man,* it is difficult to believe that she was a tomboy. "I was always doing things like that; I was *very* tomboyish. Because of the way I looked, I got away with a lot of mischief that my girlfriends didn't. One of them had a sort of coarse appearance, though she was every inch a lady. I was the one who looked like a little lady, when, in fact, I wasn't."

Shirley could never abide bullies; and she would come to the defense of those girls whom certain boys picked on "... because they wouldn't fight back. [The tormentors] didn't think I could stand up to them, and I always did," she told Mickey Herskowitz. "Bloody noses, broken fingernails... I was always coming home with my dress ripped, even on Sundays." Bloody nose or no, the local toughs quickly learned that pretty little Miss Jones was fearless, with the brave heart of a Celtic warrior.

Shirley shared this little story with me during our November 2006 interview: "I remember one day, I sat my dog in front of me and told him, heart-to-heart, that I thought it was time for a change. I cleaned up, brushed my hair and put on a frilly, feminine dress. When my mother saw me, she said- as she had so many times before, for the opposite reason- 'What happened to you!' I told her that I had decided to become the lady everyone wanted me to be... at least, I wanted to start looking like a girl."

Summers, Shirley, her friends and cousins all went swimming in Jacob's Creek, where the water was cool and the rapids not as risky as the contrary Youghiogheny River. There was camp in the summertime too. The one the Smithton girls attended was on Lake Erie. The summer Shirley was eleven, one of the camp counselors, Peggy Demler, heard Shirley sing, and the "... back of her neck tingled."

One did not have to possess a degree in music to recognize that Miss Jones had an extraordinary voice and a showmanship for delivery of her songs that was beyond her years. From the time she was four, Shirley enjoyed performing and could imitate a song she had heard once over the radio, note for note and lyric for lyric. Shirley's parents and her mother's sisters, Ina and Nell, were her first audience, and encores were the norm.

"The aunts were my first fans," Shirley has acknowledged. "They were always asking me to sing this or that, but my camp counselor, Peggy Demler, was the first person to really take my singing seriously... I was in awe of her. We would have little amateur shows at camp, and every other weekend, open house for the parents. I would always sing a solo, while Peggy played the piano. She was amazed that I was so polished at such a young age without ever having taken a lesson; so for the eight weeks or whatever I was at camp, she really cultivated my voice. When I went home, she telephoned my parents: 'Your daughter has something special, a very rare talent. You *must* give her lessons.' Peggy Demler made me aware...."

Shirley's mother arranged for piano instruction, until the persistent counselor called again, urging for voice lessons as well. "There were always people in my life, urging me on... Peggy was the first," Shirley has said.

"Mother was referred to the music critic for the *Pittsburgh Press*," Jones told me. "He and his wife were said to be, at the time, the top voice coaches in the city. His name was Ralph Lewando, and I began studying with him when I was twelve. We would drive into Pittsburgh once or twice a week, for an hour's lesson each time, and then I would practice at home with the local Smithton pianist."

Shirley's dearest friend, Charlotte Morrison-Lynn, whom she has always called "Red" due to her fiery locks, remembers: "Shirley's father was dedicated to her; nothing that involved Shirley was ever an inconvenience to him. I'd go with her sometimes on the drive to Pittsburgh; and he'd often remark to her, his expression reflecting his love and pride, 'One day, your name is going to be in lights.' Shirley would roll her eyes and shake her head... that was just a father talking."

Through most of her childhood, Shirley had entertained the idea of becoming a veterinarian, and though her intense love and respect for animals has never wavered, her career choice took an entirely different direction.

Charlotte related to me, in one of our many interviews, a little story that demonstrates Shirley's great compassion for animals. Not long past, her son Patrick telephoned her to say that he was attempting to rescue a stray dog that was navigating its perilous way across a busy intersection. Shirley rushed over, and together they succeeded in rescuing the poor animal- who found a permanent home with Shirley and Marty.

In regard to Shirley's fairytale discovery, there have been those who have said, "What luck!" Not entirely. It was more like "What talent!" Allow me to share with you some of the comments from people, from her hometown of Smithton, who have known Shirley Jones most of her life.

Diana Henry is a lovely person who has worked at Jones Brewery over forty years. She is a seven-generation "Smithtonite," whose relationship to Ms. Jones goes back to Shirley's childhood. "Shirley worked here in the office, summers," Diana told me during an interview. "All the Jones kids worked at the brewery summers for money for school things and such. As for Shirley... you could whisk her out of California, out of the Hollywood lifestyle, and put her right back in southwestern Pennsylvania, and she would fit right in. She has always been a small-town girl at heart. I have talked with her many times over the years, when she came home to visit family; and I can truthfully state that she has never put on airs. Her success, fame and fortune have not altered her one bit. Shirley has never lost that sweetness she demonstrated as "Laurey" in *Oklahoma!* And that quality was just as genuine then as it is today. There's never been anything fake about Shirley Jones.

"I remember one visit especially, when Shirley came home," Diana continued. "Her sons, the Cassidy boys, were all with her, and the youngest one wanted to visit a farm. Well, Lewis 'Bud' Barthels, who was the payroll clerk here at the brewery and the funeral director in town, came to the rescue. Bud's wife's family had a farm, and Shirley and the kids all piled into the car and off they went to see the animals. The littlest boy, as it turned out, became enthralled with the chicks; and he would not leave unless he could take a couple of those 'peepees' back to California with them. I believe Shirley ended up doing just that. I know one thing for certain; her children are everything to her. She was... *is* a fantastic mother."

Donna Kruper was the next person I interviewed. Again, I was struck by the warm reception I received from yet another longtime Smithton resident. "I've known Shirley ever since she was a young girl," Donna told me. "In fact, my husband's family were neighbors to the Joneses. My grandfather and Shirley's grandfather were best friends. Shirley grew up in the same house with her grandparents, so she had loving parents *and* grandparents to help guide her during her formative years. She was a good girl... what I would call a 'good, all-American girl.' And this was due to her proper upbringing with its strong faith in God and its strong work ethic," Donna concluded.

I knew Shirley's first serious crush had been Lewis Mologne, who went on to West Point and then to the University of Pittsburgh's medical school to become a highly decorated major general, Commander at Walter Reed, and the right-hand man to the Surgeon General. Mologne is the focus of the preceding Chronicle, "The Right Stuff," this volume. He told the Uniontown *Herald-Standard*, in regard to Shirley Jones, during a 1982 interview, "We came from the same small Pennsylvania town, where everybody knew everybody. Shirley is a very lovely lady who has charm to match her beauty."

Another former Smithton resident I interviewed was Dick Smith, whose best friends were Mologne, "Red" Morrison, and Jones. "Shirley and I have remained friends over the years and across the miles, and she has changed less than anyone I have ever known. She will always be charming and caring," Dick Smith related to me, "a great lady."

Shirley attended South Huntington (Twp.) High School located on Route 31. In 1966, the year numerous school jointures took place statewide, the old blue and gold of South Huntington High ceased to exist, amalgamating with Sewickley Township, Smithton Borough, West Newton Borough and Arona Borough to become the widespread Yough School District.

Shirley's productive high school years created wonderful memories. She and her best friend Charlotte "Red" Morrison were majorettes, and football seasons were especially filled with fun and excitement. Ms. Jones' yearbook pretty much tells the tale with inscriptions from friends reading: "To a swell girl," "To a pretty blonde," "To a great Head Majorette," and, of course, "To a girl with a terrific singing voice!"

"Miss Pittsburgh," 1952

After graduating with honors from South Huntington High in 1952, Shirley was spotted by a scout photographer for that year's Miss Pittsburgh Pageant. Kindred spirit Charlotte had encouraged her to get into camera-range of the photographer who was snapping shots of the sunbathers at a local pool. As a result, Shirley received an invitation to compete in the Miss Pittsburgh contest. She did– and she won.

"I was eighteen," she stated in her book, "one of the youngest, if not *the* youngest, of twelve contestants." Shirley won $500 and some jewelry, along with a scholarship to the drama school at the Pittsburgh Playhouse.

"As Miss Pittsburgh, I made a few appearances across the country, and then I went on to the Miss Pennsylvania competition." This time Shirley came in as first runner-up. Finishing as Miss Pennsylvania would have meant many more appearances, along with persistent duties. Coming in second in that contest was one of the best things that ever happened to her.

Shirley has often said that the real reward for the beauty contests was the chance to study drama, and she decided to take advantage of the two-year scholarship she had won at the Pittsburgh Playhouse. Her plan was to go on to college subsequent to her Playhouse apprenticeship.

In Pittsburgh, Shirley lived in a sorority house not far from Pitt campus. It was a sampling of college life, complete with a roommate and the exhilaration of being away from home for the first time and on her own. The drama students attended daytime classes. Nights, they performed at the dinner theater. Those good enough had the opportunity of putting their acting skills to work. Shirley already knew what she wanted to do with her life, and her career strategy was a good one. But then, in the summer of 1953, Destiny intervened in the guise of a trip to New York City. Suddenly, her plan was switched to fast-forward.

After borrowing $400 from her father, she headed for New York to the open audition of Rodgers and Hammerstein's stage production of *South Pacific*. Shirley was hoping to land a chorus part. When she arrived at the Broadway Theater, at the corner of Broadway and Fifty-second, the wings were packed with dancers and singers, most of them professionals who had several advantages over the teenage Shirley Jones.

In the semidark theater, the swarm of *South Pacific* hopefuls stood about, awaiting their turns to perform before a few key people in the "audience." "If they liked the person who had just sung," Shirley remembers, "they asked them to sing another song. If they didn't, they broke in after a few notes with a flat 'Thank you.' "

Over fifty girls had already auditioned when Shirley's turn came. She stepped to the spot where those who had gone before had sung, took a deep breath and launched into "The Best Things in Life Are Free." When she finished, a male voice carried across the dark and silent rows to where she stood waiting with, I am certain, bated breath. "That was lovely," the man pronounced. "Where are you from? And what have you done?"

Uncertain how to respond, Shirley hesitated. After a moment of silence, the voice asked kindly, "Have you ever been in a show?"

The straightforward Shirley answered, "No, I just got into town. I haven't done anything." She recalled, as those words fell from her lips, she became acutely aware of the bright spectrum of choruses and roles the preceding singers had rattled off from their résumés. "I thought I could sing- I *knew* I could sing- but I was not a pro. All of a sudden, I felt intimidated," Shirley related in her autobiography.

She soon discovered she was exchanging dialogue with *South Pacific*'s casting director, John Fernley. "Have you anything else prepared?" he asked then, his voice still gentle.

"Oh, yes, I do!" Shirley opened the thin folder of music she held and extracted "Lover," delivering the song in a high-soprano range, which prompted Fernley to request a third number.

At auditions, it is customary to sing familiar tunes, so the directors can better judge the performances. Shirley, however, pulled out a new love song written for her by a friend from the Pittsburgh Playhouse, Kenny Welch, who was teaching in New York, and who had accompanied her to the audition. Welch, by the bye, would go on to an award-winning musical stint with the Carol Burnett Show. His "My Very First Kiss" was *très ingénue*- very Shirley Jones- and it was, without overstatement, the *coup de theatre* that fated afternoon at the Broadway.

At the conclusion of the pretty little song, John Fernley, who had been leaning forward in his seat, sat back with an audible sigh. "Well, Miss Jones, I am *very* impressed." He also said he wanted someone else to hear her sing. The "someone" was across the street, rehearsing an orchestra. "Do you mind waiting while I call him over here?"

Shirley assured him that she did not mind at all. Then the casting director did yet another surprising thing. He announced to the assembly that he was going to need some time, and he suggested that they check back the following day. In a few minutes, the summoned man from across the street entered the theater, walked briskly up the aisle and seated himself in one of the front-row seats. After a few whispered exchanges between him and Fernley, the director asked Shirley to sing the same trio of songs she had performed earlier.

"You're just lovely, young lady," the new arrival projected from his seat, when she had finished. "You have a beautiful voice. My partner is at home, and I would like to have him hear you. Can you wait a while longer?

Shirley with her parents, Marjorie and Paul Jones

If I can reach him, it will take him about twenty-five minutes to get here."

Shirley was a tad speechless but answered in the affirmative: "Well... that's fine. And what is your name?"

The resonant voice rang out to the pretty young woman on the stage. "I'm Richard Rodgers."

"Of Rodgers and Hammerstein," it seemed to echo in the near-empty auditorium. Shirley's heart skipped a beat, but it was the only beat she missed that day. In everything else, she was right on cue. Behind her, at the piano, she heard her friend Kenny clearing his throat before he excused himself with the fact that he had a plane to catch. "That's no problem," Rodgers interposed. "I have a full orchestra across the street at the St. James."

Then, before she could say *"Oklahoma!"* she was stage-center at the stately old St. James, singing for the first time with the magic produced via a maestro's wand– before the celebrated team of Rodgers and Hammerstein. Shirley was somewhat familiar with the music– she had sung "Oh, What a Beautiful Morning" with her grade-school chorus– though she had to read the lyrics from the score someone had thrust into her trembling hands. From the moment the conductor nodded, and she opened her mouth to sing, her angelic voice carried the enchanted songs with gilded wings over the richness of the orchestra to the illustrious listeners in their front-row seats.

When she finished, there was a slight pause, which must have seemed like an eternity to the unseasoned girl. Then her tumbled thoughts were abruptly overwhelmed with a battery of rapid-fire questions: "Is this going to be your career?" "Do you intend to stay in New York?" "Would you promise not to go running back to Smithton, Pennsylvania?" Shirley answered each query– with a resounding "Yes!"

What followed was a whirlwind, fairytale dream-come-true. Shirley has said herself that those things just don't happen that way– but they did for her. She walked into the Broadway Theater that bright summer day in 1953, one of the hundreds who had come to audition for the most famous songwriting team in musical history, and signed a contract with them– all within an afternoon.

Securing a small part as one of the nurses in *South Pacific* was manna from heaven for a newcomer, because, in essence, that show had no chorus. Every member of the cast had dialogue. She was handed a script and instructed to observe the show the subsequent three days. During that same time, she was to learn *her* role, so that she could begin in the musical the following Wednesday matinee. She would be paid $120 per week. *It was all very exciting.*

What Shirley was not cognizant of was the fact that Dick Rodgers and Oscar Hammerstein had additional plans for the girl from the obscure little village in southwestern Pennsylvania. The celebrated musical team was deeply immersed in their search, via auditions and other means, for the peaches-and-cream female lead in their first big-screen musical production. Actually, the coast-to-coast quest for the right girl for the coveted role nearly equaled the search, back in the 1930s, for *Gone with the Wind's* Scarlett O'Hara. Shirley had become their leading candidate for "Laurey Williams," the pretty farm girl who falls in love with a handsome cowboy in the film version of *Oklahoma!* She certainly *looked* like their Laurey.

It was a risk, they knew, to cast an unknown. The box-office draw of a big-name star is always a consideration. Be that as it may, they also knew true talent when they encountered it; and *that* Miss Jones oozed, along with a shimmering beauty and an innocence that was downright captivating. Since *Oklahoma* was about a year away from going into production, they knew too, they would have sufficient time to groom their discovery for the female lead.

Shirley, who had been singing the songs of those legendary composers most of her life, was born to play the role of Laurey Williams. *The multitalented girl from Smithton, Pennsylvania, was on her way to the stars!*

After *South Pacific* closed, and with that stage experience under her belt, Shirley landed a featured role in Rodgers and Hammerstein's least successful show (no reflection on her), the forgettable *Me and Juliet.* No matter, for Shirley was studying, rehearsing, and learning all the while. "There is a myth," she has said, "that I kind of glided onto the scene. Well, making things look easy can be mighty hard work. I care about my craft, and I work at it every day. Never did I sail through a script or a musical score on some sort of automatic pilot."

Publicity shot of Shirley and co-star Gordon MacRae for Rodgers and Hammersteins's Oklahoma!

Perhaps what was remarkable, in addition to her talent, was the fact that on the outside, Shirley exhibited nerves of steel. "Oh, I had my bouts of nerves, but never did I churn with them. I never felt panic. Yes, I got, and still get, butterflies; however, mine are short-lived. By the time I have uttered the first words of my lines or sung the first notes, I have lost those fluttering little anxieties or apprehensions."

I want to point out that Shirley made the transition from stage to screen with aplomb. Some stage actors have difficulty making that transition, because one must exaggerate actions and expressions for theater; and that often results in overacting through the lens. Shirley never had a problem performing to the camera. "I loved the feeling of holding a thought and having it show on the screen. I loved close-ups," she told me. Many actors avoid watching themselves on the screen; but Shirley, who had never seen herself on such a scale, was instantly struck with that Pollyanna side of herself. "I loved it all. Everything connected to stage and screen excited me," she stated during our interview.

On the other hand, there were rules, regulations and restrictions. Though the era known as the "Big-Studio System" was just waning when Shirley came onto the scene, she underwent the typical Hollywood pressures. "I had a director who said I couldn't eat what and when I wanted to eat; a producer who told me what actor to be seen with. I had orders to get to sleep by eight every night, and I hated restrictions. I was young, after all, and as I said earlier, a bit on the rebellious side. Fred Zimmerman, my director on *Oklahoma,* as well as both Rodgers and Hammerstein, believed in the old star-system and were, therefore, possessive. I was their baby. I had a fierce dislike for that facet of what I saw coming."

I think it well worth sharing with you Shirley's feelings about keeping her given name. In the beginning, Richard Rodgers had wanted to change her name, stating that Jones was "too common." Again, it was that old MGM thinking; an actress needed a name that exuded glamour, such as Dorothy Lamour or Lana Turner. Despite their protests, Shirley flatly refused from the outset to let them change her name. She had grown up with the philosophy "Be yourself; an original is always better than a copy." The VIPs finally got the message.

Shirley chucked the "message" to a schlemiel reporter at Sardis not long after wrapping *Oklahoma!* The woman, known for her pretensions to cleverness, greeted Shirley with a forged smile and: "Shirley Jones. At least you could have changed your name. I mean, what could be so simple? *Shirley Jones from Smithton, Pennsylvania.*"

Our girl retorted with: "Well, I wanted to change it to Shirley Smith from Jonestown, but they didn't go for it."

There is always at least one of those types who seem to surface at life's most promising moment. Shirley's personal favorite is a press reaction penned by another Pennsylvania native, Hedda Hopper (of Hollidaysburg), after the release of *Oklahoma!* "She's a one-time Charlie. She's pretty, and she sings well; but it's a one-picture deal for this girl. She's never going to work again."

To refute Hedda, I will borrow a line from the life-affirming Shirley Jones film *April Love*: "Showin's better than tellin'!"

Shirley and I discussed, when I interviewed her for this Chronicle, how important mind over matter is, i.e., if you mind/image something, it will matter/materialize. If you have self-worth/good self-esteem, if you see yourself as a success, you can program/bring about positive results. And this reminds me of a motto of my own invention: *"Thoughts are magic wands, powerful enough to make anything happen– anything you choose!"*

Shirley was filming *Oklahoma* when she turned twenty-one. Happily, she was permitted to travel home to Smithton for the celebration. Her hometown welcomed her with open arms. Family and friends gathered at the Jones' house for the traditional cake and ice cream. The Smithton newspaper ran a feature with the headline: "Shirley Home for Birthday." The March 31, 1955, article began: "Shirley Jones, Smithton's 'Cinderella Girl' will blow out 21 candles on a home-baked cake at a birthday party here tonight."

A special telegram arrived from Rodgers and Hammerstein: "Dear Shirley. We hope to be associated with you one way or another for many more happy birthdays and meanwhile we send you our congratulations and love. Dick and Oscar."

A birthday greeting also arrived from *Oklahoma's* director Fred Zimmerman: "Congratulations, dear Laurey, in the wonderful year that lies ahead." It would be a wonderful year- *and then some.*

Before we leave *Oklahoma*, I must share with you some colorful information about the hit that was both Shirley's and Rodgers and Hammerstein's first movie. The filming was not done in Oklahoma, but in Nogales, Arizona; because the studio wanted to capture the beautiful cumulus clouds that were the area's claim-to-fame. Secondly, the studio planted corn months in advance in order to have it just the right height during filming. Trivia, but interesting *fodder*, nonetheless.

Next came Rodgers and Hammerstein's *Carousel*, the story about a pretty, innocent young mill worker named Julie Jordan who falls head-over-heels in love with a self-centered carousel barker named Billie Bigelow.

Publicity shot of Shirley and co-star Gordon MacRae for Rodgers and Hammersteins's *Carousel*

It is my contention that the storyline reflects the movement of the carousel. Everything in life moves in a circle– the seasons, the tides, as well as human cycles and emotions. Often in life, our emotions take us on a merry-go-round ride, whereby we experience a whole circuitous route of feelings. And frequently our lives come full circle. Unemployment and hard times add to Billie's moodiness, resulting in his abuse of his wife, who announces that she is pregnant. Rather than finally accepting his responsibilities as husband and father-to-be, Billie chooses to follow the advice of a "friend," who convinces him to get hold of a knife so the pair of them can liberate the mill owner from his money. Billie falls on the knife, trying to escape the authorities after the failed robbery. The death scene with "Julie"/Shirley at his side is very well executed; and, I think, illustrates, beyond a doubt, the young Shirley Jones' natural ability as an actress. *In support of my observation, Shirley was the only performer the two Broadway musical geniuses ever put under contract.*

An exuberant, carousel-riding Shirley was featured on the cover of the February 6, 1956, edition of *Life,* in which the popular magazine stated under the heading "A New Star Livens Musical's Revival": "*Carousel,* the second of the Rodgers-Hammerstein gold mine of Broadway classics to be made into a film is about to burst out all over, like June [shades of a hit song from the show]. *Carousel* is the first release in their new 55-mm CinemaScope process... but more noteworthy... is *Carousel*'s 21-year-old leading lady, Shirley Jones, who with co-star Gordon MacRae came straight from *Oklahoma!* Shirley, who plays an appealing Julie Jordan, is a show business phenomenon...."

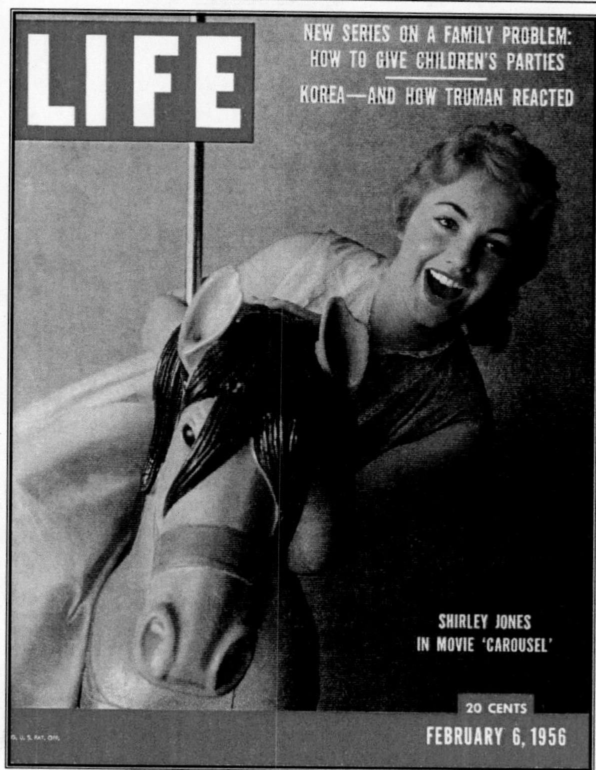

A radiant Shirley on the cover of Life

Carousel concludes with Billie Bigelow redeeming himself by returning to earth for a single day to help his fifteen-year-old daughter, whom he has never met, of course, and whom he does not want to see make the same mistakes he made. Billie leaves her- and Julie- with the eternal gift of love. At the film's conclusion, Shirley delivers the elevating song "You'll Never Walk Alone" with heartfelt emotion mirrored on her radiant features.

For one so young, as she was at the time *Carousel* was filmed, Miss Jones emoted beautifully. I could not help but think that song from her reel-life, with its powerful lyrics, was something that Shirley took out and dusted off, from time to time, in real life, whenever anxieties had to be subdued and adversity trounced.

Beginning with the mid-fifties, Shirley has appeared in a multitude of popular magazines. I came across a charming leap-year article, "Now's Your Chance, Girls," that appeared in one fifties' publication: "Shirley Jones demonstrates with a co-operative friend some *subtle* stratagems for catching a man. Let him think he's a hero... by taking a cinder out of your eye." You've got to love the innocence of the times!

Shirley was afraid of being type-cast as the wholesome sweetheart in a succession of musicals, thus after *Carousel,* she entreated the heads of Twentieth-Century Fox for roles that would give her more leeway as an actress. Their response was *April Love,* another musical, with Pat Boone.

When *April Love* was filming, the Hollywood trade papers made much of the "fact" that the married Boone declined to kiss leading lady Shirley Jones for religious reasons. Years later, in the autumn of 1997 when Shirley took part in the Fisher/Merlis production of *The Real Me* for Nostalgia Good TV, Boone, in a taped interview, told the tale of the missing *April Love* kiss. It so happens he had gotten the go-ahead from his wife Shirley to kiss his co-star Shirley, but due to the "trades," the kiss never happened. On *The Real Me,* however, Pat looked into the camera and said to a rather surprised Shirley Jones, "I'm all puckered up and ready for that kiss you owe me."

Filmed in 1957, *April Love,* though never a huge hit, is a heartwarming movie that was *perfectly* cast. The film was aptly named, I think. Full of promise, April is so like first love. The underlying theme of this story is hope. Sometimes I think that when Pandora opened that fateful box and all the evils poured out, and then she withdrew the one blessing, hope, what she really pulled from the box was April. For in many ways April is hope.

When *April Love* debuted in my hometown, I saw it about five times. It is still one of my favorite Shirley Jones vehicles. "Shirley's parents visited her on the set of *April Love*," Charlotte Morrison-Lynn informed me, "and they are identifiable in the stands in the horseracing scene that takes place toward the end of that movie." Shirley related to me personally that she did her own sulky driving in that film.

Two comedies followed- *Never Steal Anything Small* (a musical comedy) and *Bobbikins*, in 1959 and 1960, respectively. Then, just when everyone thought Hollywood had found their perfect little "goody-two-shoes," along came *Elmer Gantry*. It was the film that established Shirley Jones as an actress rather than a singer-actress. With aim and élan, Shirley walked across the street from Twentieth-Century-Fox to Warner Brothers to play, opposite Burt Lancaster, the juicy role of the prostitute Lulu Bains.

Lancaster had strongly suggested Shirley for the part after seeing her play an alcoholic in the *Playhouse 90* production of "The Big Slide," a performance that was both moving and convincing, not to mention that it earned her an Emmy nomination.

The problem, at first, with *Gantry* was that director Richard Brooks had his mind set on Piper Laurie for Lulu. Though Shirley, by that point in time, had done several dramatic television roles, "The label of 'musical lady' was a difficult one to shed," she told me.

Shirley landed the part, a detail that did not exactly thrill Brooks, who quickly made his feelings apparent before the picture even went into production. The first day of filming turned out to be Shirley's biggest *Gantry* challenge, because it was the most demanding scene for her character. To her utter surprise, she was on her own. Brooks, offering no direction whatsoever, voiced flatly: "Let's see how you do it." Shirley was convinced that he was waiting for her to fall apart, so he could fire her. Despite everything, and exhibiting the kind of grit our indomitable Shirley has become famous for, she shot all of that vital first day on *Gantry* sans any direction.

The subsequent evening, after Brooks had seen the first day's rushes, he telephoned Shirley's home, humbly offering his apologies and telling her that she might end up being the best thing in the picture." *She was.*

Publicity shot of Shirley and co-star Pat Boone for *<u>April Love</u>*

Elmer Gantry turned out to be a highpoint in Shirley's enduring career. She deservingly went home with Oscar for Best Supporting Actress that golden year of 1960 for her brilliant performance as the memorable Lulu Bains, the country girl who had gone wrong, turned vengeful, but who was still possessed of a good heart.

Again I must comment on Shirley's ability to convey sentiment via facial expressions and body language. Film, don't forget, is a *visual* art form, and that is what gives it such *impact*. As a screenwriter, I was always taught to show it more than tell it. "If you cannot show it, then give an actor a line." People do not always say what is truly in their minds and hearts, and that is *why* facial expressions and body language are so much more telling. Shirley Jones does this better, I think, than any actor I have ever observed on stage, screen and television. This inimitable artist's facial expressions and body language in *Elmer Gantry*, especially her scene with the nylon stocking, are pure genius.

There are a few human-interest tidbits I can offer in connection with *Gantry*. Burt Lancaster had been a heartthrob of Shirley's since she had been a preteen in Smithton. "We used to have a wall, each of us, in our bedrooms, where we taped images of our favorite stars," Charlotte Morrison-Lynn shared with me in an interview. "Lancaster was one of them. We even kissed those pictures 'good-night.' Who would have thought that ten years later Shirley would be playing opposite him in a movie!"

At the outset of *Elmer Gantry*, Lancaster took the anxious Shirley under his wing and reassured her. Their friendship endured until his passing. Interesting too is that Burt, an ardent opera fan, did his own singing in the film, as well as the acrobatics. A former circus acrobat, Lancaster was an excellent athlete. If you read "The Bright Path," a Chronicle about Jim Thorpe in the second volume of this series, then you know how impressed Thorpe was with Lancaster's athletic ability during the filming of the classic *Jim Thorpe- All American*. By the way, movie fans, Shirley related to me that of all her leading men, Lancaster was the best kisser.

In regard to the *Gantry* masterpiece, I think it fascinating that Shirley's ultra-supportive grandmother's name was Lulu, the appellation of the character that would win her the Oscar. [Though her given name was Loise, friends and family called her "Lulu." Later, after the grandchildren were born, this caring *grande dame* became known as "Mammie Jones."] Moreover, Shirley's mother's maiden name was "Williams," the surname of the character "Laurey" that exploded Shirley's brilliant career before the public. "For those who may be interested in numbers," Shirley told me that the Broadway opening of *Oklahoma* was on her birthday, March 31, 1943. Ten years later, on her birthday in 1953, she made her first Broadway appearance in *South Pacific.* Indeed, the name "Shirley Jones" flashed prophetically across the Milky Way before it shone along the "Great White Way"!

Shirley and Elmer Gantry co-star Burt Lancaster the night they won their Oscars, 1960

Shirley married actor-singer Jack Cassidy in the summer of 1956, whom she had met several months earlier when *Oklahoma* had gone on the road for a European tour. Their first date was in Paris, the "City of Eternal Lights," where the chestnut trees fairly sigh *l'amour.*

Shirley had been warned by just about everyone not to fall for her leading man. Nevertheless, in New York, when he had walked for the first time into her view, the picture of male elegance and sophistication, Shirley, like others before her, had been instantly captivated by his Irish wit and charm. Irrespective of his gripping first impression, it was what he said to her at the close of their first evening together that left a lasting one: "I'm going to marry you."

A year and a half after his divorce was final, the enamored couple wed, on August 5, 1956, at the New Church of Jerusalem in Cambridge, Massachusetts,

Publicity shot of Shirley and co-star Burt Lancaster for Elmer Gantry

on the Harvard campus where they had been performing together in *The Beggar's Opera.* Their characters were married on stage with every performance; and since the real marriage took place between their matinee and evening shows, the pair exchanged vows thrice that memorable August day. Shirley's best friend Charlotte Morrison-Lynn was her matron of honor, and another close friend, Shari Price, was her maid of honor.

As an afterword to this segment of Shirley's story: When Shirley related to a confidante what Jack had told her at her door in Paris, she replied: "Oh, Shirley, I'm so worried about you. He's going to break your heart. You're going to be in for a terrible time." Shirley has said that the friend meant well; but at that point in time, "It was already too late." Ms. Jones recounted in her memoirs that it would be twenty years before her friend's prediction would come to pass. To quote the insightful Mickey Herskowitz: "As bad as the bad times would get, for all the pain she and Jack would share, none of it would outweigh the happy times or make Shirley wish she could erase the past."

Upon her marriage to Jack Cassidy, Shirley became the stepmother of six-year-old David Cassidy. Shirley and Jack's union produced three handsome sons. In 1958, she had her first born Shaun, followed by Patrick and Ryan. What was surprising to me, a longtime fan, is that Shirley was pregnant with Patrick during the filming of *The Music Man.* In the movie, she certainly doesn't look pregnant. Shirley has said that she was grateful it was a period piece; the costumes with petticoats helped hide her condition. When the picture wrapped, Shirley scooted to her dressing room to slip into a comfortable robe, then she came out to say her goodbyes to the cast and crew. "Shirley, where have you been hiding *that*!" the director exclaimed, pointing to her stomach. Shirley's response was, "I told you we could do it, and we did!"

The public had clamored to see again the "good Shirley"; thus she had been cast as Marion, the librarian, in the successful 1962 *Music Man.* Robert Preston had brilliantly played the role on Broadway, and his stellar performance combined with Shirley's was pure *magic.*

I must deviate for just a second, and I don't think Shirley will mind. I saw the magical Preston on Broadway in *The Music Man.* I was only in grade school, but I harbored a secret love for him. I also caught his last Broadway play, *Sly Fox,* in 1976. The man whose voice Richard Burton so aptly hailed "golden thunder," gave forth a radiance on stage. During *Sly Fox*'s umpteenth curtain call, I focused my grandmother's opera glasses on the beaming Mr. Preston to see a face that shimmered with tears and his great love for his craft. *Robert Preston was theater.*

Publicity shot of Shirley with co-star Robert Preston for *<u>The Music Man</u>*

After the box-office success of *The Music Man,* several other winning projects followed for Shirley. The one I want to discuss next is a television movie entitled *Silent Night, Lonely Night.* Filmed in 1969, the story is a drama about two lonely people who have a chance encounter at a New England college town during the holiday season. She has come to pick up her son who is in prep school, and he to visit his wife who is in an asylum. She has recently learned that her husband has been unfaithful, and his wife is incurably insane. They discover that they are the only two people registered that

Christmas Eve at the local inn; and in their pain, and through their loneliness, they come together for a brief but poignant moment in time. Lloyd Bridges starred opposite Shirley, and the project was a huge success with Shirley winning a well-deserved Emmy.

Silent Night, Lonely Night used to air every holiday season during the decade of the seventies, and I never missed watching it. This bittersweet story remains one of my favorite Shirley Jones movies, because it is brimming with truth. So many of us have had such a juncture in our lives when a special someone turned to walk away, and we *knew* we would never see him or her again. Like history, art is truth. There are messages contained within that truth that a good writer or actor delivers via their art form. Shirley delivered to perfection in both *Elmer Gantry* and *Silent Night, Lonely Night* the soul-reaching message that, for the most part, there are no saints or devils; i.e., the quintessence of most human beings is neither lily-white nor diabolical black. Most of us are varying "shades of grey."

When I went to my computer for Shirley Jones' film, stage, and television projects, as well as her numerous awards, I was deluged with an avalanche of sheets from my printer. Some of her films for the silver screen, in addition to the above mentioned *Oklahoma!, Carousel, April Love* and *Elmer Gantry*, are: *Never Steal Anything Small, Pepe, Two Rode Together, The Courtship of Eddie's Father, A Ticklish Affair, Dark Purpose, Bedtime Story*, and *The Cheyenne Social Club,* among others. In 2006, Shirley did the voice-over for Mrs. Santa Claus in the animated, feature-film tale of a young orphan girl. *"Christmas Is Here Again"* is scheduled to be released for the 2007 holiday season.

Movies for television include: *Silent Night, Lonely Night; The Girls of Huntington House, The Family Nobody Wanted, Winner Take All, Yesterday's Child, Visions of Christmas Past, There Were Times, Dear*, and the 2006 Hallmark film entitled *Hidden Places.*

Shirley has done, to date, two television series- the 1970-1974 *Partridge Family* and in 1979-80, *Shirley.* In 2006, Shirley joined the cast of *Lifetime* TV's primetime soap *Monarch Cove*, filming several episodes in Australia. "I played a grandmother who has cancer," Shirley told me during our interview. "The role afforded me my first-ever death scene." I want to add that Shirley has made literally countless television appearances in dramas, comedies, musicals, specials, and talk shows.

Shirley's stage productions include, *South Pacific, Oklahoma!, Maggie Flynn, Wait Until Dark* (with Jack Cassidy), *On a Clear Day, Show Boat, The Sound of Music, Bittersweet, Love Letters* (with Marty Ingels), *The King and I, 42nd Street*, and *Carousel.* A word about *42nd Street* (with son Patrick): To date, this play is the only time a mother and son performed together on Broadway.

Shirley Jones' awards and achievements are also too numerous to mention in full. They include: 1972 Woman of the Year (Children's Aid Organization); 1979 Susan Award (National Leukemia Broadcast Council); Distinguished Humanitarian Award (Anti-Defamation League) (shared with husband Marty Ingels); 1986 Angels Award (shared with Ingels for outstanding humanitarian endeavor); 1986 People Award; 1986 Deedra Award (for her work in *There Were Times, Dear* about Alzheimer's); 1987 First World Citizen Award (also shared with Ingels for International Foster Parents Plan); 1987 the Diamond Jubilee Appreciation Award (shared with Ingels); 1987 El Niño Services (shared with Ingels for nonprofit child and youth counseling); 1988 Woman of the Year (Childhelp USA); 1988 Gift of Life Award (National Leukemia Council) (shared with Ingels for fifteen years of exceptional service in the fight against this illness); 1991 Honorary Doctor of Humane Letters Degree, Point Park College, Pittsburgh, Pennsylvania. In 1996, the Westmoreland College at Youngwood, Pennsylvania, established a drama scholarship in Shirley's name. In 1998, the Harvey Award was presented to Shirley by the Jimmy Stewart Museum in Indiana, Pennsylvania. In 2000, Shirley received the Community Appreciation Award at Big Bear Lake, and in 2001, the Hope Through Empowerment Award.

That same year, Shirley was the very first recipient ever of the newly created Crystal Award for *all* her outstanding achievements; and in 2005, this multifaceted icon received an Honorary Doctor of Fine Arts Degree from Washington and Jefferson College at Washington, Pennsylvania.

Of course, we must not neglect to pinnacle this list with Shirley's Oscar for *Elmer Gantry* and her Emmy for *Silent Night, Lonely Night.* Emmy nominations include: "The Big Slide" for *Playhouse 90* in 1956 opposite Red Skelton; *There Were Times, Dear,* 1983, and Hallmark's *Hidden Places* in 2006. Shirley was also nominated for a 2006 SAG/Screen Actors Guild Award for her supporting role in *Hidden Places.*

No sooner had I completed the awards' segment of this chronicle, when I noted in the newspapers that in June 2007, at the Pittsburgh Civic Light Opera's Pink Frolic Ball, *Shirley Jones will be the ninth recipient of the Richard Rodgers Award for Excellence in Musical Theater.* A joint presentation of the Pittsburgh Civic Light Opera, the families of Richard Rodgers and Oscar Hammerstein II, and the Rodgers and Hammerstein Organization, the award recognizes the lifetime contribution of outstanding talent in musical theater. Because of Shirley's close ties to the southwestern region of Pennsylvania, coupled with the fact that she is a CLO alumna, this event is especially meaningful to this exceptional performer who has always been proud to hail from the "Keystone State." *Ms. Jones is the first true Pennsylvanian to receive the prestigious award.*

The Partridge Family

As an Academy Award winner, Shirley always receives an invitation to the annual Oscar presentations. However, she has never been keen on big celebrity events, and she and husband Marty watch many of those functions from the comfort of their living room.

On Valentine's Day, 1986, Shirley Jones received her star, number 1822, located at 1541 Vine Street in Hollywood, on the gilded Hollywood Walk of Fame.

Shirley is a lady who never puts on the brakes. She is constantly on the go, filming, doing guest spots on television, live shows and concerts across America and overseas, as well as her ongoing charity work. *In fact, Shirley Jones is consistently listed as one of the top ten "Most Admired Women in America."*

Though she has always been a busy career woman, her children have always come first in her life. Shirley has often declared that they are her proudest achievements. Thus, I think it important to mention in brief what they are doing at this writing.

Shaun Paul Cassidy is the first son of Shirley and Jack Cassidy. He works behind the scenes for Touchstone Disney. Patrick William Cassidy has been in several films and numerous television shows. In 2006, Patrick, his wife Melissa, and his entire family shone brilliantly in the national tour of *Joseph and the Amazing Technicolor Dreamcoat.* Ryan John Cassidy was in law enforcement for awhile, though he has also done some acting. Presently, he is putting his talent to use behind the camera as a set designer.

Stepson David Cassidy (whose mother was actress Evelyn Ward, Jack Cassidy's first wife) co-starred with Shirley in the TV series *The Partridge Family*- which, by the way, has enamored a whole new generation in reruns. The show made David a teen idol, spiraling him to stardom. By-products of the show were hit single tunes, such as the 1970's "I Think I Love You," and albums, including *A Partridge Family Christmas,* which is one of my nostalgic holiday favorites. David is still doing concerts throughout the United States.

Actress Susan Dey, who played Shirley's daughter on the *Partridge Family,* has often expressed fond memories of that experience. She describes Shirley as the "... kindest, most generous woman," saying too that she learned about the best of herself and her acting ability via Shirley's guidance.

Shirley and Jack Cassidy were divorced in 1976. He tragically died in an apartment fire the following year. Of Cassidy, Shirley has said: "Jack had a breakdown. A real mental breakdown. He was manic depressive. But he was the one who wanted the divorce. He thought it was better for me and the kids. I never did. I would have hung in there."

In 1977, Shirley married comedian/super-agent Marty Ingels. Though I have read that theirs is an "unlikely" love story, I think that it is, at the same time, not so unlikely. It is my belief that in a successful marriage, a couple can be quite different- opposites, in fact- in temperament. Often that is preferable, as long as their philosophy of life is the same. Shirley has said that when she met Marty, he made her laugh. "He can always make me laugh... and I am never bored," she revealed. Of Shirley, Marty has quipped that though "Shirley lives and functions in a world of flowers and frenzy, she sees only the flowers."

This might be a good time to mention that Shirley and her husband's engrossing autobiography, *Shirley and Marty, an Unlikely Love Story,* will be translated to a TV movie. The date of release is yet unknown, but I can state with certainty that both Shirley and Marty are involved with the creative control.

The pair has accomplished many things together, including FAWN, their own charity, which they began in 2001, when they purchased property in the Big Bear region of California at Fawnskin in order to preserve the integrity of that rustically beautiful small town. The caring couple has turned the grounds into a lovely public park with an outdoor stage, where Shirley, Marty, and other entertainers perform concerts. A special segment of Fawn Park, displaying a portion of steel from the World Trade Center's Twin Towers, is designed as a 911 Memorial.

For further information about Shirley's charity work, her public appearances, and all other Shirley Jones data and news, please visit "The Official Internet Web Site For the Inimitable Shirley Jones." The site is continually updated and contains a wealth of images and information about "Pennsylvania's- America's- Sweetheart." Contributions to Shirley's charity can be deducted from your taxes. And with that I want to state how much I have always admired this lady for putting so much back into the system. Pennsylvania's Shirley Jones is truly an inspiration to the world, for both her enduring stellar career and her countless humanitarian achievements.

I have saved the best for last. Before concluding this section of the book, I want to share with you some of the personal memories I have gleaned from Charlotte Morrison-Lynn, Shirley's dearest friend, "Red." I was fortunate enough to be able to secure several lengthy interviews with Charlotte, and I want to openly thank her for her patience and kindness.

One of the first things Charlotte said to me was: "Shirley honored me and our friendship by choosing me as her matron of honor when she married Jack Cassidy. She could have asked just about anyone, but she chose me. Where to begin with my impressions of Shirley? She and I have been best friends for about seventy years! We are the sisters neither of us had. We started out making mud pies, under the steps of the Jones Hotel, and progressed to 'sweetie pies' with the heart-flutter-

"Pennsylvania's- America's -Sweetheart," the inimitable, indomitable Shirley Jones
The above photos courtesy Shirley Jones

Shirley and best friend Charlotte "Red" Morrison (Lynn) circa 1947, Smithton, PA

ing exhilaration of first boy friends. Shirley's was Lew Mologne, whom you paid tribute to in this volume, while mine was Dick Smith, another Smithton native you've mentioned. The four of us remained friends until Lew's sad and untimely death.

"Our high school years were very special," Charlotte stated with pleasant reverie. "Shirley and I were majorettes together, high-kicking our way through that happy era, all the while enjoying football games, parties, chorus- both school and church- and the 'high drama' of our class plays. In spite of all the activities, we both managed to graduate with honors.

"We each had loving parents who provided us with the good foundation that every child needs to carry him or her through life. Always a leader and a bit of a rebel, Shirley did give her parents a few grey hairs. Besides the famous fire-alarm episode you cited, I recall another, much earlier, incident when Shirley was six. This one took place at the annual family Christmas party hosted by her grandmother. That evening, Shirley belted out a rip-snortin' rendition of 'Frankie and Johnny,' " Charlotte laughed with the memory. "It was very bluesy and quite... *animated*. And though her parents didn't think it appropriate for the occasion, we all knew, then and there, that Shirley was multitalented."

"Frankie and Johnny" triggered another humorous episode, and after a reflective pause, Charlotte continued: "While Shirley was studying at the Pittsburgh Playhouse, and I was attending college in Pittsburgh, she asked me to accompany her on a Playhouse assignment- to critique a burlesque show at the Stanley Theater. Knowing that my parents would be upset if I skipped school- let alone to attend a burlesque show- I had my serious qualms and mentioned this to Shirley, whose reply was, 'Yes, Red, but who will ever find out?' So, off we went, on what we fancied was an exciting adventure.

"After purchasing our tickets, we entered the dark theater, taking seats in the center section. Once the sultry music came up, and the show with its dancing, prancing burlesque performers began, Shirley nudged me, whispering for me to check out the audience. After scanning our surroundings, I discovered, to my chagrin, that we were the only two females in the place! As each of the ladies on stage sashayed to the beat, I sank down into my seat, further, I think, with each bump and grind. Needless to say, we ducked out a bit early to avoid the male crowd.

"As it turned out, Shirley got an 'A' on her Playhouse assignment, and I received a

More like sisters than friends, Shirley and Charlotte "Red" Morrison-Lynn circa 1998
Photo images with Shirley and Charlotte courtesy Charlotte Morrison-Lynn

severe tongue-lashing from my parents when my mother discovered the theater stub in my sweater... but it was fun and worth the lecture. We had really felt like sophisticates." Again Charlotte's voice carried laughter on her words. "And who would have thought that, years later, a couple of those burlesque moves would be pulled from Shirley's mental file and 'Shirley-ized' for 'Lulu' in *Elmer Gantry*!

"On a more solemn note, Shirley evoked tears from those in attendance at Smithton's packed Methodist church when she sang 'The Lord's Prayer' at my wedding four months prior to hers and Jack's. A year or so later, Shirley and I shared our first pregnancies. When she was about to give birth to her first son Shaun, Shirley traveled clear across the country to be with me for the birth of my daughter Lisa," Charlotte pronounced with feeling. "What does *that* say about her love and support for a friend?

"Though Shirley has lived and worked in Beverly Hills for some fifty years," Charlotte concluded, echoing the others I had interviewed, "she is not typically Hollywood. Whenever we visit or vacation together- which is often- our conversations focus on family and children. Those times, we do all the things we have enjoyed since we were girls together in Pennsylvania. We attend movies, bargain shop, and kick back to simply relax.

"We have so much history together... it would take days to relate it all. The bottom line, though perhaps a bit clichéd, is this that comes from the very core of my soul: I am truly *blessed* to have Shirley Jones- *who is beloved worldwide*- as my oldest and dearest friend."

Shirley's live performances commence with a nostalgic trip back in time, as a projectionist lights up a big screen with a series of clips from her films. These comprise an impressive array of her leading men, including fellow Pennsylvanian Jimmy Stewart. Most of those actors are gone now, and that is why, in the wings, Shirley does not watch. "I can't; I really tear up," she confessed to me during our interview.

Shirley pays tribute to Richard Rodgers and Oscar Hammerstein in the "two or three" live performances she does per month. At Greensburg, Pennsylvania's Palace Theater, backed by an excellent orchestra conducted by her musical director, Ron Abel, Ms. Jones gave a *stellar* performance. I must interject here that Ron is more than "Abel"- he is *brilliant*. In a separate interview with him over lunch, I learned that he has written a musical soon to debut on Broadway. As both conductor and pianist on stage with Shirley, his performance is nothing short of virtuoso. *An Evening with Shirley Jones* was over ninety minutes of pure entertainment. I cannot ever remember attending a more enjoyable show.

Author with Shirley Jones, November 2006, Greensburg, PA Photo by author's husband Phillip R. Lincoln

Shirley's voice is just as resonant and strong as it was fifty years ago. The electrifying, crystal-clear notes of *Carousel*'s "You'll Never Walk Alone" literally brought me to tears; and as I glanced about, I saw that tears glittered in the eyes of audience members all around me. If ever you have an opportunity to attend a live Shirley Jones performance, I highly recommend you do. With no exaggeration, it will be *the* theater experience of a lifetime.

It is difficult to believe that this *grande dame* (at this writing) is seventy-three. Shirley never denies her age. In fact, she states it with pride. Yes, her pixie-styled hair is white now- *au natural, reflective of her personality which is untouched by her fame*- but the stunning Ms. Jones exudes an enthusiasm for life that renders her forever-young.

At the pre-show reception I attended, Shirley shared memories and warm embraces with cousins, classmates, friends and former neighbors. It was a wonderful experience for me to watch "Pennsylvania's Sweetheart" interacting with old and new devotees. Sometimes the things one cannot see are the things one remembers the most. Shirley Jones possesses a glow- a presence- that is rather indefinable. When she enters a room, she brings into that space genuine warmth. And on stage... well, she lights up a stage like no one else. It is the charisma we noted in each of her characters on both the big and the small screens; and in person, it is, in a word- *magnetic*.

That morning, during our interview at her hotel, Ms. Jones welcomed my husband and me into her suite with the kindliness of an old friend. Starstruck, I was a bit nervous; however, she immediately put me at ease. Never had I encountered a more gracious hostess. A great lady, Shirley Jones- a *lady* in every sense of the word.

Before our visit concluded, she conveyed to me this message to her fellow Pennsylvanians: "I love Pennsylvania. It thrills me when I can perform in my home state; it is always a great homecoming. Pennsylvania is the most beautiful state in the Union. *Everything here is very dear to me.* I love the charming little towns, the rich history, the rustic beauty of our woods... and since I have been living in Southern California, I miss the lovely Pennsylvania season changes. I loved traveling, when I was a girl, with my parents to the colorful Amish districts of the state, where the family-style dinners were unforgettable.

"Growing up in a small Pennsylvania town- which was like an extended, loving family- gave me solidity. I have always said that I owe my confidence and self-esteem (which equipped me with what I needed to realize my goals), as well as my strong work ethic, to my Smithton roots. I have so many wonderful hometown memories... Pennsylvania will always be my true home."

Ms. Jones has never lost touch with her Pennsylvania roots. In March 2007, she made a very special telephone call to the cast of *Oklahoma* at Belle Vernon Area High School (Westmoreland County, the Fay-West area of SW PA). The cast included two of her young cousins, Shannon Page and Krystal Page. Shirley then spent the subsequent quarter-of-an-hour on the phone with the show's main characters, answering their questions and wishing them luck. Prior to curtain, the show's musical director informed the house that they were in for a special treat, and the call was shared with the audience. What a boost for those hopeful young thespians on their opening night!

For a half-century now Shirley Jones has delighted audiences with her craft, beginning when the crown of "Miss Pittsburgh" was placed atop her golden locks. Since, she has accumulated many accolades, awards and titles; but the one that has resonated the loudest is the one of which she is most proud.

Shirley Mae Jones of Smithton *is* "Pennsylvania's- America's- Sweetheart"!

"The Wonder Dancers"

"Among other things, I was a gandy dancer before I became a professional dancer of the world-famous team of Woods and Bray, also known as 'The Wonder Dancers.' It has been a full, and I might add, a wonderful life. However, it wasn't easy. It was a long... and difficult struggle getting to the top of my profession."– Billy Bray, né Anthony Caliguire, 1974

"This biography hasn't one word of fiction," Billy Bray penned during the summer of 1974. "It is a true one, and all the particulars that are stated here are true– just as they happened."

By the end of that July, the elegant man, who could still turn heads whenever and wherever he entered a room, had just turned seventy. Billy Bray, of the world-famous dance team of Woods and Bray, was born Anthony Caliguire on July 29, 1904, in this author's hometown of Connellsville, Fayette County, Pennsylvania.

At the turn of the last century, Connellsville was at the height of her coal-and-coke boom, and the smoky town was known far and wide as the "Coke Capital of the World." A by-product of coal, coke was used to make steel; and the Connellsville coke was the undisputed best in the world for manufacturing the best steel in the world in the not-too-distant, even smokier city of Pittsburgh. There, the mills were insatiably hungry for Connellsville coke; and from the "Steel City," coal carried coal, by rail and by boat, to points all across the country and beyond.

The Connellsville Coking Basin extended from Latrobe to Fairchance and the West Virginia line. This long, narrow strip of land was devilishly dirty by day yet luridly beautiful nights when the numerous beehive ovens were in blast, and the sky was a fiery drama. In the old South, it is often said that cotton was king; but here in Pennsylvania, "King Coal" wielded his scepter for many long years. In western Pennsylvania, in the soft coal region, the "King," with his auspicious child "Coke," ruled supreme from the 1870s till the early 1950s, when the coke era finally dimmed and faded.

Though the Connellsville area was home to many millionaires during its heyday, the Caliguire family, with its ten children, was poor. There were five daughters and five sons, three of the girls coming into the world before Anthony.

"As any normal boy," he recounted in his autobiography, *The Wonder Dancers, Woods & Bray*, "I went to school, but not for long. Dad and Mother's family increased almost annually, so when I was thirteen... I was taken out of school and told to get a job to help keep the family." From that point in time, Anthony Caliguire worked nearly every day for the rest of his long, extraordinary life.

The experiences he absorbed during his early years, laboring at a wide variety of trades, would serve him well in his bright future. The first of those jobs began on the railroad. As the coke capital, Connellsville was a railroad center; and "Tony," as he was known to family and friends, easily found work as a gandy dancer, a colorful term used for those men who work on the railroad, repairing tracks, laying rails, or whatever their physical labor entailed. After several months of that toil, Caliguire sought employment in the Pittsburgh steel mills, succeeding in getting himself hired as an apprentice to a puddler. This too he realized would be backbreaking; but at least he would be inside, sheltered from the precarious Pennsylvania weather.

In essence, the puddler's job was to melt iron into steel. Before the advent of the great bulbous brute "Bessemer," these skilled craftsmen had their tasks down to a science, or perhaps I should say, an art. Puddlers oversaw the difficult mixing and heating of the ore. In the hot, yellow glare from the mill's raging furnaces, they pushed the heated pig iron around, stirred it and literally spat upon it, judging it by its color and the hue of the flames that shot out of the ovens to announce when the "cooking" was done. It was a hot, dirty job, and Tony sweated in the Pittsburgh mill until he knew he couldn't stand it another day. Again, it was time to move on.

Caliguire had a sister, Mary, in Dunmore; and there he went to work in the hard coal region, hand-digging and blasting for coal fifteen hundred or more feet beneath the earth. During this period, he was also a barefoot newspaper boy, earning a mere twenty-five cents a day, peddling papers along a five-mile route. The frugal boy sacrificed and eventually saved enough money to purchase a used bicycle. Sadly, the bike was stolen the first day he had it. "My heart was broken," he related in the above book. "It was my first and only bicycle throughout my entire life."

Next, Tony tried his hand at the restaurant business, waiting tables, and eventually managing a French-Italian eatery in Scranton. As was his way, he applied himself and saved his money. After the hard labor of his earlier positions, and due to his natural charm and charisma with the customers, he discovered he liked working with the public. He may well have stayed in that business, but Fate intervened. "An uncle came and took me away to New York City with the promise of a better position there; however, he spent all my money, treating his friends; so I deserted him and, near broke, went back to Connellsville."

Immediately Anthony found work in his hometown at an Italian bakery on Pittsburgh Street. "I had to get up around four a.m. to mix the dough in a huge wooden trough. During the mixing, I had to really work that dough and toss it from one end of the trough to the other. This required muscle. Then, once the dough was raised and ready to cut, we had to work really fast." When the bread was sectioned, Caliguire shaped it by hand and slid the loaves into the big gas ovens. His subsequent duty was to deliver it around the Connellsville area to the various stores. This he did via a covered, horse-drawn wagon.

Before too long, he found a position at a larger bakery in Pittsburgh. Though the Pittsburgh bakery paid higher wages, he still wanted better for himself. At this point in his life, he was starting to feel keenly that there was something just around the next corner. He didn't know which direction to take or what he might find, he just knew that he was eager to pursue that elusive something. Whatever it was, it would take money to discover it. That was one truth with which he had become well acquainted. Everything took money.

The best wages he could ferret out were in the ubiquitous coke ovens; thus, he landed a job hand-pulling coke from the beehives. As he expected, the work was grueling, the hours long; and there were no safety conditions to speak of. Nonetheless, he wanted to stick with it long enough to sock away a nice savings.

After hand-drawing the coke, he loaded it into a giant wheelbarrow with side gates, pushed the heavy vehicle onto the large planks that led to the top of the steel hopper railroad cars, opened the wheelbarrow's side doors, and unloaded the bright residue from the cooked coal. "Many times did I fall into the cars with the hot, smoldering coke," Caliguire recalled in his memoirs.

"After some months, I changed jobs again, laboring at one of the many coal mines that surrounded my hometown. I hated the work. My thoughts were not good; my mind was disturbed, for I was getting older. I so wanted to better myself and get away from these back-breaking, dead-end jobs."

The fact that he had toiled so strenuously at those jobs had rendered Tony Caliguire a powerhouse of a young man. Furthermore, he had acquired a wealth of information and life experience that would come in handy afterward when he became a professional entertainer with his own resort. I have not listed all the jobs at which Caliguire worked; and often, the youth had labored at more than one job at a time.

"Electrical work, plumbing, roofing, carpentry, cement mixing, painting... this hodgepodge of trades afforded me the ability to do all my own maintenance later in life. Despite this varied knowledge, I was far from satisfied. This was not what I wanted out of life. I wanted something better- something that would cause people to look up to me and marvel at my accomplishments. I wanted to be known and respected... to be somebody. That persistent thought was what prompted me to take my dancing seriously. From my early teens, I was a very good dancer; and many times, well before I became known, I danced my heart out."

After getting off work, as an escape from the dirt, sweat and misery of hard labor, Caliguire would rush home, clean up and dash to the local dance halls, attired in whatever finery he could muster. In fact, he had become known, in connection to his dancing, as the "Sheik" because he so resembled Rudolph Valentino. Later, when he began dancing professionally, he was often mistaken for Valentino.

It finally dawned on Tony Caliguire that he possessed enough talent as a dancer to do it for a living. Continuously saving his money to pay for lessons, he studied dancing in earnest, soon discovering that he was not only a born athlete but innately creative as a choreographer. He began putting together his own dance routines. Though, in the beginning, he could not read a note of music, he could easily image himself dancing to a particular tune. "But I had strong likes and dislikes in music, and I had to really like what I was listening to in order to get the inspiration I needed to start a routine," he stated in his autobiography.

When the great American songwriter Cole Porter came out with the hit tune "Begin the Béguine," Caliguire set to work creating his first stage act. Within a month, he had mastered it, after which he broke it in at the top night spot in Montreal, Quebec, Canada, at the Chez Maurice Café.

I might add that the word *béguine* comes from the French *béguin* meaning "flirtation." The romantic, hip-swaying dance, which imitates the sensual movement of the palms, originated in the twenties, in the French West Indies, on the bewitching isle of Martinique. I used to pass my summers and several holidays there back in the seventies, and the slow rumba-like *béguine* was still *très popular.*

Though the *béguine* literally set Caliguire dancing down his yellow brick road to fame, it was the tango that the Valentino-like Tony first adopted as his strongest dance.

"I started out teaching dancing, at the same time studying it, while working at Carnegie Steel in McDonald, Ohio, to pay for those studies. It was in Ohio, in 1924, where I met the most wonderful girl in the world, who later became my wife and dancing partner," Caliguire glowingly related in his book.

Born March 21, 1907, prematurely at six months, Esther Thomas had weighed a pound and a quarter at birth; and she never developed eardrums. She was totally deaf. When she and Tony met, she had never spoken a word, though she was attending a deaf-mute school in Columbus, Ohio. During her years at the school, Esther played center on the school basketball team, a team that won a championship five years in a row.

"This extraordinary girl and I took dancing lessons together to see just what could be accomplished with her handicap," Caliguire recounted. "We used to work out dance routines and rehearse them in her father's garage... this was in 1924 and 1925."

Esther, he soon discovered, was as intelligent and eager-to-learn as she was beautiful. Blonde, with a perfect hourglass figure, she was athletic, agile and exceedingly graceful. Of Welsh and English extraction, she was gutsy too. Inside her chest beat the heart of a lion. It didn't take long for Tony to teach her every type of dance he knew, and to the amazement of her family, she soon mastered each and every one of them. "We won many awards right from the beginning of our career together," he reported in his memoirs.

Esther graduated in 1926; and by this time, the striking pair was very much in love. When Tony asked Esther's parents for her hand in marriage, her mother consented immediately. Esther's father was reluctant, due to his daughter's disability; however, he eventually gave in, and the enamored couple wed on September 5, 1926.

They planned to spend their honeymoon with Tony's third sister, Frances Tripoli, who resided in Connellsville. For all their bliss, the hundred-fifteen-mile trip back to Caliguire's hometown turned into a nightmare in his well-used Model-T Ford. It poured rain the entire way, never letting up. En route, the roadster sprung a leak, requiring the couple to stop every mile or so for water. Fortunately, in those early days of auto travel, there were troughs at regular intervals along most of the roads for horses, the yet-common mode of transportation. To make matters worse, the newlyweds lost their way in the deep, dark woods of Indian Creek Valley. Over sixteen hours later, they finally arrived in Connellsville, exhausted, hungry, but undefeated.

After the stock market crash in 1929, many dance teams risked life and limb, executing dangerous moves in order to capture the attention of the news media and thus gain more gigs. A few of those dancers did succeed in making headlines with their wild antics atop high buildings, the male member of the team gingerly walking the ledge with his female partner held with one hand over his head.

While living in a dreary "cold-water walk-up" at 60th and Broadway, Tony and Esther intended, metaphorically, to top that. Their career needed a jump start, and they desperately needed a paying gig, so they began rehearsing a daredevil act on the roof of their apartment building. Actually, their flirtation with Death involved two roofs, since the buildings were close together. Esther would climb to the roof of the higher building and swan dive ten feet

The Wonder Dancers' thrilling apache dance

below, to the roof of the lower building and into Tony's waiting, well-muscled arms. The ten-foot leap went so well that the intrepid pair decided to try a fourteen-foot dive.

The first time they tried it, her body, with the strength and force it had gained via her flying leap, crashed against him like a runaway express train. To counteract the momentum, he desperately executed a quick series of shuffles and shifts, his legs working furiously to keep his balance and, at the same time, not let go of his wife. They hurtled against a skylight, nearly going through the glass, which would have resulted in serious injury or death. As it were, Tony emerged with a couple of cracked ribs. Many bruises, scrapes and cuts later, the daring duo decided to give up on such death-defying exploits to earn their living.

Now, more determined than ever to succeed in show business, the energetic couple set to work on their adagio dance to sensationalize it as much as they could. The acrobatic adagio, replete with difficult feats of balance, lifts and spins, turned out to be their best and most celebrated number throughout their theatrical career.

Times were lean in the beginning, and to save money on the road, Tony and Esther often ate in their hotel room. It was especially nice when the hotel in which they were staying had gas lights. Then he would stand on a chair, holding the little frying pan he had purchased, containing eggs or a piece of meat, over the gas flame of the wall fixture to cook their dinner.

A portable sewing machine was another essential during their travels. From the beginning, Esther nearly always made their costumes; and they were elaborate affairs that took a lot of punishment. One gown, for instance, that she designed in 1974 required approximately 30,000 sequins- hand-stitched- one at a time. Whilst Esther was their couturiere, Tony was the businessman of the team. As their career progressed, they happily discovered that he had a good head for business.

At the outset of their career, the couple was known as the "Dancing DeSondos." Later, in 1928, C.B. Maddock, a New York producer of Broadway shows, bestowed on them the stage names with which they would become internationally known- Frances Woods and Billy Bray. And it would be none other than Robert Ripley, of "Ripley's Believe It Or Not," who tagged them with the "Wonder Dancers," due to the fact that Frances was totally deaf- the only deaf dancer in the business.

You, dear readers, are likely wondering all the while how this lady could achieve a dancer's international fame with this severe handicap. Allow me to explain. Billy taught Frances to get the vibrations, the beats per measure, of their dance music through her toes and feet. He then taught her the steps to fit that rhythm.

For nearly five years, the couple never permitted the public to know that she was a deaf mute. When the news of her handicap did break, it rendered Woods and Bray the most publicized dance team in the world.

Billy successfully taught Frances to talk, spelling words as they sound, though she knew the words were not actually spelled thus. As a result, she was eventually able to carry on a conversation, providing she understood the topic of that conversation first and on condition that the others involved spoke slowly, forming the words with their lips.

A rather humorous incident occurred soon after the media got wind of Frances' deafness. At the New York theater where the couple was performing, a Syracuse doctor approached them with his own invention that he advocated was an absolute must for deaf mutes. The physician produced, with somewhat of an exaggerated flair, a piece of rubber, the approximate size of a large caramel candy, that was attached to a wire that ran to the record player. In order for this device to work, the deaf person had to place and hold the thick rubber square between the teeth; then, as the record played, he or she received the downbeat of the music. After the man demonstrated the device, Billy shook his head, stating that was a false vibration. "And how," he then asked, in light of their rigorous routines, "could anyone dance with that thing between the teeth?"

The doctor drew himself up to his full height, responding with affected dignity: "I'll have you know, young man, that I was offered seventy-five thousand dollars for this invention."

Billy's succinct reply was "My advice to you, sir, is to take it."

Another episode that took place in the early days of their career, in New Orleans, is worth mentioning. Since Frances' dancing was always so letter-perfect, a physician, who was in attendance at their club act in the Crescent City, appeared, after the show, at the door of their dressing room. The man's face was blood red, and an angry tone carried on his voice: "Aren't you ashamed of yourself permitting these announcements to be made? That woman is no more deaf than I am!"

Billy remained calm, coolly replying, "Would you like to examine my wife's ears?"

"You're dang right!" came the immediate retort.

"All right," said Billy. "Go first to get the owner and the manager to serve as witnesses, and come back here when they're with you."

Within several minutes the doctor returned with the club proprietors. He examined Frances' ears, and finding no eardrums, exited the theater, shaking his head... yes, in wonder.

Woods and Bray were one of the most unusual dance teams seen anywhere. "The male member of the duo is a combination of Sandow and Castle, strongman and dancer extraordinaire..." so read advertising cards on the tables of the hotels and nightclubs where they appeared during the late twenties and thirties. A reporter of the era wrote: "Bray handles his partner with impressive ease and grace. The waltz staged by the team is a thing of beauty and charm. Yet the audience does not realize that the most remarkable thing about the act is that its female member is totally deaf. Woods is pretty, vivacious and possessed of a most attractive figure. She seems quite carried away with the music and not once does the audience suspect during her flawless performance that she cannot hear a note...."

Woods and Bray were soon headlining the floor show on the beach walk of the Edgewater Hotel in Chicago, dancing to the champagne music of Lawrence Welk and his orchestra. Years later, on April 14, 1973, the still-striking couple would appear with Welk again at the Hollywood Palladium.

Known now as "Billy" wherever they went, he continued to choreograph all their numbers- rumbas, waltzes, tangos, adagios and their famous apache dance routine.

Allow me to elaborate a bit about both their exceptional acts- the adagio and the apache. The adagio, as touched on earlier, is a ballet duet by a man and a woman displaying difficult feats of balance, lifting and spinning. I want to reiterate that the couple's adagio is the act that literally spiraled Woods and Bray to fame.

Having no connection whatsoever to the Native American tribe of the Southwest, the word apache literally refers to a gang of Parisian ruffians, and the dance mimics the raw actions of these gangster types. It is also known as the "dance of the Parisian underworld."

Except for a scarlet-hued scarf tied round the neck, the male is attired completely in black, including his rakish beret. During the apache, the aggressive male character flings and tosses his partner about the stage, throwing her down, after which she submissively clutches his ankle as he drags her across the floor.

The female character in this scenario also sports a red neckerchief and a beret, along with black, fishnet stockings; a striped, French sailor-style top, and a tight, black skirt with a slit up the side, which allows for freedom of movement. She needs it, because the apache is an exceedingly physical dance. Woods and Bray's apache routine appeared so real that people in the audience unfamiliar with this French art form often took to throwing items from their tables at the performing Bray! At the end of their original apache, Billy would "stab" Frances with a rubber stiletto, carrying her offstage over his shoulder, as though she had perished, amidst a hail of beer and whiskey bottles, glasses, candlesticks and whatever else outraged guests could get their fingers around to hurl at him.

This reminds me of a Ma and Pa Kettle film I saw years ago, the title long forgotten, in which the bumpkins are in the audience of a classy Parisian nightclub where a rough-and-tumble apache dance is being staged. During the lively performance, Ma jumps up, a bottle, at the ready, in her hand, as she stomps across the floor toward the male dancer: "Where I come from men don't treat women like that!" Then she proceeds to christen the poor fellow with the bottle and her blessing of a few choice words followed by a swift but well-placed kick in the derrière.

Soon tired of similar treatment, Billy decided to change the ending of their apache routine. No longer did he "stab" Frances with the stiletto. Rather, she now "shot" him with a .22 pistol, pulled at the moment of truth from the scarlet garter of her black stockings. Needless to say, blanks were used. The audience really ate it up, especially the part after the "shooting," when she would snap her fingers in Billy's face, and he'd drop "dead." As Bray would fall forward, Frances pushed her shoulders into his waist, picked her partner up and carried him offstage. How that delicately exquisite creature could hoist a 180-pound man over her shoulders to cart him away at the conclusion of each performance is beyond me. This illustrates what tremendous athletic ability this couple possessed, in addition to their grace and agility. At any rate, audiences preferred the revised ending in their thrilling apache act, and no longer did they have to dodge bottles during their stage exits.

There is one more humorous (though I am certain it was not so funny to poor Frances at the time it happened) anecdote connected to the couple's famous apache. In Pittsburgh, circa 1929, Billy and Frances were booked to perform the intense routine at a hotel, where the dance floor was a rough wood. When Bray threw Woods across that floor during the performance, she picked up a tush-full of splinters. It was quite painful; and after the show that evening, it took Billy hours to tweeze them all out, with his aptly named partner across his knees!

Calamities aside, their star was ever-rising as they performed with the celebrated Paul Whiteman and his orchestra, as well as the aforementioned Lawrence Welk, Cab Callaway, Eddie Duchin, Guy Lombardo and many others. In fact, there wasn't a big band of the era with which Woods and Bray, The Wonder Dancers, did not perform. The dynamic couple danced many repeat performances, coast to coast and overseas. I would not be exaggerating when I tell you that I do not believe another headline act ever outdid these two exceptional dancers for repeat performances across the nation. Their agent kept them so busy for so many years that they appeared, time and again, at every major hotel and night spot across America.

It was in 1932 when the famous team first appeared at the summer resort called the Jack-O-Lantern in Eagle River, Wisconsin. After their first engagement at the lodge, the popular dance team was called back for the subsequent eighteen summers, booking in from the 4th of July to Labor Day, until the place finally closed its doors in 1950.

Woods and Bray came of age at the Jack-O-Lantern. They polished and fine-tuned their diverse dance numbers, together with their personal style. Already an elegant couple, the pair learned to play tennis, to shoot trap and skeet, and to ride horseback in the English manner. They became accomplished golfers. Fashionable members of the bon ton, they were now sophisticated in all the finer things of life.

It was at the Jack-O-Lantern where the idea of their own resort took seed in Billy Bray's fertile mind. He was wisely thinking ahead to a time when the very physical dances that had made them famous would become too much for them. At first, he conceived the idea of having two resorts, a winter one in the North and a summer one in the South. "I wasn't thinking in terms of making a fortune... only of security in our old age." That fortune, however, was a sparkling facet of their diamond-bright future.

"Many acts," Bray continued, "who made plenty of money during their lifetimes either lost their fortunes, gambling it away, or went on dope or drinking sprees. Many stars wound up in poverty after having made millions. I made up my mind I wasn't going to let something like that happen to us."

While still taking their act on the road, Woods and Bray opened a dance studio, in 1958, in Youngstown, Ohio, where they taught ballet, acrobatics, modern jazz and tap. The legendary pair worked well with children, and they continuously filled their classes due to the name they had made for themselves in show business. After many years of teaching young people, they decided to concentrate exclusively on ballroom instruction for adults. Moreover, they taught this type of dance at a string of country clubs across Ohio and Pennsylvania.

In my youth, I studied ballet and Spanish dance for several years with Billy Bray's younger brother, Sam Caliguire, who, following a stint on Broadway, opened several dance studios in southwestern Pennsylvania. Like all his siblings, Sam was an extremely hard worker, not to mention a fantastic dancer, especially with the Latin dances. In fact, there are those who say that Sam was an even better dancer than Tony/Billy. I didn't know Anthony, but I did know Sam. To watch him was pure joy. He moved with the graceful, liquid motion of a panther. He was a fine baseball player too. A beloved figure in the Fayette-Westmoreland-county area of Pennsylvania, Sam Caliguire was one of the most decent people I ever had the pleasure of knowing. Among incalculable others, I will always be grateful for the many things I learned from him about the performing arts.

Sam inspired his students to work hard, believe in themselves, and to reach for the stars. He told me once that a civilization is as great as its dreams, and its dreams are dreamt by artists. "Follow your heart," he said, "and your dreams will come true." Like his brother Tony, Sam taught a spectrum of future celebrities, including "Pennsylvania's Sweetheart," Shirley Jones.

The Wonder Dancers' sixteen-room resort motel, the Bray-Wood, facing Catfish Lake, was the first motel, on the chain of twenty-eight lakes in the rustically beautiful woods of northern Wisconsin, in which the rooms all had private baths. Bray-Wood boasted a sandy beach with a dock; and the guests had resort accommodations, including swimming, boating, fishing, trap and skeet, and other fun amenities.

"All this," Bray stated in his autobiography, "while we were still staging dance exhibitions and doing public appearances in clubs across the country, as well as many television shows."

The Wonder Dancers' intense adagio

In 1968, Frances required a pacemaker for a heart condition she had developed. Though their resort had always done a fabulous business, in the autumn of 1970, due to Frances' health, the couple decided to sell the place that had brought them so much happiness. A second heart operation followed in 1971.

Did The Wonder Dancers ever learn to "take it easy," as the saying goes, and retire from the limelight? Never. The phenomenal pair continued dancing professionally, very nearly to the end of their lives, though their act no longer included their world-famous adagio and apache dance numbers with the lifts and the ultra-physical routines. "It wasn't because we could no longer do them," Billy related in his colorful biography. "It was because of the danger of pulling the electrodes (wires) implanted in Frances' heart muscles."

Though their dance routines were strictly ballroom after 1968, the couple was never lack-luster. Nothing about The Wonder Dancers ever lacked luster!

In 1974, Billy penned his autobiography, at the age of seventy, from the Northernaire Hotel's Showboat, Lake Terrace Estates in Three Lakes, Wisconsin, where the couple was headlining.

During their long and very productive lives, the vibrant dance team taught the art of dancing to countless people, several of whom achieved fame of their own. Some of their students went on to become choreographers on Broadway, several to Hollywood where they put the skills learned from Woods and Bray to use in film. Others went on to television. Numerous former students became teachers of dance and opened dance studios. It must have been extremely gratifying to The Wonder Dancers to see so many of their apprentices go so far in the entertainment business they so loved.

In 1978, The Wonder Dancers, Woods and Bray, received the Ohio Governor's Award for "... achievement benefiting mankind and improving the quality of life for all Ohioans." Frances Woods' inspirational success story and the dance team's various contributions to the deaf duly earned them that prestigious award.

Frances Woods and Billy Bray continued to dance well into their eighties at various dance exhibitions and functions, including entertaining at a wide range of retirement centers and nursing homes. At each and every performance, they exhibited the creativity, skill, panache and the sheer elegance that had made them legends in their own time.

In 1991, the octogenarian Woods and Bray were interviewed on CNN, in which their brilliant career was highlighted. Then, the following year, they appeared on KDKA, Pittsburgh television, in a similar interview.

The incomparable Woods and Bray
The Wonder Dancer photos courtesy Billy Bray/Tony Caliguire's nephew, William Demiere, Connellsville, PA

Both interviews were conducted from their Ohio home. Due to failing health, the couple moved, in 1998, to Springhill, Florida.

There, in 2000, each in their nineties, they passed away only weeks apart, Billy on March 23 and Frances on July 17. The pair had always believed they were soul-mates; for, in every way, they were so perfectly synchronized.

And so, dear readers, if ever, while gazing at the night sky, you chance upon a twin-tailed comet, it might just be that indivisible duo known universally for their sparkle and dash, the inseparable, ever-luminous Woods and Bray- The Wonder Dancers.

"GHOSTWALKERS"

"The strengths cougars represent have a powerful lesson for those who are willing to learn from them."
- Nancy Wood Taber, artist

"Cougar walks as a spiritual hunter, to teach leadership, determination, independence, and, above all, courage."- Native American lore

"To me, the cougar represents, in addition to its great courage, mystery, magic and foresight.
I possess 'cougar medicine,' which translates that, like the cougar, I am ofttimes solitary - I value my privacy- and I am quite sure of my purpose in life."- Ceane O'Hanlon-Lincoln, author

I have always penned each Chronicle according to what subject strikes my mood and captures my interest at the time I am ready to begin. I write better that way; I always have. The other day, when I was looking through my desk drawer, I happened upon an article I had saved from the Sunday, January 15, 2006, *Tribune-Review* entitled "Coming Home." The piece discussed the great possibility that cougars will be returning to Pennsylvania's mountains within a few decades. Actually, there are many individuals who believe that the great cat has already made its tentative return to Penn's ubiquitous Woods. Others believe that mountain lions never completely vanished from Pennsylvania's remote mountain reaches. But lest I get ahead of myself in this discussion....

Also known, among other appellations, as mountain lions, pumas, catamounts, and panthers, cougars were prevalent across our state until the dawn of the twentieth century. They once roamed from the Atlantic to the Pacific, from South America to Canada. The originally wide distribution of this native cat has been sharply modified by human invasion, resulting in its diminished habitation- primarily the western reaches of the United States and Canada. However, human invasion of their western habitats in recent years, in the form of new housing developments and bike and hike trails (not to mention all the fires that have wrecked havoc out West) is why it is believed they are returning to the eastern mountain ranges- where they have, as they do in the West, an inherent right.

I should mention too that cougar populations in the West were diminished by ranchers aided by government-sponsored predator eradication programs of the nineteenth and twentieth centuries. Some populations of the western cats have rebounded to some extent since the 1970s when bounties on them were removed; but sadly, as of this writing, cougars can be legally hunted in eleven western states.

Nevertheless, it is important that I make my readers cognizant of this: The Florida panther, *Puma concolor coryl*- in fact, all eastern cougars, *Puma concolor couguar*- are fully protected under the Endangered Species Act.

Cougar's genus, *Felis concolor,* was recently changed to *Puma concolor couguar.* The word *concolor* applies because the cougar, like the African lion, is uniformly colored, tawny, buff, or grey on its back, with much lighter fur, to cream, on its underside and muzzle. The stunning head is marked with black on the sides of the muzzle, the back of the ears, and the tip of the tail. I have read that the ebony markings on this cat's exqui-

Confirmed Pennsylvania cougar in the winter of 1981. Photo taken by wildlife and nature photographer Dick Brown near Bellefonte; permission courtesy the photographer and John A. Lutz, director of the Eastern Puma Research Network

site face render it more fierce-looking when it snarls, growls or hisses, reminiscent of Native American war paint.

The cougar's coloring varies, depending on where it lives. Some are cinnamon, others more yellowish, still others bluish-grey. It all depends on geography. The reddish/cinnamon coat is more prevalent in tropical areas (example, the Florida panther), the grey in higher altitudes (example, the Wyoming puma). One could also state that the cougar closely resembles the coloration of the deer of the region where it preys, allowing this cat's approach- *and Cougar is a master stealth-* to be undetected until it leaps.

Like most cats, this one usually attacks from behind, fixing its claws into the neck and shoulder of its victim. Due to its muscular prowess and its long tail, thirty-six to forty-two inches in length, which acts as a rudder, Cougar's leaping skill is phenomenal. Forty-plus feet is not unheard of. This amazing cat can make a vertical jump about twenty feet, straight up!

Unlike most cats, cougars do not fear water. They have binocular vision, important for depth perception and judging distances. Their beautiful, penetrating, green-gold eyes, replete with mystery and ancient secrets, allow them to hunt both day and night. They can easily follow scent trails because the back of their nasal cavity is densely packed with olfactory cells; thus, they rely on smell first then sight when hunting. This great cat has thirty teeth. Its canines, used for delivering the lethal *coup de grâce* (usually at the back of the neck), are *impressive.* The remaining teeth are designed for slicing and shearing flesh.

The mountain lion's prey is deer, elk, moose, bighorn sheep, goats, antelope, beaver, rabbit, squirrel, skunk, and porcupine, which they wisely flip onto their backs. Indeed, cougar diet is quite varied; and these cats will even make a meal of snakes, frogs and/or fish.

Male cougars can reach a length of eight feet, including the tail, and weigh anywhere from 175 to 250 pounds. Females average around six-and-a-half feet in length, including the tail, and weigh from 100 to 150 pounds. These stats refer to those cats found in the West. Eastern mountain lions, including those recorded in Pennsylvania, are smaller, the males from 100 to 135 pounds, the females from 75 to 95 or 100 pounds. Keep in mind the difference in food source. The favorite cougar meal is a deer; and the western variety, the mule deer, is larger than the eastern, white-tailed deer. The East also lacks antelope, elk and bighorn sheep. Even the rabbits are larger out West.

Cougars are climbing cats and usually lie in wait for prey on high- on rock or on the strong bough of a tree. However, I want to state here and now that cougar attacks on livestock or humans are rare. Attacks on livestock occur if a cat is starving and too weak, for a number of reasons, to take its wild prey. Kills made by wild dogs or coyotes are frequently blamed on cougars. Proper livestock management and the use of dogs in pasture greatly reduce the chances of an attack from mountain lions, which are atypical to begin with.

With the increasing number of hikers and bikers invading what is left of Cougar's ever-shrinking territory out West, it is no small wonder that a few human attacks have occurred. Cougars, however, are *not* maneaters. Unprovoked attacks on humans make headline news because they are so rare. Rabid cats account for some of those attacks, a weak or injured cat for others. A biker or hiker who has inadvertently placed him/herself between a mother and cub(s) would certainly be another factor. Cougar has been known to go up against a towering male grizzly to protect her young!

There have been reports of cougars stealthily following a human merely out of curiosity.

All cats are naturally curious; but normally cougars are quite wary of humans, keeping their distance from us. This ghost of the forest is aware of human foray long before the human is aware of its presence. In fact, cougars are the *most* elusive of creatures and are rarely encountered in the wild, even in the areas of the West where they are more prevalent.

If ever you were to come across a cougar in the wild, do *not* attempt to outrun it. There is *no* way any human can outrun this powerful cat with its extraordinary leaping ability. And Cougar can explode into a sprint at thirty-five miles per hour. Take hold of your natural fear, and do *not* turn your back on the cat but maintain eye contact. Do not crouch, bend or stoop. Pull yourself up to your full height, making yourself as big as possible, wave your arms and shout as loudly as you can. Do *not* scream in fear; rather, use a bold *stentorian* voice. This should send Cougar in the opposite direction.

I had a good friend, John Kapolka of Connellsville, who was stalked by a curious cougar while elk hunting in the northern panhandle of Idaho. "It was in the autumn, at dusk, and I was returning to camp alone. This was a very *remote* area; the nearest town was Missoula, Montana. I had taken care to read the warning signs posted round about that I was '... in grizzly and cougar country,' " John told me. "I knew not to turn and run." The fact that he had read and absorbed what to do and what not to do in such a situation kept that cat from leaping upon him. "I had the strong sensation that the cat meant me no harm but was merely curious. After stalking me for quite a ways, he simply got bored. I may have been the first human that particular cat had ever seen."

In the wild, cougars live an average of twelve to fifteen years, but there are many intrinsic dangers for them in the wilderness. Though most of their attacks on larger animals are successful, cougars are often injured by elk, moose, and even deer, frequently to the nasal passages and frontal bones, such as the jaw. This, along with the fact that a cougar will confront a grizzly in order to protect its young, speaks of the great courage this cat possesses. By the bye, grizzlies and cougars make a point of avoiding one another in the wilds.

Minus the period spent with the mother and mating times, Cougar lives and hunts alone. Since these cats are solitary and secretive, they prefer cover, either the dark veil of forest or the rocky recesses of mountain terrain. Denning is a big part of their lifestyle. In cougar sanctuaries, hiding places are always provided so that Cougar can secret him/herself in the refuges to which he/she naturally gravitates.

Mountain lions can breed all year, though they are most active in winter and early spring, dropping their young in the warm season, as do most wild creatures. Since it takes two years to raise the cubs (one to three; two is the norm), most females breed every other year.

When it is time to leave the mother in search of their own territories, females often stay close to their mother's home range, while the males travel farther, sometimes hundreds of miles. Young cougar males are at risk of attack from all adult males, including their father.

The Erie (*Erieehronon/ Eriechronon*) Indians, discussed in "Haunted Pennsylvania," this volume, were named for the cougar, the "long-tailed cat." Before being nearly exterminated by the Iroquois, the *Erie* or *Nation du Chat*, "Cat Nation," as they became known, lived along Lake Erie's southern shore, an area where cougars were abundant.

To the Native Americans at large, these elusive "ghostwalkers" represent power, swiftness, cunning, leadership, and great courage. According to animal totem lore, Cougar is *the* energy of leadership and courage. The Seneca, who once resided in Penn's Woods, the "Keepers of the Western Door" of the great Iroquois Confederation, revered the ever-mysterious native wildcat for its stealth and bravery. The Choctaw go a step further, believing that animals are deities in disguise, here with messages to teach valuable lessons to humankind. All Natives believe that animals are our brothers, sent by the Great Spirit as messengers, teachers and guides. Indeed, by watching the swift movements of the cougar, one becomes keenly aware that no movement is wasted, no footing unplanned in this awesome cat's quest for its objective.

Incidentally, there is a difference between Native American animal guides and animal medicine. Animal spirits/guides provide humankind with guidance. Animal medicine translates as an individual's perspective on life, the way in which he or she looks at life, or reacts to life. Those who possess cougar medicine (traits/characteristics conferred by Cougar) are quite sure of their purpose in life. These people have definite goals, and they prefer solitude (so they can realize those goals). They keep their own counsel (usually), and they always seem to have an air of mystery about themselves. To read more about the cougar, its habits, other wild creatures, and Native American animal/totem lore, please read "Camelot" in the premier volume of my *County Chronicles* Pennsylvania history series.

When early European explorers came across the cougar, they were staggered by its power and mystery. There was nothing to compare with these cats in Europe. Unlike the wolf, mountain lions were found only in the New World. These pioneers likened them in looks to the lions of Africa. Because the cougar is such a powerful predator, settlers feared for their livestock and for their own safety.

Let us endeavor to understand what happened. European settlers, when they arrived in America, were at once awed and frightened by the great, dark forests of eighteenth-century frontier America. So dense were these looming woods that, in some places, sun never dappled the ground, even at high noon. The British Isles and most of the continent of Europe had not seen forests of this magnitude since medieval times. These new arrivals held, since childhood, strong beliefs deeply ingrained in their cultures about the woodlands. Traditional folklore portrayed the forest as a fearsome antagonist, the harborer of all sorts of fiendish creatures. Among the earthly snakes, bears, and wolves, "there be" the unearthly fairies, witches and goblins. Some of those tales held that Satan himself dwelt in the forest primeval under mysterious appellations, such as the "Dark Woodsman" or the "Black Hunter." Other Old-World myths told that Satan and his minions roamed the dark forests in the guise of the "fiendish" creatures that dwelled therein.

Deviltry in the dense woods of Colonial America necessitated "cleansing." Farmers these immigrants were; hence, they believed that the forest had to be tamed and subdued, beaten back to make way for their cabins, barns and crops; ever dealt with, so that it could not reach its twisted, taloned-fingers out to strangle their New-World dream. The superstitious early settlers believed there was a dark spirit in the panther, some connection to the Evil One. Its bloodcurdling scream was one of the few things that "scared the liver" out of a stalwart frontier farmer. Thus, hunting down the 'devil cat' was, unfortunately, part of that Colonial "vital cleansing."

Conversely, the Indians were never in contrast with Nature; rather, they were a part of it. The great forests and its creatures were, to them, wondrous gifts from Creator. The Woodlands actually *defined* the Eastern Natives as the "Eastern Woodland Indians." These wooded lands were their home for untold centuries- and the creatures that dwelled therein their brothers.

Readers, be mindful that the most powerful negative is fear, which is the most *dangerous* (and by consequence *destructive*) emotion we humans can feel. *This is why animals react so negatively to human fear.* It was that fear that prompted the hunting with dogs of this noble cat until it was believed they were extirpated in the eastern United States and Canada by 1900.

I must include something here about these phenomenal cats. When being tracked by dogs, Cougar has been known to take to water, walking in a stream for miles to lose pursuers. They will also leap a great distance over rock in order to shake hunting dogs from their trail.

Across the East, widespread deforestation for so many years, due to settlement, and the hunting of deer also contributed to the cougars' decline. *However, cougar sightings in remote eastern areas never completely ceased.* Could the eastern cougar, a subspecies, have survived in remote areas- for instance, in Pennsylvania's extensive forest lands? There is no hard evidence, but it is not impossible.

According to the Eastern Cougar Foundation, by the 1960s, sightings had increased to the point that the eastern cougar was believed to possibly still exist. Consequently, it was listed on the first Endangered Species Act in 1973.

An official United States Fish and Wildlife Service search for cougar signs in the late 1970s and early 1980s turned up several likely scats (droppings). Unfortunately, technology available at that time could not *confirm* them as cougar, and no other confirmed evidence was uncovered.

Then in the 1990s, DNA analysis, together with other methods, began to verify field evidence of eastern cougars. As a result, the dispute over whether cougars are present in the East has shifted. A few state and federal wildlife officials now acknowledge that some cougars may roam the eastern woods.

In addition to the survival of some eastern cougars in remote places, as well as western cats that have migrated eastward, there is another factor worth mentioning, and that is the highly likely possibility that captive cougars have escaped or have been freed into the wilds by their owners. I know for a fact that there are released cougars in the wilds, some, sadly, that have been declawed. I can say this after writing "Camelot," which appeared in the premier volume of my *County Chronicles.*

The reflective Mariah studying a rabbit at CRMLS

Dr. William Sheperd, whom I interviewed for that Chronicle (and who was actually stalked by a cougar in SW Pennsylvania's mountain wilderness), operates a big-cat orphanage near my home in the Fayette-Westmoreland-county area. This very caring veterinarian has rescued several abused cougars from their illegal captivities.

To quote Dr. Sheperd and many other individuals in the know, "Mountain lions are *not* pets!" Research and learn about them, respect them, as you should respect all of God's creatures; and leave them in the wilds where they belong. It is inexcusably cruel to confine them as pets. Captivity can be exceedingly frustrating for any big cat, often resulting in obsessive-compulsive behavior, such as incessant pacing. It can be quite difficult finding good veterinary care; and a big cat's nutritional requirements are demanding, to say the least. Cougars eat between five to seven pounds of fresh meat per day; and they need exercise and fresh air like most beings, including humans.

There are two sanctuaries that I highly recommend you visit in order to see and learn all about mountain lions. The first one is the Western Pennsylvania National Wild Animal Orphanage (in the Fayette-Westmoreland-county area of southwestern Pennsylvania) that I wrote about in *County Chronicles I.* It is operated by the aforementioned angel of mercy, Dr. William Sheperd. Visitors to his orphanage can see a variety of big cats, including cougars, tigers, African lions and lynxes. Call for information at 724-437-7838. Donations are always needed and are tax-deductible.

The second cougar facility that I can recommend is the Cooper's Rock Mountain Lion Sanctuary, which is located across the (Fayette County) Pennsylvania line in West Virginia, just outside Morgantown, near Cooper's Rock State Park. The directors of the sanctuary are Mark and Sheila Jenkins, a married couple dedicated to rescuing abused and neglected cougars. Fully licensed by both the West Virginia Department of Natural Resources and the United States Department of Agriculture, Cooper's Rock Mountain Lion Sanctuary, as Dr. Sheperd's, is recognized by the IRS as a nonprofit corporation. At CRMLS, an all-volunteer sanctuary, the mountain lions are in their natural environment; and at neither Sheperd's nor the Jenkins' will you see unhappy, pacing cats.

At CRMLS, the cougars can den, hide, climb and play; and it is a pure delight to watch them. I spent an afternoon there whilst engaged in the writing of this Chronicle; and Mark Jenkins, like Dr. Sheperd, was a terrific teacher. "We host 'Volunteer Days,' " Jenkins told me, "three to four per year. Volunteers are invited in for a full day, and sometimes for a whole weekend of sanctuary work laced with fun. Those days, we typically reserve projects that require many hands to complete. Visitors are welcome. It's not all work," Mark added. "Volunteers have a chance to meet one another and catch up on all the sanctuary news, explore the surrounding woods and waterfalls, do some rock climbing, break bread together, and, of course, visit with the mountain lions."

Special skills and donated labor, materials, (pre-approved) food, and money are always needed and thus always welcome; and as with Dr. Sheperd's orphanage, all donations are tax-deductible.

At CRMLS, you can even adopt a cougar. Of course, cougars never leave the sanctuary.

On the other hand, the "parents" never have the tremendous weight of their care. Adoption is a more direct way of helping a deserving cat, and there are several wonderful perks that go along with this help-option. If you are like me, you will fall immediately in love with all of the sanctuary's beautiful cats, bonding with one very special cougar on your very first visit. I spent a good deal of time talking to the lion named Burton. I have always been a strong believer in talking to animals, not such an oddity if you are a true animal lover.

A few words about the sanctuary's educational programs: CRMLS receives hundreds of visitors annually from schools and youth organizations from the tri-state area of West Virginia, Maryland and Pennsylvania. These students range from the elementary to the university level. Mark Jenkins offers a colorful array of educational programs and opportunities to meet any student age and just about any educational need. During my visit, he also pointed out many projects that had been executed by various scout troops. Visitors must set up an appointment, and comfortable shoes are recommended when you visit. Cameras are permitted. No fees. Donations, to reiterate, are wholly appreciated.

For further information about the Cooper's Rock Mountain Lion Sanctuary, its educational programs, scout projects, Volunteer Days, donations, visits, etc., please call Mark Jenkins at: 304-379-8908, or email him at: mtnlionwv@hughes.net.

If you cannot physically go and meet the cougars, then do the next best thing and visit Cooper's Rock Mountain Lion Sanctuary on their web site. You will be glad you did, for the site embraces a gallery of pictures of their lions, and those images speak volumes. Cougar faces with their knowing eyes are awesome in their beauty and in the fathomless mysteries they hold.

Dedicated to the recovery of mountain lions in eastern North America, the science-based Eastern Cougar Foundation, another nonprofit, all-volunteer organization, does a great deal of fieldwork; and their findings are impressive. Readers may report information pertaining to eastern cougars to their cougar hotline at: 304-664-3812. The Foundation has stated on their web site that a large amount of verified evidence is accumulating that documents the movement of wild cougars from west to east, and from Florida to points north. Missouri, Kansas, Oklahoma, South Dakota, Iowa, Illinois and other Midwestern states are reporting cougars in areas where they have not been seen in a century or more.

"As in Pennsylvania, sightings in those states never really ceased," John Lutz, founder and director of the Eastern Puma Research Network, related to me during a series of 2006 telephone interviews. "Ninety percent of the reports turned in do not have evidence. Documentation of cougar presence is difficult to come by, though not as difficult as it used to be. Cougars travel the mountain routes," Lutz continued. "They are a presence in the mountains of Pennsylvania, though not, of course, as numerous as they once were. Actually, since we began our research in 1983, we have had thousands of sightings from one end of the Appalachian chain to the other, from Georgia to New Brunswick," Lutz added. "The puma is the earth's most adaptable land mammal. They can adapt to every type of climate and terrain and are equally at home in cypress and pine swamps as they are in dense mountain forests."

To cite one proof of this, according to a September 9, 2006, "Great Outdoors" article in the Uniontown *Herald-Standard*, there were mountain lion sightings, at that time, in Palmerton, Pennsylvania, a place where two mountains were denuded from the discharge of a zinc factory about half-a-century ago. Though vegetation is coming back to that area, it is the last place one would expect a mountain lion to appear.

According to the material Mr. Lutz posted me from his network, over a thousand cougars in Pennsylvania have been reported since 1950 with documented photographic and/or confirmed track proof- despite denials from official wildlife agencies.

The Eastern Puma Research Network is the largest fact-based cougar research group in eastern North America. It too is a nonprofit, volunteer study group whose purpose is to collect, evaluate and investigate reports of big cats east of the Mississippi. Since their beginnings in 1983, they have had over 7,600 reports from credible witnesses with law enforcement, wildlife and forestry backgrounds. Their members extend from Florida to Canada.

"I have personally been researching and collecting data on cougar sightings since 1965," Lutz, a retired reporter for radio station WFBR in Baltimore, continued. "Not all the sightings we check out produce evidence, but some do. Most of those sightings have been the tan, tawny color; but about 350 of them have been reported as black, and 330 of the black ones were reported in Pennsylvania. For a fact, there are black mountain lions; but since the choice habitats of these big cats are dimly-lit areas, that could account for the color being perceived and erroneously reported as black. Of course, this type of sighting could be an exotic black panther, an illegal pet, released into the wilds. There are black mountain lions, not as common for sure; but there is such a creature. When documented evidence is collected, our science team becomes involved in evaluating the material."

Lutz related to me that he had been joined in his quest for documenting this elusive cat in the eastern regions by Dr. Ted Roth, a zoologist, who passed away in 1977. Another associate, Dr. Robert Pennington Smith, an anthropologist and biologist, passed away from cancer in 1996. Lutz' network includes several trained scholarly members who have made eastern puma research their quest.

"Critical or hardened skeptics, including many wildlife officials, continue to make outrageous claims, stating untruths. And writers for the news media continue to chase after these skeptics for their ridiculing remarks that continue to embarrass and insult the intelligence of well-meaning and often qualified witnesses," Lutz stated in the literature he sent me.

"There are many ways to tell if a sighting is authentic," the research director shared with me during one of our many discussions. "For instance, when a mountain lion brings down a deer, it will eat its fill, then cover the kill with leaves and twigs. Such a discovery is worth checking out. The cougar will return to that kill until the meat starts to spoil. Cougars never eat spoiled meat. In winter, a mountain lion will return to finish off a deer-kill down to the bone. We can tell, too, if the cat reported to us is a cougar by both the tracks and the scat. And there are questions we put to each person who calls in a sighting, so that we can determine if that report is worth following up. We know what to ask before we go to check out a sighting."

In the winter of 1996, a Huntingdon County man came across the "strange tracks of a large animal" that were later confirmed as puma. Cluster mountain-lion reports had poured in from that area. In 2005, a resident of Lycoming County sent the Eastern Puma Research Network multiple sets of pictures showing tracks in the snow where a large black cat had been reported by several area people. The photographs confirmed the tracks as those of a cougar. In addition, the authenticated photos depicted tail-drag marks in the snow. Again, there had been cluster reports, this time from the Lycoming-Montour-county area. As with most big-cat sightings, the Lycoming, Montour, and Huntingdon county information came out of dense forest regions with good water sources.

"One of the many names for this native cat is 'mountain screamer,' and if ever you have heard this sound in the wild, you would never forget it," Lutz stated adamantly.

This author can tell you, readers, that though I have never heard a mountain lion's scream in the wilds of Pennsylvania, I have heard the hair-raising scream in the Big Horns of Wyoming, verified by our Crow Native American guide, and it *is* unforgettable. I have an authentic tape of cougar sounds as well.

"The cougar's scream is often likened to a woman's frantic scream of terror," Lutz stated. "That's another thing. Over the past several years, there have been a number of police reports of a 'woman being murdered,' that have come in from remote mountain areas all along the Appalachian chain. "Any number of those cries could have been a puma, since nothing else added up after police investigations," Lutz concluded.

The cougar makes a diversity of sounds, including chirps, peeps, purrs, coos, growls, moans and whistles, in addition to their legendary screams. And I daresay the scream can sound like either a woman being murdered or a baby wailing its heart out. To be fair in this discussion, there are several other wild creatures that make sounds similar to those emitted by a cougar.

In my home county of Fayette, I have spoken to several hunters, in addition to veterinarian Dr. Sheperd, who each maintain that, over the past several years, they have seen either a mountain lion or evidence of one in the wilds of various Pennsylvania counties: namely, Fayette, Westmoreland, Greene, Potter, Cameron, Clinton and Sullivan. To quote two of those interviews: My friend Pat Beal, a veterinary assistant, told me that in 2001, her husband and son heard a panther scream while they were on a hunting trip in Cameron County. "They said it literally caused the hair on their arms and the back of their necks to rise. They will never forget it," she told me.

Tecumseh poses for visitors at the sanctuary. Photos courtesy the Cooper's Rock Mountain Lion Sanctuary

Another Fayette County resident, Dave Longanecker, recounted to me what happened to him in the late summer of 1988: "It was at Casparis in the mountains above South Connellsville where I saw the mountain lion. I was in my vehicle, on my way down that ultra-steep mountain trace when the cat ran across the road in front of me. No one has ever believed me, but it's the truth. It was about the size of a German shepherd. This was a *big* cat with a long tail, not a bobcat, which is smaller with no tail to speak of... sort of tan in color with faint spots on its side, so I figured it was a young one. The head with its black-muzzle markings was that of a mountain lion. There was no mistaking that because the creature looked right at me, though for only a second." I want to add here that mountain lions have spots until they are about ten months old.

Longanecker had another cougar experience in not-too-distant Romney, West Virginia, directly south of Cumberland, Maryland: "I was deer hunting. That time, I never saw the cat. I saw its tracks behind those of the deer I had been trailing. They were there, clear as day, in the snow. The paw marks were *not* those of a bobcat. I have been a hunter all my life, and I know bobcat tracks. These were very large cat imprints, not dog tracks that would have registered toenails. I would swear to this day they were those of a mountain lion." Lutz told me in one of our interviews that there had been cluster mountain lion reports in the Romney area in the 1980s, when Longanecker came across those tracks.

A few years ago, when scientists documented cougar populations in the Midwest, they believed the big cats would move eastward. Though most scientists would say that they have not made the move east as yet, others would vehemently disagree. Paul Beier, a cougar researcher from Northern Arizona University, said in a *New York Times* 2002 article that these big cats "...will eventually get as far east as New Jersey, or at least close."

In a 2003 article in *Outside* magazine, Maurice Hornocker, a University of Idaho biologist who is considered one of the world's foremost authorities on mountain lions, said, "Lions will hit the Mississippi within the next decade." He predicted that they would then expand even further eastward, since the Appalachian mountain range "... is beautiful cat country, full of deer and plenty of cover."

There is evidence those predictions are already coming true. "Mountain lions are showing up where they haven't lived for decades," Lutz reiterated to me. "They are in Pennsylvania, not in large numbers, but they are a presence. A cougar, however, is like a UFO with four feet. They are very, very elusive."

I read some time ago that one of the last mountain lions in the commonwealth of Pennsylvania was shot in Susquehanna County on Nittany Mountain in 1856. Since then, the cat has been on display on the Penn State campus, at State College, home of the "Nittany Lions," except when the mounted specimen was removed for a well-needed refurbishment in the 1990s. From pre-Colonial times, there has been a mystique (entangled with fear) surrounding these beautiful creatures. The University of Pittsburgh Panthers pays homage to the same big cat.

Increasingly, according to the Eastern Puma Research Network, hunters and visitors to Pennsylvania's woods are telling of sightings. Most of these folks, regrettably, do not have a camera on them to record what they see. Hunters, hikers and other outdoor enthusiasts can help prove the existence of mountain lions here in the East by reporting sightings to either the Eastern Cougar Foundation mentioned earlier or to John Lutz and his network, also a twenty-four-hour hot-line, at 304-749-7778.

"Taking along a cell phone and/or a digital or trail camera on a nature walk is on the rise, and that is good for us," John Lutz has said. "A partially eaten deer covered with leaves is evidence that needs to be investigated. A photo is good, as is scat evidence, plaster casts of tracks, and/or photographs of tracks."

Photographs can be analyzed for positive identification and authenticity. Mountain lion tracks are between three to four inches wide, four toes with a heel that registers and no registered "toenails." That eliminates most other animals. The toes go in different directions and would be four oval shapes if traced with a pencil. The palm is twice the size of each toe-oval, and the top of the heel pad is squared off. Since mountain lions have a lot of hair between their toes, and their paws are broad, they don't sink into soft earth or snow as deeply as one might expect for so heavy an animal. And be advised that the track of a bobcat is more round than the paw print of a puma. Cougars keep their claws retracted, enabling the cat to stalk quietly; and this prevents the claws from registering on their tracks. Those retracted claws are kept extremely sharp.

To learn more about mountain lions and the work of documenting their expansion, I suggest you visit the World Wide Web: Cougar Network, Eastern Puma Research Network, and the very science-oriented Eastern Cougar Foundation. These sites each provide an abundance of information and photo images, as well as related links. At the Eastern Cougar Foundation's web site, visitors will find mountain lion tracks, scat, kill-marks and other data important to proper identification.

Dr. Dennis Wydra, a retired college professor, became intrigued by the number of Pennsylvania mountain lion sightings and personally financed his own investigation in 2004. Initially joined by outdoor writer Jim Collins, the two men conducted interviews across the commonwealth. They gathered testimonials and took pictures of big cat evidence. "During the 1960s, there was a multitude of mountain lion sightings in Pennsylvania," Dr. Wydra told me in a 2006 telephone interview. "Pennsylvania lit up like a Christmas tree with mountain lion sightings during the sixties; there were so many."

Clay Nielsen, director of scientific research for the Cougar Network and a wildlife ecologist at Southern Illinois University, has been busy documenting the amount of potential cougar habitat in the Midwest, which already appears to have the runover of mountain lions that have migrated from the West. Nielsen has predicted that, as their Midwest habitat fills, cougars will move even further eastward. "Given the number of cougar confirmations actually documented by the Cougar Network during the past three years (2003-06), it is clearly time for the wildlife community to prepare for the great cat's return to the East." There continues to be an increasing number of documented episodes by witnesses having backgrounds in forestry, law enforcement or wildlife, as John Lutz has avowed, making the occurrences more credible than (not to insult their integrity) hunters, hikers and others who have reported sightings over the years.

The limiting factor here is Cougar's only predator. Will *man* permit mountain lions to re-establish themselves in the East? John Lutz makes an ardent plea to hunters: "If you are fortunate enough to see one of these elusive, magnificent animals in the wild, please don't shoot it with your gun- use your camera! *There is no cause for alarm over this information.* Cougars are more afraid of you than you are of them."

The key to this situation, as to most things, is education and the application of good common sense in wilderness areas anywhere. For instance, adults should never permit young children to wander, unsupervised, in the woods. You wouldn't allow your youngsters to wander, unsupervised, in a city either, would you?

And for you hunters: Will Cougar's return herald the demise of the deer population in Penn's vast woods? The answer to that, after interviewing several of the above experts, is an unequivocal "NO."

Certainly education has helped the Florida panther, which was designated an endangered subspecies in 1973. Hopefully, the beautiful cat will remain a part of that state's unique wildlife community. As of October 2003, the United States Fish and Wildlife Service has been considering a reclassification of "extinct" in regard to the eastern puma. At this writing, many of the above cougar-connected people I spoke with feel that the USFWS does not know what to make of these ongoing sightings and reports.

When (late 2006) I emailed the central bureau of the Pennsylvania Game Commission, they responded that, to date, they have "... been unable to scientifically authenticate the current existence of mountain lions living and breeding in the wilds of Pennsylvania; therefore, the agency continues to presume the mountain lion's extirpation within the state. The mountain lion currently is listed as an endangered species in its entire former range (including Pennsylvania) by the federal Endangered Species Act and has maintained this endangered status since June 4, 1973. In addition, the mountain lion is classified as a protected mammal under the Pennsylvania Game and Wildlife Code. Therefore, to the extent that any mountain lion(s) were found to exist in the wilds of Pennsylvania, both the federal ESA and state laws would provide a variety of protections for them, including substantial civil and/or criminal penalties for anyone responsible for, among other acts, the unlawful taking or possession of this species." Simple translation, readers: *It is illegal to hunt mountain lions in Pennsylvania under severe penalty of the law, federal and state. It is illegal to capture or own mountain lions as pets.*

Since pre-Colonial times, the folklore that has surrounded these seldom-seen cats has resulted in their persecution out of fear and misunderstanding of the important role these predators play in the natural ecosystem. Human population growth has been the primary threat to the puma's range, and this human hazard continues to diminish the quality of existing cougar habitats. We have to share this planet with a diversity of animals and humans, and if we don't soon learn that....

Each of the animals placed here on earth have messages to convey- for those wise enough to listen and observe. The owl teaches patience, the wolf (another animal that has been the victim of "bad press") how to balance individual needs with those of family; the bear's lesson is to develop and fine-tune intuition. Native American lore asserts, "Cougar walks as a spiritual hunter, to teach leadership, determination, independence and, above all, courage." A cougar will leap at opportunities. Those humans with cougar medicine (i.e., cougar characteristics) take control of their lives and circumstances the most effectively.

Ancient Native American wisdom tells us that the mountain lion is a silent stalker with the ability to fade from sight. Cougar is a solitary hunter who strikes like lightning, a quality much desired by warriors. The Cat Spirit provides fearless protection against evil. *Cougar is a strong spirit to have as an ally.*

The Native Americans successfully lived alongside the mountain lion, respecting its grace and power. Thus, I would like to conclude this Chronicle with Native American insight and understanding. "We must protect the forests for our children, grandchildren and the children yet to be born," said Qwatsinas, a sachem of the Nuxalk Nation. "We must protect the forests, too, for those who cannot speak for themselves, the trees, the fish, birds- the animals." The great American writer Thoreau was echoing Native American sagacity when he said, "In wilderness is the preservation of the world."

"Every animal the Great Manitou created has a purpose," so stated a wise *Lenni Lenapé* (Delaware) chief.

"We should understand well that all things are the work of the Great Spirit," said Black Elk, an Ogalala Sioux. "We should know that He is within all things- the trees, the grasses, the rivers, the mountains, and in all the four-legged animals and the winged peoples...."

The incomparable Chief Dan George, the First Nation spiritual leader, explained it this way: "If you talk to the animals, they, with their greater wisdom, will speak to you, and you will know each other. If you do not talk to them, you will not know them, and what you do not know you will fear- and what you fear you will destroy."

"When the animals are gone," a nineteenth-century Native sachem cautioned, "so shall we be gone- and the earth destroyed."

"MASH... Goodbye, Farewell and Amen"

"Korea is a lesson in national preparedness. Historically, in times of peace we have not prepared for war. In some ways that has been a wise course. In other ways we have paid dearly for it. Preparedness is the job of the executive branch of our federal government and of the military. The yearning for preparedness is the job of the American people. It is the prerogative of the people to demand an appropriate level of preparedness for it is the people who will pay, as they did in Korea, for our failure to prepare. Our lesson is that the extraordinary courage and sacrifices of our young men and women are not appropriate substitutes for preparedness." -A MASH surgeon in Korea, Dr. Otto F. Apel, Jr.

MASH (Mobile Army Surgical Hospital) was first established in August of 1945, at the conclusion of World War II, and later deployed during the Korean War and subsequent conflicts. The United States Army decommissioned the last MASH on February 16, 2006.

The brainchild of Michael E. DeBakey and several other surgical consultants to the military, MASH was the mobile surgical alternative to the field and general hospitals of WWII. It was designed to get experienced personnel closer to the front– in fact, as close to the front as possible– so that the wounded could be treated sooner and with greater success.

Casualties were first treated at the point of injury via "buddy aid," i.e., by Army medics and Navy corpsmen, on the field of combat, and then routed to a battalion aid station for emergency stabilizing surgery. From there, wounded were routed to a MASH unit where they would receive the most extensive treatment. This proved to be highly successful. The proof of the MASH pudding was, undeniably, Korea. During that conflict, a seriously wounded soldier who made it to a MASH alive had, after being treated, a ninety-seven (some sources state ninety-eight) percent chance of survival.

MASH made its way into popular culture via the 1968 novel *M*A*S*H* by Richard Hooker, a pseudonym for H. Richard Hornberger, a writer and surgeon who had served in the 8055th MASH in Korea. Hornberger based the character Hawkeye Pierce on himself. The 1970 feature film, based on his novel, followed by the long-running television sitcom based on the movie, both carrying the same title, made MASH a household word. The TV series' final episode (1983), "Goodbye, Farewell and Amen," is reputed to be the most-watched show in US television history. It boasted about 125 million viewers.

Actually, few people realize that there exists an earlier film which also unfolded at a MASH. *Battle Circus* (with Humphrey Bogart) debuted in 1953 at the end of the Korean Conflict. Ironically, its original title had been *MASH,* but Metro-Goldwyn-Mayer rejected it for the reason that they feared people would think it was a story about potatoes. The *Circus* part of the decided-upon name refers to the speed and ease that a MASH unit picked up stakes and moved to where the action was. *Battle Circus*, like the future *M*A*S*H,* employed humor to soften the hard-edged tragedy of war.

After Korea, MASH units continued to serve in various conflicts including the protracted Vietnam War (the longest American struggle since the Revolutionary War) that reached its bloody talons across the years from 1954 to 1975, claiming over 58,000 American lives, and over 304,000 American wounded of whom 75,000 were left disabled. Sadly, 1,300 remain missing in action, resulting in an absence of closure for their families.

In March 1991, the 159th MASH served in Iraq during Operation Desert Storm. In 1997, the last MASH unit in South Korea was decommissioned. A ceremony marked the occasion, which was attended, interestingly, by several cast members of the TV series.

The Germany-based 212th MASH became the first US Army hospital established in Iraq (2003) during Operation Iraqi Freedom. This particular MASH unit is the most decorated combat hospital in US Army history, with twenty-eight battle streamers.

Worldwide, that final MASH was decommissioned, as mentioned earlier, on February 16, 2006. The concluding deployment of the highly decorated 212th was to Pakistan to support the 2005 Kashmir earthquake relief operations. Before rotating out, its equipment was donated to the nation of Pakistan.

Today, MASH units have been replaced by CSH– US Army Combat Support Hospitals, which are, in essence, mobile hospitals delivered to the corps support area in standard military demountable containers– MILVAN cargo containers– and assembled by the staff into a tent hospital to treat wounded soldiers. The size of these hospitals is almost infinitely expandable by chaining tents together, but will typically handle between sixteen and 256 operational hospital beds. The most common configuration is the eighty-four-bed hospital.

The CSH, usually referred to as "CASH," will treat, in addition to wounded American soldiers, civilians or opposition soldiers wounded by the US military.

Unlike the MASH in Korea, the CSH is climate controlled for patients, though not for staff. Each CSH has a pharmacy, laboratory, X-Ray that often includes a CT-Scanner, as well as dental capabilities. It provides its own power from 100 KW generators.

Because of their size and the difficulty in moving them, Combat Support Hospitals are not the frontline of military medical care. Battalion aid stations, forward support medical battalions, and forward surgical teams are now the first point of contact medical care for our wounded in war.

Like the old MASH, CSH receives most of its patients via helicopters. Today, these mechanized angels are called "air ambulances." CSH stabilizes patients for further treatment at fixed facility hospitals. Ideally, the CSH is located as the bridge between incoming copter ambulances and outgoing Air Force aircraft.

As the successor to MASH, CSH is differentiated by the capability of its equipment and its size, with "CASH" being, by far, the larger and better-equipped operation. A "full up" CSH has 624 people to staff 256 beds. And CSH is commanded by a full colonel, rather than a lieutenant colonel.

Aerial view of MASH 8055, Korea

Since the focus of this Chronicle is MASH, however, let us turn the wheel of time back to 1950. By that year, budget cuts, in addition to post World War II popular disenchantment with all things military, had resulted in a sad-condition army, far below what it should have been. At the outbreak of the Korean War, only two hundred doctors were assigned to the Far East Command, and that included Japan, Okinawa, Guam, the Philippines, and Korea. This situation warranted the Doctors Draft Act of 1951.

In military medicine, I think it would be safe to say that essentially all doctors become surgeons because they are treating wounds constantly. During the conflict in Korea, the drafted doctors who entered the Medical Corps via the Doctors Draft went through a training program, which began at Brooke Army Medical Center in San Antonio, Texas. After a few weeks training at Brooke, the doctors were usually flown to Japan, by way of Hawaii, then to a MASH in Korea.

What the army needed at that time was a unit with capabilities greater than the field hospital to fill the gap in the evacuation chain between the aid stations and the evac hospitals. It needed an independent unit that could keep up with the maneuver units by using its own vehicles and providing its own supplies by tapping into the area supply channels. This medical unit would also have to keep track of its personnel through its own chain of command. MASH filled the gap and supplied the need.

When the North Koreans blitzed across the 38th Parallel on June 25, 1950, the US Army had five MASH units on paper. Then, in the hectic days after the surprise attack, three MASH units were started from scratch, the 8055, the 8063, and the 8076. A fourth unit was created a few months later. Designated the 1st MASH, it was organized in the States and deployed in September 1950 to support the Inchon landing. Less than ninety days after the war began, all four MASH units were committed in support of American and Korean troops in combat. In the subsequent eighteen months, amidst the hell of war in that faraway country, the assigned doctors and nurses would paint a clear and vivid picture of what a MASH ought to be.

For those operating in the MASH units, life was not easy. No bright lights lit operating rooms; no sterile hallways connected the tents. MASH tents were dark and cold in the severe, subzero Korean winters; dank, hot and humid in the oft-unbearable Korean summers. Incoming wounded meant that doctors and nurses labored for long hours at a stretch, all within the thunderous sounds of the guns. Except for a couple of very brief intervals, the dedicated- valiant- nurses stayed with the units at all times regardless of the proximity of combat. MASH could not be operational without its nurses.

In the push of continual relocation, following the frontline action as they did, the doctors and nurses had to be ready for anything from dysentery to massive trauma. MASH was designed to move- and move quickly- with the tactical/battlefront units, and they were always in danger of rolling into the midst of the fierce fighting that was the Korean Conflict.

One of the things I want to point out about the Korean Conflict is that war's sheer *ferocity*. Right from the outset it was savage; and it continued so to the last second, when peace talks ended it in 1953, and the North Koreans battled for the last inch of real estate. As wounded were deposited onto their operating tables, MASH personnel witnessed firsthand the agony of the young American soldiers mauled by the ferocious tug-of-war between Communism and Freedom.

Certainly they were not the first doctors and nurses to have experienced the mayhem, gore and peril of the battlefield. Clara Barton, Civil War nurse and founder of the American Red Cross; the Irish nun-nurses who served selflessly during the horrific struggle of the American Civil War, as well as the stalwart doctors and nurses from *both* world wars- *all*- remind us that medical personnel have shared the frontline experience throughout the history of warfare.

The mobility to follow the action separated the MASH combat doctors and nurses from their counterparts. The stark realities of war completely inundated the sensitivities of MASH medical personnel. For long, exhausting hours, they stood in mud or on dirt floors, over endless wounded in makeshift operating tents, searching out shrapnel or probing in flesh that looked like spaghetti for arteries to save or muscles to reattach.

One of the characteristics of MASH was improvisation. In a MASH, when things got tough, the tough got tougher, and they *always* kept going. Doctors and nurses alike did whatever they had to do to provide medical treatment and care to our troops. They slept only when there was a lull in the incoming wounded, ate when they had a chance to grab a bite at the mess tent, and laughed as often as they could to break the dark spell of Death and its sinister cohort Destruction.

The wounded were carried to MASH in every possible mode of transportation that existed. Regardless, it was always a race. Some arrived in army ambulances that, rocking from side to side, sped the short distance from the front over the hills and rutted roads that was Korea. Some wounded actually hitched rides on the backs of Army jeeps or trucks that had delivered ordnance to the front and then had been commandeered for the injured. Some of the wounded were brought into camp over the shoulders of weary comrades staggering under their loads. Others were carried in on litters. Some even stumbled in on what remained of their own strength, sometimes on improvised crutches or with the aid of a buddy. The common denominator was that they were all in need, of immediate, if not high-priority, surgical attention. I want to state that MASH were responsible for treatment of *all* wounded brought to them, including the United Nations troops, and the opposing North Koreans and Chinese. Irrespective of who they were, each and every individual attended received the best care that particular MASH had to offer.

The mode of transport we think of most in connection to MASH is the helicopter. Though the copter made its debut in World War II, it saw its first real action in Korea. Korea was helicopter country. The entire nation was crisscrossed by poor roads ravaged by tanks, bombed-out railroad tracks and bridges, and mountainous terrain with ridges up to six thousand feet. In wet weather, conditions were even worse, not to mention the subzero winters with its glaze of ice and snow. Helicopters, the only solution, became the war's mechanized angels. Those used in Korea were the H-13s, H-13Ds, H-13Es, and H-19s.

As the helicopter approached the battalion aid station to pick up wounded, it became an easy target for the Chinese-and-North Korean-Russian-trained-Russian-equipped army to pick off. Wounded pickups had to be synchronized– and swift. When the copter approached, medics on the ground set out a flare, and the wounded were loaded as rapidly as humanly possible because the smoke attracted enemy fire. A key point to make here is that wounded had to be *ready* for transport. The copter could not sit on the ground in a combat zone for long before it drew enemy guns. Too, personnel did not want to tie up helicopters that could be carrying wounded that *were* ready to be transported to the MASH units.

As soon as the chopper touched ground, the medics hastened the litter-borne wounded to it, placed the litters just above the skids, strapping them securely down, then closed the transparent protective caps over the injured on board. Straightaway, the helicopter lifted off. All this was usually done under direct enemy fire. In Vietnam this rapid wounded-pickup process was known as a "dustoff."

A humorous helicopter incident that was actually used in the TV series I discovered in yet another book entitled *MASH*. This is a personal account by Dr. Otto F. Apel Jr., an army surgeon who had served in Korea, and co-authored with his son Pat Apel. Dr. Apel was a consultant to the television show's writers for a couple of years. Helicopter pilot Jim Knighton was responsible for the real copter occurrence, one of Korea's lighter episodes that relieved the stress of war– for a few minutes anyway. The incident occurred during a quiet period when there were no incoming wounded. Those times, the doctors took a well-deserved breather, reading, chatting with one another, or playing cards. Some napped, bathed, or wrote letters home.

On that particular afternoon, several of the nurses were in the nurses' shower tent, taking advantage of the respite to refresh themselves, when Knighton's chopper, en route to the landing pad, came whirling over the pass between two towering mountains. Without cargo (wounded), he had strayed slightly out of the regular flight pattern. Though an excellent pilot, Knighton suddenly lost altitude and went nose-up into a near-stall. The engines whined, protesting loudly, as Jim struggled to regain altitude. Likely he had been caught in a downdraft caused by the wind rushing through the mountain passes. He continued to spin out over the MASH tents like a huge dragonfly hovering above a country pond on a hot summer afternoon. Directly over the nurses' shower, the tail rotor dipped under the strain of a sudden burst of power; and the chopper shuddered violently for a long precarious moment before Knighton regained control, bringing the "bubble top" to a slow climb. At that instant, however, the downdraft caught the tent below it, sending it flying– in all directions– across the Korean countryside. In its wake, in plain view of nearly two hundred doctors, enlisted men, pilots, mechanics, cooks, the chaplain, and anyone else who cared to look, were a half-dozen nurses, who, fully exposed, frantically attempted to cover themselves.

The pilot later denied that the action was executed on purpose, though, stated Apel in his engrossing book, "We looked past his denials and caught him smiling when we asked a very simple and straightforward question."

The speed and flexibility of the helicopters permitted the MASH units to centralize its doctors and nurses in specialized facilities. For instance, MASH 8076 became the place to treat extreme vascular injuries. The 8055 became the unit for head injuries. MASH 8063 handled unusual conditions, such as the mysterious fever that swept Korea in 1951-52. Cases of suspected biological or chemical warfare were sent to the 8209, later reassigned the 8225, a stable unit that did not pick up stakes and move as did the others.

In addition to wounded evacuation, helicopters were even used to make what were referred to as "house calls." Often, in the heat of battle, the wounded overwhelmed a battalion surgeon or group of field medics at a battlefield aid station. The frantic call for help would then reach a MASH; and, if at all possible, a surgeon, after having snatched up a kit bag, hurried forth via the mechanical angel. The "real" angels, the pilots, were intrepid to a man. They knew better than anyone that they were the lifeline between the front and the operating table; and to put it succinctly- *they always delivered.*

Helicopters could not fly at night or in inclement weather, thus each MASH had a motor pool, which moved with each unit. Though not as fast as choppers, MASH ambulances could navigate the bad roads regardless of the weather. Wounded seemed to come in frequently late afternoons or at night, thus ambulances were mandatory with each unit.

Living conditions in a MASH unit were rudimentary at best. Water had to be hauled with each unit via truck, and drinking water was a *precious* commodity. MASH personnel filled canteens, buckets, and army helmets from the water truck. No one dared partake from the streams or lakes for fear of what the North Koreans or the Chinese had dumped into those waters. All MASH personnel lived in tents with crates for furniture, and they used portable showers or cans of heated water to bathe. Mud or the fine powder of dust was everywhere. Nevertheless, MASH had one "luxury"- their bedding, which was better than what the soldiers at the front had, army sleeping bags. MASH bedding consisted of an army cot with its own small mattress and government-issue linens and blankets.

In spite of the comfortable bedding, there were times when the GI bedroll was preferable. In the wicked cold of the Korean winter, the nurses slept in long johns under flannel pajamas topped with a sweater, coat or both, socks, gloves, and an OR stockinet cap on their heads, in addition to anything else they could layer on. Thus bundled-up, they wormed into their sleeping bags, then piled on several blankets.

In Korea, the latrines- breeding grounds for huge green Korean flies and rats- were mostly slit trenches veiled by blankets draped between stakes for what privacy that could afford. Constantly in need of cleaning and disinfecting, the downdrafts were unbearable. Sudden strong gusts of wind could- and did- carry the blankets away, leaving embarrassed personnel in full view of whomever was in the area.

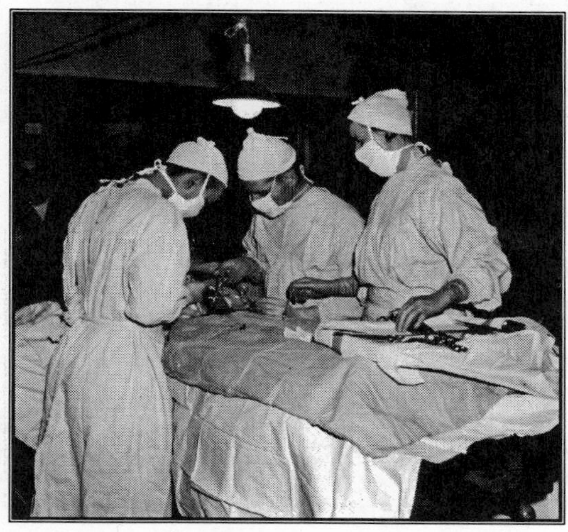

A Mash surgery at Uijonbu, Korea

Fly-and-mosquito screens were a must on all tents during the warm season, and all the facilities and incoming personnel were dusted with DDT on a regular basis. Rats, a symptom of combat and death, were a constant presence and much more difficult to control. Traps and poison were utilized, and bricks were placed on the floor along the tent perimeters. Those remedies helped, but no MASH was ever rat-free.

I was impressed with the great camaraderie that existed among MASH personnel, despite the rather rapid turnover in each unit. The average tour of duty for a MASH doctor in Korea was about a year, though some served longer. A nurse's tour extended from six to fifteen months. When a doctor rotated out, he took home, to his practice, experience that was considerable. Experience is the best teacher, and the war-experience that returned home with both the MASH doctors and nurses helped many a stateside patient.

The nerve center of any MASH was the operating tent, and I want to stress here that several improvements came to the medical profession via the ingenious MASH units in Korea. For instance, the treatment of blood-loss shock reached a high level of sophistication in the Korean MASH units.

For all the medical developments that MASH came up with, the operating tent in a MASH was unbelievably simple. Three evenly spaced operating tables occupied the center of the OR tent. The dirt floors meant that mud was a common problem in wet weather. Lights, the X-ray machines (in a nearby tent), heaters, and everything else electric were powered by one five-kilowatt and one fifteen-kilowatt generator. Surgery necessitates intense illumination. Lights and other equipment in a MASH had to be operated round the clock. Vital to any MASH, the generators *had* to run constantly.

In order to make the operating light bright enough for surgeons to work, a nurse or medic would stand behind the doctors, holding an additional light- a naked light bulb inside a tin can- directing the light where it was needed. Often, a nurse or medic held a hand-mirror that reflected from the overhead bulb onto the surgery on the table.

The hours in the OR were irregular and more often than not *brutal.* A MASH unit's shift in the operating tent began with incoming wounded and did not end until that influx ceased. If you can image the determined, sprinting nurses and other MASH personnel on the TV show's well-known overture, that picture is worth a thousand of my words when MASH units had incoming wounded. Typically, time was of the essence, and everyone hustled.

Much of the ever-needed blood came from the United States, the result of blood drives, and shipped to Korea. It gives me great pride to state that in 1951, Pennsylvania's General George C. Marshall, the favorite native son of Uniontown (Fayette County), headed a successful blood-drive crusade in which he entreated the American people to give blood for the soldiers at the front.

The post-op, a huge tent with 200 cots, was always crowded. There was no privacy; all recovering patients were together under the one tent. Since the post-op tent was moved as often as the tactical situation dictated, early ambulation was necessary. Today, this is a concept utilized after a variety of surgeries. Modern doctors and therapists get patients up and on their feet as soon as possible. The benefits of early ambulation were discovered, out of necessity, in the MASH units of Korea.

Among the brave soldiers and valiant MASH personnel, there were, as in each of America's struggles, many, many Pennsylvanians. One shining example is Dr. John H. Davis of Coraopolis, Allegheny County. Davis attended Allegheny College in Meadville. He served with honors in both World War II and Korea. During the Korean Conflict, he was a member of the surgical research team and a MASH surgeon. Thanks to his research team, MASH units began using artificial kidneys in combat zones to treat wounded soldiers with kidney failure. Necessity is the mother of invention, and I want to reiterate that medical advancement is the silver lining in all war clouds.

Tent village, MASH 8055, Korea
Photos from the "Harold Secor Memoir," courtesy the Korean War Educator web site

"Korea," the astute Dr. Otto F. Apel stated in his book, "is a lesson in national preparedness. Historically, in times of peace we have not prepared for war. In some ways that has been a wise course. In other ways we have paid dearly for it. Preparedness is the job of the executive branch of our federal government and of the military. The yearning for preparedness is the job of the American people. It is the prerogative of the people to demand an appropriate level of preparedness for it is the people who will pay, as they did in Korea, for our failure to prepare. Our lesson is that the extraordinary courage and sacrifices of our young men and women are *not* appropriate substitutes for preparedness."

I am *wholeheartedly* in accord with Dr. Apel that we need to continually employ Teddy Roosevelt's- one of America's greatest Presidents - formula for peace: "Walk softly but carry a big stick." Preparedness is vital, as are awareness and vigilance in today's world of terrorism, an enemy we will likely always have to battle. Nevertheless, I am also a great believer in America and her people. There were times in the past when we have stumbled, and we might again in the future; though our destination has always been clear, along the rocky road to history. Of all the things Freedom is, it is *not* free. Freedom has always come at a high price. But to that end, we, as a nation, are committed.

Over 1.7 million Americans served in the Korean theater of war from 1950 through 1953. Following close on the heels of World War II, the Korean Conflict was *not* a popular war, and there was no large, organized home-front effort to support the men and women who fought and served in that struggle as there had been during World War II. [See "A Sentimental Journey or Praise the Lord and Pass the Ammunition," this volume.] When Korean veterans returned home, they unceremoniously resumed their civilian lives. There was little fanfare and no heroes' welcome home. *Yet what those valiant soldiers and the MASH doctors and nurses did there should never be forgotten.*

I highly recommend my readers share the experiences of the Korean Conflict from those who were there by visiting the Korean War Educator web site: www.koreanwar-educator.org. Here visitors will find detailed accounts of the war in the memoirs and letters of its veterans and in the hundreds of photographs, as well as casualty statistics, buddy searches, and Korean War reunion information. Its learned founder, Lynnita Jean Brown of Tuscola, Illinois, holds two degrees in American history and is a riveting speaker on Korea, bringing an awareness of that war to the public. In addition to her duties as text editor on the Foundation web site, Ms. Brown works tirelessly- as a volunteer- on behalf of Korean War veterans. It all started in 1996, when this remarkable woman began interviewing hundreds of Korean War veterans. Since its beginnings in the autumn of 2000, the Korean War Education Foundation has grown in leaps and bounds. Under continual construction, veterans and their families are ever expanding the site with factual information and telling photographs.

Did we gain anything from the Korean War? You bet we did. The Korean War was one of the most important events of the twentieth century because, for the first time, force was used to *contain* communism. Communists worldwide learned that they would pay a hefty price for attempting to spread their evil. And yes, with no exaggeration, communism is an evil that spreads like a cancer to violate and annihilate the God-given, fundamental rights and privileges of human beings who reside within its totalitarian, despotic control. Subordination of the individual to the state, with strict control of all aspects of the life and productive capacity of that nation, especially by coercive measures, such as censorship and terrorism (the first methods employed by the Nazi Party in 1933) is *indeed* evil.

North Korea today remains a closed, totalitarian state, widely regarded as a threat to world peace. In fact, as I sit here at my computer, engaged in the writing of this Chronicle, North Korea is defying the international community with their nuclear testing. South Korea, on the other hand, is an economic miracle, America's seventh largest trading partner and our staunchest ally. Able to act solely for their own national intent, the South Koreans have reached an astounding level of prosperity- with the freedom to enjoy it.

The medical personnel who tended the hospitalized 103,284 wounded in Korea are held in the highest esteem by veterans of that war. The heroic Army medics and Navy corpsmen thought nothing of risking their own lives to give aid to the frontline warriors. While machine guns spat their deadly charges, and with mortars exploding all around them, those angels of mercy were there- saving the lives of our combatants.

Though civilian doctor "retreads" who had served in World War II were pulled from their specialized fields of medicine to serve again in Korea, most of the medical personnel had never before seen the kind of death and destruction they witnessed in that war-torn land. Many of the MASH doctors were fresh out of medical school, and some reservists had little or no experience with wounded. Yet, many a returning vet recounted how he had returned home alive due to a nameless "doc" who had worked magnanimously to save his life in Korea.

To every doctor, nurse, medic, corpsmen, helicopter pilot, ambulance driver and all others connected to the MASH units from Korea to 2006, America is profoundly grateful. And as MASH rolls down the road of memory and into history, we offer each of you a heartfelt "Thank you!"

Goodbye, farewell- and *amen.*

"Mine Eyes Have Seen the Glory- The National Civil War Museum"

"My paramount object in this struggle is to save the Union...."

"War... is terrible, and this war of ours, in its magnitude and in its duration, is one of the most terrible.... It has carried mourning to every home, until it can almost be said that the 'heavens are hung in black.' "

"It has been said of the world's history hitherto that might makes right. It is for us and for our time to reverse the maxim, and to say that right makes might."

"With malice toward none, with charity for all, with firmness in the right- as God gives us to see the right-let us strive on to finish the work we are in, to bind up the nation's wounds... to achieve and cherish a just and lasting peace among ourselves, and with all nations."
- Abraham Lincoln, during the course of the great and terrible Civil War

As visitors approach the entrance of The National Civil War Museum, a jewel atop a hill overlooking a sweeping vista of Pennsylvania's capital at Harrisburg, one of the first things they notice is a magnificent sculpture. The showpiece of the museum entry, the three-dimensional masterpiece, *en bronze*, by sculptor Terry Jones is entitled "Moment of Mercy." It depicts a young Confederate sergeant, Richard Rowland Kirkland, engaged in an act of incredible compassion and courage during the horrific Battle of Fredericksburg.

It was December 13, 1862, as Union General Ambrose E. Burnside's forces readied themselves to storm Fredericksburg- a strategic site on the direct road to Richmond- in northeast Virginia. President Lincoln had advised- urged- Burnside to march quickly. Since the bridges had been destroyed earlier in the war, the newly appointed commander of the Army of the Potomac could not cross the Rappahannock River until his pontoon boats appeared. In the interim, so did the Army of Northern Virginia.

An ominous fog shrouded the city. Burnside waited, and finally a weak winter sun banished the mists. Union soldiers went forth with their assault at Fredericksburg to meet an impregnable Rebel defensive.

Confederate General Robert E. Lee's forces *had* moved quickly, taking the high ground; and from behind the protective wall at the frozen slope of Marye's Heights, Cobb's Georgians made ready.

The Southerners were arrayed four-deep in some places along Telegraph Road, protected by an adjoining stone wall. Brigadier General Thomas R. Cobb, commanding there, remarked, "If they [the Federals] wait for me to fall back, they will wait a long time."

Below, the wait, under fire from the Confederate artillery, must have seemed interminable to Union General Meagher's Irish Brigade. "Not even a chicken could survive on that field once we opened up on it," stated a Rebel artilleryman. Finally, the order rang out: "Irish Brigade, forward at the double-quick!" A roar arose from the ranks: *"Faugh a ballagh!"* ["Clear the way!"] Already on their way to immortality, Meagher's Irish, indeed, went forward, their green battle flag with its distinctive gold harp unfurled by a timely breeze.

Wave after wave of men in blue went forward that grey December day, as shot and shell rained down on their ranks. Into the deadly massed fire they went, again and again. Into the face of withering artillery fire from Confederate gun positions atop the heights, and into the rapid musket fire from the sunken (from years of wagon traffic) protected road- but there was no taking Rebel defensives at Fredericksburg! The Confederates were too well entrenched.

Be advised, readers, that the rear of the men of the four-deep ranks loaded and passed forward muskets, allowing each man on the wall to keep up a near-continuous fire. And those boys were *shooters*, as were most Confederate soldiers hailing, as they were, from the rural South.

After the Irish Brigade's inconceivable assault on Marye's Heights, Cobb's Georgians (many of them Irish, a few even kin to Meagher's men) bound to their feet, raised their soft grey hats and cheered the extraordinary valor they had just witnessed, their guttural Gaelic chant "Ha-roo! Ha-roo! Ha-roo!" carrying all along their line.

In the gory aftermath, that consecrated field looked as if it were carpeted in blue. Nearly 6,300 Union soldiers lay dead or wounded in the acrid haze of gunpowder; and as the roar of cannon and the sharp reports of muskets faded, night drew a bloody curtain over the battlefield. Now, the pitiful moaning and the heartrending cries of the wounded and dying filled the cold December night. It was a miserable- hellish- night for both armies- "Macabre with an indescribable eeriness."

When the dawn broke on 14 December, the cries of agony had become too much for one nineteen-year-old Confederate sergeant in Kershaw's Brigade, whose Carolinians had reinforced Cobb's Georgians. Richard R. Kirkland rose from the cold, damp ground and hurried across the way to his commanding officer. "Sir," he said, tossing a wearied glance in the direction of the blue-littered field, "I'd like to take those boys some water."

With a disbelieving grimace, the officer replied, "Son, you're a damn fool." Then, after a weighty moment, "You can't carry a flag of truce... you know that?"

"Sir!" Kirkland saluted hastily, and before his nerve could flee him, he gathered up several filled canteens, securing the straps around his neck. Thus equipped, the Southerner muttered a quick prayer of protection and leaped the wall.

A ghostly scene stretched before him. Through the early-morning fog, the thin sunlight cast an unearthly glow on the countless hands that reached out to him from the frozen ground with its remnants of a recent Virginia snow. Instantly, the brave young man was met with a hail of gunfire from several Union sharpshooters. By some miracle of God, he was not hit. As the bullets whizzed by him, Kirkland knelt beside a wounded, blue-clad soldier, raised the man's head and pressed a canteen to the parched lips. The soothing water slid down the smoke-burned throat. No words were exchanged, but gratitude shone in the wounded man's feverous eyes; and Kirkland responded with a slight nod.

Across the way, the Union commander watched this mission of mercy in disbelief, uttering something inaudible under his breath. Awestruck, he raised his hand, and with abrupt energy, shouted in a stentorian voice to his men: "Hold your fire! Don't shoot that man! He's too brave to die!"

Oblivious, Kirkland stood and moved, on his errand of mercy, to the next wounded Federal. Of a sudden, a loud cheer rose from the Union ranks, picking up volume as it rolled down the long blue line. The brave, grey-clad sergeant passed from one suffering man in blue to the next, bounding back and forth over the wall at Marye's Heights for an hour and a half, while both sides held their fire. Finally, Kirkland returned to his fellow Confederates, behind the stone wall, satisfied that he had done all he could that day for the suffering.

The National Civil War Museum, at the summit of scenic Reservoir Park, Harrisburg, PA

Sadly, the "Angel of Marye's Heights," as the young sergeant became known, was killed less than a year later at the Battle of Chickamauga.

As for Brigadier General Thomas R. Cobb: We know from our discussion above that his brigade, his impassioned Georgians, were positioned behind a stone wall in the sunken road/Telegraph Road. It was ironic that, across the battlefield, stood old Federal Hill, the girlhood home of Cobb's mother. It was in this stately house where she had married, and it was in the yard of the estate where, during the Battle of Fredericksburg, the Federal artillery was planted– the batteries raining their fury on Sarah Robinson Cobb's son. During one of the intervals in the fighting, Cobb dismounted his horse, and was walking down the road behind the wall, encouraging his men, shouting orders for the removal of wounded, checking, with saddened heart, the number of dead, when a bullet struck him. It severed an artery, and Cobb lived only a short while, dying on the battlefield, the roar of the guns in his ears.

Our Civil War was such a terrible tragedy, yet it was replete with countless acts of human kindness. Today, at The National Civil War Museum at Harrisburg, Sergeant Kirkland's selfless act of courage and compassion has been preserved as a touching tribute to that extraordinary war of brother against brother, the war that purged our young nation of its most crippling flaw.

In the succinct description of the museum from their web site: "The National Civil War Museum is the only museum in the United States that portrays the entire story of the American Civil War. Its equally balanced presentations are humanistic in nature without bias to either Union or Confederate causes."

At the museum's entrance, "Moment of Mercy" is a fitting welcome. It is fitting too that this museum– which reminds us that the men facing one another in battle were Americans all– is Pennsylvania-based. The nation's first great melting pot, Pennsylvania has played a *major* role in every chapter of America's story. The terrible and glorious battle that turned the tide of the Civil War– Gettysburg– took place on Pennsylvania soil. Our noble commonwealth is the *Keystone* of the towering bastion of ideals that have become the great and enduring "United States of America."

Sergeant Kirkland's touching tale is but one of the vivid, action-packed episodes visitors to The National Civil War Museum will experience. Before we discuss some of the other exhibits the museum has to offer, let us talk briefly about the museum grounds. I strongly advise that when you visit The National Civil War Museum, you wear comfortable walking shoes and take the time to stroll over the grounds, which are, with no exaggeration, spectacular in the panoramic setting atop Reservoir Park. Here, you will discover, in addition to the "Moment of Mercy," the "Walk of Valor," a ribbon of red brick, symbolic of the blood shed during the Civil War. The "Walk of Valor" bears the names of Civil War veterans honored by their surviving descendants. If you would like to have your Civil War ancestor placed among those honored, contact the museum for information on how this can be accomplished.

On the east side of the museum building, opposite the entrance, you will find the "Friends Walkway," which embraces the names of the museum's supporters. Another way to be a part of The National Civil War Museum is through their membership programs. If this is something you would like to look into, please contact the museum with the information I provide below.

The museum building houses two floors with exhibits on both. The self-guided tour commences on the second floor, which is accessible via the grand staircase or elevator.

"A House Divided" is the winds-of-war exhibit at which to begin. Here, visitors can follow a featured timeline of incidents and issues that hurled our nation into the War Between the States, including comparisons of the Northern and Southern economies, the John Brown raid on Harpers Ferry, the election of Abraham Lincoln, and an easy-to-read map illustrating the nation's divisions/differences prior to the outbreak of hostilities.

A compelling video, entitled "We the People," brings visitors face-to-face and heart-to-heart with ten symbolic Americans, from a variety of milieux, who endured the privations and the adversities of the times.

The "Peculiar Institution– American Slavery" is the visitor's next stop. This exhibition presents slavery as it was during the Civil War era, including a powerful depiction of a slave auction. Visitors can ponder rare artifacts connected to slavery, along with the spoken words of those who supported and those who opposed human bondage.

I cannot help but interpose, on this issue of slavery, with a quote of Abraham Lincoln's: "Those who deny freedom to others deserve it not for themselves; and, under a just God, cannot long retain it. Whenever I hear anyone arguing for slavery, I feel a strong impulse to see it tried on him personally!"

"First Shots" carries visitors back to the bombardment of Fort Sumter (at the entrance to Charleston harbor, South Carolina), where the first hostilities took place. On April 12, 1861, Charleston residents watched the bombardment from their rooftops! This action, which forced the Federals to surrender, exploded the nation into war. A breathtaking photographic mural, covering an entire wall, vividly illustrates the dramatic overture of the American Civil War. Attention-grabbing displays discuss the aims of the conflict for each side; and more importantly, how *unprepared* both sides were for war.

Next, the "Making of Armies" focuses on the recruitment, training and equipping of both the Union and the Confederate forces.

"Weapons and Equipment" continues this focus, illustrating how the armies of the Civil War were created. Here, visitors will marvel at the museum's unrivaled collection of firearms, swords, accoutrements and ammunition, as well as both Union and Confederate uniforms of infantry, cavalry, artillery, and navy.

I stood for a timeless time before a Confederate jacket, its left shoulder marred by a bullet hole and blood stain. *What had become of its owner?* I wondered. *Did he ever make his way back home? Had he a sweetheart waiting for him? How small that tunic! Though human beings were smaller in the nineteenth century, the soldier was likely a mere boy.*

"Campaigns and Battles of 1862" proffers an overview of stratagems, tactics, and the logistics of such important campaigns as Shiloh, Antietam, and Fredericksburg.

"Battle Map" carries visitors onward through the bloody annals of 1862, from General Grant's capture of forts Henry and Donelson to the disastrous Union attack at Fredericksburg. Provided also is a memorable video narrated by famed Civil War historian, Dr. James Robertson, Jr.

A word about this esteemed educator: The great grandson of a Confederate soldier, Dr. Robertson has maintained a lifelong interest in the Civil War. A native of Danville, Virginia, and the recipient of every major award presented in the sphere of Civil War history, Robertson is the author of several award-winning books. Dr. Robertson is a regular on the Arts and Entertainment Network, the History Channel, and public television wherever and whenever programs on the Civil War air. His latest book, *Stonewall Jackson: the Man, the Soldier, the Legend,* has garnered eight prestigious awards along with an exciting film contract.

"Camp Curtin" was the largest Union training camp of the war. Over 300,000 men filtered through its gates at Harrisburg, Pennsylvania, en route to the front. This exhibit whisks visitors back in time, via its impressive diorama, to show how soldiers spent their otherwise monotonous stints in camp. So many different units passed through Camp Curtin that this segment also affords a good look at the diversity of uniforms worn by the Federals during the Civil War. The audible conversations and the invented songs of the men are historically and entertainingly telling, affording insight into camp life as well as the era.

"Why Men Fought" examines the varied motivations of the soldiers on both sides, including the many immigrants.

Due to the "Troubles" at home, there were many Irish on both sides, though the Union had considerably more. In fact, during the surrender at Appomattox, an Irishman in grey was known to have made this statement to an Irish in blue: "Sure and didn't ye win because ye had more Irish on your side!" Unbeknownst to many is the fact that both sides, in order to swell their ranks, sent recruiters to distressed Ireland.

"Why Men Fought" also tells the tale of the African-Americans who soldiered in the war- in both armies.

At the next stop, visitors can listen to the music that inspired and stirred the North and the South. "Civil War Music" includes spirituals, popular tunes of the times, and the rousing bugle calls of both the Union and the Confederate armies.

As I discussed in *County Chronicles I*, the military bugle call the most easily recognized- the call most apt to render emotion- "Taps" is a product of the Civil War. Its melody, eloquent and haunting, envelops a history that is both gripping and clouded in controversy. The "Lights Out" music was changed by Union General Daniel Butterfield for his brigade (Third Brigade, First Division, Fifth Army Corps, Army of the Potomac) in July 1862. During the Peninsular Campaign, Butterfield served prominently when, during the Battle of Gaines Mill, despite an injury, he seized the colors of the 3rd Pennsylvania and rallied the regiment at a crucial time in the action. Years later, he was awarded the Medal of Honor for that act of heroism.

As the tale goes, General Butterfield was not happy with the call for "Lights Out," feeling that it was too formal to signal the day's end. With the aid of the brigade bugler, Oliver Wilcox Norton, Butterfield wrote "Taps" on the back of an envelope either from scratch or, more likely, revising an earlier bugle call (seemingly borrowed from the French). Butterfield said he did this to honor his men while in camp at Harrison's Landing, Virginia, following the Seven Days Battle, which took place during the Peninsular Campaign.

The first "Taps" sounded on a still July night, 1862, rapidly making its accepted way through the Union Army- and verily to the Confederates. "Taps" was made an official bugle call after the Civil War ended. It must be pointed out that other versions of the origin of "Taps" exist; but this seems, to me, the most documented and accepted. Butterfield died in 1901- "Taps" was sounded at his funeral.

"The Auction Block," of the slavery display at The National Civil War Museum, is but one of many "living-history" exhibits this exceptional museum has to offer.

The earliest official reference to the use of "Taps" at military ceremonies and funerals is found in the US Army Infantry Drill Regulations for 1891, though it had been used, unofficially, before that under its former title "Lights Out" or "Extinguish Lights."

On The National Civil War Museum's main floor, the tour continues, beginning with "Gettysburg," the turning point in our nation's greatest struggle. This thrilling exhibit includes an informative video on how artillery and infantry loaded and fired their weapons. A large, detailed mural and a life-size diorama places the visitor right in the midst of the infamous Pickett's Charge!

A disastrous Confederate infantry assault, Pickett's Charge was a *bloodbath*. In truth, it is by far the most bloody single military attack in American history. Confederate offensives, the previous day and night, on both Union flanks had failed. Thus, on 3 July 1863, the final day of the Battle of Gettysburg, Robert E. Lee was determined to strike the Union center, where he felt the Federal forces were the weakest.

At a war council the previous night, Union General Meade had correctly predicted that, on the morrow, Lee would try and attack his lines in the center. There was little time for deliberation. However, the Rebel assault did not come at first-light but later in the day, preceded, as it was, by a massive artillery bombardment intended to "soften up" the Federal defense and silence its artillery. Due to defective equipment plus new/untried ordnance, the Confederate shelling, orchestrated by Lee's capable Chief of Artillery, Colonel E. Porter Alexander, was largely ineffective, overshooting its marks. Union cannons promptly answered- an ear-shattering reminder of Federal might.

Readers, the July 3 bombardment, which opened up at around one in the glare of that hot, humid afternoon, was likely the largest of the entire war, with hundreds of cannons from both sides firing- *the flashes incessant*- along the lines for over two hours. The noise was so intense that it could be heard thirty-five miles away in Harrisburg, and it is estimated that over 30,000 rounds were fired.

Confederate Brigadier General E. M. Law wrote later: "The cannonade in the center... presented one of the most magnificent battle scenes witnessed during the war. Looking up the valley towards Gettysburg, the hills on either side were capped with crowns of flame and smoke, as three hundred guns, about equally divided between the two ridges, vomited their iron hail upon each other."

Thick smoke concealed the battlefield; and when the Union's big guns ceased to answer the Confederate cannons, it was mistakenly believed that many of the Federal batteries had been destroyed. Artillery Chief Porter Alexander bore the heavy burden of deciding whether his artillery had knocked out enough of the Union's big guns for a Confederate charge to be executed. However, the Federal cannons were *not* out-of-commission but merely cooling off. The pause in the firing had also been to conserve Union ammunition.

The woods at Seminary Ridge were dark and blessedly cool, cooler, at least, than the sun-drenched fields. Under the shelter of the trees, Confederate General George E. Pickett was overheard repeating to Longstreet, "Alexander says if we're going at all, now's the time." Barked orders called weary men to their feet to form their brigades; and within a few minutes, the Confederates dressed right, line after line. Under the broiling sun, they waited to advance.

The heat was oppressive, and it was difficult to breathe. For the first time that afternoon, there were long moments of silence, lulls of an eerie stillness that in the heavy, smoky atmosphere seemed, somehow, unreal. Finally, the order carried over the cannon-quieted scene. Some of the Confederates muttered a quick prayer, others turned to exchange a final look with a friend, still others fixed their gazes to their front, perhaps trying to envision, in their mind's eye, a glimpse of home, or a beloved's face. "All right now, boys, for your wives, your sweethearts... for Virginia!"

Approximately 12,500 grey-clad men in nine infantry brigades, stretching over a mile-wide front, moved forward then- to their rendezvous with Destiny and into the raucous realm of military history. *Across the open fields they marched- for nearly a mile- under the murderous fire of revitalized Union artillery and rifles.*

When a battery fired canister- hundreds of iron balls like a giant shotgun blast- at massed men attacking, witnesses said the atmosphere, over the smoke, was shot-full of "flying arms, legs, torsos and heads," a hideous sight, "floating surreally, disembodied and spinning through the air." To die like that is unimaginable. How can we fathom such a scene? To say that it was like a raging summer storm, with crash of thunder, flash of lightning, the loud clatter of hail, and the banshee shriek of wind would not even come close to painting it in words.

During the pivotal, three-day death struggle that was Gettysburg, while a young nation held its breath and waited, soldiers on both sides the first two days (during those failed assaults on the Union flanks) had been mowed down like so many rows of grain in a grisly harvest. But "Pickett's Charge," on the third day of battle, reaps the most infamy for this kind of slaughter; when, in full crescendo, the Union Army, shooting off its cannons and nearly two thousand muskets at once, blasted thousands of grey-clad souls out of their flesh-and-blood vessels within the blaze of minutes.

Marching through that valley of death with its tempest of grape and canister and its swirl of smoke- an acrid smoke that burned the eyes red and chokingly closed the throat- the Confederates continuously filled the gaps that thundered open in their line, the mile-wide front shrinking to less than half-a-mile. All the while their leaders, waving their swords above their heads, bellowed to be heard above the deafening din, "Come on, lads! Do you want to live forever!" Banner-bearer after banner-bearer fell, as the rebel battle flag was snatched each time by willing hands before it touched the body-littered earth.

Some Confederates did miraculously manage to breach the stone wall that shielded many of the Union defenders. Though most of General Armistead's men lay dead or wounded behind him, the fiery Confederate officer sprang over the wall, waving his soft grey hat on his sword and shouting, "Give 'em cold steel, boys!" Fear never seemed to enter Armistead's heart when he was shot down, fatally wounded. He died a couple of days later at a Union field hospital. At the wall, soldiers on both sides were gored with the savage bayonet. Though they fought like wild boars, the Southerners could not maintain their hold and were repulsed. Thus ended the bloody three-day battle- and Lee's ill-fated campaign into Pennsylvania.

Dead and wounded were everywhere, and blood stood in rusty-red pools all about. I make no overstatement when I say that the earth was literally *soaked* with blood. Soon to become one of the most infamous charges in history, the Confederate assault had lasted less than an hour.

As Lee left the battlefield, the loud, derisive chant of the Federals, still behind their stone partition, pounded in his ears: "Fredericksburg! Fredericksburg! Fredericksburg!" The tide had most definitely been turned.

The Confederate casualty rate was over fifty percent. Lee's command losses were horrendous. Pickett's three brigade commanders and all thirteen of his regimental commanders were casualties. Close on the heels of losing Stonewall Jackson, Lee had now lost several more of his best officers- wounded, dead, or captured. Fearing a Union counteroffensive, "Marse Robert," as he was affectionately known to his men, attempted to rally his center. When Lee told Pickett to rally his division, repeating the command a second time, the latter allegedly replied, somewhat tearful, his voice bewildered and edged with anger, "General Lee, I have no division."

The fact that Pickett managed to escape the charge unharmed has led many historians to question his proximity to the fighting and, by implication, his personal courage. However, it was established doctrine during the Civil War that division commanders (and above) would "lead from the rear," whilst brigade and more junior officers were expected to lead their men from the front. Though this was often violated, there was nothing for the fiery Pickett to be ashamed of, if he had coordinated his force from behind. There is controversy as to *exactly* where Pickett was during the charge.

Though the assault is known to popular history as "Pickett's Charge," overall command had been given to Longstreet, Pickett being one of his divisional commanders; thus, a few more recent historians have referred to the assault as "Longstreet's Assault," or even as the "Pickett-Pettigrew-Trimble Assault," since it involved Pettigrew's and Trimble's divisions as well. Of course, ultimately, it had been R. E. Lee's decision; and he took full blame immediately. "It is all my fault," he articulated. "I thought my men were invincible." And soon afterward: "No blame can be attached to the army for its failure to accomplish what was projected by me. I alone am to blame." It was later said of Lee that he wept; likely not in the literal sense, due to the heavy documentation of his imperturbability- *but this supreme soldier and leader of men, perhaps the most beloved general in the history of American war, surely wept in the deepest reaches of his soul.*

Years afterward, when asked why his charge at Gettysburg had failed, Pickett is said to have bitterly quipped, "I've always thought the Yankees had something to do with it."

Lincoln was understandably exasperated by the fact that there was no Union follow-up offensive at Gettysburg, when lion-of-the-field Lee was at his weakest. If there had been, Federal forces may well have ended the war a lot sooner; though to be fair, some Union officers at Gettysburg believed the "old fox" Lee was planning a counteroffensive. Nevertheless, once Grant would be given charge of the Army of the Potomac, the subsequent spring, there would be no more sitting upon the laurels of battles won. The single-minded Ulysses S. Grant would accomplish in about a year what all his predecessors could not do in three.

After Pickett's ill-fated charge at Gettysburg, a devastated Lee remained on Traveller, his beloved warhorse, until well after midnight,

The National Civil War Museum houses a world-class collection of authentic Civil War weapons, uniforms, and equipment.

plotting the hazardous Confederate retreat from Pennsylvania. When he finally rode to his tent and dismounted, "Marse Robert" was so physically and emotionally drained that he clung to Traveller's muscular, grey neck to hold himself up. Neither man nor horse stirred for several minutes. [I was so moved by Lee's bond with Traveller that I wrote a Chronicle on the pair entitled "A Grey Man on a Grey Horse Rode By," which appears in *County Chronicles'* premier volume.]

From the outset, Confederate General Longstreet, whose theories on defensive warfare were generations ahead of his time, had opposed the charge across that open field at Gettysburg. He told Lee he did not believe there were "... fifteen thousand men on earth capable of taking that [Union] position." Longstreet had heard talk of Lee's temper, though it had never been vented on him. At that moment, anger flashed in Marse Robert's dark eyes, peering suddenly out at Longstreet and making him wince. Then, with resolve- one of his salient strengths- Lee had answered in his usual controlled voice, "It will break."

The reader may well ask: "What had Lee, the great tactician, been thinking?" Only Lee could wholly tell us that. Obviously, he believed that his Napoleonic assault would succeed, that the Union center would break. I do not believe that Lee ever utilized a Napoleonic offensive again after Gettysburg. Personally, I don't think Lee was over Stonewall Jackson's death. I don't think, either, that History will ever know the *complete* story of Lee's intentions at Gettysburg or what he held inside afterward. No biographer, no historian or researcher I know of ever picked the lock on that secret chamber of Robert E. Lee's heart.

I often speculate on what would have happened had the skilled Jackson been with strategist Lee at that pivotal battle. If Stonewall had been there to utilize one of his famous flank assaults....

Lee never published his memoirs, and Pickett's report was so negative, *so bitter*, that Lee ordered him to destroy it. No copy has ever been found.

The day after the battle, on July 4, 1863, George Pickett penned this poignant missive to his fiancée, revealing his shattered soul: "It's all over now. Many of us are prisoners; many are dead; many wounded, bleeding and dying. Your soldier lives and mourns, and but for you, my darling, he would rather be back there with his dead, to sleep for all time in an unknown grave."

Like so many things in history- in life- "Pickett's Charge" was the fault of no single individual. *It was Destiny.*

Before the two armies even came together to clash at the Civil War's most decisive battle, according to Jack McLaughlin in his *Gettysburg: The Long Encampment*: "Southeast, down by Littlestown and Taneytown, Union foot soldiers... plodding along, pressed through dusk into moonlight and the cool, scented sorcery of a summer night. And somewhere a rumor, an eerie 'fact,' began circulating among the soldiers, pushed on by no more than a wish for a hopeful sign: The ghost of George Washington had been seen riding a white horse leading the columns– the Other World was going to help them."

Years later, "When Major General Joshua Chamberlain, the hero at Little Round Top, was a very old man, someone asked him if there was any truth to the report that George Washington had been seen riding among them on a white horse on that [prophetic] morning in 1863 when Union troops were approaching the field at Gettysburg. The old warrior did not reply for a long while, then he said, '*Yes... yes*, that report was circulated through our lines... doubtless it was a superstition... yet, who among us can say that such a thing was impossible?' " This from John J. Pullen in *The Twentieth Maine.*

It rained at Gettysburg the night of July 3, a blessed rain after the intense heat and humidity of the day. It came out of the heavens, lightly at first, to refresh and cleanse the scene, then harder, to pound the blood into the hallowed earth for all time. A terrible wind, filled with voices and whisperings from the past, came up then, and thunder rolled in, echoing the cannon that had rumbled and roared earlier that afternoon. The sky above the battleground, with its littered dead and dying, was suddenly rent by jagged bolts of lightning– "His terrible swift sword." Those who had fought and died there had, indeed, "seen the glory."

It rained the whole night through, the weather continuing boisterous. The next day was the Fourth of July. America was "... four score and seven," a young nation "... dedicated to the unfinished work which they who fought there so nobly advanced... dedicated to the great task remaining...." Bloody and terrible, Gettysburg left no doubt in a determined President Lincoln's mind. "His truth was marching on."

Yesterday's heroes returned to Gettysburg in July of 1913 for the battle's fiftieth anniversary. Those gallant boys in blue and grey who had gone off to war a half century earlier were elderly now, many of them bearded, their faces wizened by Time. Most of them were frail, stooped a bit with advanced age and hard work; *yet each possessed some indefinable trait that set them apart from others of their era.* At the 1913 reunion, the grizzled survivors bivouacked on the hallowed grounds, reliving the great battle and swapping stories and memories.

The climactic instance of the reunion was a reenactment of Pickett's Charge. Thousands of spectators watched as the Union veterans took their positions on Cemetery Ridge. There, those men waited with bated breath as their old adversaries emerged from the woods of Seminary Ridge and hobbled toward them– across that open field– raising their hats to expose hair that shone as white as silver, the well-remembered Rebel yell on their lips. From behind the stone wall, a loud *groan*, heart wrenching in its timbre, rose from the Union vets. With sudden, overwhelming emotion, they stood; and not waiting for the ex-Confederates to reach them, they too moved forward, with as much speed as their arthritic legs could muster, to exchange with their former foes, not lead nor steel, but warm embraces– and tears.

Visitors will be riveted, at The National Civil War Museum, to the "Cost of War," which includes an in-depth look at Civil War medicine. Once again, via this museum's forté, you will be transported back in time for a glimpse of the human aspect of war. Life-size, realistic mannequins depict a surgeon about to amputate a struggling soldier's leg blackened with gangrene, as another soldier holds the victim down. Medical equipment used in the field and in the hospitals of the era, a fully equipped Civil War ambulance, crutches, artificial limbs, and the inhumane conditions that existed in prison camps, on both sides, convey the mind-boggling suffering and loss– the heartbreak– that was the American Civil War.

"Women in the War" telescopes several extraordinary women who played vital roles during the epoch– from nurses to spies to soldiers! Yes, there is documented proof that women served in the Civil War in combat! Remember that the Army did not give thorough physical exams during that long-past era.

"Navy Artifacts" is the exhibit that reminds visitors that the Civil War's battles were not all on land. The North and South faced off on the high seas, along the blockaded eastern coast, and on a number of inland rivers.

The museum's "Campaigns and Battles of 1864-65" carry visitors overland, through the 300-mile-long, 60-mile-wide path of destruction that was Sherman's March to the Sea,

The museum's beautiful rotunda, located inside the front entrance

illustrating that general's truism that "War is all hell!" and finally to the surrender, virtually four years to the day, at Appomattox– the most dramatic moment in American history.

The lighted "Battle Map" will take you through the total Civil War experience. The upstairs map covers the first half of the war, whilst the map downstairs encompasses from 1863 to the war's end in 1865. Echoing the museum's overall humanistic ambience, the video here is again narrated by distinguished Civil War historian, Dr. James Robertson, Jr.

The museum's presentation "Lincoln: War and Remembrance" is my special favorite (since my husband is a descendant of the great man). I suggest that no one miss this vibrant collage of how the war impacted our young nation, as well as how America remembers the Civil War. As touched on earlier, I was especially moved by the video herein containing vintage newsreel footage of Civil War veterans, Union and Confederate, meeting on the erstwhile battlefields of their youth, half a century or more later, to refight battles and trade, rather than shot and shell, still-vivid memories and sympathetic handshakes.

Following the Lincoln exhibit, the museum features a "Memory and Meaning" display which focuses on the Civil War's veterans. A large plaque features the words of Union General William Tecumseh Sherman, who emotionally declared at a meeting of the Grand Army of the Republic in 1880: "There is many a boy here today who looks on war as all glory; but boys, *it's all hell.* You can bear this warning to generations yet to come."

"Western Expansion" is the museum's next segment, which illustrates the push west that occurred after the Civil War. Here, the Plains Indians and the Indian wars of the Great Plains are also highlighted. During my February 2007 visit to the museum, I learned some interesting facts, via a visiting/touring exhibit, about the remarkable Black US mounted troops whom the Sioux christened (due to their hair) "Buffalo Soldiers."

The museum's theater runs a sixteen-minute film, every twenty minutes, entitled "A Nation Endures," which zealously conveys the events and emotions following the surrender, on Palm Sunday, April 9, 1865, of Robert E. Lee's Army of Northern Virginia. Those of you who read my awarding-winning "Honor Answering Honor," within the premier volume of *County Chronicles,* know what powerful sentiments– both Northern and Southern– the surrender at Appomattox captured and holds in the archives of our nation's vibrant history.

Here is an excerpt from "Honor Answering Honor," as a somber General R.E. Lee is leaving the area of the McLean house where he has just surrendered his army: "Lee turned Traveller's head precisely at the moment when Grant came rushing down the McLean front steps. As always, when he moved, the Union commander led with his head and shoulders, a determined expression creasing his brow. He started across the yard toward his tall, black horse, Cincinnati. Of a sudden, Grant realized this was *Lee* departing. He stopped; and, in silent tribute, took off and raised his hat. *Every Union soldier in the area followed suit.* Lee lifted his hat– and it seemed to those present that Time waited; the moment was so weighty with feeling– then Lee turned Traveller through the white wooden gate and out into the road.

"Compassion and admiration were stamped on U.S. Grant's rough features as he stood watching Lee ride away. His officers looked anxious to mount their horses and get back to their commands; but they remained as they were whilst Grant stood there, looking after Lee until the latter was out of sight, the westering sun burnishing the gold trim of his grey uniform."

"The Moment of Mercy," en bronze, by sculptor Terry Jones, depicting the young Confederate sergeant, Richard Rowland Kirkland, engaged in his heroic act of compassion and courage during the horrific Battle of Fredericksburg in December 1862
The above photos courtesy The National Civil War Museum, Harrisburg, PA

At the end of the visitors' journey back to the turbulent era that, for four trying years, tore our young nation apart, the museum's theater reveals, for the final time, their "We the People" cast of Civil War characters who share their war experiences and their hopes for the future.

The hopes and dreams of those who lived and survived the war bravely echo President Lincoln's second inaugural address: "With malice toward none, with charity for all, with firmness in the right- as God gives us to see the right- let us strive on to finish the work we are in, to bind up the nation's wounds... to achieve and cherish a just and lasting peace among ourselves, and with all nations."

President Lincoln's paramount objective during the war years was "to save the Union." "This," he affirmed, "is as much for the South as it is for the North." He never considered the South severed from the Union. After Lee's surrender, Lincoln did not want the South punished for what he considered was, not treason, but a rebellion. Rather, he wanted the healing process to immediately begin. Oh, had Abraham Lincoln lived to oversee the precarious Reconstruction Period!

The National Civil War Museum hosts a spectrum of annual events of which you can keep abreast by visiting their web site at: www.nationalcivilwarmuseum.org. Here, you can learn all about this incomparable institution.

At this writing, 2007, the museum is open seven days a week April 1 through Labor Day. After that, museum hours are Wednesdays to Saturdays, 10 a.m. to 5 p.m. Sundays, noon to 5 p.m. The museum is closed most federal holidays, though it is open Memorial Day, 4th of July, and Veterans' Day from noon to 5 p.m. I advise my readers to call before visiting, in order to obtain all the *current* museum information: 717-260-1861 or toll-free: 1-866-258-4729/1-866-BLU-GRAY.

The museum gift shop houses a vivid, interesting assortment of Civil War and history-related offerings, including artwork, books, clothing, jewelry and collectibles. This particular museum shop is a virtual treasure chest for the time-traveler in all of us!

For further information and directions to The National Civil War Museum, please visit their web site, telephone, or write:

The National Civil War Museum
1 Lincoln Circle
Reservoir Park
P. O. Box 1861
Harrisburg, Pennsylvania 17105-1861

Admission fees are reasonable. Group rates, senior, and student rates/school tours are available. I ardently suggest that visitors allow *at least* two hours to explore- *experience*- the museum and its grounds. Four hours is average, but each visitor can move along at his/her own pace. I appreciate this freedom because, when I tour a history site, I like to ponder and absorb as much as I can.

A lengthy interview with Director Janice I. Mullin afforded me an in-depth view of the museum. "The National Civil War Museum, which opened in February 2001, was created as a place of learning and remembrance of the American Civil War. At 65,000 square feet, The National Civil War Museum is the largest museum in the world devoted solely to the American Civil War," Mullin informed. "'National' speaks of the scope of our collections, the stories told through our displays, and the mission that our staff has dedicated itself to continue. Since our doors first opened to the public, the museum has strived to remain true to its mission of presenting an unbiased and evenly balanced view of this period of American history."

As to the impressive collection of artifacts, Director Mullin enlightened: "The museum houses a 17.5 million dollar collection of Civil War artifacts that Harrisburg has been amassing for nearly fifteen years. Approximately one third of the artifacts are on display at any given time. A large archival collection is also available for researchers and historians. Our displays are organized in chronological order, beginning with the causes of the war. From there, the museum addresses the issues of the war, from both the Northern and the Southern perspectives, portraying both military and civilian experiences. While the museum's exhibits present the facts about the various campaigns and battles, they also provide a focus on the people and the lives that were affected. Part of this insight into the personal knowledge of the war is offered through the video presentations that are placed throughout the galleries. Visitors are invited to follow the stories of the ten individuals portrayed in these videos. The characters were based upon information found in letters, diaries, and other first-hand accounts," Mullin added.

"In addition to the nearly 35,000 square feet of exhibit area, the museum has 4,000 square feet of meeting space, including two large multipurpose meeting rooms. These rooms are frequently used for corporate meetings, educational programs, receptions, and other special events. The museum also benefits from its scenic location in Reservoir Park, where visitors can appreciate breathtaking vistas of Pennsylvania's historic capital," the dedicated director concluded.

This unique facility is both educational and entertaining. I promise you that its exhibits will stir your blood. I promise too that Pennsylvanians will be proud that The National Civil War Museum is a thrilling part of the diverse and colorful Pennsylvania scene.

This museum will appeal to the staunch Civil War buff and to anyone who loves a good story well-told. Men and women, youngster to oldster, will be captivated by the light and sound shows, life-size dioramas, and the rare and varied collections of artifacts.

Come to Harrisburg; walk the museum's halls to meet the era's protagonists and share the emotions of the people who lived the war. *After all, more than anything else, history is people.*

The museum's Walk of Valor
Photo by Phillip R. Lincoln

Visitors will long remember the people they meet via this museum's exhibits, such as the compassionate and courageous Sergeant Richard R. Kirkland whom I introduced at the beginning of this Chronicle. It is my guess that those visitors will return again and again to this Civil War "time machine," where they are likely to leave a portion of their hearts.

At The National Civil War Museum- "Mine eyes have seen the glory...."

 "Kit-Han-Ne... Terror on the Frontier"

"I can take any fort that will catch fire...."
- Delaware chief Captain Jacobs, August 1756, after his destruction of Fort Granville (near Lewistown, Mifflin County, PA)

The first shots of the French and Indian War were fired in a remote ravine of my home county of Fayette, where George Washington defeated a small force of Frenchmen at what became known as Jumonville Glen, named after the French leader who was killed in the fray. The fifteen-minute battle, which took place on May 28, 1754, quickly turned into a global conflict- a war for empire between the world's, then, two superpowers, France and England.

At nearby Great Meadows, Washington oversaw the construction of a fort of necessity- thus the name of this hastily built palisades- Fort Necessity. Retaliation came, as Washington had expected, when on the third day of July of that historic year, about 700 French and Indians, led by Jumonville's half-brother de Villiers, attacked Fort Necessity with a vengeance. Washington and his men put up a fight, but they were severely outnumbered. Another problem was wet powder. The pouring rain made it near-impossible to fire their weapons. Of course, rain does not deter arrows or warhawks, tomahawks red with the blood of war. Washington had no choice but to surrender- the one and only time in his military career that he would surrender an army in the field. He and his ailing men, permitted the full honors of war, marched out of Great Meadows. And, by order of the French, the Indians burned the small, makeshift fort.

The subsequent summer, the King of England sent Major General Edward Braddock to the colonies to take the French Fort Duquesne, at what is now the Point at Pittsburgh. The Ohio River Valley was prime real estate coveted- and claimed- by both France and England. Before the advance column of Braddock's great army could reach the fort, it was waylaid in the forest, shortly after crossing the Monongahela River, by French-led Indians. Incredibly, Braddock's well-equipped, professional force was soundly defeated- in fact, virtually destroyed!

Both Benjamin Franklin and George Washington, Braddock's young aide, had warned the stubborn, haughty general not to underestimate the Native element. The sagacity fell on deaf ears. Braddock refused to speak amicably to the weighty Indian delegations when they had come to parley with him; and he refused to allow his ambushed men, when they were surprised in the forest, to take cover behind the trees and rocks to fight the enemy Indian-style.

Bunched together, as a huge red bull's-eye, most of Braddock's scarlet-vested men succumbed, falling like so many leaves in a sudden, violent storm. There, on the forest floor, the fallen remained, their bones to be discovered three years later. Then, in the autumn of 1758, the army of British General John Forbes would be successful in taking the French-held Fort Duquesne. Once the British flag would be hoisted over the Point, a detachment would be sent out to bury the remains of Braddock's long-dead soldiers. A melancholy postscript to Braddock's defeat is that a witness to this erstwhile battlefield described hearing the bones clattering under the hooves of his horse, their rattle an eerie plea that those who had died there not be forgotten.

If the Natives would have followed up after Braddock's battle, not one man would have escaped alive. But once they had their scalps, booty and prisoners, the Indians wanted nothing more than to return to their homes; thus Washington and his Virginians, in a rear-guard action, made it possible for a few of Braddock's men, including the fatally wounded general himself, to flee from the clutches of the war-whooping victors.

Bad news rides a fast horse. Word of the unexpected, horrifying destruction of Braddock's great army, at the Monongahela in July of 1755, spread across the settlements of Pennsylvania and beyond like wildfire on a howling wind, striking the hearts of those on the frontier with dismay and terror. Remote and desolate, its woods deep, dark and ever-mysterious, the Pennsylvania frontier, after Braddock's defeat, lay in watchful silence, the grim quiet broken by the occasional scream of a panther, the raucous cry of a bird, or the groan of a tall, half-fallen tree.

A favorite Indian hunting ground, Pennsylvania was an undulating, rolling landscape of impenetrable forest. In the words of Colonial writer Thomas Pownall, an "... ocean of woods swelled and depressed with a waving surface like that of the great ocean itself." Shadows wavered all about, and sunlight barely sifted down through the minute slits in the thick veil of leaves. Those passing through ofttimes related the panicky feeling they experienced that hidden eyes were watching them with ominous intent.

Due to impending Indian dangers, no one could live on the Pennsylvania frontier free of eternal vigilance after the remnants of Braddock's great army took flight, leaving the settlers on the frontier without professional military protection. With eyes that reflected the fear in their hearts, a number of settlers, cradling their children, fled in the wake of Braddock's defeated force, with little more than the clothes on their backs. In spite of this, I must relate, readers, that with the grit and perseverance that we can rightfully attribute to our ancestors, many stayed on the farms into which they had poured their blood, sweat, tears and their New-World dream, a dream that was still bright with promise, a hopeful expectation enveloped in the single word- *America.* Unlike the Euro-caste systems whence they had come, here they could be equal to their neighbors. And on the frontier, they could do as they pleased without a government boot on their necks. If that meant fighting Indians to keep the land they worked; then, by God, though harried by fear, that is what they intended to do.

In October, Indian attacks, hitherto minor in terms of actual occurrences and losses, were a wakeup call for Pennsylvanians to the danger looming on their woodsy horizon. Then, on 2 November, a substantial attack between McConnellsburg and the Maryland border demonstrated the inadequacy of the pioneer defenses. The die was now cast, and settlers prayed that the inevitable would not happen. But by this point in time, nothing could hold back the painted, feathered tempest that was about to unleash itself on the small farms and outposts that dotted the "backcountry."

The bitter cold and snows of winter interrupted the first scattered raids in the fall of 1755. I might add that winter's frosty-white cloak would provide, during the subsequent half-century of Indian warfare, somewhat of a reprieve from the terror that held the frontier in its iron grip.

In the spring of 1756, the Natives resumed their raiding in earnest. Incited and aided by the French (who actually had an older claim to the region), the Delaware and Shawnee swooped down on the widely scattered farms to burn, kill, scalp, and capture. Settlers were attacked as they labored in their fields, as they sat reading their Bibles, or at table. Even the black shutter of night did not protect them. Many were victims of the brutal warhawk as they fitfully slept in their beds.

Families were sometimes wakened in the dead of night by an express with a report that Indians were at hand. The ranger came softly to the cabin's door or the back window. Tapping, he easily roused those inside, for habitual fear rendered the frontier ever watchful. Instantly, the family was in motion. Father seized his gun and other implements of war. Mother rapidly dressed the children as well as she could, the oldest helping with the youngest. Always, *hurry* was the order of the day. In this maelstrom of violence, if the husband was away, perhaps off burying neighbors who had been the victims of attack, the women and children had to fend for themselves; and this often included fighting.

Rangers in those early days knew not the delicate art of delivering bad news. Day or night, when Indian signs were spotted, they conveyed their news succinctly without mincing words. Even children in those times of perpetual vigilance knew when they heard the word "Indian" to do precisely as their parents ordered- including keeping silent. A crying baby could and often did bring the warhawk violently down on the heads of an entire family as they attempted to flee through the forest to the nearest settler fort.

Soon after Braddock's defeat, frontier farmer Adam Hoops penned this desperate missive to the Governor of Pennsylvania: "We are in as bad circumstances as ever any poor Christians were in, for the cries of widowers, widows, fatherless and motherless children are enough to pierce the hardest of hearts. These deplorable circumstances cry aloud for your Honor's most wise consideration, for it is unspeakably shocking to the husband to see the wife of his bosom, her head cut off, and his children's blood drunk like water... in the name of God, help us!"

Braddock's ignominious trouncing had brought war to a province whose Quaker government was unwilling to take military action, whose leaders were unaccustomed to military planning. However, Governor Robert Morris had extemporized in the summer of 1755 a few local defenses in the Cumberland Valley, between Carlisle and the Maryland line. West of the Susquehanna, four forts- Fort George, Fort Granville, Fort Shirley, and Fort Lyttelton-were erected and garrisoned.

Frontier attacks reached a climax on July 30, 1756, when a force of Indians led by a Delaware chief known as "Captain Jacobs" besieged Fort Granville, the details of which I will discuss a bit later. Jacobs, a significant Delaware leader, had taken up the hatchet, shortly after Braddock's defeat, against the English and their colonists in Pennsylvania, Maryland and Virginia (including what is now West Virginia).

Jacobs' biography has many large gaps; and in consequence, this Native leader remains somewhat of an enigma. We do know that he resided for a time near present-day Lewistown in Mifflin County, where he once sold lands to a Colonel Buchanan. According to author Larry A. Smail in his book, *The Attack on Kit-Han-Ne, Kittanning, Pennsylvania, September 8, 1756*, as well as historian C. Hale Sipe and others, the above-mentioned colonel had once remarked that the Delaware leader bore a likeness to a burly German settler named Jacob who resided in the Cumberland Valley. The soubriquet stuck, and the chief became known far and wide as "Captain Jacobs."

After white colonists had settled Indian lands to the east, the mysterious Shawnee [See "The People of the South Wind" in *County Chronicles*' premier volume.] and their "grandfathers," the Delaware (*Lenni Lenapé*), migrated westward, relocating to the Mount Pleasant area of Westmoreland County, where a stream (Jacobs Creek) echoes the Delaware chief's name to conjure his tale yet today.

Readers should be made cognizant of the fact that back in 1734, William Penn's son, Thomas, claimed to have discovered a treaty, dated 1686, that the Delawares had been living on land they did not own. As I discussed in the opening Chronicle, this volume, William Penn's sons did *not* follow in their father's honorable footsteps when it came to the treatment of the Natives. William had always been fair with the Indians, a friend to them in the truest sense of the word. Unfortunately, his sons did not follow suit.

After futile parleys with the Whites, the Delawares acquiesced to a new treaty- which emerged, shamefully, as the infamous "Walking Purchase" that set the tone for many more injustices thereafter. Agreed upon by both Red and White leaders, the land in question was to be measured by one-and-one-half day's walk. Not anticipating White deceit, the Indians were unaware that the authorities had advertised for athletes to run over their land, through which a trail had been blazed, affording the swift runners easier passage.

By the mid-eighteenth century, Captain Jacobs, with many Delaware and Shawnee families, were residing principally at Kit-Han-Ne, the site of present-day Kittanning, Pennsylvania, in Armstrong County. This village was the first town founded, upon their migration into the Ohio/Allegheny Valley, by the displaced Indians.

I should interject here that the French-allied Indians who had defeated Braddock at the Monongahela were primarily from the Great Lakes region to the north. Not wanting to risk siding with the loser, the Ohio (River Valley) Indians, mostly Delaware and Shawnee, had bided their time to see who would win that contest.

It is of importance to mention that after Braddock's defeat (July 1755), the Shawnee sent, at that most *in*auspicious time, a delegation to Philadelphia to protest Iroquois concession of the Ohio country. Basically, the Iroquois had given away lands that were not theirs to give away. Though the Seneca of the strong Iroquois Confederation were the "Guardians of the Western Door" (the headwaters of the Allegheny/Ohio River Valley), those were Shawnee lands. When the Shawnee voiced their irritation over this in Philadelphia, Pennsylvania promptly hanged the delegation. Thus, the Shawnee went to war against the British and their American colonists, not so much for the French, but for themselves. In 1755, war parties struck the frontier in a wave of terror, killing over 2,500 settlers in the next two years. Peace would be made in 1759, and prisoners released in 1761; however, by that point in time, many of those captives refused to leave their adopted Shawnee families.

Established by the Delaware and Shawnee, with permission from the mighty Iroquois Confederation, it is no surprise that, after Braddock's defeat, the large Indian town Kit-Han-Ne became the staging point for a succession of bloody attacks. These raids against the frontier settlements were led by Captain Jacobs and another notable Delaware chief, Shingas.

Shingas was a chief of the Turkey Clan of the Delawares. It was widely quoted that he was a merciless and haughty leader. Here, I will let the famed Reverend Heckewelder, who lived for years among the Delaware, relate to you from his memoirs his impressions of Shingas: "Were his war exploits all on record, they would form an interesting document, though a *shocking* one... settlements along the frontier felt his strong arm sufficiently... he was a bloody warrior, cruel his treatment, relentless his fury. His person was small, but... in courage and savage prowess, he was said to have never been exceeded by anyone." [For an additional eyewitness account of Shingas and the Indian town of Kit-Han-Ne, see also "The Southern Klondike" in the premier volume of *County Chronicles*.]

The entire Ohio River Valley was ablaze; as all along the frontier, settlements were ravaged. The Indians resented the ever-increasing encroachment of the Whites, and they sought bloody revenge for layered injustices. The summer of 1756 witnessed a savage ferocity across the backcountry of Pennsylvania, where the feisty Scotch-Irish, Irish and German settlers were scrambling to organize a defense.

Native American warriors generally made no distinction between combatants and noncombatants. Women, children and the elderly were routinely killed and scalped, and prisoners were often tortured to death. Though European-Americans also waged war with cruelty, they found Indian warfare particularly brutal and frightening. The Native Americans were the best guerilla fighters this

River-view images of Kittanning today

planet has ever known, and they were *experts* at psychological warfare.

Captain Jacobs' attack on Fort Granville (present-day Lewistown, Mifflin County) occurred during the harvest of the year 1756. At that time, the fort was commanded by Lieutenant Edward Armstrong, a younger brother of Colonel John Armstrong, commander of the Second Battalion of the Pennsylvania Regiment. According to historian Sipe in his *Indian Chiefs of Pennsylvania*, Captain Jacobs' force of Indians had been lurking about the fort for some time. Well aware that the garrison therein lacked strength, the painted warriors went so far, on July 22, to taunt Armstrong's men into a fight. Needless to say, the lieutenant declined Jacobs' gauntlet. However, the Indians fired at and hit one of the soldiers, as he attempted to reenter the fort. The wounded man got inside by the skin of his teeth, after which the warriors split up into smaller war parties to terrorize the surrounding countryside.

At Baskins' settlement on the Juniata, war-whooping Indians burst through their door, instantly killing Mr. Baskins and, after plundering and torching the cabin, carried off his wife and children. Another raiding party suddenly appeared in the clearing around the cabin of Hugh Carroll; and there, they took the entire family captive.

Sometime between the third and fourth week of July, Captain Edward Ward had relinquished command of Fort Granville to Lieutenant Edward Armstrong. Ward and several men from the garrison then set out to provide a much-needed guard to area settlers engaged in harvesting their grain. Shortly after the attachment departed, what appeared to be a large force of combined French and Indians attacked and besieged the fort. I say "what appeared to be," because Native Americans often employed a form of psychological warfare known as skulking, a tactic whereby painted, war-whooping Indians would appear and disappear into the shadows of the thick foliage. The ongoing and unexpected reappearance of Indians at a scattering of locations within the assault area rendered the impression of higher numbers.

Another fact of Indian warfare is that warriors quickly became bored with sieges, a tactic they seldom used. Due to the construction of Granville, the Natives were not making much impact with their assault, and it did not take them long to form a new plan. Via a deep ravine, some of their numbers were able to creep within twelve to fifteen yards of the fort. From there, the Indians hurled burning pine knots until the log structure was aflame.

The folks inside, including a mortally wounded Lieutenant Armstrong, tried desperately to extinguish the flames, which were rapidly eating an ever-widening hole into one side of the palisades. Through the charred opening, the Indians had wounded (in addition to the commander) several others and killed at least one of the garrison. There was no doubt in anyone's mind- Red or White- that the fort would fall.

Presently, an Indian- likely Captain Jacobs himself- demanded surrender, offering to spare the lives of those inside. Upon hearing this, a man named John Turner pulled open the gates. The shrieking Indians poured inside like wine from an overturned bottle, and quickly taking possession of the fort, they captured twenty-two men, three women and a number of children (including the subsequently-controversial Girty boys). What remained of the fort was torched by Jacobs himself (by order of the French commander), and the still-whooping victors departed the area, driving their captives before them.

As an author whose milieu is the past, I often time-travel to that realm to ponder an event or a setting. Conjure, if you will, readers, those captives, secured together (via ropes looped round their necks), single-file, and heavily burdened with the booty from the fort and settlers' cabins plundered and burned. War parties with prisoners traveled fast. As this one moved through the forests, an Indian bringing up the rear effaced, with a leafy branch, any sign that they had passed that way. Anyone who showed any resistance, or made any trouble, was instantly tomahawked and scalped. Captives who dragged their feet received a right smart lick from a Native-fashioned whip. Little did those ill-fated Whites realize that their destination was the significant Indian town of Kit-Han-Ne.

In addition to being the staging center from which Captain Jacobs and Shingas sent forth their warriors to swoop down upon the frontier settlements, the large Delaware-Shawnee town was also the detention center for captives taken in those raids.

At Kit-Han-Ne the unsuspecting Granville prisoners met a cruel fate. John Turner, who had opened the gates to the Indians, endured the most hideous treatment of all. For approximately three hours, according to historian Sipe in *The Indian Chiefs of Pennsylvania* (based on earlier accounts from the annals of Pennsylvania history), "... red hot gun barrels were forced through parts of his body, his scalp torn from his head and burning splinters stuck in his flesh [rendering the unfortunate man a human porcupine], until at last an Indian boy was held up for the purpose [of sinking] a hatchet into [Turner's] brain...." Turner was burned beyond recognition at the stake, his charred remains a grisly reminder of the wide, shadowy chasm that existed between the Native and Euro-American worlds.

The fall of Fort Granville greatly boosted Native confidence in their ability to capture the scattered (and few in number) forts. The elated Captain Jacobs boasted: "I can take any fort that will catch fire, and I will make peace with the English when they teach me to make gun powder."

While Native confidence was ever-increasing, the morale of the colonists plunged to its lowest after the fall of Granville. When news of the fort's destruction reached Fort Shirley (present-day Shirleysburg, Huntington County), it was immediately evacuated. Other settler forts/blockhouses, too, were deemed indefensible and abandoned. When this information reached the ears of the Delaware leader, Captain Jacobs glowed with the light of the setting sun. His jubilation would be short-lived.

A plan to take the war to the Indians had already been contemplated by then-Governor Morris. Before Morris turned Pennsylvania's helm over to incoming Governor William Denny on the 20th of August 1756, he discussed the actual plan for an expedition to Kittanning with Colonel John Armstrong, whose younger brother had been killed at Fort Granville.

If you are wondering, readers, why there had been no such expedition carried out before this, understand that to do so would have left the scattered settler farms without their men to protect those families, homes and crops. Moreover, an expedition meant going deep into enemy territory where, every step of the way, they would be watched by that enemy. This is why, during the fifty years of virtually non-stop Indian warfare on the Pennsylvania frontier, few expeditions to Indian towns were ever carried out.

We cannot imagine life in those early days, though we might try. It was a time of terror unparalleled on a backcountry where terror had always been a shadowy presence. Mountain lions prowled the dark, thickly wooded hills. Their bloodcurdling screams, as well as the lonely cry of wolves reached isolated cabin doors. Bobcats, bears, rattlesnakes and copperheads added to the painted danger that lurked in the dusky, ubiquitous forest.

Contrary to the Indians' outlook on the thick tangle of woods that covered our commonwealth, settlers viewed the forest as an entity to be tamed and subdued, beaten back to make way for their cabins, barns and crops, ever dealt with, so that it could not reach its gnarled, twisted fingers out to strangle their dream– a dream that had required, with the exception of the Sabbath, backbreaking work from dawn till dusk.

Now the frontier was spotted with the charred, smoldering remains of settler cabins and barns; with the scalped and decaying bodies of those once-hopeful pioneers who had planted their dreams along with their grain in Pennsylvania's rich soil. In the wake of the tempest unleashed on them the previous autumn, their crops lay waste, and stone chimneys stood sentinel where the ghostly echo of laughter and fiddle music seemed to linger in the smoky air.

It was decided that an attack on Kittanning, the stronghold of Captain Jacobs and Shingas, the most aggressive of the Native leaders, *had* to be executed. It was truly a matter of do or die... or die trying. Thus, Colonel John Armstrong marched forth from Fort Shirley on 30 August 1756, with a force of nearly 300 men. This force merged with an advance party round about the 2nd of September. At this point in time, Armstrong's rough-and-ready army was made up of 307 men, Scotch-Irish mostly, from the Cumberland Valley. Author Smail tells us: "The march toward Kit-Han-Ne had begun. The distance along much of the old Kittanning Indian Trail was approximately 126 miles."

Moving along at a good clip, Armstrong's force ate up the miles between Fort Shirley and the Indian town of Kit-Han-Ne. Wisely, the colonel continuously sent his rangers out on reconnaissance for Indian sign and Native activity. Certainly he did not want to be ambushed as Braddock had been the summer before. The importance of Armstrong's reconnoiters became evident when, about six miles from their target, the scouts came across several Indians seated around the glow of a campfire deep in the murky forest. With a

These historic markers tell the tale of old Kit-Han-Ne.
Photos courtesy artist/author Larry A. Smail, Kittanning, PA

panther's stealth, the rangers moved through the shadows and out of the area to report their intelligence to the colonel.

Not wanting to alert the nearby Indian town with the loud reports from their weapons, or to have any of the "campfire" Indians escape and alarm the village, Armstrong opted to post Lieutenant James Hogg with a dozen men around those Indians, with the order to fall upon them at dawn. It was now a little before midnight on September 7. With orders to move out as quickly and as quietly as humanly possible, the main body of Armstrong's army passed through the night like specters, making a wide girth around the Indian-campfire site, proceeding on toward the large Native town of Kit-Han-Ne. There awaited several hundred more Indians, completely- and rather miraculously- unaware of Armstrong's advancing army.

Let us pause here in our tale to discuss this Indian town itself. There is some discrepancy- up to seven years- as to when this Native community originated. We will, however, be safe in stating that it was established somewhere between 1723 and 1730. We learned earlier that due to White encroachment, the Turtle and Turkey clans of the *Lenni Lenapé*/Delaware and their kindred allies, the Shawnee, with permission from the Iroquois, migrated westward from the forks of the Susquehanna to settle in the lush valleys of the Ohio River in Western Pennsylvania. The *Lenapé* Wolf Clan would initiate their migration westward, to join their Delaware brothers at Kit-Han-Ne, circa 1742.

One of several spellings in the Algonquian language, *Kit-Han-Ne* loosely translates "At the Great River." I'll remind you, readers, that this large Indian town's location was at the site of present-day Kittanning, Armstrong County. The "great river" refers to the Ohio (and/or Allegheny, since those rivers were, very early on, thought of as one), a clear, sparkling ribbon that wound its lazy way through hills covered with an abundance of trees- lofty pines and hemlocks (Pennsylvania's state tree), as well as a variety of hardwoods, such as the majestic oak, maple, hickory and walnut. White birch adorned and accented the landscape, and then (prior to the blight that destroyed them at the dawn of the twentieth century), the American chestnut was still common.

At the height of autumn splendor, Pennsylvania's gently sloping hills and forested mountains resembled then, as they do yet, a bright tapestry woven with every shade of red, purple and orange, yellow and gold, interspersed with browns, black and evergreens. Like today, the rolling meadows were latticed with the lacy patterns of dark branches; and the great timeless trees lifted intricate, multihued limbs against the intense blue of the Pennsylvania sky.

Ferns, vines, mountain laurel (Pennsylvania's state flower) and rhododendron, along with a spectrum of wild flowers and berry bushes thickly comprised the lower cover in Penn's great Woods. It was a *magical* sight, any season, the likes of which Europeans had never seen or even imagined. Game and fish were also abundant, the gifts of Creator to "The People," His Native children, who respected all living things, who never took more than they needed, who never wasted any portion of what they took.

Traders were always welcome at Kit-Han-Ne. As I discussed in the premier volume of *County Chronicles*, it did not take long for the Native Americans to become dependent on trade goods, and this was a major factor in the collapse of their lifestyle; for this dependency, as far back in time as the late 1600s, put the Old Ways on the poignant path of yesterday.

The French traders had always treated the Indians with more favor than had the English. When they came to the New World, the French actually "went native." They dressed for the woods, treated the Indians like equals, taught them their language, their religion; ate with them and partook of their festivals, even married them. Keep in mind that a major reason the Delaware and Shawnee took up the hatchet on the French side of this long and bloody Seven Years War for empire is because the French were traders not farmers. The Indians did not mind the French traders. They welcomed and, more significantly, *depended* on them. In contrast, they took a dark view of settlers on their land. The English colonists were, for the most part, farmers. And, as we have also seen- example Major General Edward Braddock- many of the English military figures treated the Indians with a haughty attitude, devoid of any, if not all, respect.

To return to the action of this Chronicle: Darkness engulfed Armstrong's army as they made their gingerly way toward Kit-Han-Ne. The otherwise silence of the night was punctuated with wild whoops and savage yells, as the Indians in the village danced into the wee hours. I have never read *expressly* why this was so. My educated guess is that the Natives were likely celebrating past victories as well as preparing themselves for their upcoming attack on Fort Shirley. Their voices and drums, however, made a fine reference for Armstrong's men to find their way to Kit-Han-Ne in the black of that night. Too, the revelry made it impossible for the Indians to become cognizant of an approaching army.

At first light, Armstrong's men moved with purpose through the tall stalks of the Indian cornfield and into their town. There was a curious smell- a pungent sweetish odor- about the place, not any worse than a White town, just different. The Indians' wood dwellings were a cross between Iroquois longhouses and crude settler cabins devoid of chimneys. Smoke holes in the roofs took the place of the white-man's chimneys, and wood smoke hung in the damp morning air. With a rain of quick shots, the men opened fire on the sleeping village.

As the Pennsylvanians discharged their weapons, the loud reports roused the Natives from their brief slumber after the long night of celebrating. From inside his lodge, Captain Jacobs sounded a bloodcurdling war whoop, returning fire through the loopholes in the log walls of his dwelling. A few Indian women and children dashed from the doors of their lodges and headed for the river. As ordered, the soldiers took aim and fired.

A steady response of gunfire continued from Jacobs' lodge. It was impossible for the soldiers to get a bead on those firing from behind the loopholes. Though the attack was a surprise, the Indians had a clear advantage, shooting as they were from behind the walls of their lodges. Several of Armstrong's men were wounded, including the colonel himself, who, whilst shouting orders to his men, took a musket ball in the fleshy part of his shoulder. Across the way, a spattering of gunfire seemed to be coming from the western bank of the river where Shingas and his warriors resided.

Bleeding, though still very much in charge, the wounded Armstrong ordered his men to ready themselves to torch Captain Jacobs' lodge. The colonel shouted for those inside to surrender. A booming voice- likely Jacobs'- carried over the chaos of battle that those inside were children of the Great Manitou and would *not* be taken prisoners. Armstrong now delivered the ultimatum, calling to the Indians a final time to surrender, to which Jacobs yelled, loosely translated, "I am not afraid of death, and I will take out four or five of you before I die!" The chief then bellowed, "I can eat fire!" Armstrong barked the order to burn the log dwelling over their heads.

As the flames hungrily devoured Jacobs' lodge, the plaintive sound of the Indians' death song drifted out to the soldiers of the 2nd Pennsylvania. A Native American's death song, in addition to invoking Creator, revealed to his enemies that he was not afraid to pass on to the "dark/shadow lands" on the other side- that, indeed, it was a good day to die.

From inside the burning walls of Jacobs' home, an anguished female voice chillingly rose over the sounds of the crackling flames and the strong stew of battle. Her cry had no sooner reached the men outside, when she was sharply rebuked by the warriors therein.

As the fire raged, becoming unbearable, I am certain, for those engulfed in its hot breath, a woman and a child, who may well have been Jacobs' wife and son, leaped from the lodge, making a mad dash for the cornfield. An immediate salvo brought them down.

Colonel Armstrong, bleeding profusely from his wound, was taken to the relative safety of a nearby hill where his shoulder was attended. Captain Hugh Mercer, who would gain recognition twenty years later with George Washington at the Battle of Trenton, also had his wound wrapped to staunch the bleeding.

From the western shore, Shingas' warriors had begun to ford the river. There was a concern among the Pennsylvanians that they would surround the troops, but the colonel would not consent to a retreat until more of the Indian lodges were torched. The Indians who crossed the river, however, were more concerned with escape than a counterattack. Those warriors quickly secured a few of the horses that had been grazing near the town and, in a hasty retreat, carried off some of their wounded. As lodge after lodge caught fire and burned- approximately thirty were in flames- a succession of ear-shattering blasts added to the cacophony, as loaded muskets and gunpowder (stored within those log dwellings) exploded, hurling Native bodies and body parts skyward. These remains would be chanced upon in the adjacent cornfield. Later too, rescued prisoners would recount that they had heard the Indians boast that there had been at Kit-Han-Ne enough arms and powder for a ten-year war against the English and their "land-grabbing" American colonists. The fires also destroyed most of the trade goods the Delawares had recently acquired from their French allies. As the six-hour battle came to a raucous conclusion, Pennsylvania gunfire brought down several more Indians. Approximately thirty or forty met their demise as they attempted to escape via the river.

Likely you are wondering, readers, what happened to those Indians who were about that forest campfire the night before. It was also learned from rescued captives that two bateaux of French Indians were to join those Natives in an attack on Fort Shirley. The 2nd Pennsylvania discovered, in addition, that about twenty-four Indians had already set out for that fort the previous evening.

Six miles distant, at what was to become known as "Blanket Hill," Lieutenant James Hogg and his twelve men had cached themselves in the depths of the forest under the preceding night's cover of darkness. Their strategy was to wait until dawn, you remember, to fall upon the Indians whom Armstrong's rangers had spotted around that campfire. The hours, under a blanket of ominous quiet, crept by with agonizing slowness, the stillness pierced only by the night creatures with which the men shared the pitch-dark woods. Though children of the forest, the apprehensive frontiersmen prayed that the sounds they were hearing were animal-emitted.

As false dawn gave way to first light, Hogg's men, who had both numbers and surprise on their side, skulked closer and closer to their objective. Through the thick underbrush, thirteen pairs of eyes fixed keenly upon the Indians until, of a sudden, one of the Natives rose and moved to within an inch of the concealed soldiers. Then a shot rang out, blasting the Pennsylvanians' chance for a surprise attack.

It was immediately realized that there were many more Indians in the forest than the three or four the scouts had seen, and subsequently reported on. Whether more Delaware (perhaps those headed for the attack on Fort Shirley) had joined that campfire sometime during the night, or there had simply been more Indians at the site than espied by the rangers is not known. One thing was for certain; the tide had abruptly- and unexpectedly- turned into a deadly counterattack against Hogg's men. The lieutenant himself was hit twice. Several of his men were killed, and two wounded in the fury that was suddenly unleashed on that hill.

The remainder of Hogg's force literally ran for their lives, whilst the wounded lieutenant dived for cover in the thick brush, hoping against hope that one of Armstrong's men from the main force would discover him before a Delaware or Shawnee did. Hogg's wish did come to pass, though not to fruition.

Retreating soldiers from the burning Kit-Han-Ne came across the wounded lieutenant, who was helped onto a horse. Just as the men attempted to skedaddle out of the area, four garishly painted Delaware warriors suddenly appeared in their path. Though Hogg shouted an order to make a stand, the soldiers panicked. Within seconds, the Indians killed one and wounded another, hitting the lieutenant a third time. Hogg slapped his mount into a full gallop and lit out, only to succumb to his wounds a few hours later. The other Pennsylvania recruits managed to escape with their lives. Later into the day, September 8, 1756, remnants of Armstrong's force made their precarious way back to the campfire site only to discover the above casualties. Due to the considerable loss of baggage, horses, and blankets left behind when the men fled, the hill was later christened "Blanket Hill."

Modern-day travelers along US Route 422 will note the familiar blue and yellow Pennsylvania historical marker bearing the name "Blanket Hill," which relates the tale in brief of 7 and 8 September 1756. There exists also a bronze marker set in stone. I must add that said markers are near to, not on, the actual site of the action that unfolded there that long-past September.

Author Larry Smail, whose great-great-great-grandfather acquired the land where the battle was fought, tells us in his beautifully illustrated account that the Blanket Hill area today is a typical Western Pennsylvania mix of woodlands and farms. As for the Indian town of Kit-Han-Ne, it, of course, is greatly changed as the site of present-day Kittanning- which, I might add, is a city pleasing to the eye, quaint and utterly charming in its appeal. An historic marker on South Water Street and the west-end Market Street Bridge reads: "The most notable Delaware Indian village west of the Alleghenies was situated here from about 1730 until destroyed by Armstrong's expedition in 1756. Its name means 'Great River,' applying to the Ohio-Allegheny." The marker was dedicated November 28, 1946.

After the attack, the Delaware and Shawnee were in total disbelief that they had failed to notice 307 men marching to destroy their town. Armstrong, in his report, noted that seventeen of his men were killed, thirteen wounded, and nineteen missing. Some of those missing did eventually make it back to the various settlements and forts, but many more perished in the wilds, dying bloody- and parted from their scalps.

As you might expect, there is no official record of the Native casualties at Kit-Han-Ne, though Colonel Armstrong reported that he believed his men killed or severely wounded between thirty and forty Indians. The force also rescued eleven captives of the reported 100 held at Kit-Han-Ne. Of that number, only seven actually returned to their homes.

A few captives were retaken by the Indians. Those ill-fated men and women met with *horrendous* deaths- a warning to other prisoners (who were forced to watch the torture) not to attempt escape. When in a dark mood, Indians sought bloody revenge for wrongs done them. After the destruction of their town, the largest Delaware and Shawnee village west of the Alleghenies, their mood was most certainly dark.

Though a costly venture, the Armstrong assault on Kit-Han-Ne was a great *morale* booster to the English and their colonists here on the frontier and was hailed as a victory in Pennsylvania. Colonel John Armstrong was ever-after known as the "Hero of Kittanning." He and his men collected the scalp bounty that had been placed on Captain Jacobs. However, the victory did have its limitations. Contrary to Armstrong's report, the attackers almost certainly suffered more casualties than they inflicted, and most of the villagers escaped, taking with them nearly all of the captives who had been held in the Indian town.

Of course, Kit-Han-Ne was no longer a staging point for attacks against the settlers; and the raid shocked the Indians, revealing their vulnerabilities. The Delaware and Shawnee abandoned their settlement at Kittanning, retreating to the protection of the French forts and to the lesser exposed Indian towns on the Beaver River. For a short while, the dreadful raids ceased. But make no mistake, readers, when the Indians took up the warhawk anew- *it was with a vengeance!*

In October 1756, the city of Philadelphia bestowed, in thanks, on Lieutenant Colonel John Armstrong and his officers 150 pounds to be divvied out in plates, swords and such, suitable for gifts. A portion of that sum went to the widows and children of those Pennsylvania soldiers who had given the fullest measure of themselves during the expedition.

A medal was struck in Armstrong's honor on January 5, 1757. The medal's obverse side depicts a shield of the old arms of the city of Philadelphia with the wording: "The Gift of the Corporation of the City of Philadelphia." The reverse side illustrates the attack on Kit-Han-Ne with the Indian log dwellings engulfed in flames, the river to the right, and in the fore, four soldiers standing over a slain Indian. The wording is as follows: "Kittanning Destroyed by Col. Armstrong, September 8, 1756." The Kittanning Medal measures forty-six millimeters.

Engraved by Edward Duffield, a Philadelphia watchmaker and engraver, and struck by Joseph Richardson, a noted Philadelphia silversmith, the original medals were done in silver, pewter, and copper. The United States Mint Kittanning Medal is bronze. I must report, readers, that there are counterfeits known in lead. A few medals in copper were struck after the dies cracked, and they illustrate the impression of the broken die beautifully. Of course, the silver medals are the rarest; and less than six are known to exist. Likely, the silver medals were issued to outstanding/highest-ranking officers, the copper and pewter to non-commissioned officers and enlisted men.

Historically speaking, the Kittanning Medal is closely connected to the early history of Pennsylvania. It is one of the earliest medals, if not *the* first, struck in Colonial America, one of the first medals, if not *the* first, awarded to soldiers for services rendered.

Thomas Penn, son of William, presented Armstrong with a sword and belt. Some years later, the city ordered a tract of land, dated March 2, 1775, surveyed and granted Armstrong, "... including the old town of Kit-Han-Ne for his arduous and successful expedition against the Indians at the Indian town... which was the first instance of carrying the war into the Indian country...."

This historic tract, replete with the vestiges of battle, was pointedly christened "Victory."

"The Flyboys"

"We are here; we are daredevils, and we don't need French discipline!"
- Commander of l'Escadrille Lafayette, Captain Georges Thenault, mimicking the attitude of "The Flyboys," spring 1916

They were dashing. They were courageous, outrageous and risk-taking. Most of them were labeled by their French commanding officers- and everyone else who encountered them- as "daredevils." They were ultra-competitive; and from the outset, they asserted their Americanisms. They were also hard drinking, rowdy and undisciplined.

Many of them had been living in the lap of luxury when World War I broke out. Several were residing in France, where they participated in competitions with their yachts or the newfangled aeroplanes. A beautiful French villa became their barracks; and there, they cavorted with their mascots, two frisky lion cubs named "Whiskey" and "Soda." These were the "Flyboys"- the first American fighter pilots.

The story of the adventurous Escadrille Lafayette fighter squadron is (surprisingly) one of the least written about but most glorious chronicles of World War I. Its thirty-eight American volunteer pilots came from all walks of life. A motley crew, they were college students- the scions of high-profile, wealthy American families- jacks of all trades, former military men, a taxi driver, cowboys and playboys. This mélange of personalities added to the unit's glamour and fame, just as their all-American, rough-and-ready spirit endeared them to the public- both the American and the French. Who were the intrepid pilots of *l'Escadrille Lafayette*? Read on and find out.

Early in World War I, a clarion call by Swiss writer Blaise Cendrars appeared in the French newspaper *Le Figaro*, beseeching all foreign residents to enlist in the French army. Several venturesome Americans were eager to fight in that "war to end all wars," but it was not as simple as it seemed.

America was not yet involved, and any American citizen who volunteered to serve in a foreign army might well have lost his constitutional rights and his citizenship. The impetuous would-be warriors decided to pay a visit to the US Ambassador in Paris, who, finding a solution, suggested that they either join the French Foreign Legion or enlist in the Ambulance Corps. Thus, many brave Americans, sympathetic to the Allied cause, offered their services to France well before the American Expeditionary Force landed on French soil in 1917. The American commander was General "Black Jack" Pershing; and his famous words at that glorious moment in time were: "Lafayette, we are here!"

Prior to Pershing's arrival, toward the end of 1915, a few of the spirited young Americans, aglow with idealistic keenness to get into the fight, were successfully transferred to the French Aviation Service. They were afterward joined by several other Americans who enlisted directly from civilian status.

Before I continue, I should define the word "escadrille." The term refers to a unit of European- here French- air command usually made up of six planes. It soon became the assertion among the Escadrille members that France should send to the front a squadron composed *entirely* of American pilots. At first, the French Government did not take kindly to the idea, which was spearheaded by a Pennsylvanian, a Pittsburgher, named William Thaw. French authorities deliberated on the matter for several months, finally agreeing; and on 20 April 1916, *l'Escadrille Américaine* was born. In their French aircrafts-Nieuports, Morane-Saulniers and SPADs- those Americans who flew for France soared into the realm of immortality, becoming one of the most famous Allied fighter squadrons of WWI.

The Escadrille's front-line duty commenced the following month at Luxeuil-les-Bains, on the edge of the Vosges Mountains in the Alsace region of France; and the group flew their first mission on May 13, 1916. Five days later, the first victory was scored by Kiffin Rockwell, when he shot down a German reconnaissance plane.

As the unit's fame grew, the German government protested to the United States– since America was yet a neutral country. As a result, France acquiesced, ordering the group, on 16 November, to change their name to the more generic *l'Escadrille des Volontaires.* The bold Americans, however, found that name much too dull for their tastes. And in December 1916, the name was changed for the final time to the more emotive *l'Escadrille Lafayette,* after the revolutionary French marquis who had aided George Washington in America's fight for Independence. Soon after France had entered the escalating European conflict that became known in the history books as World War I, that nation's role in America's winning her Independence– and Lafayette who, when he aided George Washington, preceded his country to war– were very much on the minds of the Americans who offered their services to Lafayette's homeland.

Commanded by the French *Capitain* Georges Thenault, its first-assigned American pilots numbered a mere seven. They were Norman Prince, Victor Chapman, Kiffin Rockwell, James McConnell, Elliot Cowdin, Bert Hall, and Pittsburgh, Pennsylvania's William Thaw, whom I want to discuss before we get into the core of this Chronicle.

William Thaw left Yale in 1911 to take up flying. He became one of the first Americans to learn to pilot an aircraft. In the summer of 1913, William completed his training at the Curtiss School of Aviation at Hammondsport, New York, after which he purchased with his father's money a Curtiss Model E Hydro flying boat. His intention was to pursue an aviation career in both the United States and France.

When the first hostilities broke out, no one thought the war would last as long as it did. I suppose this was said of every war that splattered the pages of history. The twenty-one-year-old Thaw, who was eager to get into the fighting, offered his services to France as a pilot a few days after the big guns of August 1914 shook the world with their ferocity. When his offer was refused, Thaw joined the French Foreign Legion (from August 21 to December 24, 1914), which, as I stated earlier, offered the readiest means to the front.

For decades, the Legion had been famous– even infamous– as the refuge of soldiers of fortune, criminals on the lam, and adventurers of every sort. Its reputation, let it be known here, was no deterrent for Americans anxious to get into action.

William Thaw penned, in a letter dated August 30, 1914, to his family in Pittsburgh: "I am going to take a part, however small, in the greatest and probably last war in history, which has apparently developed into a fight of civilization against barbarism...."

By the middle of October, Thaw's outfit was in the front-line trenches; but the action-seeking youth was already finding this life "monotonous and disappointing." Toward the end of November, a letter home to Pittsburgh read: "War is wretched and quite uninteresting. Wish I were back dodging streetcars on Broadway for excitement. Am that tired of getting shot at! Have been in the trenches now nearly six weeks. Haven't washed for twenty days...."

The trenches were filthy, louse-y, and unless the whistle blew, signaling the men to "go over the top," sated with ennui. The cure for boredom is curiosity coupled with escapade– and for that, there is no cure. During this period, William also served as a scout for his seventeen-man squad. This duty, though a reprieve from the monotony of the trenches, demanded that he march three times as far as the others, for which Thaw soon discovered he was physically unsuited. He longed to enter the air service. It was time for a change.

As soon as Thaw was able to use his influence sufficiently, he got himself transferred (one of the first Americans to do so) on Christmas Eve, 1914, as a pilot in the French flying service. Likely the fact that he had done some prewar flying aided him in his quest. At the end of that December, "Bill" (as he was known among the men in his unit) was at Mervel, attached to the Escadrille as an observer, armed with a pistol and a carbine. A WWI observer was a pilot who flew over enemy lines or raging battles to gather and report on intelligence.

Thaw's capacity for reconnaissance and his affable personality impressed the French officers. Though he hailed from a wealthy Pittsburgh family (whose fortune was made via railroads and coal), he was no slacker; and soon

L'Escadrille Lafayette and their lion mascots, "Whiskey" and "Soda," July 1917, at Chaudun, France. Standing, left to right: Soubiran, Doolittle, Courtney, Campbell, Parsons, Bridgman, Dugan, MacMonagle, Lovell, Willis, Jones, Peterson, and de Maison-Rouge (French Deputy CO). Seated, left to right: Hill, Masson with "Soda" and Thenault's dog Fram (foreground), Thaw, Thenault (French CO), Lufbery with "Whiskey," Johnson, Bigelow, and Rockwell. Henry Sweet Jones hailed from Harford, PA; David McKelvie Peterson was from Honesdale, PA, and William Thaw was the scion of a wealthy Pittsburgh family.

he was considered the undisputed leader of the Lafayette group. In fact, Bill Thaw would later command the unit a couple of times in combat whilst the French CO Thenault was on sick leave. Eventually becoming an expert fighter pilot, Thaw flew often and hard, and the men respected him immensely. Whether he was acting as a go-between or as the commanding officer of the unit, Bill genuinely cared about his fellow pilots, always putting the welfare of his men first and foremost.

A bright and enduring legend of the Great War is of the invaluable contribution made by American aviators of the Lafayette Escadrille at Verdun, the war's mightiest encounter, which took place in May of 1916. The fast-flowing stream of troops and the distressing number of speeding, swaying ambulances brought the unit the keen realization of the nearness of the gigantic battle. The aviation camps had quickly arranged themselves within a twenty-mile radius of the cacophony of the Verdun front. Each unit was given a schedule with specified flying hours, along with a field wireless (radio) to enable them to keep track of the movements of enemy planes.

Not long after the Escadrille's transfer from the Alsatian front to Verdun, Bill Thaw brought down, while on a morning mission, a German Fokker. The date of his first victory was May 24, 1916. Later that afternoon, in a pitched air battle (known hence as a "dogfight"), far behind the German lines, the entire American squadron bravely took on a superior force of German planes. Thaw and two of his comrades were wounded. Bleeding profusely, and with his arm broken, Bill miraculously managed to put his plane down just within the French sector. It was a narrow escape. In a dazed state, he tumbled from the plane and, too weak to walk, was carried to a field hospital by French soldiers, who had run toward his aircraft upon seeing it land. From there, Thaw was sent to a hospital in Paris; whence, upon his recovery, he immediately rejoined *l'Escadrille Lafayette.*

William Thaw served with the French Lafayette unit until February 18, 1918. The month before, he had been commissioned as a major in the US Air Service in France, in which he served as commanding officer of the 103d Pursuit (Fighter) Squadron until

August 10, 1918. He was then promoted to lieutenant colonel, afterward serving as commanding officer of the 3rd Pursuit Group until the Armistice was signed in November. Thaw had appealed to superiors to put all the flyers of his old (French) squadron in the (American) 3rd Pursuit Unit. In a rather bumpy transition, a few were assigned there, but several others were needed elsewhere. In other words, the "Flyboys" of *l'Escadrille Lafayette* were not taken over by the US Air Service as one unit. Rather, they were taken over individually and placed accordingly.

On April 24, 1918, Major Bill Thaw had brought down his fifth enemy plane *and* a captive balloon, both on the same banner day. Thus, he is classified as an "ace" in French and American aviation history. Colonel Thaw was notably decorated with the Distinguished Service Cross, *Légion d'Honneur*, and *Croix de Guerre* with four palms and two stars.

Remember, I said that the initial group of flyers in the Escadrille consisted of a mere seven Americans. However, during the succeeding twenty months at the front, an additional thirty-one eager, young Americans signed on as pilots. The world-wide publicity the unit was receiving attracted a steady stream of valiant men from the States; and subsequently, the Lafayette Flying Corps was created to assist Americans in enlisting in the French Aviation Service (not all of whom ended up serving with *l'Escadrille Lafayette*).

The Lafayette took as their symbol an Indian chief, in profile, wearing a full war bonnet, the mouth open in an obvious war cry. This burst of creativity occurred when Bill Thaw noticed the Indian-head trademark on crates of ammunition from the Savage Arms Company. He immediately thought it would make a fine representation for the American flyers and ordered one of the mechanics to apply it to the unit's aircrafts as a squadron insignia. In addition, the Escadrille members identified their planes with individual symbols. Thaw's, for instance, was the red initial "T" for his surname.

Every military unit has its own personalities, quirks, political intrigues, and rivalry issues. For all its exclusivity, *l'Escadrille Lafayette* was no different in that respect. The pressures and stress of combat fatigued the flyboys, and the mélange of such forceful personalities created some problems within the ranks. Rivalries, apparent from the outset, intensified, some of which became open and, at times, even a bit nasty. For one thing, there were descendants of both Confederate and Union soldiers in the unit, and this added to the dissension. As it happened, the unit's major protagonists came from wealthy northern families or the rich southern traditionalist families. Bear in mind that the Civil War was not that distant in time when the First World War commenced.

I recall a story that my Alabama-born uncle told of his father's enlistment at the outbreak of World War I: "You're not going to put on a *Yankee* uniform, are you?" shouted his grandfather, who had fought with R. E. Lee from the Wilderness to Appomattox. "I sure as hell am!" came the succinct reply.

There was, in addition, a general lack of discipline among the flyboys of *l'Escadrille Lafayette*, on the ground mostly. But in the air that defiance proved fatal on more than one occasion. Drinking became an issue for some of the men as the competition ever-increased for glory and acclaim. Though most got along with their fellow pilots, the few who clashed caused the flyboys to question one another's intentions and alleged hidden agendas.

Please do not think that it is my purpose with this Chronicle to detract from *l'Escadrille Lafayette's* bright legacy. *It is not.* The unit deserves the praise of a heroic group; however, the mark of great units is their teamwork and selflessness. Lafayette suffered, not only from a rash of discipline problems, but, even more importantly, from dissension that would cause them great pain. Some of their problems would fester and spill over into the members' postwar lives. Some transgressions and rivalries were never put to rest– and were taken with bitterness to the grave. Make no mistake; the unit *survived* this turmoil; but, sadly, it tainted an otherwise dazzling legacy.

Violations varied greatly, from disobeying direct orders in the air, which, as I said, on occasion led to deadly results, to serious problems with civil authorities on the ground. Sometimes the less severe breaches of discipline approached the comical. For example, Escadrille member Bert Hall, who gained a reputation as a colorful but far-from-reliable storyteller, had gotten himself transferred to the flight school at St. Cyr by stating that he had been the first to fly in the Turkish air service during the 1913 Balkan War. However, the first time he took off in a plane at St. Cyr, he crashed on the runway. When the French officer in charge of the training pulled him from the wreckage, he shouted that Hall had acted as though he had never been in a plane before. Bert confessed that he had not. "What in God's holy name do you mean," yelled the officer, "starting off like that?" "Well," answered Hall, calmly lighting a cigarette, "I thought I might be able to fly." The French decided that anyone with that sort of nerve deserved another chance.

Another amusing example occurred when aviator Harold Willis was shot down and taken prisoner in his pajamas. In a hurry that day to launch, he had not put on his uniform. With no rank and no uniform, Willis impersonated an officer to his captors and nearly got away with it until the Germans discovered later who he really was. His Escadrille buddies had attempted to give credence to his subterfuge by flying over a German aerodrome and dropping a bundle containing an officer's uniform and insignia accompanied by a note stating that it was for their discomfited, pajama-clad leader. The boys had figured correctly that their hapless comrade would employ such a ruse.

Yet another example, though significantly more serious, involves flyboy Courtney Campbell and the French Deputy Commander de Maison-Rouge. As de Maison-Rouge was leading a patrol back from a mission, Campbell, always a prankster, began playfully bouncing his wheels on the Frenchman's upper wing. Above the commander's aircraft, Campbell continued bouncing away; until, miscalculating, his wheels broke through the fabric of de Maison-Rouge's wing, locking the two SPADs together! By some miracle of God, Campbell was able to break free, and both pilots landed safely. However, de Maison-Rouge vented his Gallic temper in an explosive tirade toward Campbell and the entire unit of *"sauvage Américains!"*

Their French CO Captain Thenault could be a hard disciplinarian when pressed. Perhaps he tended to view his task as a bit too easy. His credo, "I had simply to treat everyone fairly and without favor," seemed to encapsulate his attitude.

Thenault's position required him to judge the right balance of discipline and latitude for his high-spirited men, and it compelled him to set an emotional barrier between himself and the American flyboys. This he did with the exception of *Sous* (second)-Lieutenant Bill Thaw, whom he considered a friend. A tough job his, but Thenault did try. He commanded the respect of his men- save when he banged away at the piano, an effort that would produce howls of protest even from the captain's faithful dog Fram.

The men seemed to look to two others as their real commanding officers, Lieutenant Alfred de Laage de Meux, the French Deputy CO/second-in-command and, as stated above, Lieutenant William "Bill" Thaw. De Laage spoke fluent English- undeniably a boon- and he took a great personal interest in the men, especially in new arrivals, whom he told individually: "I only ask that you fly well, that you fight hard and that you act as a man. I demand that you obey, explicitly and without hesitation, any orders I give when I am leading combat patrols... and I expect that you share the responsibility for the upholding of the good name of the squadron, and we shall get along quite well."

After de Laage crashed a plane on takeoff and was killed, his replacement, Lieutenant de Maison-Rouge, never enjoyed the respect from any of the men that his predecessor had received. A former cavalry officer, de Maison-Rouge was more disciplined and much more formal with the men than de Laage had been. He kept himself aloof from the Americans, one of whom described him as a "nervous, sensitive sort of Frenchman." In turn, the highly strung de Maison-Rouge referred to the Americans as *"les sauvages"* (savages). The reality was that the wild, willful and sometimes cantankerous American flyboys disliked that particular officer from the moment he set foot on "their" turf; and in fact, the boys could be quite brutal to him, as the above example illustrates.

Fear can have a serious detrimental effect on the dynamics of a unit. No pilot wants to fly with someone who will duck out of a fight. Every pilot needs to know that his wingman will be there no matter what happens. In the heat of an air battle, the load needs to be *shared.* If, due to fear, flyers lose their nerve to fight; the others in the unit are forced to carry that extra burden, adding to the stress of all. Of the first thirty-eight flyboys in *l'Escadrille Lafayette*, five, perhaps six, suffered from this problem. Those few were treated with contempt by the rest of the squadron. This was understandable; since the majority in the unit were brave men- each of whom hated having even one American among them displaying fear in full view of the French and the other Allies.

Of the *original* squadron, Victor Chapman died heroically in an aerial duel over the

Verdun battlefield on June 23, 1916. Later that same year, Kiffin Rockwell perished in a fight with an enemy ace. The following month, Norman Prince was mortally injured; and James McConnell was brought down by two enemy aeroplanes on March 19, 1917, the last American aviator to be killed by the enemy *before* America's entry into the Great War.

In September 1916, the unit took on a colorful addition in "Whiskey," a four-month-old lion cub purchased by its members in Paris from a Brazilian dentist whose patients had become unnerved by the rambunctious African feline. The cub's name was derived from another "spirited" facet of its personality- he frequently enjoyed a saucer-full of the fiery liquor. One of the flyers, desperate for warmth at night, took to sharing his bed with Whiskey, though the lion had a bad case of kitty halitosis, and his fur gave off an odor far less appealing than the *eau de parfum* with which the boys sometimes doused him.

The subsequent March, the boys returned from Paris with a companion for Whiskey, and the new cub- a lioness- got on so well with him that the Escadrille immediately christened her "Soda." Though she continued to romp companionably with Whiskey and Fram, Thenault's dog, she was surly around most human company, often hissing and showing her teeth. The playful Whiskey never bit or scratched; but to the amusement of the boys, he had a penchant for chewing up dress uniforms or the decorations attached to them. Actually, the pampered cubs chewed tunics and visors, boots, medals and anything else they could get hold of. They knocked visiting officers and dignitaries to the ground on more than one occasion, the last time choosing the wrong fellow to (literally) upset.

In October 1917, Commander Féquant had the beloved felines removed to the Jardin des Plantes, the botanical gardens at Paris, which housed a small zoo. It was a sad day, indeed, for the boys. And as they took Whiskey out for his last ride in a military *camion* (truck)- which he loved- they *knew* how much they would miss him, as well as the temperamental Soda. How heart-wrenching it was to walk away, after seeing those sad feline eyes through the bars of their cage!

The fellows visited their famous mascots whenever they had leave in Paris, and Whiskey especially always recognized them. Coincidently, soon after the Armistice was signed, both lions passed away "of loneliness," the boys stated among themselves. I think it was absolutely true.

Throughout 1916 and 1917, other American volunteers continued to arrive, so that in spite of heavy losses, the ranks of *l'Escadrille Lafayette* were never depleted. Overflow of newly trained American pilots was sent to other French units. As touched on earlier, the enthusiastic American desire to aid France during the First World War resulted in the creation of the much larger organization known as the Lafayette Flying Corps. I think this says volumes for those young, visionary American aviators and the great American warrior spirit.

L'Escadrille Lafayette's Native American emblem used on their patches and on their planes. The swastika-like symbol on the emblem was utilized by various Native American tribes and has no connection whatsoever to the Nazi symbol.
Photos courtesy the United States Air Force, from the author's personal collection

By August 1917, the Escadrille had won four *Légion d'Honneur* medals, seven *Médailles Militaire* and thirty-one citations, each citation accompanied by a *Croix de Guerre.* Stars (for exceptional bravery under fire) and Palms (repeat awards for the same basic decoration) overflowed as well. *Impressive,* to say the least. American pilots in the other French squadrons were also earning their share of decorations and awards.

During the Escadrille's tour at the front, aerial fights occurred with nearly every sortie. Most of the flyers were valiant men with nerves of steel. A few seemed downright fearless. The French who served with them often remarked: *"Ils sont braves, les aviateurs américains!"*/ "They are brave, the American flyers!"

L'Escadrille Lafayette was decommissioned on February 18, 1918, when it essentially became the first American pursuit/fighter squadron. In its beginnings, the unit, "S103," retained its French planes and mechanics.

Out of some 265 American volunteers in the French Air Force, 225 received their wings, and 180 flew combat missions at the front in French military uniforms. Most had been assigned individually or in twos and threes to the various French escadrilles. As touched on earlier, to say that they had all served in *l'Escadrille Lafayette* would be an historical inaccuracy. They were all members of the larger Lafayette Flying Corps, some of whom had gotten themselves assigned to the luminous Lafayette unit.

Fifty-one pilots of the Lafayette Flying Corps gave the fullest measure of themselves, killed in air battles over France- the battlefield in the Great War. Six were killed in training accidents, and six more perished from illnesses. The American flyers- the dashing "Flyboys"- were credited with an impressive 199 victories.

Most of the famed Escadrille's dead were buried in cemeteries scattered along the front in France, Belgium and Italy. Early in 1921, a committee was organized to search for a fitting single resting place for the glorious unit's fallen. The French government offered a large lot in the Park Villeneuve l'Etang at Marnes-la-Coquette eight miles outside of Paris- and there in 1928, a proper monument was erected.

Though Americans in the French Aviation Service were of immense value to France, I daresay their greatest contribution was in 1918 after most had transferred to the USAS/United States Air Service. As combat veterans, *l'Escadrille Lafayette* pilots were the flyers America depended on when they started sending their own "green" pursuit/fighter pilots to the front. The Escadrille flyboys were assigned to the newly arrived American units, where they passed along their combat knowledge to the fledglings. I can imagine those USAS pilots who survived their initial reconnaissance missions over the front- due to the protective guidance of the handful of their countrymen who had fought so bravely under the *Tricolore*.

It is also important to note that several former Escadrille Lafayette airmen- still possessed of their aggressive spirit- contributed their invaluable experience and service to America during World War II.

Before concluding this Chronicle, here are a few *l'Escadrille Lafayette* postscripts in regard to three of the unit's Pennsylvania-born flyers. The highly decorated Pennsylvanian David Peterson was promoted to major at the end of WWI. He was ordered home to serve as an instructor and test pilot. While thus engaged at Arcadia, Florida, he was involved in a tragic air accident in March 1919. Fellow Pennsylvanian and former Escadrille Lafayette flyer Hank Jones helped carry Peterson's casket to its final resting place in Homesdale, Pennsylvania. Peterson's proud hometown resisted efforts to move his body to the Escadrille Lafayette's memorial at its Paris *environ* in 1928.

Impressively decorated Lieutenant Henry "Hank" Sweet Jones of Harford, Pennsylvania, also returned home to the United States to serve as an instructor and test pilot. Postwar years saw Hank working for the Pennsylvania Railroad, the Transcontinental Air Transport-Maddux Air Lines, and finally for the Woolworth Company as a store manager until his retirement in 1960. Jones passed quietly away in Clearwater, Florida, in 1972.

Following his discharge in 1919, the heroic Bill Thaw returned to Pittsburgh, where he became an agent for one of his father's many business interests, the General Insurance Company. Forever an airman, Bill also involved himself in commercial aviation. When, in 1924, plans got underway for a memorial to *l'Escadrille Lafayette*, Thaw became entangled in a somewhat bitter struggle with the family of Lafayette aviator Norman Prince, whose kith and kin wanted the memorial dedicated to Prince alone. From what I've read, Norman's father persistently attempted to represent his son as the sole founder of the unit. Prince had contributed significantly to the origins of the group, but it had been Thaw more than anyone who had been its founder; and he wanted the memorial dedicated to the *entire* Lafayette Escadrille. And so it was- on the 4th of July 1928.

Bill Thaw never joined his comrades there at the great arch-memorial near Paris, where flies, yet today, two red, white and blue *drapeaux*, the French *Tricolore* and the American Stars and Stripes. After succumbing to pneumonia on April 22, 1934, Ace William

Thaw was interred in the Allegheny Cemetery at Pittsburgh.

A lifelong standard bearer for "keeping the record straight" about *l'Escadrille Lafayette,* Carl Dolan, over the years, attended all the unit's reunions and WWI ceremonies. The son of a Boston politician, Dolan had a long and eventful post-war life. After retiring from the USAS in 1920, with the *Croix de Guerre* and *Légion d'Honneur* for his WWI service, he was sent to China. Dolan trained Chinese pilots until 1925, at which time he returned home to America, where he helped design John Rogers Field in Hawaii (now Honolulu International Airport). He subsequently became involved in numerous businesses, many affiliated with aviation, including Eastern Airlines.

From 1943 to 1945, Dolan was president of Commonwealth Aircraft Company in Kansas City, Missouri, the second largest manufacturer of combat gliders during World War II.

During the Korean War, Colonel Dolan was assistant to the chief of maintenance of the US Air Force at the headquarters of the Air Matériel Command at Wright-Patterson Air Force Base, Ohio. Later, he became a USAF representative, troubleshooter and consultant.

By the time he retired to Hawaii, Dolan's countless achievements included the first insulated berths in aircraft, the first operational manual for airlines, as well as some of the first instrument landing systems. This amazing "Flyboy" also helped to write the original charter for the Civil Aeronautics Administration.

Carl Dolan's last gathering came in 1981 when he was invited to an international assembly, in Paris, of surviving WWI aces. He was eighty-six, with a sharp mind and a keen Irish wit; however, his health was not one of the valued things he still possessed. Dolan had been diagnosed with lymphoma cancer. To quote author Jon Guttman from his impressively researched book *SPA124 Lafayette Escadrille, American Volunteer Airmen in World War I:* "But he was not about to let this last honour go."

Perhaps Dolan contracted pneumonia when he visited the Lafayette Memorial while he was in Paris for that final reunion. On that bleak November day, it had been a tearful visit to the Escadrille's commemorative gravesite, almost an overwhelming one for Dolan. Shortly after he returned to his home in Honolulu, Carl Dolan passed away on December 31, 1981– the last of the thirty-eight Americans to fly with *l'Escadrille Lafayette.*

To quote again their former French comrades-in-arms: "They were brave, those American aviators!"

"The Intrepid Nellie Bly"

"Energy rightly applied and directed can accomplish anything."

"I have never written a word that did not come from my heart. I never shall. I have never had but one desire, and that was to benefit humanity, to encourage, to uplift, to point out the way called 'straight'."
- Nellie Bly

The adventurous, heroic woman who became known to History as "Nellie Bly" was born Elizabeth Jane Cochran on May 5, 1864. Bly was one of the most rousing characters of the late nineteenth-early twentieth century. While still in her twenties, she pioneered investigative journalism, becoming the most famous journalist of her day. Her fearless exposés and undaunted success helped open the profession to future generations of women journalists eager to write hard news. This woman was incredible.

She feigned insanity to be committed to an insane asylum in order to expose its horrid conditions. She circled the globe in record time, all the while taking her countless readers "with her." She designed, manufactured and marketed the first successful steel barrel produced in the United States. She ran the factories she inherited from her multimillionaire husband as models of social experiments, proving that well-treated employees are more-productive workers. She was the first woman to report from the Eastern Front during World War I. When it made her unpopular to do so, she journeyed to Europe to make a case for a defeated nation, so stirred was she by the many orphans left in the wake of the war. Forever an ardent humanitarian, she even wrote a widely read advice column, devoting herself to the plight of the unfortunate, most notably to unwed mothers and their children.

Nellie Bly's rich life- 1864 to 1922- spanned the end of the American Civil War to the subsequent Reconstruction era and late-Victorian/Edwardian period into the Great War with its disheartening, cynical aftermath that led straight to the Roaring Twenties. Nellie's roller-coaster life was never smooth. Quite often it was downright dangerous, but the ride was always thrilling!

Let's begin at the beginning- with the parents who gave birth to Elizabeth Jane, the daughter the world would come to know as "Nellie Bly." Elizabeth's parents, of the large Cochran family of Apollo, Pennsylvania, were Michael Cochran and Mary Jane Kennedy Cochran. Michael had been elected to the esteemed position of Associate Justice of Armstrong County, and in his honor the small community of Pitts Mills was rechristened Cochran's Mills at the end of his five-year term of office in 1855. Ever after, Michael Cochran was known in the area as "Judge." Though Elizabeth was born in Cochran's Mills, she grew up in nearby Apollo. Both towns are located in Armstrong County.

Judge Cochran's first wife had passed away in 1857. A year later, Michael married the widow Cummings from nearby Somerset, Pennsylvania. She had been born Mary Jane Kennedy, the great-granddaughter of the county's first sheriff, Thomas Kennedy.

When the Civil War broke out, Michael, at age fifty, was too old to serve; however, two of his sons by his first wife joined the Pennsylvania volunteers. They were both back home with honorable discharges before the future Nellie Bly made her debut into the world. With his soldier-sons returned from the war, six children (of the total ten offspring) from Michael's first marriage were still at home when second-wife Mary Jane joined the Cochran household.

The third child of the five the judge would have with Mary Jane, Elizabeth Jane/"Nellie

Bly" came along in the spring of 1864. She would live at home until she turned fifteen. It was at that age that she attended the Indiana Normal School (now Indiana University of Pennsylvania). A normal school was the name once applied to an institution of higher learning that offered a two-year course of study, chiefly for training elementary teachers. Elizabeth would never finish the training; she would be forced to drop out of the program for lack of funds. During her school years, Elizabeth Jane was not an impressive student. Despite that and everything else, she developed a keen desire to be a writer; for she had discovered early on that she enjoyed expressing herself on paper.

The Nellie Bly story is intriguing. And I am eager to relate to you the highlights of her tale; but before we get into its essence, I wish to point out that those of us interested in the past have no doubt noticed that well-behaved women seldom make history. Elizabeth Cochran was no exception to this theory. She was destined to become the most famous woman in the world by doing things that, according to the day's social standards, women were not supposed to do. It may be said that from the very beginning of her life, Elizabeth's mother groomed her daughter to know how to attract attention- and revel in it. The lessons would never be forgotten.

The vocal baby, Elizabeth Jane, was christened, not in the traditional white, but in a bright pink gown. Time, our greatest historian, assures us that there was *nothing* of the traditional about Elizabeth, who emerged Mary Jane's most rebellious child. Throughout her childhood, the rosy hue was Elizabeth's habitual color; and thus, the precocious child earned the soubriquet "Pink." To sport such a color while other young ladies wore muted tones demonstrated a rare self-confidence in one so young. The future Nellie Bly would always be, above all, *creative*, picking up her "artist's brush," i.e., her writer's pen, and obliterating the clouds- and all that business about having to stay within the lines- to word-paint across the sky her amazing life's picture with her own distinctive colors.

In a 2007 email from Elizabeth Jane's/"Nellie Bly's" great-great grand niece, artist Linda Champanier of Stamford, Connecticut, Linda informed me that, according to *A History of Apollo* penned by her great-grandfather, T. J. Henry (who was married to Elizabeth's/"Nellie's" niece, Cora Cochran), it was Elizabeth's brother Albert who dubbed his sister with the soubriquet "Pink," due to a favorite dress that she frequently wore. T. J. Henry and Albert P. Cochran(e) were lifelong best friends.

From childhood, Elizabeth was special, and her early childhood was idyllic. Hers was an affluent, comfortable home, the Victorian house on Apollo's "Mansion Row," the popular local name for Terrace Avenue. Then shortly after her sixth birthday, Elizabeth's father passed away. The sad event would dramatically alter her life and that of her family.

The judge, who had been a prominent member of the community, died without benefit of a will, leaving his wife without claim

Nellie Bly, in her signature travel togs, about to embark on her historic trip around the world, November 14, 1889

to the property, which subsequently forced the auction of his estate. At the time of Cochran's passing, there were nine surviving offspring from the judge's first marriage. When all was said and done, Elizabeth's mother Mary Jane ended up with her furniture and other household possessions, a horse and carriage (that she was forced to sell not long afterward), the cow, one of the dogs, and very little money. For Michael Cochran's younger family, his death spelled *disaster.*

Forced to auction her beautiful new mansion, Mary Jane and her five children moved to a modest home, where Pink took on the responsibility of helping her mother raise her younger siblings. I should mention here that the Cochran home still stands on Terrace Avenue in the town of Apollo. In July 1995, an historical marker was placed in front of the stately, white-columned house.

With the hope of regaining security, Elizabeth's mother remarried in January 1873, when Pink was nine and the judge had been gone over two years. Lamentably for her and the children, the new husband/stepfather, John Jackson Ford, known as "Jack," was an abusive individual with a quick temper and little patience for the brood he had taken on. Mary Jane must have been truly desperate. She was over forty at the time she married Jack, twice widowed, and raising five children on her own. She would not have had many choices, but her hasty decision to wed Jack Ford would prove catastrophic.

A telling incident that comes to mind from my research is this one which occurred on New Year's Eve, 1878. Contrary to Jack's wishes, Mary Jane and her children left the house to attend a holiday celebration at Apollo's Methodist Episcopal Church. The festivities were being held on the upper floor of the Odd Fellows Hall. As members and friends chatted in a happy holiday mood, Jack Ford, drunk and belligerent, burst into the room, made his way behind Mary Jane, and yanking a loaded pistol from his coat pocket, shouted, "I'll kill you... I'll kill you if ya were th' last woman on earth!" Though Mary Jane's son Albert and a few of the other males present succeeded in subduing the raving Ford, it would not be the last time her alcoholic husband would threaten to kill her.

Before the intense, small-town gaze and amid the rampant gossip of all Apollo, Mary Jane did the unthinkable and sued her abusive mate for divorce. Elizabeth, then fourteen, testified at the trial against her violent stepfather. According to PBS the *American Experience*, here is some of what Elizabeth told the court: "My stepfather has been generally drunk since he married my mother. When drunk he is very cross and cross when sober. I've heard him call my mother names... a whore and a bitch... I've seen her cry." Mary Jane won her case. And the child Pink was no more.

I believe that Elizabeth's future passion for women's rights was rooted in the helplessness she and her family experienced with her mother's third marriage. Perhaps this even explains why Elizabeth married relatively late in life during an era when the *raison d'être* of all young ladies was marriage.

Nevertheless, Elizabeth, who must have viewed the world through spectacles of her favorite rose hue, exhibited an extraordinary ability to defeat the sadness of her childhood. Furthermore, her choices in life would clearly display a Celtic warrior stance on the issues she was destined to champion. There is an old saying that "blood shows." I am inclined to agree with the pithy maxim.

In *County Chronicles Volume II,* I wrote about another Cochran, Margaret Cochran Corbin, in the Chronicle entitled "Captain Molly." Molly, the heroine of Washington Heights in George Washington's battle for New York, was of Clan Cochrane/Cochran, descended from Vikings who settled in Scotland (between the eighth and tenth centuries). The etymology of the surname is actually two Gaelic words that translate "battle cry" or "roar of battle." Its members were called, at the gathering of the clans, "brave fellows." The Cochrane/Cochran clan motto is "Valour and Exertion." And that clan motto clearly defines both of these outstanding Pennsylvania women to the proverbial "T."

Like most Celts, Elizabeth had a vivid imagination that became evident via her fiery newspaper articles and her brilliant storytelling. It was only a matter of time before she would proffer her profound writings to the world at large- *and her words would make a difference.*

As a teen, Elizabeth added a final "e" to the spelling of Cochran, thinking- or so I've read- that it lent sophistication to the surname. Perhaps she was also thinking that the spelling change would serve to erase the unpleasantness connected to Jack Ford; and too, the Cochranes of Apollo were a family of highly respected attorneys. Whatever her reason, her siblings and, eventually, her mother followed suit. It was about this same time, around her eighteenth birthday, that the passionate girl launched her career as a journalist.

One of the few respectable professions open to women in those days was teaching. Pennsylvania had established, at various locations, a series of normal schools for the training of teachers. Yearning for an independent life and seeking a way to support her mother, Elizabeth enrolled at the normal school in Indiana, Pennsylvania, the pride of that small town. However, the lack of funds forced her to drop out after only one term. In fact, she did not even get to take her examinations for that session. It must have been disappointing, if not downright depressing. She would now have to find another way of making a living.

The persevering young woman relocated with her mother and siblings to the smoky city of Pittsburgh, where Elizabeth hoped to find work. With so much industry in that city, there was surely a fortune to be made. A writer for the *Atlantic Monthly* said that the Pittsburgh of 1880 "... was like looking into hell with the lid off." Sadly, the hopeful girl soon discovered that the only occupations open to women anywhere were low-paying ones. In order to make ends meet, she and her mother took in boarders; but Elizabeth's dreams included so much more than housework or factory work, or the equally unhappy prospect of marriage to a factory worker. A career was on the horizon for the bright, energetic Miss Cochrane, and it all started with a letter she penned, in 1885, to the editor of the *Pittsburgh Dispatch.*

Elizabeth's missive was a lively response to a sexist editorial by the "Quiet Observer," one Erasmus Wilson. George Madden, managing editor of the *Dispatch* was so moved by the letter, signed "Lonely Orphan Girl," that he placed an ad in the Sunday edition of his paper, pleading: "Lonely Orphan Girl, will you please come forward?"

The next day, Elizabeth, with the intention of introducing herself, climbed the dark, dusty stairs to Madden's fourth-storey office. Asking an office boy, in an out-of-breath voice that threatened to abandon her, where she might find the editor, she thanked him and took her first step toward her stellar future. She need not have been apprehensive, for she landed her first job as a journalist that very afternoon.

As my readers might suspect- and in glimpse of her work to come- Elizabeth's first article was a rebuttal to the not-so-Quiet Observer's chauvinist piece entitled "What Girls Are Good For." The author Wilson had written that a woman who tries to make a living outside the house was nothing less than a "monstrosity." Elizabeth was furious, and she soundly countered Wilson's essay that a woman's sphere was her own domicile. In an article imbued with passion, she drove home the point that some women had no choice but to make their own way.

Her editor declared that her writing had "... no style, no punctuation, no grammar, but I see a spirit here... I definitely see a spirit!" Editor Madden immediately asked for a second example of her work. In spite of the misspelled words, the dangling participles, and the too-wordy text, he saw Elizabeth as a budding journalist with great promise. However, there existed one problem. She was also a woman. Allow me to deviate for a moment in order to paint you a sketch of how things were for women over a century ago.

Few things have changed more in the past hundred years than society's idea of how a lady should behave. As soon as she left the classroom or finishing school, the sole aim of every young lady was marriage, which afforded her a place in Victorian society, a position which a single woman could never attain. The Victorian age was strict and rigid in its dictates. For instance, it was not until the end of the period, often referred to as "Edwardian," when it became acceptable for ladies to dine in public places, such as restaurants and hotels. Every aspect of the Victorian lady's life was subject to custom, convention, tradition and duty. The Victorians had iron-clad dictates, and God help the lady who cast aside those rules of conduct! A lady who ignored proper protocol was risking her reputation, as well as her family's position and esteem.

What I am saying, readers, in reference to Elizabeth's job at the *Dispatch,* is that during the Victorian age, it was quite improper for a woman to write for a newspaper and make her identity known to the public. Proper Victorian ladies never cast themselves into the limelight. They rarely got their names into newspapers with the exception of birth, marriage and death. Oh, the crème de la crème got mentions on the society page, but that was as far as it went.

The managing editor of the *Pittsburgh Dispatch* solved the quandary, when he hired Cochrane as a permanent member of his

staff, by telling her that the paper would use a nom de plume in place of her own name. After several colorful suggestions from his reporters, Madden chose for his protégée's pen name "Nellie Bly." If this pseudonym sounds familiar, it is because "Nelly Bly" was the title character in the song of the same name penned in 1850, some thirty years earlier, by Pittsburgh's own Stephen Collins Foster. In his newspaper-deadline rush, Madden had not been faithful to the spelling of the song title. Nevertheless, I want to emphasize that both Stephen Foster and the journalist have their roots in the Pittsburgh area. The duly christened Nellie Bly rolled up her sleeves and got down to business.

The enthusiastic reporter discovered, to her delight, that she was a born writer. Straightaway, she put her talent to work on women's-rights issues, a theme that would echo in conjunction with her name down the long tunnel of time. In order to get the real facts, the true story, Nellie Bly invented investigative reporting. She would soon become an expert at undercover work.

One of her first articles in her now-famous series on social reform dealt with divorce. I feel certain it was based on her mother's third marriage, together with interviews garnered from other separated or divorced women. In the piece, Bly passionately argued for reform of both the marriage and the divorce laws.

Among her numerous covers, Nellie posed as a poor sweatshop worker to expose the cruelty and dreadful conditions under which so many immigrant women- and children- were forced to toil. She even posed as an unwed mother to expose baby-buying. Bly not only investigated and exposed social problems with her writings, she was always willing to suggest ways in which the problems could be solved. Her editor wrote that Nellie Bly was "... full of fire, and her writing was charged with youthful exuberance."

Nonetheless, when shop owners threatened to pull their advertising from the *Dispatch*- ads keep newspapers afloat- the editor bounced Nellie over to the fashion beat. Pushed now to the women's pages, Nellie reported on the haute couture of the day, the society news, the arts, and gardening- the usual stuff for the few nom-de-plume female journalists of the day. Bly dug into her garden research, at first, with renewed energy, writing a perceptive admonition to Pennsylvanians to begin planting trees or risk deforestation of Penn's Woods. She praised Governor Pattison's decision to declare April 16 Arbor Day, and then pointed out that this was the state's only official act regarding trees since 1681, when William Penn had required the preservation of one acre of forest for every five acres cleared.

Quickly though, Bly's new duty at the paper filled her with ennui. I've said it before, but I'll repeat it here again: The cure for boredom is inquisitiveness spiked with escapade, and for *that*, there is no cure. In her own words, Nellie expressed it like this: "I am too impatient to work along at the usual duties assigned women on newspapers." Bly then took the initiative- something she would do for the remainder of her life- and lit out for Mexico to serve as a foreign correspondent for her paper. Her road there and back would be a bumpy one, though it was taking her in the right direction in her life.

Then twenty-one, Nellie spent nearly half-a-year south of the border, reporting on the lives, traditions and customs of the Mexican people. Mexico was mysterious, exotic, even dangerous- Bly's kind of place- and for a while anyway, she was in her element. Her dispatches were later published in book form under the title *Six Months in Mexico.* In keeping with her emerging trend, Nellie wrote about poverty and corruption. But when she openly protested the incarceration of a local journalist locked up for criticizing the Mexican government, she opened a Pandora's Box!

Under the iron grip of former General Porfirio Díaz, the Mexican government, at that time, was a dictatorship. Authorities threatened to toss the outspoken American reporter into the local jailhouse- which would have meant tossing away the proverbial key as well. Nellie had no choice but to flee the country. Back home in America, she soundly denounced Díaz as a tyrannical leader who suppressed his people and controlled the press.

After her scorching Mexican story, Nellie could not get her teeth into anything substantial. Again, the paper "burdened" her with what she called "theater-and-arts reporting." Enough was more than enough. In 1887, Bly left the *Pittsburgh Dispatch* for good. Whilst she had been in their employ, Nellie had mastered the foundations of journalism. Now it was clearly time to move on. Her destination was New York City.

Then, as now, New York was the nation's publishing capital. Nellie set her goals high- she aspired to land a job with one of the city's top newspapers. The note she had penned to Erasmus Wilson/the "Quiet Observer," with whom she had cultivated a close friendship, pretty much said it all. In fact, it was *pure* Nellie Bly: "Dear Q. O., I am off for New York. Look out for me! Bly."

Four lean months passed. Nellie found herself, not only jobless, but penniless. She had knocked on the doors of New York's newspapers, exhausting them all, from the prominent to the inconsequential. Rejecting a retreat to Pittsburgh, the persevering girl turned her predicament into the propulsion to finally land a job.

Fast-talking Nellie persuaded the guards who barred her way into the office of Colonel John Cockerill of *The New York World* to grant her an audience. Once inside the managing editor's inner sanctum, the golden-tongued girl wasted little time. Her bright ideas radiated from her like fairy dust, settling over the newspaper executive and working their magic on him. Cockerill promptly paid her twenty-five dollars to retain her services, whilst he discussed "his discovery" with Joseph Pulitzer, the paper's owner.

Bly's foremost idea had been to travel to Europe and return steerage, so she could report firsthand on the excruciating experiences of an immigrant. That idea, though a good one, was rejected- the paper had something else in mind for the daring Nellie.

In September 1887, Nellie officially joined the staff of the famed *New York World*, where, in 1888, her first major assignment would bring *her* fame. In order to investigate reports of brutality and neglect, Nellie and her editors felt that undercover just might be the best way to gather information for an accurate story on the treatment of inmates at the Women's Lunatic Asylum on Blackwell's Island (known now as Welfare Island). It was a bold challenge- and one the intrepid Nellie readily accepted. Immediately, she set about concocting the strategy for getting herself committed.

After an evening spent practicing deranged expressions in front of a mirror, Bly checked into a working-class boardinghouse under the alias "Nellie Brown." There she acted her role to perfection. For instance, she refused to ever go to bed, telling the mistress and the other boarders that she was afraid of them, that they all looked crazy to her. The other residents soon decided that *she* was the crazy one. The police were summoned, followed by a hearing, wherein Nellie pleaded amnesia. The judge concluded that she had been drugged. She was then examined by several doctors, who all declared with certainty that she was insane. "Positively demented," pronounced one of their numbers. "I consider this girl a hopeless case. She needs to be put where someone will take care of her."

At New York's Bellevue Hospital, the head of the insane pavilion echoed the court examiners when he declared her "undoubtedly insane." All the while, the New York newspapers were having a field day with the story. Just who was this pretty yet sadly unbalanced girl? The *Times* posed the question "Who is the mysterious waif with the wild, hunted look in her eyes?" And all the papers echoed her desperate courtroom cries: "I can't remember! I can't remember!"

Committed to the hell of Blackwell's asylum at her peril, Bly experienced the horrific conditions of that aptly named institution firsthand. The vermin-infested food- if one could call it food- was gruel broth, spoiled meat, and bread that was little more than dried dough. Nellie found it inedible, though many of the famished women made an attempt to eat the slop. Mustard and vinegar were put on the rancid meat and in the gruel, to cover the smell and the taste, which only served to worsen the horrible fare. Fish was simply boiled in water and given to the inmates with no salt, pepper or butter. "Anyone who refused to swallow the food was threatened with punishment," Nellie would write later. "In our short walks," she stated in a subsequent report, "we passed the kitchen where food was prepared for the nurses and doctors. There, we got glimpses of melons and grapes and all kinds of fruits, beautiful white bread and nice meats, and the hungry feeling would be increased tenfold."

The inmates were forced to sit up straight for much of each day on rock-hard benches with scant protection from the cold. The nurses were mean and physically abusive, often shouting at the patients to "shut-up!" Beatings and agonizing ice-cold baths were common. Speaking with fellow residents, Bly was convinced that some of them were as sane as she. On the effects of her ten days in the mental hospital, Nellie penned: "People in the world can never imagine the length of days to those in asylums. They seemed never-ending, and we welcomed any event that might give us something to think about as well as talk of.

"I always made a point of telling the doctors that I was sane... but the more I endeavored to assure them of my sanity, the more they doubted it. They would not heed me... the insane asylum on Blackwell's Island is a human rat-trap. It is easy to get in, but once there- it is *impossible* to get out."

In conclusion, she wrote: "What, excepting torture, would produce insanity quicker than this treatment? Here is a class of women sent to be cured. I would like the expert physicians who are condemning me for my action... to take a perfectly sane and healthy woman; shut her up and make her sit from 6 a.m. to 8 p.m. on straight-back benches; do not allow her to talk or move during those hours; give her no reading and let her know nothing of the world or its doings; give her bad food and harsh treatment, and see how long it will take to make her insane! Two months would make her a mental and physical wreck!"

After ten days, Bly was released from the asylum at *The World's* behest. Cockerill had promised her that he would find a way to get her out when the time came. Her haunting account, later published in book form as *Ten Days in a Mad-House*, caused a jolting sensation and brought her lasting renown, propelling Nellie Bly into the limelight of New York journalism.

While embarrassed court and hospital physicians and staff fell over one another to explain how so many professionals had been duped, a grand jury launched its own investigation into conditions at the Blackwell asylum, inviting Nellie to assist. The jury's report recommended the changes she proposed. And its call for increased funding for the proper care of the insane prompted an $850,000 increase in the budget of the Department of Public Charities and Corrections.

At only twenty-three, Nellie Bly demonstrated enormous courage to be put into the asylum at Blackwell. Her description of the place as a "human rat-trap" was an apt metaphor. Once a person was put into that wretched place, there was no way out, unless released; and release was quite rare- in effect unheard of. During that era, one could be committed to asylums- ofttimes maliciously- by family members. At Blackwell's, Nellie met a woman who had been put there by her husband who accused her of being unfaithful to him. Nellie also discovered that some inmates were suffering from physical illnesses rather than from mental problems. Bly's scathing attacks on the way patients were treated at Blackwell's Island resulted in much-needed reforms.

Fame afforded Nellie new opportunities, and a subsequent piece she wrote for *The World* became the seed for her one-and-only novel *The Mystery of Central Park.* Though the cover bore the promise "The Nellie Bly Series," there were no sequels. The novel drew some derision from the literary critics of the day with no known literary acclaim. The idea for the book's main character was based on a real-life Central Park stable foreman. The stableman had allegedly plied New York's cops with beer "to look the other way" whilst he cruised the Park in a horse-drawn hansom cab, looking for unsuspecting girls (usually new to the city) with the intention of luring them into prostitution.

Whatever the critics might have said about her novel, Bly's first year in New York was a colossal success, especially when one considers that she was a young girl in her twenties, alone in that big city, with little education and no formal training as a journalist. Those jealous called what she did "stunt reporting." Irrespective of what it was called, what she did sold newspapers. Succinctly put, everything this ultra-talented writer would do from this point on in her life would sell papers. She always seemed to know how to choose the assignment that would propel her stage-center. It was one of Nellie Bly's greatest gifts.

Her mad-house quest had made national headlines. Nellie's next daredevil adventure (a few months later, in 1889) would make *global* news. After having read Jules Verne's *Around the World in Eighty Days,* Nellie suggested to Joseph Pulitzer that his newspaper should finance an attempt to break the record illustrated in the popular book. Pulitzer liked the idea and hoped to use Bly's journey- of course, *she* was the reporter selected to make the trip- to publicize *The New York World.* The best-selling *Around the World in Eighty Days* had been out since 1873, but no one until Nellie Bly had dared to attempt what Verne's fictional Phileas T. Fogg had achieved within its thrilling pages.

As soon as she was asked to make the trip, Nellie made a morning beeline to Ghormley's *Robes* and *Manteaux* (the French designer's dresses and coats), the city's most fashionable couturier whose studios occupied the Rue Richelieu in Paris and Fifth Avenue, New York. She ordered a traveling costume that would be sturdy enough to withstand three months of constant wear and still look chic. She wanted it within twelve hours. When the elite designer, his hands appealing to the heavens, shrieked, *"Mon Dieu! Mademoiselle, c'est impossible!"* He explained in French-laced English that such things require more time. Undaunted, Nellie exclaimed with an impatient wave of her hand, "Nonsense! If you want to do it, you *can* do it!" That was, of course, Nellie Bly's personal motto; and I daresay from what I've read about this fascinating woman, she did seem to take a perverse delight in asking for things to be done in dreadfully short notice. 'Twas her *manner* of asking that usually produced the desired results!

By noon, the blue plaid broadcloth travel gown was boned and shaped. Nellie had her final fitting late that very afternoon. At the same time, her regular dressmaker fashioned for her a lighter weight, basic brown frock for warmer climates- which was also ready within a day. In addition, she purchased a plaid ulster (overcoat) for extra warmth, a gossamer-light "waterproof" (raincoat) for rain, which meant that she needed no umbrella; and she sported a "very English" double-beaked cap, *à la* Sherlock Holmes, for her head. From her ears dangled seventy-year-old, family-heirloom earbobs. Her only other adornments were a simple silver bracelet and a gold "twist" ring. On her thumb she wore her "lucky ring," which she had worn the day *The World* hired her. She also took a much-needed watch. The photographs I've seen render Nellie quite spiffy. She looked ready for anything!

Her office gave her a total of 200 pounds in English gold and banknotes which she would keep on her person at all times, the gold in a deep pocket, the banknotes in a small chamois pouch tied round her neck and cached under her clothing. She also took some American money. She intended to see where it could be used. She would carry one small piece of hand luggage- a gladstone bag- about sixteen inches wide and seven inches tall. She was determined, she said "... to confine [her] baggage to its limit."

At 9:40 a.m., November 14, 1889, Nellie Bly departed New York from the Hoboken pier on the Hamburg-American Company liner *Augusta Victoria*. Her glowing face beneath her plaid Sherlock-Holmes cap reflected the promise of the success of her mission- to break the record set by Jules Verne's legendary character Phileas Fogg. From the ship's deck, Bly enthusiastically waved her goodbyes, as the ship glided gracefully into the Atlantic's autumnal embrace.

When a fellow passenger asked her later if she ever got *mal de mer*, Nellie answered in the negative, but that was all it took to bring on the nausea. At dinner, she sat bravely on the captain's left at his table, albeit a little pale. When the queasy feeling became too much, she bolted for the railing. Upon her third return to the table, a little cat smile playing at the corners of her mouth, the room exploded with applause and a warm "Bravo!" After a good night's rest that stretched till four the next afternoon, Nellie acquired her sea legs, after which she became quite the little sailor.

No special considerations were afforded Miss Bly as she hopped from ship to train to boat to rickshaw or sampan, to donkey or carriage then steamer and train on her 24,899-mile journey. Her vibrant travel experiences were published daily in *The World*- and eagerly read by thousands of readers. It was all very exciting!

I feel the need to interject in our tale the fact that Nellie Bly/Elizabeth Cochran(e) shaved three years off her life by stating on her passport that she had been born in 1867. Sans compunction, she would adhere to that little white lie for the remainder of her life. I can forgive this peccadillo in our heroine. Her life's accomplishments would far outweigh her little faults.

During Bly's journey, *The World* initiated a contest for their readers to guess her travel time; the grand prize a free trip to Europe. And at the request of the famous author himself, Nellie met Monsieur and Madame Jules Verne in France during the course of her trip. "Why do you not go to Bombay, as my hero Phileas Fogg?" M. Verne asked Bly, to which our girl succinctly replied, "Because I am more anxious to save time."

At Singapore, Bly spied a tiny monkey for sale and knew she had to bargain for it, though the rascal did cause some havoc on board ship. Her only other souvenirs were jewelry purchases which added no real weight to her gladstone. Giving in to the temptation of Ceylon's sparkling gems, Nellie wrote: "No woman who lands at Colombo could possibly leave without a few new rings selected from the mountains of deeply-dark emeralds, fire-lit diamonds, exquisite pearls, rubies like drops of blood, the lucky cat's eye with its moving line, and all set in such beautiful shapes."

Nellie was taking in the major tourist sites along her route. But lest we forget our girl was a born humanitarian, there were other sites/sights as well. On Christmas morning, Bly visited a leper colony in Canton, China. She passed New Year's Eve with her fellow passengers on board her vessel in the Pacific, where they endured a brutal sea storm. No matter, Nellie was ever determined to succeed, stating at one point, "If I fail, I will never return to New York. I would rather go in dead and successful than alive and behind time."

When her ship, the *Oceanic*, docked in San Francisco harbor, and a rumor reached Nellie's ears of a smallpox quarantine on board, the feisty Bly leaped with her little monkey "McGinty" into a tugboat and sped away for land. A special train awaited her arrival. With more than 20,000 miles behind her, there were yet over 3,000 to go!

On Saturday, January 25, 1890, the timekeepers stopped their watches at seventy-two days, six hours, eleven minutes and fourteen seconds. Nellie Bly had beaten the legendary Phileas Fogg by nearly a week!

The beaming, waving girl arrived back home greeted by the press, crowds of cheering fans, booming cannons, exploding fireworks, and blaring bands. Her speed, including stops, was figured to have been about 22 miles per hour. *The World* crowed that their reporter had broken every record for circumnavigation. Now followed a seemingly endless agenda of interviews and parades. It was all quite heady.

The World released an "authentic biography" of Nellie Bly. Her personal account of her travels, *Around the World in 72 Days,* was destined to become a best seller. Her travel ensemble, especially her double-beaked cap, became all the rage in women's fashion. Advertisers clamored to utilize her name and image on their products. Trade cards carried clever verse and caricatures of Nellie attired in her long, plaid traveling coat that had already become her signature outfit.

Nineteenth-century trades were 3 X 5 colorful cards printed, as stated above, with poems and ofttimes with humorous advertisements that customers could pick up at stores and save and/or trade. For Nellie, there was a whole series created in 1890, right after she concluded her trip around the world. I love the Bly trade-card rhymes! One depicts Nellie in her traveling togs, her gladstone in hand, her arms out for balance, walking a mystical cord stretched across the stellar universe. It reads: " 'O bye and bye,' dreams Nellie Bly/ 'Along a strand of light I'll hie/ And stars and gleams will follow too/ But they must hustle if they do!' " [*Hie* translates "hurry."]

Another trade card shows Nellie in her signature travel ensemble with her gladstone in one hand, an American flag in the other, as she sets off across the globe, leaving Jules Verne's Fogg in her wake. This card bears the verse: " 'O Fogg, goodbye,' said Nellie Bly/ 'It takes a maiden to be spry/ To span the space 'twixt thought and act/ And turn a fiction to a fact.' " Nellie was now a symbol of American pride and power.

The acclaim, from all corners of the globe, was exhilarating; yet from *The World,* she received "nothing." Or so she believed. Nellie's stories from around the globe had increased that newspaper's circulation so significantly that Bly supposed a bonus of some sort was due her. Dismayed and disgruntled by the lack of appreciation from her editors, Nellie tendered her resignation.

As much as I respect this Pennsylvania heroine, it seems to me that she had become a tad full of herself at this juncture in her life, neglecting to count all the perks her trip had garnered her. *The World* published her biography, and their sponsored journey served to increase her fame from a national to a global celebrity. Immediately upon her return, she became a sought-after speaker. In fact, for the rest of her life, she was a resounding success as a lecturer, surprising initial audiences with her self-assured delivery and amusing anecdotes. Irrespective of all the positive fallout the trip had showered upon her, Bly vowed and declared she would never return to *The World.* It would not be long, however, before she had a change of heart.

Soon after her book's release, *Around the World in 72 Days* sold out, and Nellie prepared for a second printing in late summer of 1890. One would think that there would have been marriage proposals and one or two amorous encounters by this point in her life. If there were, Bly was ultra-discreet.

In the autumn of 1893, Nellie made a comeback at *The New York World.* As her heart ever dictated, her pieces focused mainly on issues regarding women's rights and social injustices. Her first piece, upon her return, was her famous interview with Emma Goldman, the close compatriot and live-in lover of Alexander Berkman, who had endeavored to murder Henry Clay Frick during the deadly Homestead Steel strike the previous summer. For a thrilling, detailed account of both the strike and Berkman's attempted assassination, I entreat you to read those segments found in my *County Chronicles Volume II.*

"Do you need an introduction to Emma Goldman?" Nellie asked her readers in the opening sentence. Clearly captivated by Emma's passion and sincerity, Bly painted a unique portrait of the anarchist, dubbing her the "modern Joan of Arc." Though her sympathetic description implied no personal politics, Nellie bestowed on Goldman full forum to vent on controversial ideas, the subjects ranging from marriage to murder. When Bly asked Emma (who, along with Berkman, advocated free love) what she thought should replace the institution of marriage, Goldman replied, "The marriage of affection... that is the only *true* marriage. If two people care for one another, they have a right to live together so long as that love exists. When it is dead, what base immorality for them to keep together?" One can imagine how this kind of talk went over in that Victorian era!

Alluding to H. C. Frick's attempted murder, Bly blurted at one point during the Goldman interview, "Do you think murder is going to help your cause?" Goldman pondered the undiluted question a pensive moment, and then answered gravely: "That is a long subject to discuss. I don't believe that through murder we shall gain, but by war, labor against capital, masses against classes, which will not come in twenty or twenty-five years. But someday, I firmly believe we shall gain; and until then, I am satisfied to agitate, to teach. And I only ask justice and freedom of speech."

Now Bly authored her own column. "All my own! Herein every Sunday I may say all I please and what I please. Is it not a joy!" Above the text of the column, *The World* published, in an oval frame of intertwining flowers and vines, a fetching image of Nellie. In large letters her name unfurled from a banner above and beneath the festooned girlish likeness: "Nellie Bly's Column." The whole idea suited her perfectly. By this instant in history, Bly was revered by her editors because her stories sold papers. Above all, her writings ever boosted public awareness of social problems, resulting in reform.

Nellie Bly was never afraid to expose corruption. When she wrote about the plight of unwed mothers, she became the unanimous spokesperson for all women. Nellie revealed shady lobbyists and the way women prisoners were treated by police. The compassionate reporter always sided with the poor and the disenfranchised, as when she journeyed to Chicago in 1894 to cover the Pullman Railroad strike. She was the *only* reporter who told of the strike from the perspective of the strikers. As was her habit, Nellie infused her own reactions, feelings and keen observations into whatever subject she was covering.

Bly's increasing fame afforded her evermore opportunities to interview celebrities. She profiled boxer John L. Sullivan and suffragist Susan B. Anthony among other big names of the era. All in all, it was, for Nellie, a wonderful nearly-two-year comeback.

Then, on April 5, 1895, when she was just about to turn thirty-one, Nellie surprised and shocked the world by eloping with a man forty years her senior. Her husband was Robert Livingston Seaman, a multimillionaire industrialist from Catskill, New York, who was as well-known in New York business circles as she was in the world of journalism. Those who knew them both were incredulous. Bly took a husband in the same burst of energy with which she did most things in her life. The marriage caused "no end of talk."

I can imagine that Nellie armored herself for the onslaught of his family's barbs, and that was why, I am fairly certain, the marriage took place in Chicago rather than in New York City or Catskill. Though Seaman's heirs were opposed from the outset, and Nellie's reason for entering into the union can only be speculative, the couple remained married until Seaman's passing ten years later. Upon her marriage, Bly said she would retire from journalism– or so she intended.

For now, a new life awaited her. As wife to a celebrated multimillionaire, she was now "mistress of the mansion" at her husband's residence in New York City's prestigious Murray Hill district, as well as at his holiday "cottage" set on manicured lawns amidst terraced gardens above the Hudson. There was also her husband's country estate which sprawled over 300 of Catskill's lush picturesque acres.

Was Nellie's marriage a success? Only she could tell us that. My guess, based on my research, is that it was neither gloriously happy nor miserable. My speculation– and it is only that– is that Nellie saw a chance, marrying a multimillionaire industrialist, to make yet another difference. The marriage had its challenges in the first few years. In fact, before her husband's health failed, Nellie went back to writing for *The World* in order to have an income of her own. But after Seaman's health weakened, and Nellie took care of him, they drew close. He had apparently stopped listening to the negative comments of his family, and began regarding his wife with a whole new consideration.

Seaman changed his will for the final time in November 1896, clearly indicating the dramatic extent of his respect for the exceptional woman he had married. Therein, he stated: "I have given and willed to my wife Elizabeth C. Seaman all of my property entire and absolute to hers alone and to do with as she wishes. In view of the repeated threats of certain persons that they will break my will and take my property from my wife, I desire to make this statement, which I shall swear to and sign in the presence of witnesses and which I intend to be used in court as my affidavit, if any attempt is made to carry out the threats to take my property from my wife and divide it among those who have no right to it and to whom I am taking every precaution it should not go." Here, Robert Seaman went on to elaborate on all that he had done during his life for his brother, nieces and nephews, and grand nieces, though a codicil did instruct that the nieces and grandnieces each get a one-time gift of $1,000 apiece. The important point to make here is that Nellie Bly was back where she felt the most comfortable- in control.

After her husband's death, Bly took over his business interests, running the Iron Clad Manufacturing Company, where she immediately made radical changes for the benefit of the employees, including the building of a recreation center, the establishment of hunting and fishing clubs and an employee library. She eliminated all piecework, i.e., work done by the piece and paid for at a set rate per unit. Nellie bestowed fair weekly wages, hours, and benefits upon her workers. Unfortunately, her good intentions and radical reforms were overshadowed by her lack of banking and accounting knowledge, and the Iron Clad Manufacturing Company eventually went bankrupt.

The reason for the company's financial problems was due, not to the reforms that Nellie made, but to the forgeries and draining of funds from Iron Clad by unscrupulous people in positions that afforded them the opportunity to steal. People tend to perceive others the way they are. Very simply put, Nellie was honest; thus, she did not readily conceive of dishonesty in others. When the auditors decoded and uncovered mysterious entries in the Iron Clad books, such as expenditure for a $25,000 yacht, Nellie declared: "I cannot blame myself enough for not having learned banking methods and commercial accounting when I first went into the Iron Clad."

For nearly ten years, however, Bly managed two multimillion-dollar companies. She introduced the steel barrel to the distilling process in America. Most importantly, she recognized the value of treating her workers well. She ran her plants as social experiments, initiating physical fitness and health care to her workers, even mental health and vitality by providing staffed libraries to teach employees how to read and to pass examinations for diplomas. She so wanted her employees to be able to enjoy intellectual pursuits, and hence improve their lives.

In order to escape her tangled business problems, and likely her creditors, for a few quiet weeks, Nellie set sail for England in 1914. She was expecting to restore her vivacity by bringing herself back to her fighting weight so she could solve her financial dilemma once and for all. What she was not expecting was the outbreak of a world war.

Trapped in Europe and never one to pass up an opportunity, Nellie seized the chance to apply her flying fingers to the typewriter clatter of correspondents reporting on the "war to end all wars." *The New York Evening Journal* carried Bly's reports under the logo "Nellie Bly on the Firing Line," parceling out her accounts (nearly every word she wrote) of what was happening on the war's Eastern front. There was nothing else like it in the newspapers.

In her new role of war correspondent, Nellie was her old self. Fearless- she came under fire more than once- impervious to her own hardships and discomforts, she was willing and able to endure anything for the story- for the truth. Moreover, she was eager to tell the world about this war that was supposed to end barbarism between nations. In keeping with her style, her reflective, sensitive reports were replete with compassion and the war's human element. Bly, who had reinvented herself yet again, remained in Europe until 1919.

At the war's end, Nellie received word that her mother had fallen ill. She immediately sailed for home.

Revitalized by the high drama of journalism, Bly would continue adding brilliance to her star-studded career. She was still writing for the *New York Evening Journal*. The dynamic writer seemed to take up right where she had left off, beginning with the cause of widows and orphans that the horrors of war had created. As an editorial columnist, Nellie Bly's comeback warranted a four-column headline; and her first piece put her name slap on the front page. It was a colorful interview with Jack Dempsey. "The king is dead," she wrote on July 5, 1919, after the Willard-Dempsey bout, "long live the king! Willard's day is done. Dempsey's has begun."

"The go-getting-woman-braves-a-man's-world" facet of Bly's reporting had lost its novelty by this point in time, but *The Journal* trusted in what it hoped was the enduring power of her byline to draw and hold a large segment of the newspaper-reading public. A fresh idea, however, was taking shape in Nellie's fertile mind.

When a woman who had fallen into despair over her financial circumstances wrote the paper, asking Nellie if she should give up her two-year-old son, Bly answered her, strongly advising against it. Nellie's advice appeared in the paper, though the woman's real identity was never revealed. Soon, the compassionate journalist found herself a clearinghouse for women in distress. *The Journal* provided her with a private office and secretarial help in handling the avalanche of mail the paper was receiving to her attention. Of a sudden, a whole new facet of Nellie Bly's diamond-bright career blazed.

I love what she advised her readers on November 6, 1919: "Know yourself. That is the first essential for success. If one would become great, two things are absolutely necessary. The first is to know yourself, the second is not to let the world know [the real] you.... If the world knows you, you are... prey. Your heart and soul are exposed and unprotected...."

I suppose focusing on the troubles of others in her help/advice column served to take her mind off her financial woes. At any rate, she was good, as usual, at what she was doing. Characteristically, she threw her whole self into her current project. Now, Bly opened hearts and homes to abandoned children, while she advised and gave purpose and direction to unwed mothers.

I should relate to my readers that Nellie was always good to her own family. She insisted that Robert Seaman agree, before she married him, to supporting her mother and sister. She convinced him to improve her position in his will thrice, which, of course, was for their sakes as well as hers. Bly also saw to her own nieces and nephew's education. She gave her brothers jobs. In essence, she demonstrated- by example- to her mother Mary Jane how a responsible woman manages a family and cares for loved ones. I do not think Bly ever completely forgave her mother for not insisting that Judge Cochran make a will providing for his younger family. The five-year horror of living in a house with the drunken, pistol-packing Jack Ford had left an indelible mark on Nellie's soul. Mary Jane's weaknesses in protecting and managing her family in that early period reached its long arm into later years, pitting Nellie's siblings against one another.

Bly rarely used the telephone, always preferring to do her interviews and other work connected to her column in person. She dashed about even in the worst weather, often skipping meals and generally neglecting her health. When she did come down with something, she usually refused doctors and/or medicine. More than once during her long and enduring career she risked her life to grab headlines and the nation's attention.

In 1920, a treatise she wrote for the paper on happiness read: "To be happy, to know how to find happiness under all circumstances and out of all conditions is the acme of wisdom and the triumph of genius. Only those who have mastered the art of happiness can prosper and progress. The happy spirit sees no obstacles, is not blinded by gloom and thus invokes the strength and ambition that surmounts all difficulties. The world would be... better... if everybody cultivated happiness.

Don't be a grouch and waste life; don't be disgruntled and dissatisfied; don't be a growler; don't be a crank."

Good advice that. It was the old counsel of filtering out the inevitable negatives in life, of the "mirror image," i.e., negative attracts negative, and positive attracts positive, coupled with the ability to garner life's perfect moments.

The happy person is one who basks in the joy of a special moment. Happy people do not dwell on the past, nor do they worry about a future that may never come to pass. They live, as much as possible, in the *present* with the apprehension that is why it is called such; for the appreciation wrapped round it render it a true gift. Reading Nellie's wisdom, the thought crossed my mind that a happy life is a collection of precious moments all strung together like a pearl necklace. Reminiscent of a string of pearls, these collected moments/memories are worn over the heart, enticing the repeated touch of the wearer. Something else just occurred to me. I wonder if, years later, that was Glenn Miller's thinking when he wrote the now-classic WWII hit "String of Pearls" as an anniversary gift for his wife.

The New York Evening Journal published Bly's final column on January 9, 1922. In it Nellie recounted the tales of two women, eerily named "Mary" and "Jane." In Bly's vivid account, the two had begun life on equal footing, but ended up in vastly different circumstances- as did their offspring. The piece was to show that people make their own luck, their own destinies. As Bly had avowed so many years before, "Energy rightly applied and directed can accomplish anything." *It could have been her epitaph.*

On the frosty morning of January 27, 1922, Nellie Bly- who had never minded moving on to a new place- passed away of pneumonia at the age of fifty-eight.

Among a myriad of American newspapers, every one of the New York and Pittsburgh papers acknowledged her passing with elaborate obituaries. After all, Bly was one of their own. *The New York World* ran a lengthy story, noting her close friendship with another of their alumni, Erasmus Wilson, the "Quiet Observer," whose piece on "What Girls Are Good For" had prompted Nellie's fiery entry into journalism so many years before. How ironic that Wilson's death had occurred a mere two weeks prior to hers!

Nellie Bly image and trade cards from the personal collection of the great-great grand niece of Nellie Bly, Linda Champanier, Stamford, Connecticut

The most elaborate tribute came from another good friend, Arthur Brisbane, who devoted his entire column in *The New York Journal* to Bly's memory, calling her the "best reporter in America" and concluding: "Her life was useful, and she takes with her from this earth all that she cared for, an honorable name, the respect and affection of her fellow workers, the memory of good fights well-fought and of many good deeds never to be forgotten by those who had no friend but Nellie Bly. Happy the man or woman who can leave as good a record!"

The pretty, petite female journalist, who had given birth to investigative reporting, emerged the personification of media exposé. Before the muckrakers of the twentieth century publicized corruption, and before modern investigative reporters started seeking the "story behind the story," Bly paved the way to valuable journalism. In the 1880s and 1890s, she courageously went behind the scenes to sweep out into the open, from all the shadowy, dark corners, the grime of society's ills and evils. The first reporter ever to go after the real story, Bly's fame was worldwide, her readers everywhere.

Nellie Bly's life was so remarkable that I have only touched upon the events herein. There have been several books written about her amazing story. Two that I strongly suggest and that appear in the selected bibliography, this volume, are *Getting the Real Story: Nellie Bly and Ida B. Wells (Women Who Dared)* by Sue Davidson, and *Nellie Bly: Daredevil, Reporter, Feminist* by Brooke Kroeger.

Nellie will live on wherever a journalist is ferreting out the truth, undercover and behind the scenes, and wherever, amidst shot and shell, a war correspondent is reporting from the firing lines. The rebellious little girl from the obscure hamlet of Cochran's Mills, Pennsylvania, who could hardly spell or punctuate a sentence, was proclaimed in the end– the "Best Reporter in America."

In 1998, Nellie Bly was inducted into the National Women's Hall of Fame in Seneca Falls, New York. To echo the Stephen Foster song from which Elizabeth Cochran(e)'s erstwhile editor extracted her pen name: "Nelly Bly! Nelly Bly! Bring de broom... we'll sweep [it] clean... Nelly Bly had a heart warm as it can be...."

And to quote actress Muriel Nussbaum: "I wonder when they'll send a girl to travel 'round the sky, read the answer in the stars– they wait for Nellie Bly!"

"The Ringing Rocks"

"The Native American attitude is that everything is animated through Divinity."
- Author Ceane O'Hanlon-Lincoln

Nestled in a grove of woods in Bucks County, not far from where George Washington made his famous crossing of the Delaware River, lies a strange phenomenon- a large clearing- ten feet thick and seven acres in size- strewn with reddish-brown boulders of various shapes and sizes. Strange too is the fact that this rocky field seems devoid of any vegetation save the lichens growing on the boulders. But the real oddity is a trait of the rocks themselves- *they ring*. When struck lightly with a hammer, these rocks issue sounds not unlike the delightful chiming of bells.

Why they ring is a mystery. I should state here that not all the rocks ring, though they all seem similar in appearance and composition. Only about a third of them generate a musical sound when struck. Those that ring are termed "live" rocks, and those that do not are referred to as "dead."

There is an uncanny sense of mystery and the *élan vital* about this fascinating place, heightened, of course, by the unique musical quality of the rocks. I would not be exaggerating when I say that these boulders possess a crystalline nature which produces characteristic tones that positively mesmerize. *It is intriguing that the note from each rock is so distinct that musicians have created whole concerts here!*

Inhabitants have been cognizant of the fact that these rocks ring for quite some time. In 1890, Dr. J.J. Ott collected enough rocks with different pitches to play some pretty lively tunes for the enjoyment and resultant delight of the Buckwampum Historical Society. Accompanied by the accomplished brass section of the local Pleasant Valley Band, that just may have been the first-ever rock concert. By the way, Ott discovered what other investigators have since concluded- the rocks need not be in their natural location to ring, nor do they need to be wholly intact.

Native Americans used to go to the Ringing Rocks area to gather rocks for their sweat lodges and ceremonies. I could not find, in my research, if the Indians knew these rocks ring. Nonetheless, it is my theory that they believed the site to be a sacred place that Earth Mother had provided for their medicinal and spiritual needs.

More recently, local musicians have organized jam sessions on the rocks, striking them with various implements, including hammers, railroad spikes, and even other rocks. A few of those concerts were featured on the Learning Channel's *Strange Science* series. That was, in fact, where this author first discovered Pennsylvania's Ringing Rocks.

According to the Unmuseum, "In 1965, a geologist named Richard Faas from Lafayette College in nearby Easton... took a few of the rocks back to his lab for testing. He found that when the rocks were struck they created a series of tones at frequencies lower than the human ear can hear. Only because the tones interact with each other is a sound [generated that is] high pitched enough to be audible. Though Faas' experiments with the rocks explained the nature of the tones, he was unable to figure out the specific physical mechanism in the rock that [created those tones]... though scientists suspect it has something to do with stress within the rocks."

Where did these boulders come from? That is a good question. Some folks believe these rocks fell from the stars. Could these heavenly tintinnabulations cached in rock have been meteors? Others think that, though the glaciers did not reach this far, a unique paraglacial climate that lasted here till about 7,000 BC produced periods of freezing and

Ringing Rocks vistas. Note the surrounding forest.

thawing, allowing volcanic intrusions to heat and crack the bedrock, leaving "rivers" of rock. A simpler-stated explanation is that the ringing boulders possess a high content of iron and aluminum and were formed by the slow process of weathering and erosion.

Though this is more than likely a *natural* phenomenon, some writers have attributed supernatural reasons for the boulder field. I am certain this is due largely to the lack of vegetation and the observation that no animals or even insects inhabit the seven-acre rock-strewn area. That, however, is not surprising, since the boulder field is inhospitable to wild life. It is, for instance, much hotter than the surrounding forest in summer; and the barren area provides no food or shelter. Too, I assume the bolder-strewn field would be difficult, if not impossible, for most animals to navigate.

Claims have been made that compasses do not work at Ringing Rocks. From what I have read, attempts to see if the area has any unusual properties, beyond the rocks themselves, such as high background radiation, abnormal magnetic fields, or strange electromagnetic activity, have yielded next to nothing.

Though I cannot answer many questions about these resonate rocks, I can tell you where to find them. They are located at Ringing Rocks Park at Upper Black Eddy near Easton, Pennsylvania, Bucks County. The site is a 120-plus acre park, including the Ringing Rocks acreage and Pennsylvania Game Lands. Upper Black Eddy can also boast Bucks County's largest waterfall.

If you plan to visit Ringing Rocks, the most well-known location is southeast of the Allentown-Bethlehem area. From Easton, go south along Route 611. Continue until you arrive at the intersection with Route 32 at Kintnersville. Take Route 32 south to Narrows Hill Road then to Ringing Rocks Road. Watch for the clearly marked signs for Ringing Rocks Park.

The town of Upper Black Eddy is one of many small Delaware-River hamlets located in the northernmost regions of one of our commonwealth's most charming as well as historic counties. While visiting Bucks County, make certain to take in the site of Washington's Crossing. If you read "Surrender Never!" in the premier volume of my *County Chronicles*, then you know how replete this spot is with the thrills and chills of Pennsylvania's rich, layered history.

Not too distant is Pennsbury Manor, the home of William Penn, which I included in the opening Chronicle, this volume. At Perkasie, visitors to the area can take in the Pearl S. Buck House, which is nestled on the sixty-acre Green Hills Farm. This is the home where the award-winning author wrote many of her books. Buck is one of only two women to win *both* the Pulitzer Prize (1935) and the Nobel Prize (1938). In the homestead's library is the ornate, hand-carved Chinese desk where this exceptional American novelist wrote *The Good Earth*.

Visitor tapping a "live" rock with a hammer to hear its musical/ringing timbre
Photos courtesy Golden Pheasant Inn conveniently located next to Ringing Rocks Park in magical Bucks County, PA

Once known as Upper Black's Eddy, Upper Black Eddy borrows its name from the Black family prominent in the history of the region. The area now known as Point Pleasant was once called Lower Black's Eddy. The region is mostly rural, residential and rustically beautiful, with a few businesses scattered among the quaint homes. One of Pennsylvania's three original counties (the other two are Chester and Philadelphia), Bucks County abounds with Bed and Breakfasts. Each is unique; many are charmingly pastoral; all are magical, and some provide a magic carpet ride all the way back to the eighteenth century!

The Pennsylvania Canal flows down from Easton, passes through Upper Black Eddy (where it was known as "Candy Bend") and continues on its southerly way to New Hope and beyond. Though railroads, trucking and oil heating all contributed to the abandonment of the canal in 1931, the Pennsylvania Canal still exists, notably as a tourist attraction. Much of Upper Black Eddy had its beginnings parallel with the canal's heyday. As the town grew and prospered, the Upper Black Eddy Hotel was erected. This was the preferential vacation spot for President Grover Cleveland, the twenty-second (1885-89) and twenty-fourth (1893-97) President of the United States.

To return to our main focus: Southeastern Pennsylvania is littered with places where rocks ring like bells when struck with a hammer or hammer-like implement. These sites include the Stony Garden at Haycock, Bucks County, and the Devil's Race Course located in Franklin County.

Strictly speaking, the marvel of ringing rocks is not quite limited to Pennsylvania. These mysterious rocks have been found scattered all over the world. And what's even more captivating is the fact that ringing rocks at other locations are often composed of different materials. What physical characteristics they have in common with Pennsylvania's unusual rocks might well explain why the rocks ring- which is still unknown to geologists.

To quote Edgar Allan Poe, at this point in "... time, time, time/ In a sort of Runic rhyme/ To the tintinnabulation that so musically wells/ From the bells, bells, bells.... "

The mystery continues.

"INCIDENT AT MUDDY CREEK"

"Every day we have accounts of such cruelties and barbarities as are shocking to human nature."
-George Washington

Washington's quote with which I chose to launch this Chronicle really set me to thinking. The great man had seen plenty of action by the period following America's War for Independence. He had experienced much in the horrors of war, so for him to speak those words, the situation on the frontier must have been *appalling*.

The end of the Revolutionary War did not terminate the numerous Indian attacks against the frontier settlers in the Ohio River Valley. In fact, due to continuous British encouragement, raids *increased* until President George Washington sent General "Mad" Anthony Wayne to take the war into the Ohio/Indian country. There, at the Battle of Fallen Timbers in 1794, Wayne would crush the multi-tribe coalition, finally ending the half-century of Indian wars on the Pennsylvania frontier.

The frontier farmers understood hard work, sacrifice and struggle. And they understood war. It was in the blood of those hawkish Celts, English and Germans. Like the Indians, they were fighting for more than just land- though the owning of the land they worked was a dream come true for these folks who had escaped the caste system in Europe. They were also fighting for a way of life. The settlers were unlike the Indians, however, in the way in which they waged war.

The Indian raids on the frontier had begun with the Seven Years'/French and Indian War (1754). The attacks had thundered, virtually nonstop, down the tunnel of time with the subsequent, far-reaching Pontiac's War (1763) and the vengeful Dunmore's War (1774), followed then by the long Revolutionary War with its bloody aftermath. What the white settlers were not used to- what they could never accept or tolerate- was the fact that the Indians conducted *total* warfare when they took up the hatchet.

The Natives made no distinction between combatants and noncombatants. Women, babies, children, the elderly were all fair game. Understand, the Indians were not profiling, to use a word we hear a lot today. This was how they treated *all* enemies, Red and White. As a Pennsylvania governor of the era described it: In war, the "Indians... make no distinction as to age or sex... all are alike the objects of their cruelty- slaughtering the tender infant and frightened mother with equal joy and fierceness."

Not to say that the frontiersmen never took the war to the Indians. There are certainly incidents of this happening in our history. The September 1756 destruction of the large Shawnee-Delaware village of Kit-Han-Ne (Kittanning), Pennsylvania, about which I wrote, this volume; the shameful murder of the peaceful Conestogas by the "Paxton Boys" (Scotch-Irish frontiersmen) during the winter of 1763; the Revolutionary War-prompted Sullivan Expedition into Seneca lands, which I included in *County Chronicles Volume II*; and the March 1782 massacre of the Delaware village at Gnadenhutten, discussed in *CC I*, are four prime examples.

The Indians at Gnadenhutten were peaceful converts, baptized by German Moravian missionaries. However, the settlers discovered that the marauding Indians used Gnadenhutten as a way station for their raids, and they wintered there. To clinch it, when the militia arrived at the village, one of the men in the party who had just lost his wife in a raid found her bloody clothes in one of the lodges. That was all it took. The frontiersmen, after disarming the Indians via trickery, fell upon them, brutally killing about ninety men, women and children. Gnadenhutten, like the surge of the visceral beat of the war drums, incited the Delaware and Shawnee to an all-time high-point in their hostilities. The thirst for revenge had carried from the White settlements to the Native villages and back again (as we will soon see in this Chronicle).

Once more the lonely settlers were beset with Indian violence. The raucous cry of a jay, the desolate call of the crow, or even a sudden stillness in the forest would cause callused hands to reach swiftly for Pennsylvania Rifles. What more could they do other than keep vigilant? Leaving their women and children on their small, scattered farms unprotected to ride away to the far-off Indian villages to wage war was not the common practice for the frontier farmers. They knew they would likely be *watched* by the enemy during their entire trek en route to those villages. Overall, "taking the war to the Indians" was not always the wisest thing to do. And there are several examples of failed- in fact, *disastrous*- expeditions to prove my words, such as the Crawford Expedition that took place shortly after the incident at Muddy Creek.

The Indian manner of conducting war both shocked and enraged the settlers. Those fiery Scotch-Irish, Irish, Welsh, English and German frontiersmen often went insane with fury (fueled, more times than not, by their heavy indulgence in 100-proof rye whiskey). One minister spoke for all when he said of his parishioners: "What could I do with men heated to madness? All that I could do was done; I expostulated, but life and reason were set at defiance...."

From the settler point of view, the Native style of warfare was downright demonic. The grisly images of a grown man, a warrior, dashing a baby's head against a tree or burying a tomahawk into the scalps of terrified children, women and the aged were burned forever into their souls. They never forgot. Most never forgave. They carried these images- these tortured memories- with them ever-westward- where, tragically, the watchword "The only good Indian is a dead Indian" continued to fester and spread.

Let me remind my readers that most of the guerrilla raids were launched from the Ohio region. Throughout the entire Ohio River Valley- the site of the bloodiest Indian invasion in American history- hundreds of frightful tales unfolded. During those turbulent years (1754-1795) of eternal vigilance, all too often the natural sounds of the forest were overwhelmed by sudden, ferocious war cries interspersed with the screams of settler women and children and the sharp reports of gunfire.

Colonel William Crawford, who would later be hideously tortured and burned to death by the Indians, penned this telling missive about the dreadful conditions in the Ohio River Valley: "They killed and scalped one man at Raccoon Creek about twenty miles from this place [Crawford was writing from Pittsburgh.]; forty-five miles down the Ohio, they killed and scalped a man and burned a woman and her four children; at Wheeling, they killed and scalped another man, the body of whom was much mangled with tomahawks; at Dunkards Creek, they killed and scalped one man and a woman and took three children...." It was a routine account among hundreds of such reports.

Here, allow me to relate the incident that occurred on Muddy Creek, now known as Whiteley Creek, in Greene County, Pennsylvania.

The focus of our tragic tale is the Corbly family (also Corbley, though the more accepted spelling is "Corbly"). The head of the family was Reverend John Corbly. This steadfast, persevering man had been born in Ireland in 1733, and had come to the New World as an indentured servant at age fourteen, agreeing to serve for seven years the man who had paid his passage. After the completion of his indenture, Corbly journeyed down the Great Valley, better known as the Shenandoah Gap, through the magical Blue Ridge to Virginia. He located in or near Culpepper County, where he converted from either Catholicism or the Presbyterian faith to the emerging Baptist persuasion.

Arrested and jailed with others who refused to pay tithes to the colony of Virginia's Anglican Church, Corbly preached from his jail cell. After his release, he settled in Pennsylvania- which had always welcomed all faiths- and founded the Goshen Baptist Church, later renamed in his honor the John Corbly Memorial Baptist Church. Historically, Corbly was the first pastor of the first recorded religious congregation (organized sometime prior to April 1777) in Greene County, Pennsylvania. The present, red-brick church was erected in 1862. It is noteworthy to mention that John Corbly was an ardent patriot during America's long struggle for Independence.

Not long after his first wife had passed away, John remarried Elizabeth Martin, with whom he had seven children.

I set this account down before you with empathy for each of its protagonists. The date our story unfolds is May 10, 1782. The British General Lord Cornwallis had ignominiously surrendered to General George Washington the previous October, but peace would not be signed until 1783; and though the Revolutionary War was winding down, the Indian hostilities were not- would not- until 1795.

It was a Sunday, the "second Sabbath" in May, on that particularly fine (1782) spring morning. The Corbly family had just set out walking, en route to "meeting" at nearby Garard's Fort. The settlers' fort/blockhouse, where the service was scheduled to take place, was only about a half-mile distant from the Corbly cabin. The sun was shining brightly, and the new grasses were lush and intensely green. Many of the trees had blossomed, sweetly perfuming the air. How sweet the scent of lilacs that fateful day! In the surrounding woods, the redbuds were in full rosy glory. Violets and mayapples covered the forest floor. The whole family reveled in the delights of that glorious morn, the girls, in their usual manner, giggling and exchanging chatter among themselves.

The pleasant music of birdcalls pierced the otherwise near-silence. Little did the Corblys realize that a few of those joyful sounds were an ominous signal for what was about to befall them. Oblivious, the reverend's mind was focused on his sermon, which he reviewed in his usual speaking voice. Partway through the delivery, he paused, mentally making a last-minute change to what he had written the evening before in the candle-glow of his cabin. As a result, his family got ahead of him on the forested trail.

Actually, there are two versions why John became separated on the trail from his family. The first I have already mentioned. The other account suggests that Corbly had given the family Bible to his wife to carry to meeting. No sooner had they started out, when she realized that she had left it behind. The reverend turned back to retrieve the Bible from the cabin, attempting subsequently to reunite with his wife and children on the trail.

His reason for lagging behind may have been a combination of the two. I chanced upon a letter that Corbly penned to his brother on July 8, 1785, in which he stated that he was carrying his Bible, but he was also going over his sermon.

At any rate, we know the reverend was about 200 yards behind his family, who had just disappeared over the brow of the hill on the path leading toward Garard's Fort. At that point, the fort was about 700 yards away. Noting that the family had vanished from view, John hastened his steps to catch up with them when he was suddenly, in his own words, "... greatly aroused with their frightful shouts and screams."

A small war party had been hiding in the gully, waiting to spring upon anyone coming along the trail. The red, black and yellow paint on their faces and bodies, coupled with their terrifying war cries, rendered them diabolically fierce.

Imagine, readers, a warrior covered entirely in vermilion except perhaps for a black soot-mask or a jet-black hand painted over his face. Picture another painted *entirely* black. Such a warrior meant either to take life or die trying.

As the Indians leaped into view, whooping and brandishing their weapons, Elizabeth and her children shrieked. The youngsters, bunching together against their mother, gripped her skirts and one another for protection.

Startled out of his reverie, the minister caught sight of two Indians running, one of whom let out a bloodcurdling yell. His eyes vainly seeking a club, Corbly dashed forth to within forty yards of his family, and what he saw must have paralyzed him, because he briefly froze on the path. As he stood at the top of the hill, looking down on what must have been a gruesome sight, his wife's frenzied voice reached him, "John, save yourself! Run! Get help!"

For that protracted moment, as often happens in the most horrible of nightmares, the reverend could not move, so traumatized was he. "My wife had a suckling baby in her arms..." whom an Indian violently snatched from her. With "Baby Nancy's" feet in his hands, the Indian, yelling his spine-tingling scalphulloes, dashed the screaming child's head against a tree. "They... then scalped this little infant," related Corbly in his affecting memoirs.

Elizabeth, her arms still extended for want of her infant, let out a heartrending scream, keening her anguish. As John would pen later, "They then struck my wife several times... not getting her down." One of the Indians saw the reverend on the path and aimed to shoot him. It was at that instant when his wife had yelled, "John... run ... get help!"

John Corbly (surname spelling most accepted today) historic marker in fore of the church he founded sometime prior to April 1777

"The Indian who aimed to shoot me," Corbly would later record, "ran then to Elizabeth and shot her through the body and scalped her."

Stripping off his coat, and armed only with his Bible, the reverend, in a burst of adrenaline, ran all-out for the fort through the woods with one of the Indians close on his heels. I am certain the hopeful thought was racing with him that, more often than not, the Natives took children captive for the purpose of adoption. He needed to get to the fort as rapidly as his legs could carry him to muster a rescue party!

Simultaneously, unbeknownst to the clergyman, another of the warriors sunk his tomahawk into the skull of Corbly's only son, Isaiah, after which he scalped the six-year-old. The little boy would perish the following day. The toddler Mary Katherine was brutally killed and scalped within moments. Elizabeth and Delilah, the two older girls, attempted to escape. Pursued by a warrior who overtook her in several giant strides, Elizabeth did not get far when the Indian caught her, taking a piece out of her cranium and sinking his warhawk into the back of her neck.

Delilah, who had sprinted into the woods, cached herself in a hollow log about twenty yards from the rest of the family. There, she "watched the whole proceedings." Seeing the Indians leave the area, or so she thought, she crept out of her hiding place only to be espied by one of the painted foe. The Indian ran up behind her, and knocking her to the ground, grabbed her by her long auburn hair, viciously jerking her head back. The frenzied girl struggled then ducked beneath the ferocious tomahawk blow aimed at her, raising her hands to ward it off. The blade skimmed across the back of her head, slicing through her thick hair and skin but not damaging her skull. Both Elizabeth and Delilah were scalped. Elizabeth never recovered from her physical injuries or the terrifying psychological ordeal she underwent that violent May morning. She died a few years later. Corbly's daughter Delilah did recover.

All the while the reverend was racing for all he was worth to the fort, his pursuer was steadily gaining on him. John was more than halfway to the blockhouse, when the Indian caught him, and the two grappled. Corbly dropped his Book, as boyhood memories of fisticuffs on the Old Sod returned to his clenched hands. Knocking his opponent out, he seized his Bible and dashed again for Garard's, shouting to those inside, as he neared the blockhouse's stout log walls.

Margaret, the eldest of his children, was already at the fort, where families from round about had congregated for the Sunday service. Hearing her father's frantic voice, she shouldered her way through the assembly and rushed forward to meet him, as he stumbled through the gate, out-of-breath and pale as the Angel of Death. Margaret's hand flew to her mouth; and she shivered with apprehension at what her father shouted- his words coming in sudden spurts- to the men gathered around him.

"Reverend!" One of the men called, thrusting something smooth and cold into John's grasp. Despite himself, his fingers gripped the gun with a response he never knew he possessed. Time was of the essence. Their Pennsylvania Rifles in hand, those rough-and-ready farmers hastened after Corbly to the spot where his family had been attacked.

There, on the fresh green floor of the forest trail, the frontiersmen and their minister discovered Corbly's wife Elizabeth dead in a pool of blood- her babe, its brains dashed out, thrown across her breast. Mother and child lay near a tree, the trunk of which was covered with horrible spatters. Only inches apart, three other Corbly children lay mangled and dead. Several feet distant, one of the men stopped abruptly and raised his hand. There, the two oldest girls, bleeding profusely, looked near-death. As previously revealed, they had all been scalped.

The large family dog also lay dead on the blood-soaked path. He was the reason the reverend's daughters Elizabeth and Delilah were still alive. When the Indians had jumped them, and one of their numbers caught hold of the smallest girl to tomahawk her, the dog seized the warrior by the leg with his bared teeth. The faithful canine had continued fighting- to the death- to save the children he so loved.

Forcing back nausea, John knelt beside his wife's body, slipping his hand behind her neck, under the gore-covered kerchief that Elizabeth had bleached with care for this day, now white no longer. He bowed his head, and his lips moved in silent prayer. A firm hand gripped his shoulder, then another. Behind him, he could hear the other men conferring in low tones. Tears wet his cheeks; but when he stood, his face was like iron. Later, his grief would nearly engulf him; and he would struggle against wave after wave of regret and sorrow. For the moment, there remained the sad work of burying the dead.

Margaret, the Corbly daughter who had met her father at the fort's gate, describes the grisly scene when her family was brought in: "Mother was... dangling across the withers of a horse, the skirt of the dress, a black silk, had been cut off close to the waist, and she was frightfully mangled and smeared with gore, presenting a spectacle more ghastly than language can portray. Isaiah lived twenty-four hours and revived enough to cry deliriously for the Indians to spare his life...."

It was ascertained afterwards that there had been seven Indians involved in the massacre. As I mentioned earlier, at the time this incident took place, the Indians had been committing terrible ravages against the inhabitants on the Pennsylvania frontier. The Corbly tragedy was one of many incidents in typical Indian warfare.

Three years later, the reverend's troubles commenced again, when he was accused of siding with the "Whiskey Boys" during the Whiskey Rebellion of 1794. He was arrested and jailed, along with other insurgents, in the new nation's capital at Philadelphia. Along with the others, he was released about a year later. An historical marker, at Corbly Memorial Baptist Church, Garards Fort, Greene County, was dedicated on November 15, 1994. The text therein reads: "A noted Baptist minister serving area congregations, Corbly was among some 150 men arrested by federal troops on the 'Dreadful Night' of November 13, 1794. A local opponent of the excise tax on whiskey, Corbly was the area's best known participant in the Whiskey Rebellion and was seen as a threat by the Federalists."

If you are wondering why November 13, 1794, was termed in Pennsylvania history the "Dreadful Night," you must read the thrilling account in my *County Chronicles Volume I.* President George Washington sent an army of over 12,000 to southwestern Pennsylvania to arrest the "Whiskey Boys." The insurgents were rousted from their beds in the wee hours and marched- as they were, many barefoot and in nightshirts- through mud, snow and the killing frosts of autumn to Philadelphia. No

The Corbly family massacre site. The Indians had been hiding in the gully that runs left to right in the background.

blankets, boots, clothing, nor much else were provided them during the agonizing month-long march. Upon their arrival in the former capital, Christmas day, to the blast of cannons, church bells ringing, the sick and weary captives were paraded through the streets, past Washington's house, amidst jeering crowds, who had gathered "to see the hairy yahoos."

Philadelphia discovered, however, to its chagrin, that witnesses brought over the mountains were unwilling to testify against their neighbors. Absent from their families and farms for nearly a year for trial, the prisoners were finally released for lack of evidence, though at least one man had died. Later the unfair tax was repealed.

I should mention here that since it was such an unfair tax, most of the frontier clergy sided with the so-called "Whiskey Boys."

For Western Pennsylvania settlers, all other crises had been secondary to the terrifying Indian situation on the frontier. During the bloody years from 1754 to 1795, frontier families lived in constant fear, as I have often reiterated. The Quaker government in Philadelphia had only half-heartedly attempted to quell the Indian threat. Not surprisingly, the connection between Indian depredations and the unfair federal tax on whiskey seemed *obvious* to these settlers. Both were symbolic of the lack of influence the Western settlers had with the Eastern political establishment in Philadelphia. Animosity towards the Federal government swept through all social groups on the frontier. About two-thirds of these folks were Scotch-Irish who were especially outspoken about their beliefs and their rights.

For some time after the Indian attack on his family, Reverend Corbly was inconsolable. "Grieving I must bear," he related in that 1785 missive to his brother. John eventually married for a third time. Ultimately, he recovered and recommenced with his ministry, serving in that capacity until 1803. By the time of his death, at age seventy in June of that year, he had founded a number of Baptist churches in western Pennsylvania. What finally brought him back to his work was the realization, after much sorting out, that God had spared him for a reason. While the apprehension quieted his troubled soul, ever after when alone with his memories, the terrified screams of his beloved wife Elizabeth and his children shattered many a tranquil moment.

Today, a monument depicting the massacre of the Corbly family stands at the yet-rustic, wooded site where the reverend's wife and children were slaughtered. The monument is located on the east side of the village of Garard's Fort, adjacent to the Garard Fort Cemetery. When I visited this lonesome spot, I could almost hear Elizabeth's frantic voice echoing, across the broad span of time that separates us, and through the tall, wind-stirred trees: "John, save yourself ... run!"

Reverend John Corbly, his children, and his wife Elizabeth sleep their eternal sleep within that historic graveyard. The stone on Elizabeth's grave bears this poignant epitaph: "Beneath the Indian tommy hawk/Me and my babe we fell/Was hurried suddenly away/With Jesus for to dwell."

The situation in Pennsylvania had drastically changed from the days when William Penn had walked, unarmed, among his Indian friends. Keep in mind, readers, that by this point in time, the Native Americans had experienced *layered* injustices. There had been, by the generation of our tale on Muddy Creek, numerous broken treaties and land swindles, as well as cruel White-perpetrated incidents that equate with the above Red-executed event. In history, as in life, there are rights and wrongs on each side of a conflict. There is an old

Close-up of the Corbly memorial stone with depicted massacre. Note the dog defending the family.

The Corbly family gravesites. Ground markers, fore, left to right: (daughter) Elizabeth, Mary Katherine, Isaiah, Baby Nancy. Standing markers, fore, left to right: (wife) Elizabeth and (with flag) Rev. John Corbly. John's third wife rests to his right (out-of-view). Photos courtesy the author's husband, Phillip R. Lincoln

Native American saying that "War does not determine who is right, only who is left."

The Eastern Woodland Indians, whose basic law of life focused on respect, had lost that consideration for the Whites. It had become difficult, if not impossible, to believe white men anymore. I am sharply reminded of the words a Native leader spoke at a peace conference during the angry era the Muddy Creek affair took place: "How smooth the language of the Whites, when they can make right look wrong and wrong like right!"

What is always tragic in history is that the good suffer for the wrongs done by the wicked.

The Shawnee leader Tecumseh, discussed in this volume, saw that his people were as rabbits before a pack of wolves, running in every direction, each nation on its own. He saw that as the great tangle of forests were giving way before White encroachment, so too were the Native Americans. "Our lands," he said, "are in the hands of the Great Spirit. We are determined to [unite and] defend our lands; and, if it is His will, we wish to leave our bones upon them."

The educated Mohawk Chief Joseph Brant, when he visited England in 1775 soon after the hostilities of the American Revolution had begun, declared to King George III: "Our wise men are called 'Fathers,' and they truly sustain that character. Do you call yourselves 'Christians'? Does the religion of Him whom you call your savior inspire your practices? *Surely not.* It is recorded of Him that a bruised reed he never broke. Cease then to call yourselves 'Christians,' lest you declare to the world your hypocrisy! Cease too to call other nations 'savage,' when you are tenfold more the children of cruelty than they...." Brant finished by telling the king that he bowed to no man, but he would shake his hand.

I will conclude this segment with the serene and comforting words of a venerable Algonquin sachem: "The first peace, which is the most important, is that which comes within the souls of people when they realize their relationship- their *oneness*- with the universe and its powers, when they realize that at the center of the universe dwells the Great Spirit and that this center is really everywhere. *It is within each of us.*"

"Historic Connellsville"

I wrote about Mac's barbecue stand and airfield in *County Chronicles Volume II*; however, at the time, I was unable to ferret out any photographs of the historic Connellsville landmark. Then, at a book signing when *CCII* debuted, I had the good fortune to meet Mac's granddaughter, Margaret Coughenour, who graciously supplied me with photos of her maternal grandfather, William H. McAfee, Fayette County's famous "Mac."

Mac's-Convict-Bar-B-Q; the first building

Popular in the 1920s and 30s, Mac's-Convict-Bar-B-Q and Air Field [sic] was located between Connellsville and Uniontown. Mac's was unique for a variety of reasons. Firstly, the place carried an atypical theme. All the windows and doors bore bars and padlocks; and its employees sported black and white, striped convict uniforms. To complete their garb, the staff's heads were topped with the round, striped, beakless/pillbox caps that convicts wore in that era.

It is my guess that the prison theme emerged due to the fact that Mac's was established during the "Roaring Twenties," when Prohibition saw the rise of organized crime with gangs who competed for the distribution of unlawful liquor. Moreover, Mac's was the spot where the state police took their meals *and* their calls, so perhaps *that* is what gave McAfee the idea for his unusual eatery.

According to Mac's granddaughter, Gladys Addis, Mac's was a great place to dance as well as to eat. There was a jukebox and a large dance floor. Patrons sat in prison-like "cells" rather than commonplace booths. "I remember that the dances at Mac's on Saturday evenings were pretty lively," Gladys told me in an interview. "Those nights, my grandfather always tried to hire a good Western band. The dances were held in the back, at the barn where there was a stage, which reminds me– Saturday nights also meant 'Amateur Hour.' Those who won received the grand prize of a dollar. Once *I* won the dollar... nobody else competed that night," Gladys laughed with the memory.

I should make it clear to my readers that Mac's was not an airport; rather, it was a grassy airstrip that extended approximately 2,500 feet in length behind the barbecue stand. Located across from the present-day campus of Penn State Fayette, on the then-two-lane Route 119, the site became popular in the late twenties for "fly-ins." Pilots began congregating there to gas up, chat and compare notes. These early aviators enjoyed the excellent, reasonably priced food Mac dished up, especially the ham barbecue that made him famous in the Connellsville-

Mac's-Convict-Bar-B-Q; the second building. The airfield was behind the building and to the right. Note the bars on the windows and doors.

The staff at Mac's always dressed as convicts. The woman to the far left is Mac's wife, Gladys M. McAfee. Photos courtesy Mac's maternal granddaughter, A. Margaret Coughenour, Connellsville, PA

William H. "Mac" McAfee and friend "Mac" at the airstrip, circa 1937

Uniontown area. On a par with Depression-era prices, the thick, succulent barbecue sandwiches cost all of fifteen cents. Mac's generous-sized hamburgers were a dime. Quite literally via word-of-mouth, Mac's Air Field became a favorite to a number of pilot clubs.

If my Fayette-County readers are wondering: The Connellsville Airport did not exist during Mac's *heyday.* That airport was established in 1935, toward the end of Mac's reign, when aviation had begun to see systematic regulations. Mac's operated from circa 1926 to 1939. During that period, in addition to his food stand and the airfield, Mac owned a share in a charter plane. Margaret Coughenour showed me photographs of the impressive aircraft from which happy, holiday-attired passengers are disembarking on an airfield at what may be the Cayman Islands.

What was really interesting to me is that Mac used the local Connellsville *coke* (a by-product of coal) to cook his hams, because the coke made no smoke, and it would stay red-hot. Many local old timers in the Fayette-County area remember taking their first airplane rides at Mac's. The rides averaged ten minutes and cost fifty cents for children and a dollar for adults. Passengers had a choice of whether they wished to fly over Connellsville or Uniontown.

One bright summer day, circa 1928, Mac hosted a very famous visitor. The icon was none other than Charles Lindbergh. After Lindbergh's historic solo flight across the Atlantic to Paris (May 20, 1927), he was constantly besieged by autograph seekers everywhere he went; thus, the shy pilot soon tired of the pressing crowds at airports. That is how he came to land at Mac's. And, like so many others, the famous aviator became an instant fan of Mac's tasty barbecue.

"I can vividly recall meeting Mr. Lindbergh," Mac's granddaughter Gladys related to me. "When he was at my grandfather's place, people always gathered around him. One time, he had his wife Anne with him, who often served as his copilot. This was before their baby was kidnapped. I recall that they both seemed somewhat reserved... reticent. But they were very nice... especially to us kids."

For years after, a framed dollar bill hung on Mac's wall, the first that "Lindy" spent there. I should mention too that Amelia Earhart was another celebrity pilot who flew in at Mac's. For more information about Mac's Air Field and Charles Lindbergh, please read "The Lindbergh Connection" found in *County Chronicles Volume II.*

About the Author

Ceane O'Hanlon-Lincoln is a native of Connellsville, Fayette County, Pennsylvania, though she resided in neighboring Westmoreland County's Ligonier Valley for eighteen years, where she taught high school French until 1985. Already engaged in commercial writing, she immediately began pursuing a career in writing history, as well as historical fiction. "History has always been my first love," the dynamic author has stated. "I'll read a history book the way many read a novel."

In 1987, O'Hanlon-Lincoln won honors at Robert Redford's Sundance Institute, when two of her screenplays made the "top twenty-five," chosen from thousands of nationwide entries. In 1994, she optioned one of those scripts, along with her partners on that work, to Kevin Costner; the other screenplay, *A Toast to Destiny*, she adapted, with a fellow teacher, to a compelling mystery novel of the same title.

Ceane has also had a poem published in *Great Poems of Our Time*. Winner of the Editor's Choice Award, "The Man Who Holds the Reins" appears in *County Chronicles II* and in the fore of her anthology, *Autumn Song*, a medley of stories threaded by their destiny themes and autumnal settings. A Fayette County English professor said of her *Autumn Song*: "The tales rank with those of Rod Sterling and the great O. Henry. O'Hanlon-Lincoln is a *master* storyteller."

Robert Matzen, writer/producer of Paladin Films said of *Autumn Song*: "I like the flow of the words, almost like song lyrics... very *evocative*."

From February 2000 to March 2002, Ceane authored, in her hometown newspaper, *The Daily Courier*, her own bimonthly column, "County Chronicles," in which she focused on local history. A vivid assortment of places, people and events that affected and shaped Pennsylvania, *County Chronicles*– the series– is the result of the numerous requests for a compilation and continuation of her exciting Chronicles.

Author Ceane O'Hanlon-Lincoln with her Athena
Author image courtesy the author's husband, Phillip R. Lincoln

In February 2004, O'Hanlon-Lincoln won the prestigious Athena, an award presented to professional "women of spirit" on local, national and international levels. The marble, bronze and crystal Athena sculpture symbolizes career excellence, community leadership and the light that emanates from the recipient.

Soon after the debut of the premier volume, Ceane won for her *County Chronicles* a Citation/Special Recognition Award from the Pennsylvania House of Representatives, followed by a Special Recognition Award from the Senate of Pennsylvania. The talented author has also made the *International Who's Who*.

Ceane shares "Tara," her restored, century-old Victorian home, with her husband Phillip and their champion Bombay cats, Black Jade and Black Jack O'Lantern. Her hobbies include travel, nature walks, theater, film, antiques, and reading "... everything I can on Pennsylvania, American, and Celtic history, legend and lore."

Called by many a "state-of-the-heart storyteller," Ceane is currently hard at work, preparing subsequent keepsake volumes of her Pennsylvania history series. "I hope readers will want the complete set of the very collectible *County Chronicles.* Pennsylvania is home. There is *no* place like home... and there are so many more Chronicles to share!"

~ ~ ~

WHAT READERS HAVE TO SAY...

"Dear Ms. O'Hanlon-Lincoln: *County Chronicles* is a beautiful book that demonstrates the love and loyalty you have for your very special home area.... I am sharing your fine book with members of my staff.... I appreciate your passion for honoring... the history of our great commonwealth."
– Pennsylvania Governor Edward G. Rendell

"A true state-of-the-heart storyteller, Ceane O'Hanlon-Lincoln is an *exceptionally* gifted writer with a talent for bringing history alive like no other author I have ever read. In each of O'Hanlon-Lincoln's books, I am *there.* I have smelled the coal smoke drifting on the Pennsylvania winter air. In each *County Chronicles* volume, I have smelled the smoke of battles fought and heard the roar of guns. I have *experienced* history; and thus, understand it better. And I have come to know the *human* side of many of our historic figures."
– Judy D. Reed, teacher and Mayor of Connellsville, PA

"Ceane O'Hanlon-Lincoln's *County Chronicles* is the perfect bedside/fireside reader. The more I read, the more I want to read. I *know* what kind of painstaking research goes into work like this. In *Autumn Song* and in each volume of *County Chronicles,* O'Hanlon-Lincoln's style is fascinating, from beginning to end. *She is a master storyteller.*"
– William Colvin, English teacher (Ret.), Connellsville, PA

"What an interesting and well-researched chronicle!" (Regarding "George Washington's Secret Weapon," the Pennsylvania Rifle, in *County Chronicles'* premier volume)
– Stephen Molstad, author of *The Patriot,* the novelization, Los Angeles, CA

"Ceane O'Hanlon-Lincoln, I applaud you for your initiative and vision in bringing area history to new audiences! Keep up the good work!"
– Robert Matzen, Paladin Productions, Pittsburgh, PA

"Ms. O'Hanlon-Lincoln: Your chronicles on Washington and Lee are excellent! 'Honor Answering Honor' is a fantastic piece– interesting, warm, memorable, moving... congratulations on excellence!"
– President Thomas Burish of Washington and Lee University, Lexington, VA

"Ms. O'Hanlon-Lincoln: I found your chronicle on George C. Marshall, 'Soldier of Peace,' most interesting, well-written and accurate. We are happy to include it, along with its wonderful photos, in our permanent files in the Marshall Research Library."
– Joanne Hartog, Director of Research Library/Archives, Marshall Foundation, Lexington, VA

"Ms. O'Hanlon-Lincoln: The *County Chronicles* Pennsylvania history series is a welcome addition to the Pennsylvania Senate Library. The rich history you provide will help anyone researching Pennsylvania."
– Jay Craig, Pennsylvania Senate Library

"*County Chronicles* is a wonderful collection of stories that fills a void in ... Pennsylvania history, a region with as colorful and varied a past as any in the USA. Each volume is stocked to the brim with stories worth telling over and over again. Many of the chronicles touch historical events and lives that go far beyond [Pennsylvania]... this series deserves a place on any bookshelf that is concerned with American history."
– George Baldrose, Director, the Balmoral School of Piping, Pittsburgh, PA

"I minored in history in college, and I want to say that *County Chronicles* is well-written, well-researched... a very *fine* work. I personally congratulate Ceane O'Hanlon-Lincoln on a job well done."
– John Y. Woodruff, Gold Medalist, 1936 Olympic Games

"The historical facts come alive with the author's account of vivid details. This series is a *must* for anyone interested in the development of Pennsylvania– of America! It is obvious that Ceane O'Hanlon-Lincoln puts her heart and soul into her beloved Chronicles. Read, learn, and most of all- *enjoy*!"
– Frank C. Gyimesi, M.D., Lost Creek, WV

"*County Chronicles* reads like whip cream; it is so smooth! It is my contention that this Pennsylvania history series should be a supplement for the local history courses taught across our commonwealth."
– Gloria Rock, Connellsville, PA

"*County Chronicles* is a writer's treat. The book is meticulously researched, beautifully written and artfully presented. Each page turn takes the reader to another event, era and tale from Pennsylvania's exciting history. I have truly enjoyed every moment spent with this book, and it will be a dear friend that I visit many times in future. Beyond that, however, is the fact that this is a tremendous research resource. I thought that they no longer made books of this quality until I purchased the premier volume of *County Chronicles*. I am glad to see that quality writing and publishing have not gone out of style. I plan to own and enjoy each of the books in the *County Chronicles* Pennsylvania history series."
– Patty A. Wilson, Author/Historian, Bedford, PA

"We were honored at *The Daily Courier* to be the *first* to publish many of Ceane O'Hanlon-Lincoln's 'County Chronicles.' Her exhaustive research and writings provide readers with detailed insight into what life was like for our ancestors in an area rich with American history."
– Barry A. Martin, former General Manager of *The Daily Courier*, Connellsville, PA

"Ms. O'Hanlon-Lincoln, you write history as a story! Such an approach is interesting reading and far more enlightening than accounts primarily concerned with dates and figures. Your thrilling description (*County Chronicles'* premier volume) of George Washington's dark-night journey to meet Half King prior to the Jumonville skirmish is a perfect example. I also appreciate that you have obviously done your homework. Few books mention things like the fact that Washington built a crude palisade near Gist's settlement before the battle at Fort Necessity. My favorite stories of *County Chronicles II* are "The Long Flight Home" about Jimmy Stewart, "Into the Woods," "A Tragic Victorian Romance," and "Wings of Athena." These tales are special because they are seldom told. I found them well-written, with nice "tight" writing, and quite interesting."
– Bob Cole, Author/Historian, Hilton, NY

"Ceane, every chance I get I read a Chronicle or two– or three. I always find myself wanting more; and if you remember me from school, I was not big on history. But the way you capture it makes it so interesting. In fact, I think it's great!"
– Roseann Carbonara, Alexandria, VA

"Ms. O'Hanlon-Lincoln: Recently, I finished reading *County Chronicles Volume II*. How I enjoyed reading about all the famous people connected to Pennsylvania! I especially enjoyed the Chronicles on Jimmy Stewart, Charles Lindbergh, and Henry Frick.... your books bring history alive for me! I am looking forward to each new volume. Thanks for including a map of all the counties in Pennsylvania. That is so helpful!"
– Andrea Corsillo, Alexandria, VA

"Ms. O'Hanlon-Lincoln: I just finished reading *County Chronicles Volume II*. I told my husband how much I enjoy your books. The funny thing is I was totally uninterested in history in school... but after each of your Chronicles, I want to hop in the car and visit the place I've just read about. I never realized how much history we have in Pennsylvania! You are my favorite author. Please keep writing, and I'll keep reading. I love your *County Chronicles*!
– Nancy Anderson, Uniontown, PA

Selected Bibliography

In addition to a myriad of interviews with rangers at historical sites, curators of museums, tour guides, other authors, reenactors, history teachers and professors, as well as with the many individuals connected to the people and the subjects of the Chronicles in this volume, I want to highlight my nearly two-hour personal interview with Shirley Jones, November 25, 2006, at Greensburg, Pennsylvania.

I also drew from and recommend further reading in the following...

Books

Anderson, Fred. *Crucible of War.* New York, NY: Alfred A. Knopf, 2000.

Apel, Otto F., Jr., M.D. and Apel, Pat. *MASH, an Army Surgeon in Korea.* Lexington, KY: University Press of Kentucky, 1998.

Asfar, Dan. *Ghost Stories of Pennsylvania.* Edmonton, Canada: Ghost House Books, 2002.

Bachelder, Louise. *Abraham Lincoln, Wisdom and Wit.* Mount Vernon, NY: The Peter Pauper Press, 1965.

Bakeless, John. *America As Seen By Its First Explorers.* New York, NY: Dover Publications, 1961.

Breuer, William B. *Unexplained Mysteries of World War II.* New York, NY: John Wiley & Sons, Inc., 1997.

Cole, Bob. *The Land of Dayaogeh.* Apollo, PA: Closson Press, 2006.

Couch, Ernie and Jill. *Pennsylvania Trivia* (Revised Edition). Nashville, TN: Rutledge Hill Press, a division of Thomas Nelson, Inc., 1995.

Davidson, Sue. *Getting the Real Story: Nellie Bly and Ida B. Wells (Women Who Dared).* Emeryville, CA: Seal Press, 1992.

Deleon, Clark. *Pennsylvania Curiosities.* Guilford, CT: The Globe Pequot Press, 2001.

DeMay, John A. *The Settlers' Forts of Western Pennsylvania.* Apollo, PA: Closson Press, 1997.

Eckert, Allan W. *That Dark and Bloody River.* New York, NY: Bantam Books, 1995.

Griffing, Robert. *The Art of Robert Griffing, His Journey into the Eastern Frontier,* with text by George Irvin, Editing and Additional Text by Ann Trondle-Price, Introduction by Donald Miller, and Conclusion by Ted Brasser. Ashville, NY: East/West Visions, Paramount Press, Inc., 2000.

Gummere, Amelia Mott. *Quakerism and Witchcraft, a Study in Social History.* Philadelphia, PA: The Biddle Press, 1908.

Guttman, Jon. *SPA124 Lafayette Escadrille, American Volunteer Airmen in WWI.* Osceola, WI: Osprey Direct USA c/o MBI Publishing, 2004.

Hoops, Roy. *Americans Remember the Home Front.* New York, NY: The Berkley Publishing Group, 2002.

Jennings, Francis. *Empire of Fortune, Crowns, Colonies & Tribes in the Seven Years War in America.* New York, NY: W. W. Norton & Company, 1988.

Jones, Shirley & Ingels, Marty with Herskowitz, Mickey. *Shirley & Marty, an Unlikely Love Story.* New York, NY: William Morrow and Company, Inc., 1990.

Kelly, C. Brian. *Best Little Stories from World War II.* Nashville, TN: Cumberland House, 1989.

Kirk, Robert. *Through So Many Dangers (The Memoirs and Adventures of Robert Kirk, Late of the Royal Highland Regiment).* Edited by Ian McCulloch and Timothy Todish, Introduction by Stephen Brumwell, Artwork by Robert Griffing. Fleischmanns, NY: Purple Mountain Press, Ltd., 2004.

Kroeger, Brooke. *Nellie Bly, Daredevil, Reporter, Feminist.* New York, NY: Random House, 1994.

Loudon, Archibald. *Loudon's Indian Narratives.* Lewisburg, PA: Wennawoods Publishing, 1996.

McCullough, David. *Brave Companions, Portraits in History.* New York, NY: Simon and Schuster, 1992.

McCullough, David. *Truman.* New York, NY: Simon and Schuster, 1992.

McLaughlin, Jack. *Gettysburg: The Long Encampment.* New York, NY: Appleton-Century, 1963.

Miller, Arthur P., Jr. and Miller, Marjorie L. *Guide to the Homes of Famous Pennsylvanians.* Mechanicsburg, PA: Stackpole Books, 2003.

Miller, Randall M. and Pencak, William. *Pennsylvania, a History of the Commonwealth.* University Park: The Pennsylvania State University Press *and* Harrisburg, PA: The Pennsylvania Historical and Museum Commission, 2002.

Moore, Frank. *Women of War.* Hartford, CT: SS Scranton & Company, 1866.

Nesbitt, Mark. *Ghosts of Gettysburg.* Gettysburg, PA: Thomas Publications, 1991.

O'Hanlon-Lincoln, Ceane. *County Chronicles* (Volume I). Chicora, PA: Mechling Books/Mechling Bookbindery, 2004.

O'Hanlon-Lincoln, Ceane. *County Chronicles Volume II.* Chicora, PA: Mechling Books/ Mechling Bookbindery, 2006.

Pullen, John J. *Twentieth Maine.* Philadelphia, PA: Lippincott, 1957.

Seitz, Ruth Hoover. *Amish Country.* New York, NY: Crescent Books, 1991.

Seitz, Ruth Hoover. *Pennsylvania's Historic Places.* Intercourse, PA: Good Books, 1989.

Seitz, Ruth Hoover. *Philadelphia & Its Countryside.* Harrisburg, PA: RB Books, 2003.

Sheets, Georg R. *Pennsylvania Heritage.* Harrisburg, PA: RB Books, 2001.

Sipe, C. Hale. *The Indian Chiefs of Pennsylvania.* Lewisburg, PA: Wennawoods Publishing, 1999. (Originally published in 1927, Butler, PA)

Sipe, C. Hale. *The Indian Wars of Pennsylvania.* Lewisburg, PA: Wennawoods Publishing, 1995. (Originally published in 1931, Harrisburg, PA)

Smail, Larry A. *The Attack on Kit-Han-Ne, Kittanning, Pennsylvania, September 8, 1756.* Chicora, PA: Mechling Books/Mechling Bookbindery, 2006.

Swatzler, David. *A Friend Among the Senecas.* Mechanicsburg, PA: Stackpole Books, 2000.

Truman, Harry S. *Truman Speaks.* New York, NY: Columbia University Press, 1960.

Wallace, Paul A. W. *Indians in Pennsylvania.* Harrisburg, PA: The Pennsylvania Historical and Museum Commission, 1999.

Wallace, Paul A. W. *Indian Paths of Pennsylvania.* Lewisburg, PA: Wennawoods Publishing, 2003.

Wilson, Patty A. *Haunted Pennsylvania.* Laceyville, PA: Belfry Books, 1998.

Wilson, Patty A. *The Pennsylvania Ghost Guide Volume I.* Waterfall, PA: Piney Creek Press, 2000.

Wilson, Patty A. *The Pennsylvania Ghost Guide Volume II.* Roaring Spring, PA: Piney Creek Press, 2001.

Yellin, Emily. *Our Mothers' War.* New York, NY: Free Press/a division of Simon & Shuster, Inc., 2004.

Booklets, Magazines and Newspapers, etc.

Adams, Richard. *The Delaware Indians, a Brief History.* Saugerties, NY: Hope Farm Press, 1995.

Bray, Billy. *The Wonder Dancers, Woods & Bray.* Printed in Three Lakes, WI, 1974.

Daily Courier. Connellsville, PA: "Local Woman Was a WASP." Judy Kroeger. November 11, 2004.

Daily Courier. Connellsville, PA: "Something Special." Judy Kroeger. February 21, 1998.

Herald-Standard. Uniontown, PA: "Great Outdoors." September 9, 2006.

Herald-Standard. Uniontown, PA: "Lewis Aspey Mologne." September 30, 1982 and "Connellsville's Mologne, a Military Hero Worth Remembering." February 20, 2006.

Tribune-Review. Greensburg, PA: "Coming Home." Sunday, January 15, 2006.

Tribune-Review/USA Weekend Magazine. Greensburg, PA: "Declaring Our Freedoms." Sunday, July 2, 2006.

Videos and Films

The American Experience. "Nellie Bly," PBS Television.

April Love. Twentieth-Century Fox, 1957.

Carousel. Twentieth-Century Fox, 1956.

Elmer Gantry. United Artists, 1960.

The Flyboys. MGM, 2006.

The Music Man. Warner Brothers, 1962.

Oklahoma! Twentieth-Century Fox, 1955.

Silent Night, Lonely Night. MCA Video, 1969.

Witness. Paramount, 1985.

Web Sites

The American Experience
The American Revolution
Bagpiping.org
Butler County Historical Society
Carnegie Museum of Art, Pittsburgh, PA
Cooper's Rock Mountain Lion Sanctuary
Cougar Network
Eastern Cougar Foundation
Eastern Puma Research Network
Encyclopedia Smithsonian: The Smithsonian from A–Z
Eyewitness– History Through the Eyes of Those Who Lived It
Ghosts of Gettysburg
Ghost Tours
The Golden Pheasant Inn, Erwinna, Bucks County, PA
HersheyPa.com
The History Net
Korean War Educator: God Bless the "Docs"
Mechling Books/Mechling Bookbindery
National Museum of the American Indian
Ohio History Central
PaDutch.com
Pennsbury Manor
Pennsylvania Maple Festival
Pittsburghpiper.com
Ringing Rocks Park, Bucks County, PA
Roadtotheisles.org
SACO (The Sino-American Cooperative Organization)
Senator John Heinz Pittsburgh Regional History Center/Heinz History Center
Shawnee Traditions, Language, Culture, and Ethnohistory
The National Civil War Museum, Harrisburg, PA
The Smithsonian Institute
The Smithsonian Magazine
The United States Military Academy at West Point
United States Olympic Committee
WASP, Women Pilots of WWII
Westmoreland County Historical Society
Wikipedia
Women's Military History

~ ~ ~

In Memory of

John A. Kapolka

1948 – 2007

Pennsylvania County Map

COURTESY FAYETTE COUNTY MAPPING DEPARTMENT
DAVID M. DOMEN, MAPPING SUPERVISOR